*The Green Thumb Book
of
Fruit and Vegetable Gardening*

By the same author

THE GREEN THUMB GARDEN HANDBOOK

THE GREEN THUMB BOOK OF
INDOOR GARDENING

The GREEN THUMB

Book of

Fruit and Vegetable

Gardening

by

George Abraham

PRENTICE-HALL, INC., ENGLEWOOD CLIFFS, NEW JERSEY

10 9 8 7 6 5

To millions of busy, malnourished Americans,
who are about to learn the thrill of

- Eating a chin-trickling tomato
- Picking a sun-sweetened peach
- Munching a juicy, red berry

—all raised by their own hands!

ℭONTENTS

INTRODUCTION
TO
HOME FRUIT CULTURE

CHAPTER I

Fruit Growing for the Home Gardener

Fruit is nature's storehouse of vitamins and good health! Ever since man began he's depended upon fruit for maintaining his well-being. Modern man can dispense with pep pills, vitamin tablets, and other artificial crutches by turning a portion of his backyard into a miniature fruit farm.

Many homeowners, unfortunately, fail to look into the merits of including fruits in their original landscaping plans, and find out too late that all fruit trees and many of the small fruits can do double duty as producers of food while adding beauty to the surroundings, even on very small lots where each square foot is important.

Apples, pears, peaches, plums, nectarines, apricots, sweet and sour cherries, Chinese chestnuts, black walnuts, and English walnuts all provide bountiful shade in summer plus delicate traceries of color and grace in early spring when the blooms appear. Yet they require very little more care than trees that are purely ornamental.

The little more care that is required for fruit trees involves spraying for insects and disease, helping them receive proper pollination, if necessary, and somewhat more than casual pruning. Recent developments in spray materials make it possible to reduce this former chore to a few pleasant hours in the yard on a fine day now and again, and the pruning will not only improve the quantity and quality of fruit you can pick in your own yard, but will enhance the beauty of your landscaping.

Small bush fruits such as currants, gooseberries, quinces, and blueberries may serve as a decorative planting in a sunny corner of the yard; grapes and raspberries (red, black, and purple) can serve as hedges on property lines if trained to grow on or between wires. Strawberries, the most glamorous of the small fruits to most people, should not be attempted unless the planting can be moved about every 2 or 3 years and a minimum of 100 square feet of garden space allotted for each 25 plants to be set out.

Small fruits must have a year to settle in for fruit production. Full-size fruit trees will, of course, take longer to bear. The following chart will give you a rough idea of when (from time plants are set out in your garden) to expect fruit, as well as the relative planting distances and height for the trees, bushes, or plants.

KIND OF FRUIT	AGE OF BEARING	DISTANCE APART	HEIGHT	YIELD PER PLANT
Apples, Dwarf	2 yrs.	15 x 15 ft.	15 ft.	2 bu.
Apples, Standard	2 to 14 yrs.	18 x 30 ft.	25 ft.	5–10 bu.
Apricots	3 yrs.	20 x 20 ft.	15 ft.	½ bu.
Blackberries	1 yr.	6 x 6 ft.	4 ft.	2 qts.
Blueberries	1 to 2 yrs.	3 x 6 ft.	4 ft.	4 qts.
Cherries, Sour	2 to 3 yrs.	20 x 20 ft.	20 ft.	30–60 qts.
Cherries, Sweet	3 to 4 yrs.	25 x 25 ft.	30 ft.	30–90 qts.
Chinese Chestnuts	3 to 4 yrs.	35 x 35 ft.	40 ft.	8 qts.
Currants	2 yrs.	4 x 4 ft.	3 ft.	3–4 qts.
Gooseberries	2 to 3 yrs.	4 x 4 ft.	3 ft.	3–4 qts.
Grapes	2 yrs.	8 x 8 ft.	4 ft.	½ bu.
Peaches & Nectarines	2 to 3 yrs.	20 x 20 ft.	20 ft.	1–3 bu.
Pears, Dwarf	2 yrs.	15 x 15 ft.	20 ft.	1 bu.
Pears, Standard	3 to 4 yrs.	20 x 20 ft.	30 ft.	1–3 bu.
Plums	2 to 3 yrs.	20 x 20 ft.	20 ft.	1 bu.
Quinces	1 to 2 yrs.	15 x 15 ft.	15 ft.	½–1 bu.
Raspberries	1 to 2 yrs.	3 x 6 ft.	4 ft.	1–1½ qts.
Strawberries	1 yr.	2 x 2 ft.	1 ft.	1 qt.
Walnuts, Black & English	3 to 4 yrs.	35 x 35 ft.	40 ft.	½ bu.

FROST POCKET

POOR

GULLY
OR VALLEY

GOOD

Fruit trees need good air drainage. Cold air flows downhill and collects in low places. (University of Arkansas Cooperative Extension Service.)

Planting Fruit Trees: Fall or spring are ideal times to plant fruit trees, and the way you set them out spells the difference between success and failure of your venture. First, dig holes large enough to spread the tree roots without twisting or crowding. Put the topsoil you dig up in 1 pile and the subsoil in another. Dig the holes deep enough to set the tree 2 inches deeper than it grew in the nursery, with the bud or graft about 2 inches below ground level. (Dwarfed trees are an exception to this rule, as the bud union must remain above ground level to prevent scion [the top part of the graft] rooting and to permit the dwarfing root system to have its influence throughout the life of the tree.)

Now place 3 or 4 inches of topsoil in the hole you have prepared and prune the roots of your new tree lightly. The idea is to remove all ragged tips and expose firm lively root structure to the soil to encourage the sprouting of new fine roots. If you are planting in fall, leave the top-trimming of the new tree for spring, except to remove 1 or 2 branches that might rub together or limbs that grow from the trunk at a narrow angle.

Set your tree in the prepared hole as straight as you can. Some small trees are crooked when dug from the nursery rows, but they will straighten considerably as they grow. Mix the remainder of the topsoil you have dug with the subsoil, thoroughly. Fill the hole ⅔ full with the mixture and tramp it firmly. Pour in a bucket of water. After the water seeps away, fill the hole completely with soil, leaving a saucer-like depression to catch the rain. Be sure to remove the nursery tag from the little tree, or the wire will cut into the wood as new growth is made, retarding or possibly even killing the limb to which it is attached.

Fertilizing Fruit Trees: The greatest danger in fertilizing fruit trees is that you may stimulate overproduction of new growth in late fall, very likely to result in winter injury of the trees. Time your feeding program to avoid such late growth, and start as early as December to feed for the growing year ahead.

A complete or balanced fertilizer is used on trees that are not yet bearing. For bearing-age trees, in general, you can use ammonium nitrate, nitrate of soda, or a liquid plant food. You can also use a liquid plant food foliage spray applied with the insecticide. If available, you can apply manure around the base of the tree in winter. Here is a good rule of thumb on the amount of fertilizer to use: ¼ pound of 16 percent nitrate of soda for every year of the tree's growth. So, if the tree is 12 years old, it will take 3 pounds of nitrate of soda. All types of fertilizer can be applied over a mulch in the spring. Never put fresh manure in a hole where it will come in contact with the roots of the tree.

The best time to apply nitrogen fertilizers is in April or early May. This early feeding helps set fruit, improves color, and encourages bloom. For apples 3 to 5 years old, use ½ pound of 10–10–10 fertilizer or nitrate of soda, scattered around the base of the tree. Trees over 5 years old can get 1 to 2 pounds of ammonium nitrate or 3 to 6 pounds of 10–10–10. Pears 1 to 5 years old get ½ pound of ammonium nitrate or 2 pounds of 10–10–10. Peaches and sour cherries 5 years old can get 3 or 4 pounds of 10–10–10 and prunes 5 to 10 years of age, 1 to 2 pounds.

These materials are readily available in most garden-supply stores, but if you cannot get them, try something close to them, because actually you can feed your trees any kind of plant food and get results. To feed with a substitute is better than not to feed at all. Scatter the food around the base of the tree, going as far out as the spread of the branches. It is not necessary, incidentally, to punch holes in the ground to feed your trees.

Many fruit growers I know use a liquid plant food, 23–19–17, at the rate of about 1 pound per tree. Diluted with water, 1 pound makes 30 gallons of food, which is applied in 3 equal doses: when the buds have just begun to show color, in early full leaf, and once more in the summer. Liquid foliage fertilizer may be applied over the whole tree and what drips to the ground will be absorbed by the roots. Liquid foliage food may also be mixed in pesticide sprays, combining 2 operations in 1.

All-purpose Spraying: Commercial growers spray apples anywhere from 7 to 14 times or more a year, to grow clean fruit, but you don't have to spray that much. The introduction of a "homemade all-purpose" formula which will control most bugs and diseases has vastly simplified fruit growing for the home gardener. This formula can be used in all applications after the leaves have developed, and on all fruits and ornamental shrubs.

INGREDIENTS—"ALL-PURPOSE SPRAY"

CHEMICAL	1 GALLON OF WATER	25 GALLONS OF WATER
Malathion (25% wettable powder)	2 tbsp.	½ lb.
Methoxychlor (50% wettable powder), Sevin	3 tbsp.	¾ lb.
Captan (50% wettable powder), Ferbam	3 tbsp.	¾ lb.
Sulfur	2 tbsp.	½ lb.

Timing the Spray: The timing of a spray for fruit pests is important. Try to spray at about the same time commercial growers spray, as shown in the following chart.

TIME TO SPRAY	APPLES	PEACHES	PLUMS	CHERRIES	PEARS
Green Tip	X				
Prebloom	X	X	X	X	X
Bloom	NO	NO	NO	NO	NO
Petal Fall	X	X	X	X	X
First Cover	X	X	X	X	X
Second Cover	X	X	X	X	X
Third Cover	X			X	
Fourth Cover	X	X			

"Green tip" means when buds are broken enough to show color.

"Prebloom" means when blossom buds begin to show color, but before petals begin to unfold.

"Bloom" is when blossoms are open. Never apply any insecticide during blooming period, though fungicides, which will not kill pollen-carrying bees, may be used.

"Petal fall" is when last petals have fallen from the blossoms.

First cover means 10 days after "petal fall."

Second cover through fourth cover—10- to 14-day intervals. Cover sprays may be continued until 30 days before harvest.

If you're discouraged with the effort involved in the spray program, remember that the most important sprays are prebloom and petal fall and you can do some fertilizing right along with the control program.

The all-purpose spray formula, applied through the growing season, will check most major pests, and with 4 or 5 sprays properly timed, you should be able to eat your fruit in the dark with an easy mind! Malathion controls the plum curculio and other beetles; methoxychlor or Sevin will check leafhoppers, codling moth, fruit moth, and other worms. Captan or ferbam are included to prevent cedar rust and leaf spots, and sulfur to control apple scab, brown rot, and mildew. To control psylla on pears, and aphids on all trees and shrubs, it's a good idea to add nicotine sulfate at the rate of 2 teaspoons per gallon. Nicotine is very volatile and will not retain its strength if not stored in sealed containers. All of these materials are available at your local feed and seed stores, or you can purchase prepared all-purpose formulas. Sometimes you will see Chlordane, DDT, or Sevin used in place of methoxychlor, but in the main, all-purpose formulas are pretty much the same.

Methoxychlor is usually a safer substitute for its controversial "cousin," DDT. Methoxychlor has many of the advantages of DDT and only a few of the disadvantages. It has lower toxicity to humans and other warm-blooded animals. It has a long residual action and is not injurious to crops. In fact, methoxychlor is 50 times safer than DDT, and there is no evidence that it accumulates in the body fat, as DDT does.

At the present time, methoxychlor has been established by USDA for use on apples, apricots, blackberries, blueberries, peaches, and dozens of other fruits as well as vegetables.

How about rotenone? It's more toxic than DDT or methoxychlor, so don't think you can use rotenone on your fruits and vegetables without washing it off. All pesticides are toxic. That's why they are used for killing bugs.

DORMANT SPRAYING

What's a dormant spray? It's simply a spray applied while plants are dormant. That is, while non-evergreens are bare, and before evergreens have started new growth. During the dormant period plants can tolerate a stronger spray than when in active growth. Many hard-shelled scale insects pass winter on twigs, other insects, such as mites and aphids, pass the winter in egg stage on buds, twigs, and trunks. If you kill these pests before they get a chance to hatch you can prevent serious outbreaks. Dormant spray will protect all fruit trees from scale, peach leaf curl, cherry aphid, mites, and others. Will also protect ornamentals such as arborvitae, elm, maple, yews, lilacs, evergreens (such as junipers), willows, and dozens of other. Some evergreens are susceptible to dormant spraying (see following).

Kind to Use: Ordinarily there are 3 types of dormant sprays: Lime sulphur, oils, and the dinitro or DN compounds. Lime sulfur comes as a dry mix or in liquid form. The dry forms are usually diluted at the rate of 1 part lime sulfur to 9 parts of water. Oil spray can be either miscible ("mixable" with water) or an oil emulsion. Scalecide is an example of a dormant oil spray. Dinitro (short for dinitro-ortho-cresol), available in powder or paste form, will kill eggs of aphids and other pests.

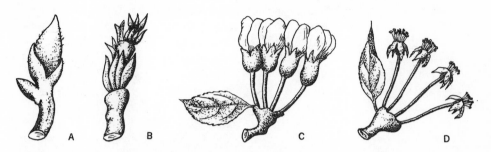

Stages in spring fruit-tree spraying: (A) Dormant stage. (B) Delayed dormant or "green tip," bud has broken a little. (C) Prebloom, buds show some color but petals have not begun to unfold. (D) Petal-fall or calyx stage.

Time to Apply: All dormant sprays should be applied on dormant trees, before buds show green—anywhere from March through April, just as the buds begin to swell. At that time insects are more vulnerable and trees can withstand the strong sprays. NEVER APPLY DORMANT OIL SPRAYS WHEN TEMPERATURE IS BELOW 40°, nor in late afternoon, when there is a possibility the temperature will drop down to 32° that night.

Dangers to Watch: Do not use dormant oil sprays on Japanese maple, sugar maple, magnolia, black walnut, douglas fir, true firs, hemlock, yew, or larch. Follow manufacturer's instructions. On plants susceptible to dormant oil spray, you can use lime sulfur, a compound diluted with water before application, usually at rate of 1 part to 9 parts of water. Lime sulfur will stain paint, sidings of houses, so be careful with it. Apply the dormant spray once during each spring. Do not mix oils with lime sulfur.

Spray Equipment: What sort of equipment would you use for dormant spraying? The same types of equipment used in summer spraying, but to invade the sleeping quarters of those hibernating forms of insect and fungus life, your spray equipment should develop pressures high enough to shoot a wetting solution some distance and still cover all surfaces thoroughly, driving the spray into corners, crevices, and other protected areas.

Spraying fruit tree using trombone slide sprayer. Pail holds spray material, pressure for spraying is built up by operating slide. (National Sprayer and Duster Association)

Compressed air sprayers at pressures of 30 to 50 p.s.i. (pounds per square inch) will do a satisfactory job of applying dormant materials at close range. But, in comparison, a slide sprayer, which develops 150 to 200 p.s.i., will reach 20 feet or more into the tops of trees and provide the penetration needed for thorough coverage. Some slide sprayers use separate buckets from which to draw spray, others include attached tanks. Most of them have adjustable nozzles to control the pattern and direction of the spray.

A small power sprayer is ideal for spraying more extensive areas. It has plenty of pressure to reach the pests, plus all the advantages of effortless operation, big payload, and speedy application. For dormant spraying, it's best to pick a calm, sunny morning when the temperature is at least 40° above and there's little danger of it dropping below freezing before the plants can dry off. In applying a strong dormant spray, the droplets should be large enough to drench the surfaces thoroughly. Spraying can only be as effective as it is thorough.

Summer Spraying: While lime sulfur is a fungicide, it acts as an insecticide, controlling scale and red mites on fruits, spider mites on ornamentals. Liquid lime sulfur can be diluted to 1 to 50, for summer spray. Never use it within a month of using oil.

You can also use a miscible white oil summer spray, for white fly, mealybugs, red mites, scale crawlers, at rate of 2⅔ tablespoons to a quart of water. We've found this safe on fruit trees including citrus, ornamental shrubs, evergreens, and conifers. Does a fine job. Mix in Malathion, 1 teaspoon to a quart, for added insecticide value. Always FOLLOW DIRECTIONS OF MANUFACTURER, AND BE SURE TO TEST MATERIAL ON SMALL SCALE BEFORE SPRAYING ALL YOUR PLANTS.

Note: Fungicides containing carbamates (Fermate, etc.) can be used as dormant spray for leaf curl, and others, with good results. Never use dinitro on active trees—just dormant trees, before buds show green.

Preventing Fruiting of Ornamental Trees: "Gardeners are told how to care for fruit trees, but we would like to have them only for their shade and their flowers in spring. Is there anything we can spray on the trees to keep them from forming fruit and littering the ground?"

The use of synthetic hormone sprays containing naphthaleneacetic acid and sold under trade names as App-L-Set, or Parmone, etc., eliminates or greatly reduces fruit setting, retards fruit development, or causes the dropping of young fruits of many kinds of flowering trees without causing any apparent damage to the health of the tree.

These materials can be used to prevent fruit from setting on western catalpa, horse chestnut, Carolina poplar, Norway maple, tree of heaven, maidenhair tree (ginkgo), Kentucky coffee tree, purple crab apple, as well as the apple, pear, quince, etc.

Usually the time to apply is when the trees are in full bloom, or on tiny developing fruits. It only takes a small amount of spray to do the job. Not much research has been done on this for the home gardener, although hormone sprays are a regular part of commercial growers fruit-growing practices. Experiment and find out which works best for you.

SHOULD YOU PLANT DWARF FRUIT TREES?

If you are an average gardener you are rightly intrigued by the new dwarf fruit trees which number compactness among their virtues—

you can plant them 6 to 12 feet apart; their low-growing nature makes them easy to prune and spray as well as to harvest, and they are well adapted to the small lot. They bear their fruit sooner after planting than the standard fruit trees, and may be trained to grow on trellises (espaliered). Dwarf apple trees yield up to 2 bushels of fruit per tree.

Apples and pears are more frequently dwarfed than other varieties of tree fruits. Peach, nectarine, plum, apricot, and sour cherry trees as ordinarily grown are small in comparison with well-developed standard apple trees and come into bearing sooner, without the dwarfing process to speed production.

In deciding on dwarf fruit trees, some consideration should be given to the rootstocks that have been used to induce dwarfing. Apples grown on the most dwarfing of all the rootstocks, known as Malling IX, require bracing or support because the root system is brittle and will break off easily. Apples grown on the semi-dwarfing Malling VII, and dwarf peaches and plums, do not require support. Your nurseryman will be glad to tell you the name of the dwarfing stock used in the trees that interest you and to explain that apples dwarfed on Malling IX will grow no taller than a man, while fruits dwarfed on Malling VII will attain the size of a small peach tree.

Still Confused about Dwarf Tree Terms?: Nearly all dwarfing rootstocks for apples used in this country were first developed at East Malling Research Station in England, and are labeled with such terms as EM (East Malling) and M (Malling) I, II, IV to X.

1. M (or EM) IX. The smallest dwarf. It can be maintained at 8 to 10 feet tall.

2. M (or EM) 26. A little larger than IX, this rootstock causes trees to be productive, but is not fully evaluated in this country.

3. M (or EM) VII. Grows to about ½ the size of a standard tree; today probably the most popular dwarfing rootstock. It may sucker badly from the ground.

4. MM 106. A cross of Northern Spy and Malling I. A little taller than M VII. It doesn't sucker and is resistant to wooly aphids.

5. M (or EM) II. About ⅔ the size of a standard tree, well anchored, does best on well-drained soils.

6. MM III. About the same size as M II, resistant to drought and an early and heavy producer.

M IX, M 26, M VII, and MM 106 should all be anchored or staked. Most dwarfing rootstocks are smaller and weaker than standard rootstocks.

Among apples, try Lodi, Yellow Transparent, Red and Golden Delicious, Baldwin, Wealthy, and Rhode Island Greening—all resistant to scab fungus. Cortland and McIntosh are good dwarfs but must be sprayed as they are very susceptible.

Planting Dwarf Trees: Since dwarf trees are grown on rootstocks that restrict the growth of the fruit-bearing top, it is important that the graft union (place where the variety was grafted to the dwarfing rootstock) be planted above soil. DO NOT PLANT BELOW GROUND LEVEL. If this graft union is in constant touch with the soil, roots will develop from the top part and the dwarfing effect of the rootstock will be lost and you get a much larger tree.

Time of Planting: Plant as early as possible in the spring. If trees show signs of dryness when received from the nursery soak the roots in water for a few hours before planting.

Where to Plant: Plant in garden or on an open, well-kept lawn. Apple trees need full sunlight. Never plant in a shady location. Do not plant near large shrubs or tall trees which will shade and rob the fruit tree of moisture and other nutrients, or close to the eaves of buildings where the trees may be damaged by ice and snow from the roof.

Do not use any chemical fertilizers in the hole when planting the tree or burning will result and may kill the tree. Bone meal can be used with no danger of burning and is a good fertilizer to use. The first year an adequate supply of water at all times is much more important than using fertilizers. Be sure to water newly planted trees whenever rainfall is deficient. When you water, soak the soil thoroughly. Too little water is worse than none at all. A good watering once each week during dry periods will contribute greatly to tree growth. An old pail is very useful in watering. Punch some holes in the bottom and the water will run out slowly, soaking in the ground without packing it or running off.

Divide your property with this apple-growing fence. Dwarf apple trees can be trained to a wire trellis for a screen or boundary marker, and for a supply of crisp, juicy apples. Ideal for small area. Set posts 12 feet apart with 4 wires strung 1½ feet apart.

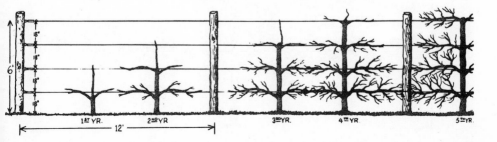

Mulching: Dwarf trees grow very well under a mulch system. Straw, old hay, lawn clippings, peat moss, or any other material that will make a good ground covering is good. This should be applied early in the spring, under the tree and out a little farther than the branches extend. It will conserve moisture and keep the soil temperature in summer at a constant and favorable temperature for growth. (See section on mulches.)

Pruning: Allow 1 top or leader to grow. Cut out superfluous branches and those that crisscross or rub against each other. Spray using the all-purpose formula (see All-purpose Spraying).

Training Dwarf Apple and Pear Trees as Espaliers: Interest in training trees as espaliers is zooming in America. First, you must start out with dwarf varieties. Study the illustrations, and you'll find it easy to espalier (pronounced "espal-yer" or "espal-yay") your trees. Espaliered fruits will need trimming in the dormant season and during the growing season. Heaviest pruning is in early spring, just before sap flows (dormant or winter pruning). Summer pruning consists of shearing off or cutting back the side shoots at least once a month, in July, August, and September. In mild climates, extend it into November. Don't be discouraged with your first results. Try 1 or 2 trees first, and after you get the hang of it, you'll be qualified to teach your neighbors all about espaliering dwarf fruit trees.

How to espalier a young apple tree. Black marks show places tree can be pruned.

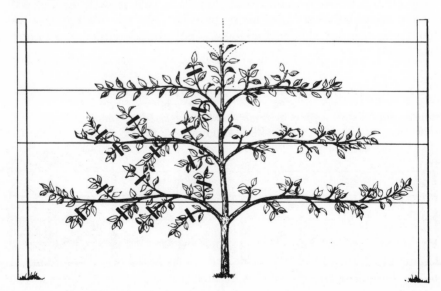

CHAPTER II

Common Fruits of
Temperate Regions

APPLES (*Pyrus malus*)

"An Apple a Day": The apple is perhaps the most important fruit grown in our part of the world. There's something to the old expression "An apple a day." Present-day research indicates that the pectin in apples helps reduce cholesterol in the bloodstream. Apples contain vitamins A and C, thus aid skin problems and help prevent viral infections. The fact that apples are healthy (actually any fruit is good for you) was learned many years ago, back in Devonshire, England, where it was decreed: "Ate an apfel avore gwain to bed. Makes the Doctor beg his bread." Next year, why not plant an apple or 2 in your backyard.

How to Grow Good Apples at Home: Many gardeners refuse to plant apple trees because of the bugs and diseases that bother this fruit. There was a time not too far back when you could raise apples without spraying, the kind of fruit you could eat in the dark. But you can do this no longer. Yet, don't be discouraged from planting this fruit tree. Apple trees make good shade trees, so why not kill 2 birds with 1 stone? We have chemicals which do a good job of helping you produce the kind of fruit you can eat without worrying about biting into a juicy worm.

Varieties: As for which variety to grow, it doesn't make much difference. Commercial growers are favoring red sports because the color appeals to the consumer, but there's no reason why you cannot grow Greenings, Yellow Delicious, or any variety you want. There are summer, fall, and winter varieties. For a summer variety, you might want to try Red Duchess, Red Astrachan, or Yellow Transparent. For autumn varieties, try Pound Sweet or Red Gravenstein, and for winter apples (varieties which keep well in winter storage), there are Baldwin, Monroe, Northern Spy, and Rome Beauty. Study your nursery catalog for best varieties for your purposes and locality.

Cross-pollination: Many varieties of apple cannot be fertilized by their own pollen. For best fruit yield, plant 2 different varieties, 1 of which will serve as a "rooster" tree.

Some varieties produce pollen that's sterile, others bloom early, so their pollen is scarce when other varieties are in bloom. Some varieties produce pollen which is not compatible with the blooms of certain other varieties, hence no fruit in spite of lots of apple blossoms in spring. Plant a rooster tree of a good pollinator variety, one that blooms at the same time as the trees which are to be pollinated. Golden Delicious, Red Delicious, Cortland, and Jonathan are good pollinator trees to have.

One commercial grower who had a case of "The Absent Apples" solved the problem by placing live Golden Delicious pollen in the entrance of beehives. The bees walked through the pollen and carried it to nearby Jonathan and Stayman apple trees. Result? Yields increased by 68% and some yields were even doubled! This happened in a well cared for, 15-year-old orchard which produced a lot of blossoms annually but an unsatisfactory yield of fruit.

All fruit trees do better if interplanted with a rooster tree. One tree by itself seldom produces a full crop. The variety of rooster tree chosen will not affect the appearance or characteristics of your crop.

We have found it relatively simple to overcome the pollination problem, for apples, and other fruits, by borrowing a bouquet of fresh fruit blooms from a neighbor and placing them in water in a sunny spot where the insects like to work. Cut the bouquets when the most advanced blossoms are open, and the sooner you can get them in water, the better. Keep the blossoms fresh, for when they wilt they are valueless. It goes without saying that if you wish to pollinate apples, you must secure apple blossoms, pear blossoms for pears, etc.

Age to Buy Trees: You can buy 1-year-old and 2-year-old trees from your nursery, but make sure they aren't any older because older trees do not take hold as quickly as younger trees. Watch out for door-to-door peddlers who tell you that the older the tree the sooner it comes into bearing. Young trees (1 and 2 years old) come into bearing sooner after planting than the older ones, and as far as we can see, nothing is gained by planting "bearing-age" fruit trees.

Age of Bearing: Many gardeners have a mistaken idea as to when their newly planted fruits will bear. Standard apple trees rarely bear much before they are 6 to 7 years old, the age of the tree being reckoned from the time the nursery-started tree is planted in your garden. Apples vary in their bearing age—from 2 to 14 years, depending on the variety. There isn't much you can do to hasten bearing (except ring the bark with a knife, to be explained later). Over-pruning a young tree will delay bearing. Just be patient and yours will bear when ready.

Apples from Seed: Growing apples from seed can be an interesting hobby, but if you start it, be sure someone in the next generation will be on hand to evaluate your work. Your chances for edible fruit are slim, and the home gardener would be foolish to nurse a tree started from a seed. The seedling would probably grow into an inferior, "common" fruit, unless you do what nurserymen do: bud and graft cultivated fruit on the wild seedlings (see Fruit Propagation).

Multiple-variety Trees: The so-called 5-in-1 (5 varieties in 1) can be used for home planting, producing in 3 to 8 years. Prune for uni-

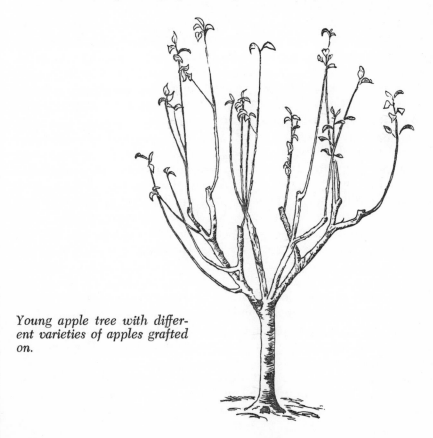

Young apple tree with different varieties of apples grafted on.

formity, so that 1 variety doesn't grow more than the other, otherwise you'll have a lopsided tree. If 1 branch is weaker than another, prune it more lightly than the vigorous kind. With the 5-variety apple tree, since different varieties have different rates of growth, it often happens that the strongest-growing varieties will outgrow the others and eventually take over the whole tree. The 5-in-1 is generally less satisfactory than trees which carry a single variety. The most obvious advantage in the multiple-variety fruit tree is the readiness of cross-pollination between varieties.

Should you be especially interested in the tiny "man-sized" apple trees, do not be put off by the need to support the tree (some are shallow-rooted). All that is required is a strong stake driven into the ground near the tree, which is then firmly tied to the tree with a broad band of cloth or rubber hose.

New Facts About Old-fashioned Apples: I'm often asked, "Why can't we get those good, old-fashioned apple varieties anymore?" This is one way of saying that new interest is being shown in the old apples. Years ago it was common for everyone to have a planting of Snow Apples (Fameuse), Black Gilliflower, Pumpkin Sweet, etc. People grew these fine-quality apples for their own use. That was before the day when fruit growing became a specialized business. Many of the "fine old varieties" disappeared since they were only suitable for home plantings. They had to give way to modern varieties, which must have the following attributes: (1) productivity, (2) attractiveness, (3) ease of handling, (4) disease resistance, (5) good keeping quality, (6) dual usefulness, for dessert and processing.

Here are some old favorites and why they faded out of the apple picture: Black Gilliflower ("Sheepnose"): a conic shape, mild-flavored, good quality. Has a dark, dull, unattractive color, a reason why it faded away. "Strawberry" Apple (Chenango): fine-flavored, but bruises easily and has poor keeping quality. Early Harvest: most popular variety of a century ago. Small size, uneven ripening, and difficulty in handling, bruises easily. Esopus Spitzenberg: fine quality, still rates with the best as dessert. Tree lacks vigor, is unproductive. Fameuse ("Snow Apple"): before McIntosh the most highly valued of all table apples, pure white flesh, a fine eating apple. McIntosh probably has some Fameuse blood in it. Lady: small in size, very beautiful, high in quality. Has been known for more than 300 years. Mother: considered by some to be the finest dessert variety. Has uneven ripening and short storage life. Subject to winter injury, tendency toward biennial bearing. Maiden Blush: yellow with crimson cheek, has short storage and poor dessert value. Porter: fine-quality fall variety, tender flesh. Pumpkin Sweet: large yellow ("Pound Sweet"), fine eating and baking. Tree not too hardy and subject to sunscald.

Roxbury Russet: one of several russet varieties with tender flesh and sprightly flavor. Color, though distinctive, is blotchy, thus not too attractive. Fine eating. Golden Russet and Roxbury keep until spring in ordinary home cellar. Make wonderful cider. Seek-No-Further: does best in area having a longer and warmer growing season, fine quality. Swaar: tops in quality, but has greenish-yellow fruits flecked with russet, thus not too attractive, low productivity. Tolman Sweet: one of best winter sweet apples, small size greenish-yellow color. Wagener: fine pollinator, but fruits are small and tree is short-lived. Yellow Newtown: fine quality, but tree does not thrive in some colder regions. Baldwin, a fine winter apple, and Northern Spy are losing out due to biennial bearing habits and unproductivity. Rhode Island Greening: is being grown for processing. Twenty Ounce: staging a comeback. Wealthy is coming back in spite of its biennial bearing habits (controlled now by blossom-thinning sprays).

Here are some other dessert apples worth growing in the home orchard: Akero, Almata, Calville Blanc D'Hiver, Cox's Orange Pippin, Dr. Matthews, Early Joe, Grimes Golden, Irish Peach, King (Tompkin's King), Lamb Abbey Pearmain, Lyman's Large Summer, Muster Orenco, Red Gravenstein, Summer Rambo, to name a few. The list is almost endless.

How to Prune a Young Apple Tree: When you buy a young apple tree from the nursery, it usually needs pruning before planting. Never

How to prune a young fruit tree at planting time: (A) Shorten the tip or leader. (B) Shorten branches that might outgrow the leader. (C) Leave branches that are properly spaced. (D) Cut at a point where there is a bud pointing outward. (E) Remove branches that are too close to ground. (F) Remove broken or injured roots. Snip ½ inch off each so new feeder roots will form quickly. Note how branches are well spaced, and narrow-angled crotches removed.

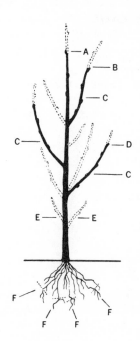

plant one unless it's been trimmed back, both top and roots. Pick out 3 to 5 husky side branches that are spaced 6 to 8 inches apart along the trunk of the tree. Branches at wide angles to the trunk are better than those with narrow angles. They are stronger and will make up the "scaffold" or main branches of the tree. Cut the top branch or "leader" back ½ to ⅓ of its length, and the side branches should be cut back proportionately. Then cut off all the remaining branches. It's a good idea to cut off an inch or so from the tips of the roots, so no ragged ends show. This encourages new fine roots to sprout. Train your tree right when small and the framework will develop properly, and you won't have to prune so much later. (See illustration.)

How to Prune the Old Apple Tree: A good many home gardeners have old apple trees in the backyard, trees too tall, too crowded to produce good fruit. Commercial growers even tell you they can't make money on a tree that can't be picked with a 12-foot ladder. A tree thick with branches won't let sun or spray materials in to cover leaves, and it may have so much weak wood that it bears a large percentage of small apples.

Old trees which have not been pruned for years are usually filled with branches of thin diameter, many of which hang downward. This is especially true with Wealthy. Such branches are usually found between the larger main limbs in the lower half of the tree. They usually have very weak fruiting branches (spurs) and produce apples of less than 2¼ inches in diameter, unprofitable to grow. All these branches should be removed.

(A) *Here's what happens if you don't make undercut first. Limb tears, stub is left.*
(B) *Undercut (1) made first, then top cut (2), and final cut made flush (3).*

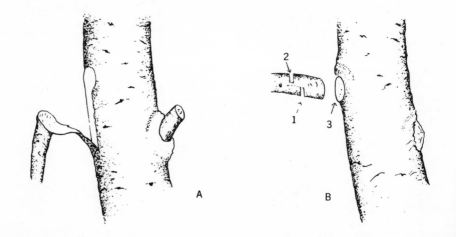

A   B

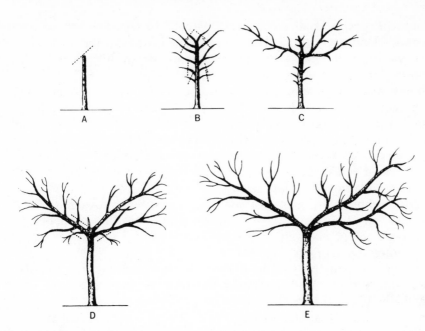

Steps in pruning a young fruit tree: (A) Young tree planted. (B) Second year after pruning. (C) Third year. (D) Fourth year after pruning. (E) Fifth year—note open center to let sunlight in.

In winter or spring, take out limbs that are dead, broken, or too high or too low, and those which rub or crisscross one another. Skinny weak limbs should come out, also those which will not allow light to get to the center. The pruning job can be done in winter or late fall, after leaves have dropped. Don't cut out a lot of big branches at once or you'll have a lot of suckers or water sprouts to contend with. This kind of operation should be done gradually over a 2- or 3-year period.

Don't prune young trees too much as it encourages non-fruiting wood and will delay the time when the tree will come into bearing. Over-pruning of any age tree can result in lack of fruit. Crab apples need very little pruning, except to remove dead wood, and limbs which make bad crotches.

Keep your apple tree as low as possible. Suppose you have a Red Astrachan apple that's 4 or 5 years old, and about 8 to 10 feet high. It should be kept low by pruning out the top shoots, and at the same time you can prune out (moderately) any long, leggy branches on the sides of the tree so it will be nice and bushy. The central leader or tip can be left longer than any of the side branches, at least while the tree is young (say from 5 to 7 years old). After that, the leader can be cut back to keep the top of the tree open for sunlight to enter, so apples will color up.

Note to Pruners: If all this sounds "Greek" to you, keep these points in mind: Don't overprune. Many trees have been dwarfed and delayed in flowering and fruiting because of aimless severe butchering. HEAVY PRUNING OF NON-BEARING TREES DELAYS THEIR FRUITING AGE. Small wounds made in pruning while the tree is young will heal over quicker than larger ones made later. If you want to paint pruning wounds, you can use shellac, Bordeaux-water paint. If you prune in spring, wounds heal most readily and are least likely to enlarge because of winter injury. DON'T TRY TO PRUNE A NEGLECTED APPLE TREE IN 1 YEAR, because the bark of newly exposed limbs may be hit by sunscald, and trees with severe sunscald seldom recover.

Over-pruning also brings on lots of suckers. Some suckers or "water sprouts" are desirable to replace the worn-out fruiting branches. You will want to cut out some of the suckers in 2 or 3 years, leaving only the strongest at 3 or 4 feet apart.

In short, open the tree to permit the sun and spray materials to penetrate and cover all the leaves and fruit. A good reason for lowering the height of the tree.

Whitewashing Trunks: Painting the trunk with whitewash will help prevent "southwest injury" (winter injury), but has no value in keeping insects or disease down. Painting with pine tar may keep out borers (due to odor of tar) but cannot be relied upon to keep out leaf-chewing pests.

Factors Affecting Bearing Age: Gardeners often ask: "How come my apple tree doesn't bear?" Varieties vary in their bearing age. For example, McIntosh apple trees come into bearing at the age of 6 or 7 years. Golden Delicious begins to fruit at a younger age, 4 to 6 years. But Northern Spy begins to fruit very late; trees of this variety rarely begin bearing until they are 12 or more years of age.

Aside from this inherent varietal characteristic, a number of other factors affect the development of flowers and fruit setting. Apple trees which are grown on a dwarfing rootstock, such as the East Malling IX rootstock, are not only dwarfed in size but also begin to bear at an earlier age than trees on the standard seedling rootstocks. Northern Spy trees with EM IX roots begin to bear at 8 to 10 years of age, in spite of the variety's tendency to begin bearing late.

Tricks to Hasten Fruiting or Bearing Age: Tying Branches: Many commercial growers tie down the branches of young apple trees, to hasten fruiting and produce a much better-shaped tree, easier to spray and pick. The following procedure is used. Drive a stake into the ground, put a slipknot on a piece of rope and tie it to the end of an upright branch. Then pull branch down until the branch is more or less horizontal and tie to stake in the ground. Spreading the branches down-ward will help the limbs initiate fruit spurs and will give heavier, early production of fruit. It also encourages a tree to develop a more dominant leader (center limb that grows straight up) and thus be a stronger tree. Crotch angles in some apple varieties in early growth tend to become narrower and branches tend to bend upward or in-ward. Tying down the branches prevents this. The twine on the ends of the limbs will not cause girdling, as you might suspect, since the twine touches only the top surface of the branch.

Bending of branches induces earlier fruiting, and causes more abun-dant flower production. In amateur gardens in England and on the European continent, the tying down of branches of apple trees is prac-ticed extensively. It is used there to shape the tree into small space as well as to cause early bearing. Growers in those countries train apple trees as cordons, to which are tied trellis-like grapevines.

The theory behind bending: It acts just as knife ringing (see follow-ing) would do, restricting movement of carbohydrates from the outer portion of the limb toward the roots. The resulting accumulation of carbohydrates in the limb and slowing down of growth beyond the bend is favorable to flower-bud formation. Before the bend, less carbohydrates are available; but more water and nitrogen from the roots are present and this results in vigorous shoot growth in this area. Branches which are tied down in the spring of 1979 will have excess accumulation of carbohydrates in the summer of 1979.

Note: Although bending of branches may cause earlier bearing, it may also stunt the growth of a tree, a good thing for home gardeners since most of them want dwarf trees. Bending can be done any time during the dormant season or after growth starts in spring. The IMPORTANT thing is, it must be done before the end of May so that a chance is given for the carbohydrates to accumulate prior to the time of fruit-bud formation at the end of June.

Ringing Hastens Fruiting: Ringing is often useful in inducing a tree to begin to bear early. About June 15, a ½-inch section of bark is removed from the trunk of the tree. This is done by cutting through the bark right around the perimeter of the trunk (be sure to cut through the bark only, and not the growing tissue, or "cambium," underneath). After a second cut around is made ½ inch higher on the trunk, a half-inch ring of bark can be removed. The wound is covered with tape to prevent drying. The removal of this ring of bark prevents the food materials made by the leaves on the treetop from traveling to the roots. The additional carbohydrate material remaining in the top causes increased flower-bud formation for the following season. Thus, if a tree is ringed on June 15, 1979 it would be expected to cause increased fruiting in October 1980. Simply scoring bark around the trunk with a knife is almost as effective as removing a section of bark.

Slitting the bark, a technique sometimes used on cherry trees, is not recommended to induce earlier bearing of apples. Its effectiveness is questionable.

Mulching: A mulch of straw, sawdust, grass clippings, etc., is desirable but be sure to keep a wire screen around the base of the tree to keep mice and rabbits away. Mulches encourage mouse troubles.

Thinning Fruits: Too many fruit sets on apples prevent flower-bud formation for the next season and result in alternate bearing, or a heavy crop of small-sized fruits one year and no crop the next. This is common with Golden Delicious and others. Prevent by early thinning.

Thinning of fruit allows the grower to take off the blemished, worthless or crowded fruits early in the season. It lightens the tree load and prevents limb breakage. It reduces the number of fruits in proportion to the number of leaves which will nourish these fruits. Thinning assures more food and moisture to make large, sweet and well-colored fruits. Leaves make sugars and these sugars cause fruit color.

Nature may take care of the thinning job if the trees are not properly sprayed for insect and disease control. If left unsprayed the fruit will drop heavily from the trees before maturity.

While commercial growers use chemical thinning sprays, hand removal of the little fruits is most practical for the home gardener. To thin properly, break off each unwanted fruit with the fingers.

Apples can be spaced from 4 to 6 inches apart, leaving a single fruit on every third or fourth cluster. It doesn't take long to thin and you get improved size, quality, and repeat blooms each year. You can thin apples by using a hormone, naphthalene acetamide (better than naphthaleneacetic acid, which sometimes injures foliage and over-thins the fruit).

Dropping Apples: Most varieties lose some apples in the "June drop" —more fruits are formed than the tree can nurse. You can prevent dropping of premature fruit just before harvest by spraying with hormone or "preharvest" sprays on the market. So we have hormone sprays that thin fruit and hormone sprays that prevent fruit from dropping.

Immature apples may drop for other reasons:
1. Lack of pollination
    (a) lack of bees
    (b) lack of proper pollen. In a 5-variety tree, this is not likely.
2. Lack of food
    (a) improper care of tree, with resulting poor leaf surface. For example, if there is a lot of scab, the fruits will drop.

(b) lack of soil nutrients. A little nitrogen fertilizer might help.
3. Disease and insects
4. Low-temperature injury
5. Lack of water. If last summer was dry some of this year's fruits may drop off.

Alternate Bearing ("Every-other Year") of Apples: One group of apple varieties are classified as annual bearers. That is, these varieties tend to produce a medium-sized crop every season. This group includes such varieties as McIntosh, Cortland, and Delicious. However, there is a second group of apple varieties which are classed as biennial bearers. Very strongly biennially bearing varieties include Wealthy, Baldwin, and Golden Delicious. Unless some controlling device is used by the grower, these varieties tend to bear a heavy crop in one year and essentially no crop the following year. The reason for this alternate-bearing habit lies in the food mechanism within the tree itself. The buds which eventually develop into the fruits are initiated a full season ahead of the time of fruiting. Thus the blossoms which are to produce the 1980 crop are being initiated in June of 1979. If an apple tree is carrying a heavy load of crop during 1979, this crop tends to compete for the available food with the formation of blossom buds for the 1980 crop.

Fruit thinning can reduce alternate bearing. During the year of heavy fruiting, remove by hand ½ or up to 75% of the fruits. This increases the food (carbohydrates) available for forming fruit buds for the next year. Ringing the bark with a sharp knife (run it all the way around the trunk, without removing bark) will induce annual bearing. Ringing must be done 2 weeks after bloom in the year of heavy cropping.

Naphthalene acetamide, naphthaleneacetic acid, and Sevin are thinning chemicals which can be sprayed on the tree 2 weeks after full bloom.

The fruits can also be thinned by hand. This should be done about the last week in June. All of the fruits except 1 should be removed from each cluster on the tree. Furthermore, fruits should not remain closer than 6 inches apart on the tree. Sometimes this is equivalent to removing 50 or 60% of the fruits on the tree. Hand-thinning should not be delayed until mid-July because at that time the fruit buds are already initiated for the following season's crop. However, late thinning will increase the size of the fruits in the present season.

Why Apples Bear on 1 Side of Tree: It's very common for some apple trees to bear heavily on 1 side one year and on the opposite side the following year. In fact, in almost every year on Baldwin trees, 1 side of the tree will carry a heavy crop and the other side will have none

and in the next year the reverse will be true. This is linked to a carbohydrate deficiency.

Cause of Late Blooming: The blossoming of apple trees in late summer commonly occurs in very dry seasons. Apple trees as well as many
other woody perennials require a period of dormancy before they will
push open blossoms. A very dry summer will artificially provide this
necessary period of dormancy and a few blossoms will open in the fall.
In apples certain varieties such as Idared are more apt to do this than
other varieties.

Coloring Your Apples: "Blushing" or coloring in apples is linked to
the amount of light the fruit gets. The more sunlight that gets to the
fruit, the redder the color. That's why it's a good idea to prune out
the center or inside of your apple tree so that sunshine can get in and
color your fruit. Center limbs produce shade and apples on them do
not get good exposure to sunlight. Apples get their best color in seasons with bright, clear days and cool nights. During hot seasons, McIntosh apples may ripen before they develop a good red color. If apples
are spread on the ground under the trees, after harvesting, they will
develop a good red color. Don't leave them there too long or their
keeping qualities will be impaired.

So get out your trimming shears and saw, and open up the center
of that apple tree. You'll have better-colored fruit next fall.

How to Pick Apples: Stems should be left on the fruit. Apples with
stems left on last longer. When you pick an apple and tear the stem
off in the process, you break the skin and make the fruit susceptible
to rot. Stem pulls are much more apt to stimulate decay than many
so-called "rots" that develop in storage. In some states, apples from
which the stems have been pulled are considered culls.

A simple way to pick apples is to raise the fruit to one side with the
fingers and twist the wrist. If apples are hard to pick, the end of the
thumb or forefinger should be placed against the stem at the point
where it is attached to the fruit spur or twig. When you twist the fruit
off you prevent breakage of the fruit spurs. When apples are yanked
off, quite often some of the spurs come off with them, thereby reducing the crop for next year.

How to Store Apples over Winter: With the modern heating plants in
most homes it's difficult to keep apples for over a month or so. If you
have a hankering for apples in winter you don't have to worry about
heated cellars. Store them in your garden. They'll stay tree-fresh
throughout the winter months.

Many use a garbage can sunk in the garden for keeping apples.
This is a simple and inexpensive way to keep choice apples.

Select a good keeping variety such as Northern Spy, Rhode Island Greening, Rome Beauty, or Baldwin. Make sure the apples are free from cuts, bruises and disease.

Dig a hole in your garden; a shady spot is preferable. Place a galvanized garbage can (new, or well cleaned and dried) in the hole just deep enough so that the lip of can is slightly above level of ground. Fit can with tight cover.

Place apples inside garbage can, put the top on, and cover with a pile of straw or leaves to a depth of 2 feet. A board or a few stones may be placed on top to hold the leaves or straw. Apples will last until May, and even though the ground is frozen around the can, or barrel, the apples will not freeze. Apples give off enough heat to protect themselves. It's a good idea to keep the apples in an unheated room or garage until ground temperature gets cold, also keep them moist by spraying lightly with water, before placing in the storage can.

My neighbor has the slickest storage for apples. He took an old refrigerator, knocked the lock off and made himself an apple keeper which protects against subzero temperatures. A hole was dug in his garden, and the refrigerator placed flat on its back so that the door remained flush with the soil surface. Bushels of apples can be set inside the refrigerator (shelves were removed). After the door is closed, he places a layer of straw or leaves over as added protection. ALWAYS BE SURE TO KNOCK THE LOCK OFF ANY USED REFRIGERATORS. Too many lives have been lost by failing to do this.

Apples keep well all year long in old refrigerator buried in ground.

Failure to Bear: Due to lack of pollination in poor weather during full-bloom period. At temperatures below 65° bees do very little flying. May be due to vigorous growth of foliage, cause of no fruit setting. End shoots should grow 6 to 8 inches annually; if they grow 18 to 24 inches, tree is getting too vigorous. Cut down on fertilizer. Failure to spray causes leaves to shed in summer, and tree is not able to set blossom buds.

Bitter Pit: Physiological disease—causes little brown hard spots in flesh. Worse in dry summers. Baldwin and Spy are very susceptible; Red and Golden Delicious quite resistant. Bitter pit, stippin and Baldwin spot are all same trouble. Cause not known. Control: Grow varieties not highly susceptible. Apply only small amount of nitrogen. Don't thin too heavily as larger fruit is more susceptible than small ones. Don't prune too heavily. Store apples quickly at 33° if possible (see directions in How to Store Apples over Winter).

Fire Blight: Causes leaves to turn brown and remain dead on twigs. Often worse after a hailstorm. Control: Spray trees with streptomycin when buds are in full pink, repeat at 4-day intervals until petals fall. Make applications at night since the drug's potential is reached only then.

Small Apples: Due to overcropping, or failure to thin. Apple trees often produce more fruits than will develop into proper size. Thin fruits early in spring (see Thinning Fruits).

Green Apples Fail to Ripen: Due to too rich a soil or too much nitrogen. Early varieties tend to ripen over a 2- or 3-week period. Late-ripening varieties mature their fruits evenly, and whole tree of ripe fruits can be harvested in a single day.

Wormy Tunnels in Apples: Called railroad worm or apple maggot. The maggot has usually left the apple before harvest and cannot be seen in the fruit, only his trail. Spray with methoxychlor or Sevin (see All-purpose Spray) every 2 weeks starting about June 20. No. 1 pest of apples.

Lots of Blossoms But Few Fruits: Lack of pollinator trees (see Crosspollination). Rooster trees help all fruits.

Water Core Inside: Inside watery or icelike. Worse on Spies, Greenings, Delicious, and in regions of intense sunlight and high temperatures. Control: Harvest crop before it has become completely mature, since this condition is not present in apples somewhat immature. Not serious, fruit is edible. May disappear after storage.

Apple Russet: Caused by pear leaf blister mite. Spray with Malathion or Kelthane.

Apple Scald: Skin has scalded look. Worse after high temperatures prevail during last 4 to 6 weeks of growing season. Control: Wrap ap-

Apple deformed and russeted by pear leaf blister mites.
(USDA Photo)

ples in oiled paper or dip in diphenylamine. Worst on Cortland, Greening.

Apple Scab: Causes black scabs on skin. Use Captan in the all-purpose mixture.

Tent Caterpillars: Cut out and burn entire twig. DO NOT BURN IN TREE.

Cedar Apple Rust: Leaves have yellow or orange spots. Destroy cedars nearby.

Apple Tree Borers: If you see piles of sawdust around base of trunk, it's flatheaded tree borer. Spray with Sevin or Chlordane, or squirt some borer paste into holes and seal off with putty.

Cracked Bark: Winter injury, caused on bright sunny day in late winter. Painting trunks with whitewash helps ward off this "southwest injury," as the trouble is called, since it is most common on the southwest side. No control.

Dying of Apple Tree in Midsummer: Due to girdling by rabbits, mice, etc., winter before. May be due to hoe, or cultivating machine, lawn mower, injuring and killing the tree. Also wet soil, or dry soil. Waterlogged soil shuts out oxygen.

Holes in Trunks: This is the work of the sapsucker, a bird which drills holes to induce sap to flow. This sap attracts bugs which the bird likes to feed on. Holes are the size of a lead pencil and often clustered in a ring 2 inches wide, and you find the holes confined to the upper parts of the tree trunk where the bark is younger and not so thick. As for control, there's nothing you can do to keep out the sapsucker.

Woodpeckers, on the other hand, dig out and feed on borers and bark beetles in the tree, thus being helpful. They'll chisel holes in dead and dying wood in search of food.

USES

Apples on the Half Shell: 3 to 4 large ripe avocados, salad greens, 2 (6½-ounce) cans crabmeat, ½ cup slivered toasted almonds, 1½ cups diced, unpeeled red apples, ½ cup mayonnaise, ⅓ cup sour cream. Halve avocados, set on greens, fill with mixture of remaining ingredients.

Apple Potato Salad: 6 tablespoons yellow prepared mustard, 3 tablespoons evaporated milk, 3 tablespoons sugar, 3 tablespoons vinegar, ½ teaspoon salt, 4 cups cubed cooked potatoes, 1 medium onion, finely chopped, 1 cup sliced celery, 2 cups diced, unpeeled red apples. Combine first 5 ingredients, beat until light and fluffy. Combine remaining ingredients, add mustard dressing immediately, toss until thoroughly mixed. Serve on crisp salad greens. Serves 6 to 8.

Boiled Apple Cider: Useful for making elderberry and other pies, also as syrup for pancakes and waffles. To make, take fresh sweet cider and boil slowly over low heat as you would sap to make maple syrup. Boil until consistency of molasses, put in glass fruit jars and seal while hot. Gallon of cider makes about 1 pint.

Cape Cod Baked Apples: 1 can whole-berry cranberry sauce, 6 large baking apples, ½ cup miniature marshmallows, ⅓ cup finely chopped pecans. Spread ½ the cranberry sauce in shallow baking pan. Add enough water to fill pan to a depth of about ½ inch. Core apples, peel about ¼ down from stem end, place peeled side down on cranberry sauce in pan. Bake at 250° for 30 minutes. Turn apples peeled side up. Combine remaining cranberry sauce, marshmallows, and pecans. Fill apples heaping full. Return to oven and bake 15 minutes longer or until apples are tender. Serves 6.

Pork Chops with Jellied Apple Slices: Panfry or bake 6 loin pork chops. Core red apples, do not pare, cut in 12 thick slices. Place apples in large frying pan. Dissolve 1 (8-ounce) glass currant jelly in ½ cup boiling water, pour over apples. Cook over low heat, turning occasionally, until tender and well glazed. To serve, surround chops with apple slices and garnish with parsley.

Sliced Baked Apples, Dixie: 8 cups thinly sliced apples, ½ cup golden seedless raisins, 1 cup orange juice, ⅓ cup flour, ⅓ cup sugar, ½ teaspoon cinnamon, 2 tablespoons butter or margarine, 2 tablespoons grated orange peel, ¼ teaspoon salt, 4 tablespoons peanut butter, ½ cup salted peanuts. Pour apples into 2-quart casserole. Add raisins and orange juice. Combine remaining ingredients, except peanuts; mix until crumbly and sprinkle over apples. Scatter salted peanuts over all. Bake at 375° about 45 minutes, or until apples are soft. Serves 8 to 10.

APRICOT (*Prunus armeniaca*)

If you can grow peaches, you can grow apricots. Their blossoms will withstand about as much frost as peach blossoms. However, the apricot blossoms about a week earlier than the peach, and the blossom shucks are shed earlier, leaving the small green fruits exposed at an earlier date, when frost is more likely to occur. The small fruits are killed by a temperature of 29°, therefore it is important to plant apricots on frost-free sites if possible. Generally speaking, culture for apricot is same as for peaches.

Planting: Select, deep, well-drained soils. Plant 2 varieties for cross-pollination. In spring, cut top back ⅓ and mulch with straw or sawdust. Feeding is same as for peaches (which see). Harvesting should start when fruits are well colored and firm. If picked too soon the fruit will be dull in appearance and/or have poor flavor.

TROUBLES

Winter Injury: Southwest side of tree is split open, due to extreme drop in temperature. Wrap trunk with burlap or whitewash trunk, to prevent winter injury.

Wormy Fruit: Due to plum curculio. Spray with methoxychlor when fruits are size of marble.

Peach Tree Borer: Mothball crystals or Malathion on trunk.

Brown Rot (see illustration): Spray with Captan when blossoms are in ballon-pink stage, and at petal-fall stage.

Verticillium Wilt: Sudden wilting and dying of limbs. Avoid using land for apricots that has been used for raspberries, strawberries, tomatoes, potatoes, peppers, or melons in the past 5 years.

BLACKBERRY (*Rubus*)

If you aren't lucky enough to have access to the wild blackberry then you should plant a few cultivated varieties in the backyard. Darrow, Bailey, and Hedrick are good varieties.

Blackberries are biennial. That is, canes grow one season, fruit the second, then die and are replaced by another set of canes. They'll grow in any well-drained soil. Plant in spring or fall.

Pruning: Berries are borne on leaf branches arising from canes of the previous season's growth. In spring (before growth starts) cut out weak and broken canes. Thin the remaining vigorous canes to 8 or 10 in a row not over a foot wide. Cut back the branches to 12 buds. In early June new shoots will come along, and when about 3 feet high, pinch the tips off to force side buds into growth and produce squatty, well-branched canes. After crop is harvested, canes which produced fruit can be removed at any time.

Harvesting: Let berries become dead ripe before harvesting, since the riper fruits are sweeter.

TROUBLES

Orange Rust: Remove infected plants and burn as soon as discovered. Grub out and burn suckers coming up from base of infected plants. Nearby wild plants should be pulled and burned.

Tarnished Plant Bug: Causes imperfect berries. Spray with Sevin just before first flowers open.

Tree Cricket: Punctures stems, which break. Remove affected stem and burn at pruning time.

Red-necked Cane Borer: Causes swellings or galls. Cut off and burn during dormant pruning season.

Wild blackberries harbor many insects and should be eliminated near cultivated stands.

BLUEBERRY (*Vaccinium corymbosum*)

You can grow big, fat blueberries right in your own backyard. Resistance to low temperatures, varieties that produce plump juicy blue fruit in abundance, and handsome reddish-brown foliage in fall are working their magic to increase the popularity of homegrown blueberries, only 45 years from the completely wild state to domestication for easy growing. As a rule, blueberries need no spraying, can thrive in sun or semi-shade, and produce fruit a year after planting. They are, however, soil-fussy, and demand a humus-rich acid soil.

Blueberries require cross-pollination for better crops. At least 2 varieties should be planted. To provide a long picking season early, mid-season, and late varieties should be selected.

Note: Garden "huckleberries" (which see)—also called seed huckleberries, sunberries, wonderberries, garden berries—are not huckleberries or blueberries, but belong to the genus *Solanum*. Incidentally, huckleberries and blueberries are not the same, belong to different plant genera. Huckleberry has 10 large seeds, each of which has a bony covering which crackles the teeth. Blueberry has 50 to 75 small seeds which are not noticeable when eaten.

Buying Plants: For best results, buy rooted plants from your nursery. Prune the branches back ½ at planting time.

Soil: Blueberries like a moist soil, neither too sandy nor too heavy with clay. The secret is to incorporate a lot of humus, peat, or sawdust in the soil. Plants do well in sun or shade and should be planted 3 feet apart in rows 6 feet apart. Blueberries like a VERY ACID SOIL. Soil that is alkaline can be acidified by adding powdered sulfur, or aluminum sulfate. If your pH reading is over 5.0, here's how much aluminum sulfate to use (for each 100 square feet, spaded in).

PRESENT pH	TO CHANGE TO pH OF 4.5 (BEST FOR BLUEBERRIES)	
	ON SANDY SOILS	ON LOAM SOILS
5.0 (your county	add 2.4 lbs.	add 7.2 lbs.
5.5 agent will test	add 4.8 lbs.	add 8.3 lbs.
6.0 your soil to find	add 7.2 lbs.	add 21.0 lbs.
6.5 out pH reading)	add 9 lbs.	add 27½ lbs.
7.0	add 11.4 lbs.	add 38.8 lbs.

You can, of course, have a soil test made to determine the acidity of your land (see Liming and Soil Acidity), but for the small home garden, we like the method devised by Michigan State University for growing blueberries in tubs; you are, after all, going to plant at least 2, but probably no more than 4 blueberry plants of at least 2 varieties for cross-pollination: the Concord variety for early, Rancocas for midseason, plus a choice between Rubel and Jersey.

Feeding: Sulfate of ammonia is the best material for feeding blueberries. A tablespoonful spread in a circle close to each plant every 2 or 3 weeks during the growing season is good. Blueberry plants cannot convert or use the nitrogen in nitrate of soda. Don't use nitrate of soda, or ammonium nitrate. If leaves are yellow-looking, plants make no growth, even though you feed them, then switch to ammonium sulfate, because blueberries can use the nitrogen in that form. Just scatter the sulfate of ammonia (or sulfur) over the surface of the ground or surface of soil mulch. Two ounces per plant is O.K., giving that much more each year until mature plants 5 or 6 years old are getting ¾ pound a year. They need this acid plant food.

Pruning: Prune back ½ at planting time, and give them a pruning yearly after the third year to maintain big, fat berries. HEAVY PRUNING IS IMPORTANT. Your object is to reduce the crop, to prevent overbearing, which causes small berries and poor bush growth. Proper pruning also prevents bush from being too dense and twiggy. Prune in early spring before bushes come into bloom. All short twiggy growth is taken out, leaving vigorous new shoots 6 inches or more in length. If these contain too many fruit buds, some can be cut to leave only 3 or 4 buds per shoot. This gives marble-sized berries, more vigorous shoot growth, and a better-producing plant the following year.

A comparison of the results obtained from light and heavy pruning of mature blueberry plants:

Light Pruning:
> Greater yields
> Smaller berries
> Later maturity

Heavy Pruning:
> Smaller yields
> Larger Berries
> Earlier maturity

Some fruit can be harvested the third year. Full production is reached by the sixth or seventh year and the plants can be expected to bear for at least 30 years.

Do your blueberry pruning in early spring before the bushes bloom. A good rule of thumb is to allow 1 fruit bud for each 3 inches of new shoot growth, thereafter removing all sucker shoots and twiggy branches. The vigorous new shoots remaining should be about 6 inches in length and well spread.

Keep your blueberry plantation free of weeds, and remove flowers for the first and second year after planting to help the bushes develop quickly.

Mulching: Blueberries have roots close to the surface, therefore need a mulch of sawdust. Any kind of sawdust is O.K., hardwood, soft-

Pruning blueberries is simple. Prune back vigorous new branches as shown by black marks. Shortened branches will send out new branches the following year and produce flower buds.

Left, Blueberries grown in metal drum. (Michigan State University)
Right, Blueberries grown inside tire, and mulched with sawdust.

wood, fresh or weathered. You can't grow blueberries without sawdust or similar mulch (see section on Mulches). Peat moss is good. Oak leaves are good because they leave an acid residue.

Propagation: If you want to start your own plants, it's simple. Use hardwood cuttings from dormant wood, using 1-year shoots. Take cuttings in late fall, using "whip" shoots 10 to 30 inches long. Store them in the cool, moist cellar, in old sawdust or sphagnum moss. Cuttings should be taken from the shoots, and these are usually 3 or 4 inches long, and from ⅛ to ¼ inch in diameter. Thicker or thinner wood does not do well. Root in a mixture of sand and peat moss in the greenhouse. Maintain a high humidity until roots form. Cuttings may also be taken in April and rooted in a sand-peat mixture in a cold frame. Shade from direct sun. Rooted cuttings can be left in the propagating bed over winter and protected from alternate freezing and thawing by a straw mulch.

Growing Blueberries in Tubs: For tub culture, you use oil drums cut in half with the bottom and tops removed. Sink the tubs in the soil and fill with a mixture of ½ bushel of sawdust or peat moss mixed with good garden soil. This mixture may then be acidified by adding from ¼ pound to 1 pound of ammonium sulfate or sulfur—the former for solids already acid, the latter for very alkaline or nearly neutral soils. Into these specially prepared tubs you then set out your blueberry plants, early in spring, trimmed back to little more than ½ the size the nursery sends you. Trim off ragged root ends also, and set the plants just a little deeper in the soil than they were in the nursery row, as indicated by the soil line on the plant.

Picking: Berries continue to grow and enlarge for some time after they appear ripe. Too early harvesting results in reduced yield. By allowing berries to become fully ripe, the flavor is improved. Berries should be blue all over. Overripe berries shrivel and may drop badly.

TROUBLES

Small Inferior Fruit: Due to lack of pruning. Pruning is important to good blueberry culture, as the plants have a tendency to overbear, producing small fruit. A large number of fruit buds form on new shoot growth and if all these fruit buds, each producing a cluster of 5 to 8 berries, are permitted to mature, your fruit will be small and inferior.

Ordinarily, blueberries need no spraying. However, there is the blueberry stem borer, comes in June or July, wilts plant. Grub mines entire length of stem, enters the roots, and comes up in other stalks. Control: Remove infected part and burn. Last week in July is good time to do this. Cut wilted tips off well below girdled area. Spraying with Sevin in May is helpful.

Bird Damage: Cover with netting, cheesecloth, tobacco netting, anti-bird mesh.

Mummy Berry: Causes berries to harden and shrivel, and tender shoots to die. Control: Stir up soil mulch 2 or 3 times in early spring to bury mummies at least an inch.

Stunt Disease: Spread by leafhoppers. Spray or dust with Sevin. Pull up and burn stunted, diseased bushes as they never recover.

Botrytis Blight: Causes blighting of blossoms in wet weather. No control.

Phomopsis Twig Blight: Girdles shoots and causes shriveling. Remove and burn weakened twigs.

Blueberry Maggot: Same as blueberry fruit fly. Larvae (grubs) get in the flesh. Control: Dust with rotenone or Sevin starting when berries begin to color up.

Fall Webworm: Insect spins a dirty white web in late July or August. Remove webs by hand and destroy caterpillars.

Yellowing of Leaves (Chlorosis): Due to iron deficiency. You can apply iron chelate (pronounced "key-late"), ¼ pound around base of each plant in fall.

Sour Fruit: Picked before ripened. Allow to ripen fully on the bush.

BOYSENBERRY, DEWBERRY, AND LOGANBERRY

You hear a lot about boysenberries, dewberries, and loganberries, but few people ever take the trouble to explain what they are and what they'll do for gardeners. All are bramble fruits (family Rubus). The loganberry is a hybrid originated in California by a Judge Logan, who produced a cross between a western black dewberry and a red raspberry. The result: a loganberry, a plant not altogether hardy in northern gardens, unless you take the trouble to mulch it heavily with straw.

Boysenberries are a cross between loganberry, raspberry, and blackberry. Berries are tremendous—often more than 2 inches long, and very delicious. Canes are long and thorny and must be covered in winter if fruit is to be produced. If you're willing to fuss with it, you can protect the canes and grow them on trellises in summer. Plant them 6 feet apart.

If you want to try dewberries, grow the Lucretia, not hardy in north unless you give it protection. Then there's the youngberry, similar to the boysenberry, and it comes with spines and without spines. The youngberry and the boysenberry are replacing the loganberry. There's also a nectarberry, which is similar to the boysenberry, and there's a thornless boysen for your garden. Don't go overboard on the thornless sports since they are not as productive as the thorny plants.

In general, all these brambles take about the same care. Try not to grow boysenberries where tomatoes, eggplants, or peppers have grown recently, since these crops sometimes have a wilt disease which may carry over in the soil.

Boysenberries and its relatives are started by layering tips of new canes in fall. They root in spring and can be cut from the mother plant. Mulch the plants with sawdust, straw, plastic sheet, or whatever is available, to keep down weeds, conserve moisture, and give juicy berries. Feed same as you do raspberries (which see).

Supports Needed: At the beginning of the second growing season a trellis must be erected to support the trailing canes so that the fruit will be easy to pick and kept out of the soil during splashing rains.

A suitable trellis may have the lower wire about 2 feet from the ground and the upper wire 1½ feet higher. If a trellis is not convenient, posts 6 feet high may be used. In spring 5 or 6 of the largest canes are cut back to a length of 6 feet and tied up to the wires or to the posts. The remaining canes are cut out. In early August after the crop is harvested the canes which fruited are removed, as they are no longer of use to the plant. The new canes which grow during the current season are allowed to trail on the ground until the following spring when they in turn are trellised in preparation for bearing the next season's crop.

Winter Mulching: In the states north of Washington, D.C., it will be necessary to winter-protect the boysenberry and its relatives. In the milder regions of the northern states the canes may occasionally come through the winter without injury if unprotected and provided there is abundant snow cover. Since this is uncertain, winter protection should be provided. Either soil or straw may be used for covering, 2 or 3 inches over the canes is sufficient. Wheat straw, marsh hay, or similar materials may be piled on the prostrate canes to a depth of 3 or 4 inches. In the spring if desired, the straw cover may be left on the surface of the soil as a summer mulch. The canes should be covered before severe cold weather sets in and uncovered before much warm weather occurs. In the latitude of New York City, December 1 to about the end of March is the period when protection is needed.

Pruning: see Raspberry.

SWEET AND SOUR CHERRIES (*Prunus avium* and *P. cerasus*)

Every homeowner should have a couple of cherry trees around the place. If you can grow peaches, you can grow cherries. Both the sweet and sour varieties can live on a wide diversity of soils, provided they are well drained. The cherry is sensitive to a poorly drained soil and you'll be wasting money trying to grow them in a heavy clay soil.

Sour cherries are easier to grow, and have a wide range of uses in cooking, baking, and canning. Sweet cherries cannot be beaten for fresh, delicious, out-of-hand eating.

Varieties: Sweet cherry varieties range from the pink-fleshed, black-skinned Windsor, and all pink and golden Royal Ann (called Napoleon in most catalogs), to the large, black, and temptingly juicy Black Tartarian and Schmidt's Bigarreau. Montmorency is the most widely grown sour cherry. Duke cherries are hybrids of sweet and sour cherries, and have some of the characteristics of each.

Cross-pollination: Sweet cherries do not pollinate themselves and need the rooster proclivities supplied by either Windsor or Black Tartarian, or both. In considering sweet cherries for your garden, figure on 2 varieties, or your best efforts may come to naught. Montmorency is self-fertile, but may not be used to pollinate sweet cherries, which bloom earlier. Likewise, sweet cherries will not pollinate sour ones. Both sweet and sour cherries will pollinate the Duke varieties.

Planting: Spring's the good time to plant, although many plant in fall. Set the tree in the hole slightly deeper than it was in the nursery. Tamp the soil around the roots and move the tree up and down to help settle earth in around the roots and exclude any air pockets. As the hole is being filled, the soil should be stamped firmly. Most failures in planting are due to insufficient or improper firming of the soil about the roots.

At planting time all branches that form narrow angles with the trunk should be removed. If allowed to remain they are almost sure to split under the loads of fruit, weight of snow, or during heavy windstorms. Also, winter injury is worse in such narrow-angled crotches.

Pruning: Proper pruning at planting time will save you a lot of trouble later on, since a mature cherry tree needs little pruning except to remove crossing limbs that rub against one another, and weak crotches which are apt to split. Weak unions are common in most varieties of sweet cherries, and that's why you should save all the wide-angled crotches, removing all those that grow up against the trunk. Over-pruning delays bearing so don't be "prune-happy" with any fruit tree. In a nutshell, a mature cherry needs just a light heading back of main branches and moderate thinning out of fine wood. Except for rotted or broken limbs, that's all the pruning you should worry about. Early spring is a good time to do the job.

Before you plant the 1- or 2-year-old cherry, trim the top back ⅓ and cut out weak-angled crotches. Also, trim the roots back an inch or so, to remove scraggly ends and to encourage tiny feeder roots.

A wrinkle little known outside the trade in cherry-growing is to spread the branches of the tree with notched boards when the tree is young and supple. This makes a broad and open tree and produces extra fruit. Apple growers do this on varieties which tend to grow straight up.

Feeding: Nitrate of soda or ammonium nitrate can be applied in spring or fall. Nitrate of soda is used at the rate of ⅓ pound for each year of the tree's age. For example, a 6-year-old tree would be given 2 pounds of nitrate of soda. Use ammonium nitrate at ½ this rate.

Dwarf Potted Cherry: Prunus jacquemonti is a hardy shrub growing 6 feet high. Edible fruit similar in appearance to common sour cherry, but smaller, ¼ to ⅛ inch diameter. Will bear in a pot, but don't expect a big crop from this novelty. Bears when 3 or 4 feet high.

Homemade Cherry Pitter: Want a good cherry pitter for less than a penny? Try using a hairpin or a paper clip to remove cherry pits. Nothing beats them for doing the job quickly.

TROUBLES

The all-purpose spray program (see Fruits for the Home and Garden) will control most of the major troubles you will encounter in growing your own cherries, with the possible exception of those years in which late frosts (against which there is no practical protection for the home gardener) take the blossoms. Should this happen to your cherry program, you will have to resign yourself to waiting for the next year's crop. Birds are often a greater menace to sweet cherries than all the insects, diseases, and inclement weather combined. Use a netting over trees. Also plastic owls, fur pieces, "snakes," flashing items in trees. (See section on Animal Control.)

Winter Injury: Sweet cherries are more susceptible to winter-killing from extreme drop in temperature (shows up in summer). Bark is shriveled and split, separates from the tree; vital cambium layer has been killed. Much of the winter injury results from the cherry's susceptibility to improper soil drainage. Trees on heavy, poorly drained soil become weak, suffer from adverse conditions during the growing season, and are more susceptible to winter injury. Cherries must be grown on well-drained soils.

No Fruit: If your trees bear 1 year, none next, it may be due to late-spring frost killing the buds, or winter injury. Only a few fruits means imperfect pollination. If your cherry tree has small green cherries which fall before maturing, your trouble may be due to a shortage of rooster trees in the neighborhood. Sometimes a sweet cherry tree has only a few large fruits on, or none at all, and this trouble can be eliminated by introducing a pollinator tree. A sour cherry bears 3 or 4 years after planting, a sweet cherry 1 to 6 years.

Among sweet cherries Napoleon, Bing, Lambert, and Emperor Francis varieties will not cross-pollinate one another, and you have to have a third rooster tree nearby, such as Windsor, Black Tartarian, or Giant when you plant any 2 of these.

Plum Curculio: Brownish adult beetle lays eggs on fruit, which hatch into tiny worms that feed on the fruit, often causing it to fall from the tree. Spray with Malathion.

Brown Rot: The disease that hits your sweet and sour cherries with violence right after a rain, being worse on sweets. If you spray your trees with a preblossom spray (just before the blooms open) using lime sulfur, you'll check brown rot disease before it starts.

Cherry Fruit Fly: The pest that lays eggs in the flesh of the fruit, and these eggs hatch into tiny, whitish legless maggots (that's the "worm" you bite into). Spray with the all-purpose spray (which see) just as the cherries are forming and again before they just start to show color. Wash the fruit before eating.

Black Cherry Aphid: The pest that causes leaves to pucker up, turn brown, and die. The aphids secrete a honeydew, too, which collects on leaves and fruit, and a sooty fungus grows in the stuff, making the fruit practically inedible. Control: Lime sulfur while buds are still brown will kill the eggs. If a dormant treatment has been omitted, spray with nicotine sulfate, 1 teaspoon to a quart of soapy water at the green-tip stage (when the leaves of the blossom buds are bursting and show ¼ inch of green color). This will catch most of the aphids.

Cherry Leaf Spot Disease: One of the worst problems yet, causes holes in leaves, which yellow and fall, and makes the trees susceptible to winter-killing. Control: Spray with Bordeaux mixture or Fermate or Captan in the petal-fall stage, again 2 or 3 times in the foliage in July. LOWER SURFACE OF LEAVES MUST BE SPRAYED TO PREVENT LEAF INFECTION.

Cherry Yellows: Caused by a virus which makes the leaves drop, especially in cool weather. No control.

Powdery Mildew: Can be checked by using the all-purpose formula, or Bordeaux mixture. Those gum boils you see in the bark are due to injuries, also work of borers. Scrape off the bubble and poke the borer entrance with hot wire.

Cracked Fruit: Due to rain after a dry spell. Causes pressure which forces skin to burst. No control.

Trees Dying in Summer: Usually due to winter-killing. Trouble does not show up until summer. Cut tree down and plant new one. Plant 2 if sweet cherries are wanted.

USES

Preparing Cherries for Freezing: Look over, pit if necessary. Wash and pack in freezer containers. Add sugar to taste either before freezing or when ready to use.

Cherry Cheese Cake:

Crust: ¾ cup butter or margarine, 3 tablespoons sugar, ⅛ teaspoon salt, 1½ cups sifted flour. Cream butter or margarine with sugar and salt, add flour and blend well. Press crumb mix in bottom and sides of 10"x6" cake pan. Do not cover rim of pan.

Filling: 1-pint can sour pie cherries, ½ cup sugar, 3 tablespoons flour, ⅛ teaspoon red food coloring. Drain can of sour pie cherries, combine sugar and flour in saucepan. Add cherry juice and blend together. Mix well over medium heat, stirring constantly until thick. Add food coloring and cherries. Bake in preheated oven (350°) for 15 minutes.

Topping: 8-ounce package cream cheese, softened, 1 egg, ⅓ cup sugar, ½ teaspoon vanilla. Combine cream cheese, unbeaten egg, sugar, and vanilla. Beat until thick and creamy. Pour in pan on top of cherry filling with small openings in a few places. Bake in preheated oven, 350°, for 30 minutes, until cheese is golden brown. Cool before cutting into small squares for serving.

Cherry Cinnamon Cobbler:

Filling: ½ cup sugar, 2 tablespoons red cinnamon candies, 2 tablespoons cornstarch, 1-pint can sour cherries, drained. Mix sugar, candies, cornstarch, and juice from cherries. Cook until mixture thickens, then add cherries and pour into 8"x8" square pan.

Dough: 1½ cups sifted flour, 2 teaspoons baking powder, ½ teaspoon salt, 6 tablespoons brown sugar, ½ cup shortening, ⅓ cup chopped pecans, 1 egg, 2 tablespoons milk, 1 tablespoon soft butter, ¼ teaspoon cinnamon, ½ cup powdered sugar, 1 tablespoon lemon juice. Sift together flour, baking powder, and salt, add 3 tablespoons brown sugar. Work in shortening and pecans. Add slightly beaten egg and milk. Roll out to 14″x12″ and brush with butter. Sprinkle with 3 tablespoons brown sugar and cinnamon. Roll up and cut in slices and place on top of first mixture. Bake in preheated 400° oven for 30 minutes. Serve warm with Lemon Glaze.

Lemon Glaze: ½ cup sifted powdered sugar, 1 tablespoon lemon juice. Combine sugar and lemon juice, pour on cobbler while hot.

Cherry Cream Cheese Pie:

Pastry Shell: 1 cup flour, sifted, ⅓ cup shortening, ¾ teaspoon salt, 2 tablespoons water. Sift flour, add shortening and salt and cut into mixture. Add water and roll out. Bake in 9-inch pie pan at 425° for 8 minutes, cool.

Filling: 2½ cups frozen cherries, ¼ cup sugar, 2 tablespoons cornstarch, 3 ounces cream cheese, ½ cup powdered sugar, ½ teaspoon vanilla, 1 cup heavy cream. Drain cherries, mix sugar and cornstarch. Add syrup from cherries (1 cup). Cook sugar, cornstarch, and syrup for 2 minutes. Remove from heat and add cherries. Cool, whip cream until stiff. Beat cream cheese, powdered sugar, and vanilla together until smooth. Carefully fold whipped cream into the cream-cheese mixture. Turn into the prepared pie shell, spreading evenly. Spoon the pie filling evenly over top. Chill thoroughly before serving. Serve chilled as a dinner dessert or a buffet luncheon.

Cherry Jubilee:

Meringue Cups: Beat 2 egg whites till frothy. Add 1 teaspoon vanilla, ½ teaspoon cream of tartar, ¼ teaspoon salt. Mix well. Add to this gradually ½ cup sugar. Beat until stiff peaks are formed. Drop by spoonfuls on cookie sheet. Sprinkle ½ teaspoon confectioners' sugar on top of each one. Bake in preheated 250° oven.

Filling: Drain can of frozen cherries, reserving few for top. Whip together ½ pint cream, 3 tablespoons sugar, ½ teaspoon vanilla. Fold cherries into whipped cream, add ½ cup nuts, mix together. Spoon mixture into meringue cups. Top with cherry. Bake at 250° for 1 hour.

Cherry Kuchen:

1 egg, beaten well, ½ cup sugar, ¼ cup milk, ½ teaspoon vanilla, 1½ cups biscuit mix, 1 (1-pound) can pie cherries* (1½ cups) drained

---

*Frozen fresh cherries may be used without changing recipe. Drain cherries before and after chopping.

and chopped, ¼ cup flour, ½ cup light brown sugar, ½ teaspoon cinnamon, 3 tablespoons butter, ½ cup chopped nuts. Combine beaten egg, sugar, milk, and vanilla. Add biscuit mix and stir until smooth. Pour into an oiled 8″x8″x2″ pan. Sprinkle drained cherries evenly over batter. Mix flour, brown sugar, and cinnamon well; cut in butter until like cornmeal, add nuts, and sprinkle over cherries. Bake at 375° about 30 minutes. Serve as coffee cake or as a pudding with cream. Serves 9.

Easy Cherry Fluff Pie: 1 9-inch baked pie shell, 1 package cooked vanilla pudding mix, ¼ cup sugar, 1-pint can pie cherries, 1 cup whipping cream. Combine pudding mix and sugar. Drain cherries. Add water to juice to make 1½ cups, add gradually to pudding mix, mixing well. Cook over medium heat to full boil, stirring constantly. Add drained cherries and cool thoroughly to room temperature. Fold in stiffly beaten cream. Pour into baked pie shell and chill. Serves 6.

CURRANTS AND GOOSEBERRIES

Currants and gooseberries all belong to the same family (Ribes). Because these are so easy to grow, more home gardeners should plant them. Usually you can plant them and forget them. There's a red, white, and even a black currant.

Currants will grow on soil too wet for other fruit. In dry soils gooseberries and currants suffer from premature falling of foliage and fruit. Some states require you have a permit to plant both currants and gooseberries because they may carry the white pine blister rust fungus, a disease that spends part of its life cycle on the canes of the fruits. Check with your county agent or nurseryman. No currants or gooseberries should be planted within a 900-foot radius of white pine trees, or within 1,500 feet of any nursery where white pine seedlings are grown.

Varieties and Planting: For a current, try Red Lake; Pixwell is a good variety of gooseberry. Set plants out in spring, or you can dig up clumps and transplant them in early spring. You can start new plants by layering, covering a branch with soil and allowing it to root. Both currants and gooseberries lose leaves early in fall. Both are self-fruitful and you need only 1 bush of either.

Pruning: Annual pruning is relatively simple. Usually more canes are formed than are needed for a shapely bush. During the dormant season some of the weakest ones should be removed close to the ground. All canes should be taken out when they become 4 years old, since at that age they become weak and not fruitful. It is rarely necessary to do any cutting back of terminals. Of course, in pruning, any dead or broken canes or branches will be taken out. It is well also to remove branches that are so low that when loaded with fruit they will touch the ground. A well-pruned currant bush will have about 5 1-year shoots, 4 2-year, 3 3-year and 2 or 3 4-year canes, if they are still vigorous.

Soil can be cool and moist. They don't like hot, dry situations. Partial shade is good. Feed in spring, using a balanced fertilizer such as 5-10-5, a couple handfuls per bush.

Propagation: Currants can be propagated by cuttings, 8 to 10 inches long, made from well-matured shoots of 1-year growth. They are collected in late fall or early winter, stored in moist sand, sawdust, or peat moss in a cool place where they will remain dormant until early spring, then planted about 6 inches apart in garden and grown for 1

Currant bush after pruning. Dotted lines indicate branches which have been pruned out or cut back.

to 2 years before planting in a permanent spot. When planting cuttings, all but the 2 upper buds are covered with soil. Gooseberries are propagated most readily by mound layering (see illustration in Raspberry section), and by hardwood cuttings.

TROUBLES

Rust: Do not plant near white pine trees (5-needled pine).

Currant Borer: Works inside canes. Cut infected cane back and burn.

Currant Aphid: Causes leaves to curl downwards. In fall, spray leaf undersides with Malathion, as leaf buds are opening or later if needed. Aphids are worst pest of currants and gooseberries.

Currant Fruit Fly: Causes wormy currants and gooseberries, berries drop off before ripening. Control by spraying with Malathion as soon as most of the flowers have wilted.

Birds: Bird damage can be checked by placing netting over bushes.

Powdery Mildew: Leaves show furry white patches, a problem on gooseberries. Control: spray with Bordeaux mixture or dormant spray of lime sulfur.

Leaf Spot Disease: Appears as small, dark-colored spots on older leaves, resulting in defoliation of the plants in late summer. Treat with Bordeaux mixture, spraying as soon as the disease appears. If plants were defoliated, the following year spray just after blossoms fall, again after fruit is picked, and again 3 weeks later. Or you can use zineb (75%), 6½ tablespoons per 5 gallons water, applied after harvest.

Imported Currant Worm: Larva is green spotted with black, will strip the bush in a few days. It attacks in early summer, so keep close watch and as soon as injury is seen, dust or spray with Sevin.

ELDERBERRY (*Sambucus canadensis*)

If you don't happen to have access to wild elderberries, you can grow the luscious cultivated varieties along the edge of your property. Nothing beats elderberries for homemade pies and jams. Cultivated elderberries are juicier and more prolific than wild elderberries.

Elderberries grow in any soil, especially good in wet spots. Might be a good idea to plant 2 for cross-pollination. Grow in full sun.

Pruning: Cut out dead wood, and any that crisscrosses.

Propagation: Start new plants from dormant cuttings 10 to 18 inches long. For best results make sure each cutting has 3 sets of opposite buds. Stick the cuttings into the ground in early spring. Bury entire cutting (except pair of top buds) in ground and water. Cuttings root fast. Home gardeners can start a cutting simply by sticking it in ground in its permanent location.

TROUBLES

No Berries: Lack of pollination.

Spindle Worm or Elder Borer: Tips of shoots turn black and fall off. Control by cutting out dead wood and burn.

Birds: Can be a problem. Place cloth netting over the fruits.

USES

To the gardener who would eat his herbs and have them too, elder is a banquet. From the time the first leaf buds appear in the spring, through the period when the fragrant flowers open wide in June, and on until the ripening fruit is made into jelly, this plant is edible. The young leaves may be scalded with boiling water and added to green salad served with French dressing. Elder flowers dipped in batter and browned in deep fat like fritters are a European delicacy.

Elderberry Blossom Fritters: Select the blossom heads just about the time they are turning into berries. Leave an inch or 2 of stem to use as a handle. Dip the blossoms into thin pancake batter and then fry in deep grease until golden brown. Shake off excess fat and sprinkle powdered sugar on top, and eat. Taste like waffles and the kids will enjoy them.

Elder Jelly: The half-ripe berries make tasty jelly which needs no added pectin. If it is later than you think when you get around to gathering the fruit and they are all deep purple, with no green ones to insure the jell, add apple juice or pectin.

Elderberry Pie: 1 heaping cup elderberries, ⅔ cup sugar, 2 to 3 tablespoons Boiled Cider (see apple recipe section), 1 tablespoon flour for thickening. Mix ingredients well and put in unbaked pie shell. Cover with top crust and bake at 375° until crust is done.

The first time I ever had this delectable pie was when I came home on furlough during World War II. My mother-in-law made it for me as a special treat. It has been one of my favorites ever since.

FIG (*Ficus carica*)

(For indoor culture in northern areas, and outdoor culture in southern areas, see elsewhere.) It's hard to believe that you can actually grow figs in regions where the winters drop to zero or lower. Many of our gardening friends have good luck growing figs in their backyard.

Where to Get Plants: You can purchase dwarf fig plants from various nurseries which sell rooted plants. Or you can get a plant from your friend who has one, by layering. Bend a branch over in early spring so that a portion 2 years old may be fastened down and covered with soil. Keep this covering moist and roots will form by summer. The new plant may then be detached and planted.

Soil and Care: Figs like full sun, well-drained soil, liquid feeding, plenty of moisture. Enrich the soil with humus, rotted manure, or peat. Many gardeners grow figs in tubs and move the tubs indoors in fall. Figs need little pruning. Train to 3 or 4 branches, making sure that they are as close to the ground as possible. Most of the pruning is done while the tree is young. Even if you don't grow them in tubs, you may get as much as 8 quarts of fruit from a single tree.

Figs pollinate themselves so you don't have to worry about cross-pollination. The fruit must ripen before you pick it. Wait until it starts turning a light purple and then pick. Sometimes an early frost threatens, but when it does you can cover the bush with a plastic sheet and uncover it the next day. There is nothing you can do to force figs to ripen earlier. Some varieties, such as Brown Turkey, mature fruits earlier than others.

Winter Treatment: Trick #1: In fall, cut some of the longest branches back a bit. Take some snow fence and wrap it around the bush tightly. Tack heavy insulation to the snow fence and tie the whole bush tightly with rope, packing straw and leaves in between the branches first. Straw is also packed around the roots. Some folks pack straw on top of the entire bush, covering the whole thing with canvas. Tarpaper is wrapped around the outside of the snow fence and on top of the bush. Tie the whole works up tightly with a good wire or rope. In spring, after danger of frost is over, unwrap, removing the straw, leaves. Soon new leaves will start to come out. You may have a couple bare branches, killed by the winter, but these can be cut off.

Trick #2: Dig a large hole alongside the tree, large enough so that the tree can be bent or pushed into the trench and buried. Place a rock over the tree. Cover with leaves, straw, hay, etc. and mound with a foot or more of soil. In spring, uncover the tree, push it back up so it's straight, and pack soil around it. It may be helpful to train the plant so its branches grow close to the ground.

TROUBLES

Figs are relatively free of insects and diseases.

Scale and Aphids: Apt to be troublesome. Spraying with Kelthane and syringing the foliage regularly while the bush is growing outside will help to keep these pests (and red spider mites) down.

GARDEN HUCKLEBERRY (*Solanum nigrum*)

Gardeners who raise the "garden huckleberry" (also called sunberry or wonderberry) will tell you the fruit makes the finest huckleberry pie you ever tasted. Garden huckleberries are not related to regular blueberries or huckleberries. One year I suggested that the fruit wasn't particularly tasty, and hundreds of letters came in, stating I was a poor judge. Garden huckleberries are not good for eating fresh, but many feel they are a good rival for the blueberry for pies and preserves. They can be quick-frozen or canned for future use.

If you're interested in this novelty, start seed indoors (or you can buy plants from a seedsman). Plant outdoors when all danger of frost is over, setting them about 3 feet apart. Give plenty of plant food and water often. If fruit is to be cooked for pies or canning, it can be picked a week after turning black.

USES

Garden Huckleberry Pie: 1 quart of garden huckleberries, 2 cups sugar, 2 tablespoons flour, 3 slices of lemon, 1 tablespoon butter, pinch nutmeg. Mix flour and sugar dry and add the fruit. Cook thoroughly, mash up the berries, and fill the pie. Some use 1 tablespoon of vinegar in place of lemon. It makes a good pie either way.

GRAPE (*Vitis labrusca*)

Since my home is in the very midst of a great grape-growing area of New York State—the Finger Lakes Region—I am particularly enthusiastic about grape culture and the pure delight of grapes as a fruit. I personally feel that no yard or garden should be without at least 1 or 2 grapevines.

Varieties: Among the many varieties of grapes you can grow, a few have outstanding qualities with which you should be familiar. Ontario, an early white grape, and Buffalo, a midseason blue grape, have the virtue of needing no spraying. Interlaken Seedless is a semi-early California white grape that is utterly delicious and sensational as a conversation piece over the back fence with your neighbors. Delaware and Brighton are excellent red grapes, but do not plant Brighton alone. It is self-sterile and needs another grape variety nearby for pollination. Steuben and Sheridan are Concord-type grapes, ripening late. Sheridan is an excellent keeper and can be held in cool storage sometimes until Christmas.

Soil: Grapes are not soil-fussy, but since they live and produce for as long as 60 to 80 years, you will want to do all you can to maintain high organic content of the soil in which you plant your grapes. This can be done by adopting a biennial program of mulching around the plants with waste hay, sawdust, wood chips, compost, or peat moss.

Planting: Select either 1- or 2-year-old grapevines for setting out and locate your vines away from frosty pockets, in full sun, and considerably out from under the shade of trees to prevent mildew of the vines. Where growing seasons are short, ripening can be hastened by planting on the south side of a building and training the vine against the wall.

Heat radiated from reflected sunlight on the wall will make the fruit ripen as much as a week earlier.

Usual spacing for grapes is 8 feet by 8 feet, but if space is limited you can set the plants on 7-foot centers. Holes should be dug 12 to 14 inches deep and 16 inches in diameter. I like to put some rotted compost in the bottom of the hole before planting the vine. Prune the top back so that you have 2 buds remaining. If you plant grapes in fall, hold the pruning over until spring; but in either season, trim off broken roots and any roots that are too long to fit without crowding into the hole you have provided.

Set the pruned vine into the hole so that the 2 buds are just above soil level, tamp soil firmly around the roots and into the hole, and water well. You can either mulch or cultivate the first year.

No trellis is needed for the vines the first year since they can be trained on stakes placed next to the base of the plant. The second year, you will need support for the growing vines. I use metal posts about 8 feet long, driven 2 to 2½ feet into the ground. On these posts 2 wires should be strung, one 5½ feet from the ground, and the second 2 feet below the top wire. This spacing will provide maximum exposure of leaf area to the sun and promote early ripening of the fruit.

Pruning Is Simple: So much has been written about pruning grape-vines there is little wonder that the home gardener is afraid to tackle it. But tackle it you must, because there is no one thing so completely disastrous to your efforts to grow grapes as vines that have not been regularly and (preferably) properly pruned. Better to be brave and hack away at your vines in good spirit than to say "I don't know how to do it" and neglect them entirely. The purpose of pruning is to limit the production of fruit and control cane growth so that cane and fruit are in balance at all times.

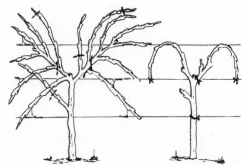

Pruning a mature grapevine looks complicated, but if you make the cuts as indicated, you'll be sure to have a bigger and better crop.
(J. E. Miller Nursery)

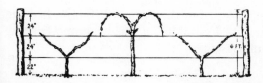

Train your grapes to grow on a trellis in this way and you'll have all the grapes you want. Use plastic-coated wire twists to secure the vines to the wire.
(J. E. Miller Nursery)

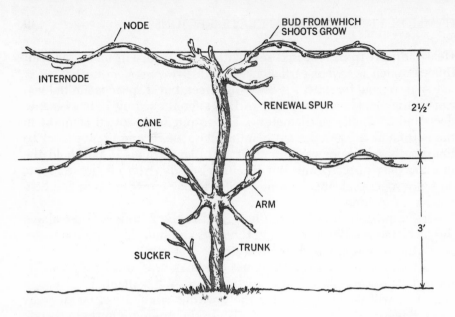

NODE

BUD FROM WHICH SHOOTS GROW

INTERNODE

CANE

RENEWAL SPUR

2½'

ARM

SUCKER

TRUNK

3'

Parts of a grapevine. The average home gardener can avoid a lot of confusion by selecting 4 good canes, and cutting out the rest. Try to prune your vine according to the diagram and you'll have a good crop. (Michigan State University)

In the main, the canes you want to save are those of last year's growth that are about 5 to 8 feet long and about as thick as a lead pencil, or slightly thicker and fairly short-jointed. Those buds near the center of the cane produce more than those at the base of the cane or near the tip. Thus, cut off the tips of the canes, leaving 8 to 12 buds. Remove all unnecessary old wood as well as less vigorous canes of last year's growth. That is the general idea of grape pruning. Specifically, here is what to do:

1) At planting time, prune canes back, leaving only 2 buds.

2) Second year prune off all growth except 1 strong cane and leave 3 to 5 buds. Tie this cane to the bottom wire of the trellis or support.

3) Third year leave 2 fruiting canes of 6 to 8 buds each, tied to the bottom wire.

4) Fourth year, leave 2 longer fruiting canes of 10 to 12 buds each, tying them to the bottom wire of the trellis.

5) Fifth year, leave 3 fruiting canes of 10 to 12 buds each, tying the longest cane to the top wire of the trellis.

In selecting the fruiting canes to leave, use those which have grown the previous year. You will also want to leave a "spur" for each cane —a spur being simply a cane cut back to 2 buds. The reason for this procedure is that the canes growing from this spur will be the fruiting canes to select from next year, and by following this program, fruiting canes are kept near the trunk of the vines.

Ordinarily, a total of 4 canes per vine is enough to leave on. A weak vine can support about 40 buds and a thrifty vine about 60. This is called "balanced pruning." If your grapes are a whole mass of canes, don't be discouraged. Select 4 of the best canes per vine and cut out all the rest. Choose canes of last year's growth which have buds at reasonably close intervals. After you have finished a good pruning job, you should have a lot of brush to clear away, which is as it should be, and not a sign that you have just completely ruined your little vineyard.

Feeding: Feeding grapes has just a few tricks to it that you should keep in mind. On vines that are making exceptionally strong growth, use fertilizers sparingly or you'll get all brush and no fruit. On top of that, overfertilized vines won't harden off properly for winter and may kill back. Grapevines have long roots that extend as much as 8 feet from the base of the vine, with most of the feeder roots 3 to 6 feet out from the base. Therefore, fertilizer applied to the base of the trunk will do almost no good at all. You must fertilize widely for grapes.

Grapes need potash, do not respond to phosphorus, and are fairly nitrogen-hungry at all times when yields are wanted. Provide the nitrogen needs of the vines by applying ⅓ pound of nitrate of soda or ⅙ pound of ammonium nitrate to each vine as soon as the buds start to swell in the spring. Potash should be supplied by the application of 2 pounds of potassium sulfate per vine.

Gibberellic Acid to Increase Bunch Size: Home gardeners often want to treat vines with gibberellic acid, a material which will increase the size of the bunches, but so far this is still in the experimental stage. If you want to experiment with it, fine, but gibberellin cannot offset the effects of frost, or take the place of good cultural practices. If used, follow manufacturer's directions.

Cutting the bark, or girdling, is an old practice (reported as early as 1776), consists of removing a narrow ring of bark, usually about ³⁄₁₆ inch, from the vine. Girdling interrupts the normal movement of food materials so that carbohydrates (plant foods) tend to accumulate in the vine above the wound. The wounds heal in a short time, so to be most effective, girdling should be timed to about the fifth or tenth day after full bloom. We don't recommend gibberellin or girdling, except for those who want to experiment.

TROUBLES

Most of the grape troubles you will encounter in the backyard planting can be controlled by spraying early with Bordeaux mixture, to which has been added 2 ounces of 50% wettable methoxychlor and ¼ ounce of spreader per 6¼ gallons of Bordeaux. Spray again with this mixture just before blossoming in mid-June, and a third time just after blossoming. For best results, spray grapevines when the leaves are dry. You'll find that Bordeaux mixture, and copper sprays (purchased in garden stores) are effective, even if they are old pesticides.

Flea Beetle: (see illustration p. 185). Use Malathion or methoxychlor in early spring.

Black Rot and Downy Mildew: Spray prebloom (just before blossoms open), using Captan or Bordeaux mixture.

Powdery Mildew (grayish fuzz on leaves): Use Captan or Karathane, immediately after bloom.

Grape Berry Moth, Leafhopper: Spray with methoxychlor immediately after bloom, and again about last week in July.

Do not blame bees, wasps, and hornets for damage you may find in your grapes. These insects will do no damage to sound fruit, but are simply sharing your enthusiasm for grapes—tempted to the vines by fruit that has popped open due to weather conditions. You will find this condition most often after a long drought followed by heavy rains late in the season. The grapes will build up pressure under these conditions, causing the fruit to pop open and drop to the ground.

Birds: Pick the flesh open and the sweetness attracts bees and hornets. Control: First, keep the birds out by using a nylon anti-bird netting. You can also go to the trouble of putting a paper or plastic sack around each cluster during ripening period to keep out the birds and the bees. There is no chemical control for this problem.

Caution: All effective bird repellents in the past have eventually failed due to overexposure. Any scarecrow, whether it be a piece of fur, polyethylene hawk, or "snake," should be used only when necessary and not flown constantly throughout the growing season. Birds get wise, fast.

Grapes Ripen Slowly: What makes some grapes ripen so slowly? There are several reasons for this. In the first place, grapes just won't grow and ripen well in everyone's backyard. They're sensitive to location and elevation. The plants need full sun to ripen fruit.

Another cause is weed-killer injury. Grapes are extremely sensitive to 2,4-D and may be injured by tiny amounts carried hundreds of feet in a wind from the roadside or from a neighbor. Weed killers cause grapes to ripen unevenly or not at all.

Another possibility is the way the vines are pruned. Home gardeners with 1 or 2 grapevines often do not prune adequately, the vines become overloaded, and the fruit does not ripen properly. Usually, such vines ramble all over a fence or an overhead arbor. Next spring prune your vine so that you have only 40 to 60 buds per vine.

The following recipes have been sent to me by readers, listeners, and gardeners all over America. While I've tested many, others have not been tested in my own kitchen. We hope you like them.

Brussels Sprouts and Grapes: 1 pint fresh or 1 (10-ounce) package frozen Brussels sprouts, boiling salted water, ¾ cup seedless green grapes, 1 small red onion, thinly sliced (optional), 2 tablespoons butter or margarine, ⅛ teaspoon salt, ⅛ teaspoon pepper. Cook Brussels sprouts in boiling salted water until tender. Add grapes, cook over low heat for 5 minutes or until grapes are plump and hot. Drain. Add butter or margarine and seasonings. If desired, add onion rings. Toss lightly until butter is melted. Serves 4.

Fresh Grape Salad: 2 packages lime-flavored gelatin, 2 cups boiling water, juice of 2 oranges and 1 lemon (put in cup and fill up with ginger ale), additional cup ginger ale, 1½ pounds seedless grapes, shredded cabbage (optional), salad greens. Dissolve gelatin in boiling water, add fruit juices and ginger ale. Stir. Put in washed grapes, add some shredded cabbage (if you like). Refrigerate. Remove from mold onto platter, garnish with greens. This salad is delightful served with nut or brown breads.

Grape Butter: 1 quart grapes, 1 quart sugar, cook for 15 minutes from time it comes to a good boil. Put through fine sieve while hot. Butter is thick and has good grape flavor.

Grape Cheese Pie: 1 (8-ounce) package cream cheese, 1 envelope (1 tablespoon) unflavored gelatin, ⅓ cup sugar, ¼ teaspoon salt, ¾ cup orange juice, 1 egg, separated, 1 tablespoon lemon juice, 1 tablespoon sugar, 1 cup halved, seeded Tokay grapes or halved green grapes, ½ cup heavy cream, whipped, 8- or 9-inch baked pie shell. Let cream cheese come to room temperature. In small bowl, whip cream cheese to fluffy texture at high speed. Blend gelatin, sugar, and salt in heavy sauce pan, add orange juice and slightly beaten egg yolk. Cook over medium heat, stirring constantly, until mixture comes to a boil. Boil 1 minute, add to cream cheese while beating at low speed. Add lemon juice, chill until mixture mounds when dropped from a spoon. Beat egg white in a small bowl until frothy, gradually add 1 tablespoon sugar and continue beating until stiff. Fold into cream-cheese mixture. Fold in grapes and whipped cream, spoon into baked shell. Chill until firm, about 2 hours. Garnish with whipped cream and additional halved seeded grapes. Serves 5 to 8.

Grape Compote: 6 pounds grapes, 6 pounds sugar, 2 pounds seeded raisins, 4 large oranges chopped fine, 1 pound English walnuts, cut fine. Cook all ingredients to a jelly.

Grape Cream: 4 cups unsweetened grape juice, 1 cup sugar, 3 tablespoons cornstarch. Bring juice and sugar to a boil, mix cornstarch with small amount of water, stir into juice and bring again to boiling point. Cool, cover, and serve with milk or cream.

Grape Crumb Pie: Wash and remove grapes from stems, use 3 cups crushed. Place in saucepan, boil until tender, rub through a colander to remove seeds. This should make 2 cups sieved grapes. Add ½ cup granulated sugar, mixed with 4 level tablespoons cornstarch, cook until thick, allow to cool. While this is cooling you make crumbs and pie shell. Make pie shell of your favorite crust recipe, either plain dough or graham-cracker. For crumbs take ½ cup flour, 2 level tablespoons brown sugar, and 2 tablespoons soft (not melted) butter or margarine, rub together like pie dough until well blended. Pour cooled grapes in unbaked pie shell and top with crumbs, bake in oven heated to 375° for 30 minutes or until crumbs are brown.

Grape Juice: Wash and pick grapes over, put 1 cup grapes and ½ cup sugar in clean quart jar, fill with boiling water, use 2-piece lids and screw band on tight. Ready to use in 2 months.

Grape Juice #2: Wash well-ripened grapes, crush, and simmer until fruit is well cooked (add a little water if you wish). Drain in flannel jelly bag. To each quart of juice add ½ cup sugar, pour into clean sterile jars and process in hot water bath 30 minutes. Mighty nice served mixed with ginger ale.

Grape Marmalade: 1 quart grapes, picked off stems, 4 tablespoons water. Cook crushed grapes with water until tender, run through sieve, add 2 pounds sugar, simmer 10 minutes.

Grape Pie: 3½ cups Concord grapes, ⅛ teaspoon salt, 1¼ cups sugar, 4 tablespoons flour (or 2½ tablespoons tapioca), 1 teaspoon lemon juice, dash cinnamon (optional). Wash grapes and slip from skins, bring pulp to boil and cook slowly 3 minutes, stirring occasionally. Press through sieve, add strained pulp to skins, combine other ingredients and add to grapes. Pour into unbaked pie shell, top with pastry which has small steam vents pricked in the top. Bake in hot oven (about 425°) 35 to 45 minutes. Makes 1 deep 9-inch pie.

Green Grape Pie: ¾ cup sugar, 3 tablespoons cornstarch, 1 quart seedless green grapes (stems removed), ¼ cup sugar, 1 tablespoon lemon juice, 9-inch baked pie shell, 1 cup sour cream, 1 tablespoon sugar, 1 teaspoon vanilla. Combine sugar and cornstarch in saucepan, add grapes and water. Cook over low heat about 5 minutes, stirring constantly until thickened. Remove from heat, stir in lemon juice, chill thoroughly, and pour into cooled pie shell. Mix sour cream, 1 tablespoon sugar, and vanilla, spread evenly over top. Chill 2 to 3 hours, serve garnished with whole or half fresh green grapes.

Homemade Communion Wine: Put 1 cup washed, cleaned grapes in quart jar (scalded), add 1 cup sugar, and fill jar with hot water. Seal. In 24 hours shake jar until sugar has dissolved. Let set for 2 months or so.

Mulled Grape Juice: ½ cup sugar, 2 cups water, 2 sticks cinnamon, 12 whole cloves, 1 quart grape juice, ⅓ cup lemon juice, rind of ½ lemon, sliced. Combine sugar, water, and spices in saucepan. Place over low heat, bring to a boil, and simmer 10 minutes. Add grape juice, lemon juice, and rind, bring to boil. Strain. Serve in small cups. Yields 10–12 servings.

Never-Fail Grape Butter: Wash and drain grapes, then take 2 quarts grapes, 2 quarts sugar, 6 tablespoons water. Let come to a boil, boil fast 15 minutes, put all through sieve, then put in jelly glasses.

Spiced Grapes: 7 pounds grapes, 3½ pounds sugar, 1 pint vinegar, 1 tablespoon each cinnamon and cloves. Skin grapes, boil pulps and strain, add the skins, boil together with other ingredients until thick, put in jars.

Unfermented Grape Juice: Put grapes in a boiler with enough water to cover, boil till soft, then put in a cheesecloth bag, and let it drain overnight. Do not squeeze bag. In morning take 1 quart juice and 1 cup sugar and boil slowly for ½ hour. Bottle and seal while hot. (We are told this was served as grape juice for Communion, as these folks did not believe in strong wines for the Church.)

MAPLE SUGAR AND SYRUP

While not strictly a fruit, maple sugar and syrup are from a tree, and are mentioned for the benefit of those who want to tackle the job of making them from scratch.

You can gather sweet sap from nearly all the maple varieties, although the hard or sugar maple (*Acer saccharum*) furnishes about

75% of commercial syrup and sugar. Unless you're doing it to give the kids an education, it's cheaper to buy your syrup and maple sugar. Tapping a tree, gathering sap, and boiling it is good experience, but a lot of work.

Usually March or April are the best sugar-making months. Tapping should be done early enough to catch the first real run of sap. Tap the maple trees in several places without worrying about injury to the bark or vigor of the tree. You will need from 33 to 40 gallons of sugar sap having a 3% sugar content to make 1 gallon of syrup. Boiling sap in the kitchen is a mess. Sap from a single tree will produce enough refined syrup to serve a family of 4 for 1 meal—about a cup of table syrup. For full information on tapping and processing sap, write to your state college of agriculture.

MULBERRY (*Morus*)

Nothing is easier to grow than white- or black-fruited mulberry. Trees are weak-wooded but fast-growing, heavily fruited. Will grow in sun or shade on almost any type of soil. Berries are more or less sweet and flat-tasting, lasting all summer. Just plant and forget it. Will attract birds which at times can create a messy situation.

TROUBLES

No Fruit: The mulberry tree is a dioecious plant, which means some trees have only female parts of the flower while other trees have only male parts. This is in contrast to such trees as the apple tree, which has both female and male parts on the same tree as well as within the same flower. Thus in a mulberry planting both male and female trees are usually necessary to produce fruit, although a single tree may be self-fruitful. When the tree has only female parts, you can do either of 2 things: (1) plant a male tree, or (2) secure sprays of male blooms and place them in bottles filled with water. These are then tied in the tree or located about the tree. Then insects should do the rest.

NECTARINE

Many people have never eaten a nectarine. Some call the fruit a "fuzz-less" peach because this is what it looks like. Many believe that the nectarine is a cross between a peach and a plum, but it isn't. Even to pomologists, the classification of nectarines is confusing. Some insist they are a species by themselves, others say they belong to the same species as peach, *Prunus persica.*

The truth of the matter is that the origin of the nectarine is unknown. It is probably a "sport," or mutation developed from the peach. It's not a new fruit, having been known centuries ago. They used to be white-fleshed only, but flesh of the newer varieties is a golden color, and the fruit is larger and firmer. Rivers Orange is a yellow-fleshed nectarine you might try. You get the same variation in nectarines that you get in peaches—color of flesh, season of ripening, hardiness, productiveness, etc. Nectarines and peaches can be budded and grafted to each other, and they will also cross-pollinate each other.

Hardiness of the nectarine is about the same as the peach, will tolerate about 15° below zero. Tree is self-fertile, one only is needed to produce abundantly.

A gardener wrote: "Years ago my mother purchased nectarines and she saved 2 pits which looked just like peach pits. She planted them and it took 5 years for them to bear. What do you think they bore? Nice large black delicious plums! That's why I believe that nectarines are from a peach grafted to a plum rootstock. Am I correct?"

No. It is impossible to obtain plum trees by planting pits of nectarines. However, it is possible to obtain nectarine trees by planting pits from certain genetic types of peach trees.

Nectarine trees do not develop when a peach is grafted onto a plum rootstock. Nectarines will develop when nectarine buds are budded into plum rootstocks, although this combination is quite incompatible. It is usually recommended that neither peach nor nectarine be budded into plum rootstocks because they often die after a few years of growth.

Plums will not pollinate either peaches or nectarines, according to Prof. Roger Way of the Department of Pomology, Cornell University.

Boiled down, nectarines can grow from pits which were borne on a peach tree. But only when the pollen (male element) parent of the pits is a nectarine and only when the peach already has some nectarine in its ancestry.

Still confused? Don't worry about it! If you can grow peach trees, you can grow the fuzzless peach (nectarine). Set out a couple this spring.

PEACH (*Prunus persica*)

Peaches are very easy to grow, provided they are given the right care at the right time, and on this will hang the success of your peach production. You start with any type of soil for your peach trees, but be sure the drainage is good. Peach trees will not stand wet feet, thus fertile sandy loams are preferable, although heavier soils will do.

Hardiness: Peaches seldom thrive where winter temperatures go below 15° below zero. There is a range of hardiness in peaches. Veteran and Prairie Dawn, very hardy. Golden Jubilee, Hale Haven, Red Haven, Triogem, hardy, Elberta, medium hardy, and J. H. Hale, tender.

Best varieties for your home garden will probably be Golden Jubilee, Hale Haven, or Elberta. J. H. Hale is an excellent variety but will need a rooster peach nearby of another variety to produce fruit. Most peaches are self-fruitful. Be sure and plant trees of named varieties, unless you like to take a chance with seed.

Classes of Peaches: There are 2 classes of peach varieties. Those with melting flesh (Elberta, Golden Jubilee, etc.), and those with "cling" stones. Cling types have firm, rubbery flesh and pits which do not separate easily from the flesh.

Some of the cling types look fine on the outside but flesh is hard and rubbery, making them practically worthless for eating from hand. Canned store peaches are mostly of the cling variety. If the fruit of your tree is poor-tasting, rubbery, nothing can be done to change the variety. Bud new limbs on, or plant a new tree of a variety with melting flesh.

If you're interested in white-fleshed peaches (many prefer their characteristic flavor), some good varieties are Early-Red-Fre, Raritan Rose, and Champion.

Pruning: Planted in spring or fall, peaches need very little pruning until they are 3 or 4 years old. Then you aim at having an open-center

Pruned peach tree. Dotted lines indicate branches that have been removed. Top has been cut back, center cleared out, and side branches thinned.

tree with 3, 4, or 5 scaffold branches arising from the trunk no higher than 36 inches from the ground. Most peach trees bear the third year after planting, and since the fruit is borne from side buds on 1-year-old shoots, you'll need to do some regular pruning each year from now on to force out the new shoots. Old, neglected peach trees can be cut back to wood 3 years old or more and started again from there.

To start the open-center formation of your peach tree, the central leader or main branch of the tree should be held down. This is done throughout the life of the tree, beginning the first year after planting. The scaffold branches are allowed to grow with less pruning, the lowest of which may be no more than a foot from the ground. Don't let branches lower than this remain on the tree. Now remove limbs that tend to fill up the center of the tree or make any part of the tree too dense. Head back any tall, ungainly limbs. The best time to prune peach trees is in March.

Peaches from Seed: A gardener writes: "I plant the dried 'stones' [seeds or pits] in a sunny spot in November, about 4 inches deep and a foot apart. In July or August of the following year plants will be about a foot high, and then I transplant them to a sunny, well-drained location. Mothballs are placed around the base of the tree when the plants are only 5 or 6 inches high. By the time the trees are 3 or 4 years old I can pick some dandy homegrown peaches, just as good as those you buy. Try it and you'll be surprised."

Normally when you plant seed from peaches, apples, cherry, and other fruits you do not get sweet-tasting crops. They are more like the fruit that grows in the wild. That's why nurserymen have to bud or graft their fruit trees. They do this by sowing seeds such as apples, peaches, etc., and when the seedlings are a couple feet tall, they take buds from a known variety and bud them onto the wild seedlings.

Thinning: Peaches often set several times as many fruits as the tree can possibly develop. Such overloading should be avoided, as it ruins the trees. About 30 good leaves are needed to produce 1 peach, spaced 6 to 8 inches from its nearest neighbor. So it is an important part of peach culture to think in terms of hand-thinning them right after "June drop"—the time that nature elects to thin the trees by letting many small peaches drop from the trees that are loaded beyond capacity. At this time you should look over the peach tree, limb by limb, and remove any peaches that are small, poorly shaped or damaged, or closer together than 6 to 8 inches.

Feeding: If soil is sandy, add some nitrate of soda, 2 or 3 handfuls. A complete fertilizer such as 10–10–10 can be used for peaches in the home garden, especially if they are grown in grass sod, where the rate of application is greater. Try 5 handfuls around each tree. Study the growth status of your tree. If the terminal growth is of green color, less plant food is needed. If yellowish, add a little extra. Put wire cage around trunk to keep out mice and rabbits. Use poisonous baits in sod lands.

Picking: Don't pick peaches too early (green); pick when fruit has changed to greenish-yellow, with up to 25% blush color. Suppose you picked 100 bushels of not-ripe peaches today. If you left them on the tree, in 2 days they would yield 109 bushels. Five days later, they'll make 116 bushels, and if you left them until a week later you could pick 124 bushels. Don't pick peaches when green! Red color is not a sign of ripeness! A pale, pale peach can be riper and sweeter than one with deep red cheeks. Blush depends upon variety. For most varieties, a soft, creamy-to-gold under-color of the yellow part is the sign of ripeness. Medium to large, firm-ripe peaches are generally best for flavor and quality. They bruise less easily and will ripen fully to sweet, juicy goodness at room temperature.

When picking peaches from the tree, cup the fruit in the whole hand and twist gently. If it comes off easily, it is ready to pick. If not, leave it. This eliminates the thumb and finger bruises so often seen on peaches.

Spraying: The most savage attacks of insects and diseases on your peach trees can be pretty well controlled by the all-purpose spray and program. You can buy all-purpose sprays or mix your own (see instructions in Fruits for the Home and Garden). All-purpose spray can be used during the summer for pests such as curculio and leaf spot diseases. It cannot be used for dormant spray. Give your peaches a spray at the pink stage (just before the blossoms open), and also at the petal-fall stage (when the last of the petals are falling). Another spray about 3 or 4 weeks after petals fall will do wonders.

TROUBLES

Peach tree borers, leaf curl, and brown rot are the most common enemies of good peach production, and each is prevalent enough to make at least a minimum spray program necessary.

Peach Tree Borer: There are 2 borers, one found at soil level and the so-called lesser peach tree borer, which you find higher up on the trunk and scaffold branches. Those gum "boils" you see are usually the work of borers. The borer found at the base can be licked by using Chlordane or Sevin (also paradichlorobenzene crystals around base; use ½ ounce for trees 3 or 4 years old, ¾ ounce for trees 5 years old, 1 ounce for trees 6 years old). The borer found on the trunk and above needs

Malathion. MALATHION WILL CHECK BOTH. Spray entire tree, starting in mid-June, giving 3 or 4 doses, using Malathion (25% wettable powder), 1 teaspoon to 2 quarts of water. Spray trunk, scaffold branches, and soil at base of tree. REMOVE ALL GUM BOILS.

Many use old-fashioned method of digging or worming out borers from their holes. Cut away gum boils, poke red-hot wire up into holes and stab borers. Remove sod 3 or 4 inches away from trunk base, scatter Sevin or Chlordane in it. If your tree suddenly wilts and dies, you can usually blame it on borers working in trunk.

Peach Leaf Curl: Causes leaves to curl, turn yellow or reddish, pucker up and fall. Very serious but can be checked easily. One dose of Bordeaux mixture in fall or winter (or you can use lime sulfur or ferbam) will knock it out. Spray bud scales as well as entire tree. DON'T WAIT UNTIL LEAVES START TO PUCKER AND COLOR. Spray in winter while tree is dormant.

Brown Rot (see illustration): If fruit rots before you can pick it, brown rot disease is present, one of the worst diseases of stone fruits. Spray with Captan or wettable sulfur when buds are showing pink color, and again during bloom when rains threaten. Keep a coating of one of these on peaches at all times, at least before they touch one another at maturity. We like Captan because it does a good job and is unlikely to cause cracking of skin. Remove dried mummies on tree or ground and burn.

Peach Scab (see illustration): Apply Captan when fruits are size of golf ball.

Flat Taste: Due to picking too early (see Picking). Leave peaches on the tree until almost soft. They will have a better flavor and be

*Brown rot
of peach.
(USDA Photo)*

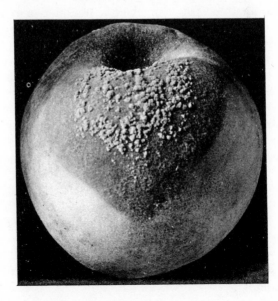

Peach scab, a common fungus disease of peaches. (USDA Photo)

juicier than those picked green. Green peaches will ripen up at room temperature, but keep them away from direct heat or sunlight.

Yellow Leaves: Due to peach leaf curl (which see) or nitrogen shortage. A lack of nitrogen reduces fruit size and yield. Scatter 3 or 4 handfuls of ammonium nitrate under your peach trees so they can soak up the nitrogen and make big fruits. Keep in mind that too much nitrogen might delay maturity, and cause a flat flavor in varieties that do not color up too well.

Split Pits: Happens often with J. H. Hale. The J. H. Hale is a fine, extra-large freestone peach. It is one of the few peach varieties that must be cross-pollinated with some other peach. The J. H. Hale is subject to split pits, especially when there is a light crop. Due to insufficient pollination. You can place a bouquet of peach branches in the Hale tree at bloom time to improve the set of fruit. This will in turn decrease the number of split pits.

Another factor that might be involved has to do with the nutrition of the tree. If your peach is overfed and over-vigorous, making more than 18 inches of tip growth a year, this might accentuate the problem. Also, severe pruning would tend to bring on splitting of pits. Anything which tends to increase the number of fruits set will help reduce the proportion of split pits. If you plant a rooster tree nearby, such as Elberta, you should have better pollination and fewer split pits.

USES

The National Peach Council tells us we should eat peaches as we do apples, plums, or apricots. Don't bother to peel peaches. They can be sliced without peeling. Leave the skins on for fruit plates and salads. Why cheat yourself of the many vitamins and minerals in the skin and just under it?

To Prevent Darkening after Peeling: For canning: 1 tablespoon salt or lemon juice to a gallon of water. Do not let stand in salt water for more than an hour or peaches get too salty. For fresh sliced: Sprinkle with lemon juice, cover with ice, then refrigerate. Keeps that bright fresh-sliced look and makes the flavor perky. Or, cover with orange, lemon, or pineapple juice or any lemon- or orange-drink concentrate, diluted to taste. Drain before serving to let the peach flavor come through.

Easy Ways to Crush Peaches: A small can (such as a juice-concentrate can with both ends cut out crushes peaches with admirable efficiency. A mesh-type potato masher or pastry blender does nicely too. Or spin peaches in an electric blender.

Last-minute Peach Crisp: 4 or 5 peeled, sliced fresh peaches, 1 tablespoon lemon juice, ½ cup sugar, ½ cup graham-cracker crumbs, ½ cup slivered almonds, 1 teaspoon cinnamon, 2 tablespoons butter. Preheat oven to 350°. Spread peaches in 9-inch pie pan. Drizzle with lemon juice. Mix sugar, graham cracker crumbs, almonds, and cinnamon, sprinkle over peaches. Dot with butter and bake 30 minutes. Serve warm or cold with cream or ice cream. Serves 4 to 6.

Molded Peach and Blueberry Ring: 1 package peach-flavored gelatin, 1 cup boiling water, ¾ cup cold water, 1 tablespoon lemon juice, 1 cup fresh blueberries, 2 or 3 peeled, sliced fresh peaches, salad greens, ½ pint cottage cheese. Dissolve gelatin in boiling water, add cold water and lemon juice. Chill until partially set. Arrange fruit in lightly oiled 1½-quart ring mold or 8-inch square pan. Spoon gelatin over and chill until firm. Unmold on a large platter lined with crisp salad greens. Garnish with cottage cheese. Serves 6.

Peachalade: 1 medium orange, 1 lemon, 2 pounds peaches (about 5 or 6 medium-size), 1 cup water, 7½ cups (3¾ pounds) sugar, ½ bottle liquid pectin. Squeeze juice from orange and lemon. Grind rinds or chop in electric blender. Put peeled, pitted peaches into bowl. Crush fine with mesh-type potato masher or small can with both ends cut out. Add fruit juices to peaches. Let stand.

Put ground orange and lemon rinds into 5- or 6-quart kettle. Add water. Cover and simmer over medium heat for 10 minutes. Blend peach mixture and sugar into cooked rinds. Bring to full rolling boil. Boil 10 minutes, stirring often. Remove from heat and stir in pectin. Alternately stir and skim to remove foam for 5 minutes. Pour into clean, not dry, jelly jars. Seal at once with self-sealing lids. Or cover at once with a ¼-inch layer of melted paraffin. Store in cool, dark place. Makes 8 half-pints.

PEARS (*Pyrus*)

Pears are among the easiest of tree fruits to grow in the home garden, almost as hardy as apples and well acclimated to heavy clay or loam soils. Pears will even tolerate a little wet feet, but a well-drained soil will produce best growth. It is not generally known that the flavor, aroma, texture, and keeping quality of pears is influenced more by the soil than anything else. Pears that are sour, dry, and bitter are most likely to be the result of poor soil conditions. Pear trees also need good air drainage for disease and frost damage prevention. Thinning of fruit is not usually necessary, but if you wish, thin some out by hand as soon after the June drop as possible. Use the all-purpose spray and program (which see) for insect and disease control.

Varieties: Bartlett, Bosc, Clapp's Favorite, and Seckel are excellent though quite different pear varieties. If you choose Bartlett and Seckel to grow together (a favorite combination), do be sure to provide a pollinator—either by planting a third pear variety, or by blossom bouquets of a compatible variety. Bartlett and Clapp's Favorite are very susceptible to fire blight so if you plant these varieties, be prepared to watch for and deal with this disease. All pear trees need cross-pollination.

Feeding: A complete fertilizer such as 10–10–10 is suitable for pears. Use 2 to 3 pounds for trees 5 years of age; for trees 5 to 10 years of age, use 3 to 5 pounds per tree. But go easy when fertilizing pear trees! Too much feeding stimulates strong growth and makes the tree more susceptible to blight. Rather, put a screen around the base of the tree and use a mulch of sawdust, ashes, peat moss, etc., to keep weeds down and moisture in.

Actually, pear trees can do without feeding. A quick look at the end growth of twigs (10 to 12 inches) and color of the foliage (good dark green) should be your guide as to whether feeding is necessary.

Picking: It seems almost elementary to say anything about how and when to pick pears, but actually no other fruit requires so much care as this one. Just about every pear we know should be picked long before it is ready to eat. It is hard to say just when green pears should be picked to have the perfect flavor of ripe pears. A fair rule of thumb is to pick when the stem parts from the branch when the fruit is lifted. Some folks wait until the seeds are brown. If your pears don't keep well, chances are you are picking them too late, causing the fruit to be mealy or gritty. You might watch the wormy pears, if you have any. When wormy fruit begins to turn yellow, that is the time to pick the green fruit, as injured fruit will ripen first. To ripen your pears after they are picked, cover them with newspapers and keep them in the garage or on a cool porch. They ripen best at 65° and 85% humidity or higher, which means a cool, humid place.

To Prevent Fruit: Pears and apples produce beautiful blossoms, and some folks would like the trees for decoration only, without the fruit. Older people do not want to rake up the fruit and often want a spray to "de-fruit" the pear and apples.

Fruit trees can be de-fruited with the same chemicals commercial growers use to thin their trees. Homeowners who wish to de-fruit pears and other fruits can use napthaleneacetic acid (sold as NAA in farm stores), at a concentration of 10 parts per million (the same as 4 grams per 100 gallons of water, or ⅘ teaspoon per 100 gallons of water) applied a petal-fall stage. Petal-fall stage is when the last petals have fallen from the blossoms.

This spray may cause temporary wilting of the foliage and distortion of tender shoot tips, but recovery is rapid and there is no cause for alarm.

Some varieties of pears (and other fruits) differ markedly in their susceptibility to the NAA treatment, and it is possible that the recommended rate will not completely de-fruit the trees. If this is the case, the rate can be increased the following year. However, increases in the rate should be modest because excessive applications of NAA can cause severe leaf injury.

TROUBLES

Lots of Blossoms, Little Fruit: May be due to lack of pollination (poor weather at blossom time). Pears need cross-pollination. Flowers of one variety must have pollen from flowers of another variety, transported by bees and other insects, in order to set fruit. Place a branch of flowers of another variety in a pail of water and hang in tree. Repeat operation each year. Bartlett and Seckel will not pollinate each other.

Gritty Cells in Flesh: A varietal characteristic. All pears have grit cells.

Mealy Flesh: Picking too late. Pick green and ripen *off* the tree in a cool cellar, 65° (see Picking).

Rotted Core: Due to late picking. Pick pears sooner, when the green color of fruit just begins to take on a yellowish tint. Ripen at temperature of 65° and 85% humidity (see Picking).

Russet Rings on Skin: Appear on apples and pears. Due to frost occurring a week or more after bloom, after young fruitlets have begun to develop. Frost kills the surface cells of skin and the russet is healing, similar to a scab on wounded human skin.

Stained Fruit: Due to pear psylla. Spray fruit with Sevin. Psylla secretes sweet honeydew which attracts black fungus growth. Causes leaves to shed prematurely.

Gnarly, Knobby, Goose-necked Pears: Due to fruit tree leaf rollers. Spray with dormant spray (which see) in early spring.

Knotty, Deformed, and Dwarfed Fruit: Due to pear plant bug, "false tarnished plant bug." Control: Spray with Sevin in June when fruits are small.

Pear Scab: Similar to apple scab, black spots on fruits. Spray with Captan before blossoms open. Also rake up leaves and burn. Spray ground.

Aphids: Spray with dormant DN sprays in early spring, in summer spray with Malathion.

Yellow or Reddish Blisters on Leaves: Caused by pear leaf blister mite. Apply dormant spray (which see), which will also control psylla and thrips.

Leaf Spot Disease: Spotted foliage. Keep leaves sprayed with Captan.

Holes in Trunk: Pear tree borer, causes tree to weaken, branches die, and tree succumbs. Control: Malathion sprayed on tree and trunk about June 10, and again 2 weeks later.

Scorched Leaves: Due to hot weather or sulphur sprays.

Fire Blight: Fire blight is easily recognizable by dead blossoms, leaves, and twigs that turn black and remain on the tree. Cankers and mummified fruit may also be found. Radical treatment is called for. Inspect your pear trees and cut out infected wood. Make all cuts 6 to 8 inches below the visible edge of the fire blight because the bacteria are frequently a considerable distance ahead of the visible symptoms. Further, tools should be dipped in disinfectant between each cut, for fire blight spreads easily. Sodium hypochlorite (household bleach) is cheap and effective for this purpose.

Disinfect your pruning tools after this chore by thoroughly soaking in 1 part of bichloride of mercury in 1,000 parts of water (¼ tablespoon per gallon).

Antibiotic spray of streptomycin checks blight. Also, avoid heavy pruning of pear trees, as it causes fast growth which is susceptible to blight.

PERSIMMON (*Diospyros*)

The native American persimmon (*Diospyros virginiana*) is not reliably hardy, although some varieties will mature early enough to ripen fruits in northern gardens. I have found persimmon tricky to grow; the fruit falls off before ripening. But the cultivated persimmon is sweet and well worth the effort. A hard frost before the fruit is ripe will ruin it. After the fruit has ripened, a frost won't harm it.

Persimmons grow on poor soils. There is a male and female tree. Some of the female (pistillate) trees produce seedless (parthenocarpic) fruits without benefit of cross-pollination. You can start persimmon seeds yourself, although you might be disappointed with the results. Just sow them in a pot of sand and peat moss, and leave them outdoors for the winter, preferably in a cold frame.

I'm often asked, "Why is it when we buy persimmon fruit at stands it tastes bitter?"

Many varieties of persimmon are astringent until dead ripe. One way to overcome the astringency is to place unripe persimmons in a polyethylene bag with several ripe apples and subject them to room temperature for up to 4 days. The gas escaping from the apples will help to ripen the persimmons.

Many have found that the persimmon is hard to transplant.

It has a long taproot which is difficult to ball and burlap. That's why most specimens shipped from nurseries are sent bare root. One way the long taproot problem is overcome is by planting the original rootstock seed on galvanized or aluminum mesh wire so that the taproot is automatically cut off as the seedling grows and the resultant calloused stub forms a ball of roots.

PLUM

The plum is a fine fruit tree, well suited to most conditions in the north, where the tree is hardy. Home gardeners have a choice of many species and varieties of plum, and they provide a greater range of flavor and color than any other temperate-zone fruit except the grape. There are types for every state and much of Canada. The European plum is the most important in the world, and is used for fresh fruit, as well as dried into prunes.

Among the hardiest of all plums are the sand cherry-plum hybrids. And there's the beach plum of the dunes of the Atlantic Coast, good for jelly and seashore planting.

Varieties: There are 2 Damson-type plums, French and Shropshire, which are blue with green flesh, and 2 Japanese-type plums, Burbank and Formosa, with red or red-yellow skins and yellow flesh, that are popular garden types. Burbank and Formosa need rooster trees for pollination and should be grown with one of the other varieties of Japanese type, for fruit production. Formosa does not produce good pollen and you need 3 varieties of Japanese types when growing Formosa. Shiro is one of the better Japanese plums to try. (See plum variety chart.)

There is some confusion over "when is a plum a prune?" Prunes are a special class of plum which, because of their sugar content, may be successfully dried on the pit. Most popular for home growing in the Northeast are the Stanley prune, the French and German prunes, and the Italian or Fellemberg prune. These varieties produce more if grown with another plum variety nearby for pollination. For the rough-and-ready gardener, the Stanley is probably the best to try, as it is self-fruitful.

Don't be impatient for the fruit from plum trees. It will take anywhere from 5 to 7 years after setting out before they start to bear—and they cannot be pushed! Prune the branches only enough to remove those that are crisscrossing or crowding one another, and wait it out.

Planted in well-drained soil, sprayed with the all-purpose spray (see All-purpose Spraying) plus Bordeaux mixture, and fed about ⅛ pound of ammonium nitrate per tree per year of age, plums will come along with little effort and yield delicious fruit for fresh eating, canning or preserving for many years.

TROUBLES

Small Fruits: Result of overloaded tree. Thin crop for quality plums. Reduces rot and limb breakage. Thin just after the "June drop," leaving remaining fruits spaced 3 or 4 inches apart. While thinning, remove insect-injured or otherwise inferior fruits. A light annual pruning helps give stronger limbs, bigger fruits.

Brown Rot Disease: Serious, rots fruit in wet, humid weather. Control: Sulfur or Captan applied just before the blossoms open, again when the shucks fall from the young fruits, and a third about 3 weeks later. Gather all rotten fruits by hand and burn.

If you should see a gummy, gelatinous material on plum fruit, you can be sure that your tree is under attack by the curculio insect. The best way to fight this pest is to gather and burn fallen fruit, since the worm is inside the dropped fruit.

Humpbacked Beetle: Not only lays eggs in apples, plums, and cherries, but causes small green prune fruits to drop before they ripen. Control: 1 spraying when fruit shucks begin to split, 2 more at 10-day intervals. Use Methoxychlor, 1 tablespoon to a gallon of water, with a few drops of detergent.

Black Knot: Large, distorted, ugly growths on limbs. Cut out and burn as soon as it appears. Make cut 4 inches below the gall. Wild or neglected plum and cherry trees in vicinity should be removed. Spray plum branches with ferbam in early spring.

Cracks in Bark: Due to winter injury. Wrap trunk in winter with aluminum foil or material, whitewash trunk.

Suggest reference to your state university's latest extension bulletin for pests and sprays in individual areas.

Variety	Time of Bloom	Ripening Date*	Fruit Size	Fruit Color	Dessert Quality	Stone Freeness	Flesh Color	Pollination Requirement
EUROPEAN TYPE								
BRADSHAW	4/28	−15	Med. large	Purple	Fair	Free	Yellow	Self-unfruitful
French Prune	4/28	3	Small	Red	Good	Cling	Green-Yellow	Self-fruitful
German Prune	4/29	4	Small	Blue	Fair	Free	Green-Yellow	Self-fruitful
ITALIAN PRUNE (Seitenberg, Fellemberg)	4/29	4	Medium	Blue	Fair	Free	Green-Yellow	Self-fruitful
IMPERIAL EPENEUSE	4/28	1	Medium	Red	High	Semi-cling	Green-Yellow	Self-unfruitful
Reine Claude	4/26	19	Medium	Yellow	Good	Semi-cling	Yellow	Self-fruitful
STANLEY	4/28	5	Medium	Blue	Fair	Free	Green-Yellow	Self-fruitful
DAMSON TYPE								
FRENCH	4/27	8	Small	Blue	Tart	Semi-cling	Green	Self-fruitful
SHROPSHIRE	4/27	5	Small	Blue	Tart	Semi-cling	Green	Self-fruitful
JAPANESE TYPE								
Burbank	4/22	−18	Medium	Red-yellow	Fair	Cling	Yellow	Self-unfruitful
Formosa	4/20	−37	Large	Red	Good	Cling	Yellow	Self-unfruitful
Methley	4/20	−43	Medium	Purple-red	Fair	Cling	Red	Self-unfruitful

Those varieties which appear in capital letters, such as STANLEY PRUNE, are the ones that are considered as the most reliable commercial varieties. The other varieties are of value for extending the season or for special purposes. (Courtesy Ohio Agricultural Experiment Station)

*Average ripening date in days before or after the peach Elberta

Old-time Plum Crumb Pudding: 3 pounds fresh blue plums, 1¼ cups sugar, 1⅓ cups sifted flour, ½ cup butter, ¼ teaspoon salt. Wash and quarter plums (there should be 6 cups). Combine ¾ cup of the sugar and 4 tablespoons of the flour, and mix with the plums. Turn into a 10″x6″x2″ baking dish. Mix remaining sugar and flour. Add butter and cut into a crumb consistency. Sprinkle over plums. Bake at 375° for 1 hour, or until fruit is tender and crumbs are brown. Serves 6.

Plum Rum Jam: 1 quart of cut-up plums (pit but do not peel), ½ cup lemon juice, 6½ cups sugar, ½ bottle fruit pectin, ¼ cup rum. Put plums and lemon juice in blender or chop very finely. Put in large saucepan, add sugar, and bring mixture to full rolling boil, stirring well. Boil 1 minute, stirring constantly. Remove from heat, add fruit pectin, stir well. Add rum. Put in scalded glasses. This makes 6 large glasses or about 9 or 10 small ones. If you use light rum use ⅓ cup instead of ¼ cup.

QUINCE

For the home gardener, this is one of the easiest shrubs to grow. You can grow 2 kinds of quince, the flowering type (*Chaenomeles*), a handsome ornamental with crimson and white blooms, and the edible quince (*Cydonia*). No quince is edible out of hand, but the fruit is popular for jelly.

The most commonly grown edible quince is the variety Orange, which is self-fruitful, while many of the flowering quinces are not. There is also a dwarf Orange quince, which can be grown as a bush or a small tree. Fruit is large, golden yellow, ripens in September. Excellent for preserves.

Quince grows 12 feet high, can be trimmed to any shape or height. Has thorns so is useful in a hedge, may be clipped if desired. Prefers a well-drained soil.

Propagation: Both flowering and edible quinces are usually propagated vegetatively, as seedlings vary greatly. Cuttings, layering, or division may be used. In spring take some cuttings about 6 inches long and insert in ground. Cover with glass jars. Or seed can be sown in spring. To start a plant by layering, simply grab a branch and peg it down on the ground. Cover the pegged part with soil and by fall you'll see lots of roots on the pinned branch. Cut it off and set it in a permanent spot.

Quince Honey: 1 cup fruit of the Japanese flowering quince, 1 quart cold water, 6 cups sugar, pinch salt. Pare, core, and wash quince well, chop fine, put into 4-quart kettle with water, sugar, and salt. Bring to boil. Boil until pinkish color appears in kettle. Must be watched so it doesn't get too dark pink or it will be scorched. Pour into hot, sterilized jars and seal. Delicious? Just try it.

Quince Jelly: Remove cores and blossom and stem ends from about 3 pounds of fully ripe (yellow) quinces. Do not peel. Grind, add 4½ cups water, bring to a boil and simmer, covered, 15 minutes. Place in a jelly bag, squeeze out juice. Measure 4 cups juice into a large saucepan. Add ¼ cup lemon juice and 7½ cups sugar, mix well. Place over high heat and bring to a boil, stirring constantly. Stir in ½ bottle liquid fruit pectin. Bring to a full rolling boil and boil hard 1 minute, stirring constantly. Skim off foam with metal spoon, and pour quickly into glasses. Cover at once with ⅛ inch hot paraffin.

RASPBERRY

Raspberries probably give the home gardener as good a return in delicious fruit as he can get from any fruit plant. There is no substitute for homegrown raspberries and other small fruits. Always fresh and firm, homegrown berries are far more tasty than those crated and shipped in. The returns from a high-yielding raspberry patch warrant the best land you have for planting.

Soil: An ideal soil is a sandy or gravelly loam, with lots of humus. It must be well drained. If your soil is clayey, don't be discouraged because good crops may be obtained on it if you can provide drainage. Type of soil isn't too important, if it's well drained.

Poor drainage means winter injury. The root system of a raspberry plant extends to a depth of 3 feet, but the bulk is in the upper 2 feet. Wet soil stimulates late-autumn growth which fails to ripen and will winter-kill. Air drainage is needed also. "Pockets" or low land spots surrounded by higher ground or dense growth of trees stops the downward flow of air, and diseases such as anthracnose and mildew are apt to be serious.

Varieties: Latham, Taylor, and Newburgh are good red raspberry varieties, Bristol is a recommended black, and Sodus a favorite purple. There are also fall-bearing red raspberries, which bear 2 crops of fruit—one in early summer and one on the new canes in the fall (to be discussed later).

Red raspberries have different growing habits than the black (called blackcaps) and purple raspberries and require slightly different care and pruning. It is also well to remember that nothing can get out of hand and into a bramble faster than a neglected raspberry planting! You must be the boss in your raspberry patch, or the plants will quickly take over, become diseased and provide you with nothing but small seedy fruit and you will regret that you ever set a plant.

Time to Plant: Berries should be planted as early in spring as possible. Some folks advocate late fall plantings. Early fall plantings are often subject to severe winter injury, because the plants haven't had a chance to harden and mature fully. Growth of new shoots from the base of the canes starts early and you may not get this with late-spring planting, so do the job early. If you want to set them out in fall, the last week in October and the first 2 weeks in November are the best for fall planting. Do not plant if soil is too wet. It's best to store plants in a cool place and wait until the soil dries enough so that it will not pack.

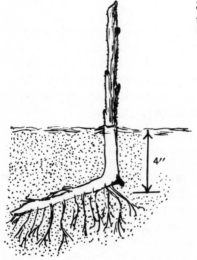

Set new raspberry plants in well-prepared soil at least 4 inches deep.

How to Plant: Plants are spaced 3 feet apart, with rows 8 feet apart, for commercial plantings. For home gardens the space in the row should be 3 feet, but 5 feet between rows is wide enough for the home garden. When you set out young plants, dig a small hole or open a shallow furrow to a depth of 4 inches. Cover the roots with fine loose soil and firm the earth around the roots with your foot or hand. Then fill in the rest of the soil to the proper level, leaving this top layer loose so that buds growing from below the ground level can grow out easily. You can water them well. Never allow the roots to dry out. Do not place any fertilizer in contact with the roots when planting.

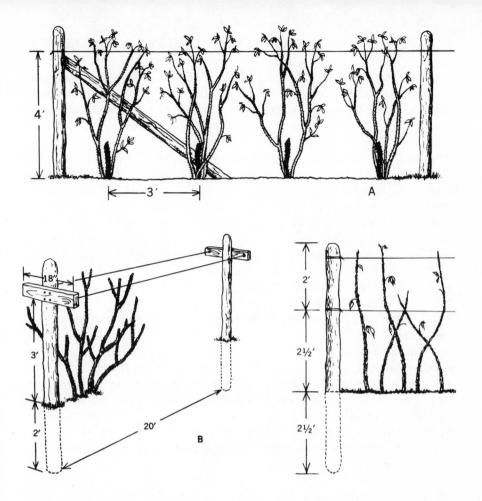

Three ways of trellising bramble fruits: (A) single wire, and (B and C) 2 double-wire methods.

Mulching: Use sawdust or wood chips to increase fruit size and yield. If sawdust or straw is used for mulching either berries or strawberries and allowed to remain on the ground, a decrease in plant growth may occur because of a depression of available nitrogen. Therefore it is necessary to add extra nitrogen when this type of mulch is applied. For every ton of straw or sawdust, it may be necessary to add from 75 to 100 pounds of ammonium sulfate or its equivalent, or about 1 handful per bushel of sawdust or per bale of straw.

This nitrogen will feed the plants while the bacteria are decomposing the mulch material. After the mulch has decomposed, then it will give back the bacteria used.

Feeding: Nitrate of soda or ammonium nitrate are good. Nitrate of soda is applied at rate of 250 pounds per acre, or 2 ounces per plant. Ammonium nitrate, 125 pounds per acre or 1 ounce per plant. Apply these as soon as the buds begin to swell in spring. Do not place too close to roots, spread fertilizer evenly by hand so entire root system will be able to use it. Roots on mature bushes extend 3 to 4 feet from base of plant.

Pruning: The first thing to know about pruning all raspberries is that the canes that bear the fruit grow one year, produce the fruit the next year, and then die. Once a raspberry cane has produced fruit, its function in life is over and it should be cut off at ground level, removed from the patch, and burned. The burning, while not a total disease and insect control, helps immeasurably.

All raspberries profit by a summer "topping," or pruning the tops of the new shoots off when the canes have reached a height of from 2 to 3 feet. Black and purple raspberries should be topped at 2 feet, before they make a long, spindly growth which arches over until the end touches the soil. It is at this point that the blacks and purples will get out of hand, for the tip of the long cane will form a new plant and thus a whole new family of canes and arches and new plants. It takes only a couple of years to produce the massive bramble mentioned earlier if summer topping is neglected. One-year-old plants set in spring will not be ready to top off until July first, or later. These first-year plants should be topped when the canes are about 12 inches high. THE PRACTICE OF TOPPING (cutting out the tip) of black and purple raspberries DOUBLES THE YIELD OF FRUIT AND MAKES A COMPACT, SHAPELY BUSH.

(A) *Black or purple raspberries. Left, unpruned. Right, pruned.*
(B) *Red raspberries. Left, unpruned. Right, pruned.*

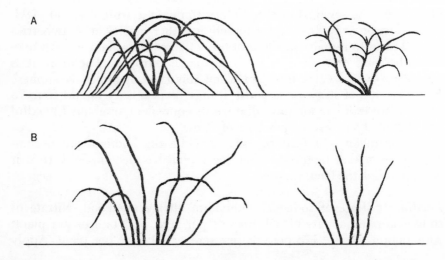

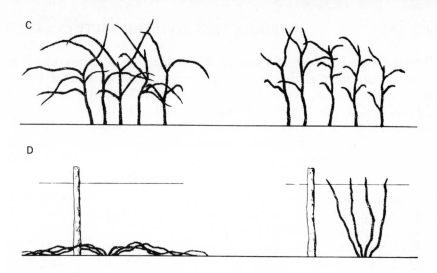

(C) Blackberries. Left, unpruned. Right, pruned.
(D) Trailing blackberries. Left, unpruned. Right, pruned and trained.

Red raspberries do not tip-root, but make suckers. These sucker plants should be trimmed out every year, allowing the new canes to set no closer than 8 to 10 inches from one another. All raspberries need good air drainage and should not be allowed to grow too thickly. During the winter or before growth starts in spring, the side branches or long canes should be pruned. Cut the canes off, leaving them 6 to 8 inches long. (See drawing). Then remove the pruning (called brush) and burn it in piles.

If all this sounds "Greek" to you, let's boil pruning of red raspberries down to the following:

Cut out all diseased and damaged canes. Next step is to remove all old wood, meaning canes that grew any time before last season. You can tell them easily. They are darker in color and the outer layers are frequently broken, flaky, or split in appearance. Third step is to thin out the young canes, those that grew last year. These are lighter in color and have the outer layer intact. Average spacing for canes that are left should be about 6 inches. In all of these steps the canes should be cut off at ground level. The remainder of the red raspberry canes can be sheared off at hip height.

Cultivation: Clean cultivation of the raspberry planting should be kept up until about the time the blossoms form. Then the plants may be mulched with straw or sawdust, which does double duty, keeping down weeds and preserving soil moisture for the promotion of large fruit. After harvest of red raspberries, mulch should be thinned to allow the new shoots to come up straight and true for the following year's crop.

Chemical Weed Killers: If you raise black or red raspberries on a bigger scale than most gardeners, then you might want to resort to herbicides (weed killers). We've had good luck with Simazene at the rate of 2 tablespoons per 3 gallons of water, applied in spring before growth starts. A knapsack sprayer can be used. Apply the chemical in the row and it will kill sprouting seed. Simazene is also useful on asparagus, grapes, and blackberries.

Propagation: Red raspberries are started "suckers" that come up from roots. Dig up rooted suckers early in spring before they make too much growth. Dig up a piece of old root with them.

Black and purple varieties are started by tip-layering, called "tipping." Late in summer, about end of August, the ends of the canes drop to the ground and tips become somewhat snakelike. Where they touch they root. You can help the rooting process by burying the tips in a small hole 3 inches deep and pressing soil against it. By fall the tip is well rooted and the following spring you can dig it up and sever it from parent plant. DO NOT LET TIPS DRY OUT. Tips grown on sandy or mellow soils are better than those grown on clay. While raspberries are producing fruit they are also struggling to perpetuate themselves, and suckers and tip-roots must be watched carefully by the tidy gardener to keep things under control.

Mound layering is another simple way to increase plants. Mound soil over the base of the plant, after you scar or slit the stem bark. Roots form in the wounded areas and the newly rooted plants are severed and set out.

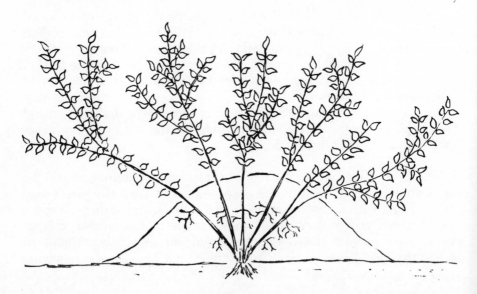

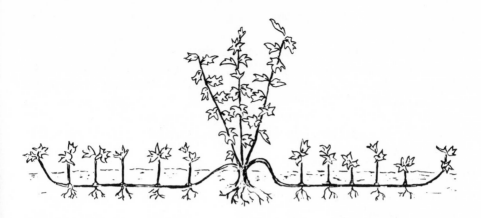

Multiple layering consists of bending and burying branches, slitting in several places.

How to Pick: If picked too early raspberries will lack flavor and some varieties crumble badly when pulled loose. For home use, fruit can be left on plant longer. Pick in cool of morning but not while fruit is wet with dew. Use thumb and first 2 fingers in picking and hold very few berries in the hand at one time. Pick canes every other day.

Fall-fruiting Raspberries (*"Everbearers"*): You can have raspberries until frost by setting out autumn-fruiting raspberries, or everbearers. Everbearers produce a good midsummer crop of berries, but it is for their fall crop that they are most outstanding. The fall crop begins to ripen in early September and continues until frost.

Some people harvest both crops, but others prefer to cut back the fruiting canes drastically in spring and concentrate on the fall crop. Fall-fruiting raspberries should be supported as the berries are borne high on the cane tips, which have a tendency to drag on the ground, bruising and dirtying the fruit.

Some everbearing varieties have been disappointing to home gardeners, but the newer varieties are excellent. September and Fall Red are 2 good red everbearers. September is about a month earlier than Indian Summer, another fall-fruiting type. The fruit of September is medium-sized or about as large as that of Latham. It is bright red and firm and free from crumbling. It clings tightly to the bush until fully ripe, however. Purple Autumn is a fall-fruiting purple variety with delicious fruit and heavy yield.

TROUBLES

Lots of Blossoms, No Fruit: Due to mosaic virus disease, which causes sterility. No cure. Dig out plants and burn them. Try planting certified plants following year in different location.

Fruits Half-developed: Due to tarnished plant bug, which injures young, developing berries and mature fruit. Spray foliage with Malathion before blooms appear. Note: Preblossom sprays are IMPORTANT! One spray thoroughly applied before blossoms open may be effective against several injurious pests.

Hard Seedy Fruits: Due to mosaic virus. Grow certified plants, rather than attempt to use possibly diseased ones donated to you. Dry weather also causes seedy fruit.

Soft Crumbly Berries: Due to mosaic, anthracnose, or winter injury. Some varieties are softer than others.

Wormy Fruit: Raspberry fruit worm, which shows up as small grubs in fruit. Apply Sevin when the first blossom buds appear and again just before the blossom buds open.

Fruit Rot: Worse in wet seasons. Berries turn brown and dry up before they ripen, or may rot. Not much you can do to check it.

Rotting of Fruit Cluster: Due to anthracnose (see Shot-hole Effect on Leaves).

Lack of Berries: Due to winter injury of buds. Immaturity of wood in fall, late-spring killing. Causes partially injured canes to collapse in summer just about fruiting time, leading gardeners to think that a fungus blight is present. Poor soil drainage (heavy soils) is contributing factor in winter-killing.

Leaf Curl: Virus disease spread by aphids on undersides of leaves. Inspect, and pull up and burn plants as soon as detected.

Wilt: Due to soil-inhabiting fungus which causes wilt of tomatoes, peppers, eggplants, and potatoes. Causes canes to droop, turn yellow, shed leaves. No control. Do not plant on soils where these vegetables have grown.

Yellowing of Leaves: Mosaic virus disease ("yellows"), worse on reds, but also bad on purples and blacks. Causes stunting of plants, fruit dries up or crumbles on picking.

Control: Spread by aphids from wild and tame raspberries. Since red raspberries carry the mosaic virus without showing symptoms, do not plant red and black varieties close together—separate by at least 20 rows or further. Mosaic also causes crumbly fruits. Since aphids are spreaders of the virus try controlling them with Malathion (25% wettable powder, 2 tablespoons per gallon of water) right after the petals fall.

Orange Rust on Leaves: Spreads from native brambles to cultivated ones, affects black raspberries, seldom reds or purples. Pull up plants and burn.

"Shot-hole" Effect on Leaves: Due to anthracnose fungus. Causes canes to dry out and die during winter or break off during fruiting. Leaves develop irregular spots, turn reddish, then brown. Leaf tissue in diseased spots drops out, giving the shot-hole effect. Also called "cane spot" disease.

Control: Grow raspberries where air drainage is good. Remove weeds between rows. Cut "handles" (stubs of old plants) off new plants. A portion of the parent cane (called "handle") is left on newly rooted plants by nurserymen to make planting easier. These "handles" are often infected with anthracnose. Cut them off and destroy them before new growth appears. A dormant spray of lime sulfur, 1 pint to a gallon of water, will give control. Apply in early spring just as leaves are exposed ½ to ¾ inch. Grow resistant varieties such as Milton, Marcy, or Indian Summer.

Holes in Leaves: Due to anthracnose (see previous discussion) or raspberry sawfly. Pale-green worm feeds on leaves, chews out irregular holes. Spray with Sevin or Malathion early in season.

Blackened Tips of Canes: Due to cane borer. Restricts flow of sap, causing blackening, lopping over of canes. Control: Cut off wilted tips several inches below girdled portion as soon as found. Spray with Sevin just before blossoms open. Cane maggot causes similar injury. Cut off infested cane and burn.

Galls: Cane gall, crown gall, or root gall, caused by bacteria in wart-like growths. Difficult to control. Keep plants watered and fed and they'll bear even if infection is heavy.

Rodent Injury: Mice and rabbits nibble on canes. Difficult to check. Fencing with 2-inch mesh wire netting 30 inches high keeps rabbits out.

Wind Breakage: Worse on new shoots of blacks and purples. Use trellis to support canes.

Winter-killing of Canes: Due to poor soil drainage. If diseases are serious, it weakens leaves and invites winter injury.

General Control Measures: Diseases such as crown gall, orange rust, and mosaic cannot be controlled by spraying. There are certain practices recommended, however, to aid in preventing these troubles:

(1) Avoid planting new stock where diseased plants have recently been grown.

(2) Plant resistant varieties purchased from certified plantings.

(3) Plant red varieties as much as 300 feet away from black varieties.

(4) Pull out diseased plants and burn when spraying would be ineffective.

(5) At planting time, cut off old stubs of 2-year-old nursery stock and "handles" of young purple and black raspberries.

(6) Burn old fruiting canes immediately after harvest.

STRAWBERRY (*Fragaria*)

Strawberries are the most commonly grown small fruit and perhaps return more per square foot of garden space than any of the smaller fruits. And there's no reason why you can't make some extra pin money growing them in your backyard for local trade.

Strawberry plants need water, full sun, and protection from the birds (see section on Animal Control; try anti-bird mesh) when in fruit. Weeds must be kept down in the berry patch, plants should be spaced as they form, the bed should be mulched over winter, and some kind of protection against frost should be available when the blossoms are out. Plant food is needed, of course, but care must be taken as to the time and amount applied. In spite of all of this, many people grow strawberries in the home garden with little or no effort, delighted with the fact that a strawberry picked and eaten ripe from one's own patch is a thing of great enjoyment. The persistent plants will give you some fruit no matter how neglectful you are of the things you should do for the best berries.

Soil: Strawberries need soil that is well drained and very well supplied with humus. The more humus, the better. If you have manure, use it for strawberries. Horse, cow, sheep, or hog manure is good, at the rate of 1 bushel for every 50 square feet, before plowing. If no manure is available, use 5–10–5 fertilizer worked in the fall or early spring, ahead of plant-setting time. Or after first cultivation, you can apply it as a side-dressing to help plants get a vigorous start. Apply evenly and brush off any that may get on the leaves. Six pounds per 100 feet of row or 700 pounds per acre is ample. A light feeding of nitrate of soda during late August does a lot to help flower and fruit buds to form.

Do not grow strawberries on ground which has had a crop of tomatoes, potatoes, peppers, or eggplants on within the past 4 or 5 years. These crops are likely to have verticillium wilt, which lives in the soil and this fungus disease stunts strawberry plant, sometimes kills them.

Systems of Growing: There are many systems of planting. One most often used by commercial growers is the matted row. Plants are set out 24 inches apart in the row and allowed to multiply as they will. You get a fair amount of large berries on outside of rows, smaller ones on the inside, but you get more fruit to the acre than with the hill system. With the hill system you get big strawberries. Here the plants are set 12 to 18 inches apart in rows and all runners are cut off as fast as they are formed, and no new plants are allowed to form. Then there are spaced or hedge row systems. You allow 2 to 6 runner plants to form from each plant, and remove all other runners (see illustration). With this you get a high yield of big, fancy fruit. If you're a busy gardener and want lots of berries, resort to the matted-row system.

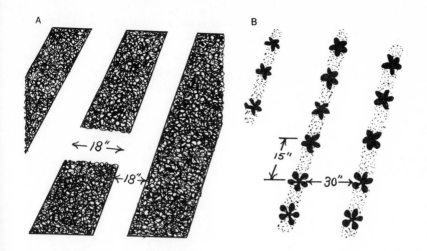

Systems of training strawberries. (A) Matted-row system. Most commonly used in home gardens. Rows are spaced 3 to 4 feet apart, and plants set 18 to 36 inches apart in the row. Allow runners to form a mat 15 to 18 inches wide, with plants 4 to 6 inches apart. (B) Hill System. Takes more hand work than matted-row system. Space rows 2 to 3 feet apart with plants 12 to 15 inches apart in the row. (Michigan State University)

Planting: Very early spring is the best time to set out strawberries. Buy your plants from a good nursery, preferably a grower, where you can get freshly dug sets. Choose from amongst the heavy-yielding good varieties such as Midland, Empire, Catskill, Fairfax and Sparkle (late). If you can plant only 1 variety, try Sparkle. Add Midland for a second variety and Fairfax for a third.

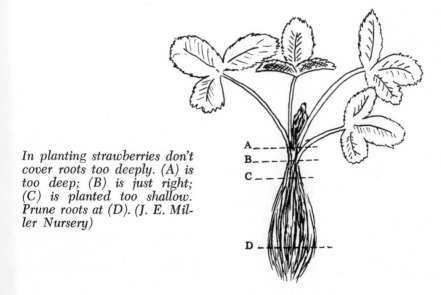

In planting strawberries don't cover roots too deeply. (A) is too deep; (B) is just right; (C) is planted too shallow. Prune roots at (D). (J. E. Miller Nursery)

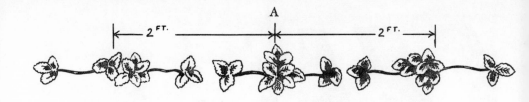

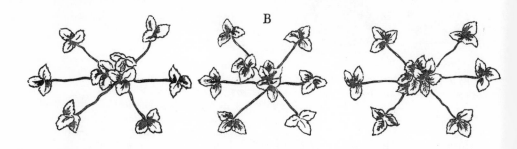

(A) *Single hedge row. Set plants 2 feet apart in rows spaced 3 feet apart. Each original plant is allowed to make 2 runner plants which are layered on opposite sides of the mother plant, all in line with the root.*

(B) *Double hedge row. Plants are set 2 feet apart in rows spaced 3½ feet apart. Each original plant is allowed to make 6 runner plants, which are laid out like spokes in a wheel. (R. M. Kellog Co.)*

If you do not intend to spend a lot of time with your strawberry plants, allow 2 feet between each plant and 1½ feet on each side of the plant row. All of this space will be well covered with plants by the end of the first growing season, and you will wonder in the next summer where you can put your feet when picking. Do not underestimate the ability of the strawberry to spread itself wherever there is ground! You should provide 25 plants for each member of your family for enough strawberries to eat at any one time. At the height of the season, you will have some extra for preserves or freezing out of this size planting. You can include the rows in your vegetable garden rotation, as strawberries are seldom fruitful more than 2 or 3 years and new rows should be set at least every third year. Do not plant strawberries where you have recently grown tomatoes, potatoes, peppers, or eggplant.

When setting strawberry plants, trim off ragged root ends. Make a slit in the soil and hold a berry plant with roots fanned out against 1 side of the slit, the "crown" or thick part of the plant just even with the top of the slit. Now stamp the slit closed with your foot, firming the soil around the roots and leaving no air space at the bottom of the slit. The crown of the plant should not be covered with dirt nor should the roots show above the ground. Most successful planting of strawberries is done by 2 people, 1 doing the digging and 1 setting the plants. A good soaking right after planting will do much toward settling in the plants. Hold off the fertilizer until the plants are established in the row and growing. Do not set plants in ground that has been freshly fertilized.

Frost Control: Irrigation for frost control can mean the difference between an 80% crop and a 20% crop. Spring frosts are always a hazard to strawberry crops during the blossom stage. Sprinkling the strawberry bed will help protect against frost. Don't get alarmed if ice forms on the plants—just keep on sprinkling and the plants will usually come through in good shape. Leave the sprinkler on until all the ice has melted from the plants.

Another trick to thwart frost is to cover the bed with plastic film, which comes in rolls 12 to 32 feet wide and 100 feet long. The thicker weights are easier to handle, especially if a breeze is blowing. Between frosts the film can be piled up in accordion-style pleats between rows and held down with bricks, rocks, or whatever is handy. The film method is practical where berries are too remote from a water source, or for gardeners who don't want to get up early in the morning to turn the sprinkler on. Just roll the plastic sheets on at night when you feel frost threatens and go to bed without worrying. Burlap, painter's dropcloth, old curtains, etc., can also be used.

Feeding: After plants show signs of new growth in the leaves, you can commence a feeding program, using a complete formula fertilizer, either applied in liquid form or around the plants, about ½ handful to a plant, hoed in lightly and then watered.

Removing Blossoms: When blossoms appear on newly set plants, they should be cut off the first year to throw all possible strength into the plants for a good fruit crop the second year. Shortly after the blossoming season, runners will spring from the center of the plants, at the end of which, in a few days, a new plant will form. If you want highest possible yields of fine big strawberries, no one plant should be allowed to make more than 6 of these new runner plants, which you space evenly around the plant in the row. All other runners should be removed as they form. This runner removal should be kept up all summer long. If you do not keep at it, your berry patch will quickly get out of hand.

Weeding: Weeds are your worst strawberry pest. The hoe is still a handy weed killer. Hoe away from the plant, and the earlier the better. You can cut the weedlings off easily when they're little. As for weed killers, keep 2,4-D away. Sesone is good, known as a "pre-emergence" weed killer. It won't kill grown weeds, but it does kill the germinating seeds before they have a chance to get big, also the small seedlings. Apply anytime you wish, although early spring is very effective. For every 100 foot of row, mix 2 level tablespoons of Sesone to a gallon of water. Sprinkle on with watering can. You won't harm the strawberry plants. Give another treatment in late August. Sesone won't kill weeds after they're up—it kills the seeds, so get it on before they have a chance to germinate. Geese do a wonderful job of weeding strawberry patches. If you raise ⅛ of an acre or more, put in a goose or 2 before the strawberry fruit comes on. One goose for every 1,000 strawberry plants.

Picking: The strawberry patch should be harvested daily. Birds can be a real problem, best method of control is cheesecloth or nylon anti-bird netting. After picking, refrigerate fruit immediately for use, or freeze.

Keep fertilizer away from the berry patch until the crop of fruit is off, as feeding at this time tends to make the berries soft and encourages rotting before they ripen. Do supply the plants with frequent watering (an inch of water per week) all through the berry season, soaking the patch after you pick. This increases berry size wonderfully. Should a frost threaten when your strawberries are beginning to bloom, cover the rows overnight with newspapers or burlap bags. The blossoms are very sensitive to frost and a late frost can take the crop if the patch is not protected.

After the patch has produced its first crop of berries, dig out small and unthrifty plants, filling the spaces with the new runners that will again form this second year. Once the spaces are filled, however, again continue the runner removal all through the season—and the feeding program you used in the first year. Some people like to cut the plants back by removing all but a few leaves from each plant after fruit harvest. This is not necessary but does give a cleaner-appearing patch. Winter mulch (see section on Mulches) is applied to the rows and removed in spring.

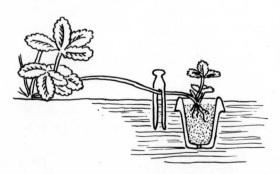

You can root the tips of strawberry runners in a 4-inch clay pot sunk level with soil surface and filled with good soil. Clothespins or stones hold runners in place until roots secure them.

Black plastic mulch on a strawberry planting. (Monsanto Plastic Products Division)

Fruit of second crop will seldom be as fine as that of first-year crop, due to grass and weeds, but you should get 2 crops from the same planting. If your plants are good and clean, free from disease, there's no reason why you can't use them to start a new patch. If disease is in them, you might better buy new plants from a good firm. Most plants from nurseries are virus-free.

After the second fruit harvest it is well to dig the plants under and work on a new patch. Some diseases may take hold of an old patch about this time and the plants will be spindly. Grass and weeds are a more serious problem.

Mulching for Winter: In late fall, before temperatures drop to 20°, cover the entire strawberry bed with a 2-inch blanket of straw or marsh hay. Do not follow the advice given in some of the older books and bulletins: "Wait until the ground has frozen about 1 inch and hard enough to drive on it and then apply the mulch." This advice, followed for many years, resulted frequently in severe crown injury which showed up the next spring in poor yields of berries. Leaves should be used as a last resort as they tend to mat and may smother the plants. This mulching is very necessary, as strawberries that are not covered over winter tend to heave out of the ground as it alternately freezes and thaws; this heaving will eventually break off the roots of the plants and kill them.

Mulching for Summer: Early in spring, the following year, just as plants begin to grow, the mulch may be gradually removed. You can tell when to take off the last of the mulch by watching the color of the foliage. When it starts to turn a sickly green under the mulch, the plants need light and it is time to fully expose them. Keep the mulch you take off the plants right in the berry rows around the plants. This will serve to keep the fruit off the ground and keep it clean. Sawdust, either hardwood or softwood, makes a good summer mulch. If plants show a yellowish tint, it may be due to lack of nitrogen. Sprinkle with some water-soluble plant food, or nitrate of soda. From ⅓ to ½ cubic yard of sawdust is needed for every 100 square feet of planted area. Plastic mulch between rows cuts down on weeds, increases yields. Anchor with soil on edges, or stones. Any mulch will keep weeds out, water in, and produce clean fruit (see section on Mulches).

Some Unusual Strawberry Plantings

How to Grow Everbearing Strawberries: What are they? They are varieties that produce a crop of fruit in the spring, and another in the fall. They also have ornamental value when planted along walks and foundations, or in a strawberry barrel or pyramid. While not recom-

Sawdust mulch is excellent for everbearing strawberries grown by the hill system. (Arthur J. Pratt)

mended commercially, they can be grown for limited local sales. Ever-bearers cannot equal the best spring-fruiting varieties in yield and quality, but since you can pick them off-season, they still taste good!

How many should be planted? For an average family, at least 50 everbearing plants is enough for fresh fruit. Under good conditions, the best variety produces about 1 quart of berries per plant in spring, and 1 pint in the fall. Hot summers will lower yields.

What are best varieties? Hard to say for your area, but here are a few we've liked: Geneva (cross between Streamliner and Fairfax) and Red Rich (Wayzata x Fairfax). Fruit ripens in June, later in July, and continues up until October. Red Rich has high-quality, honey-sweet, extra-large fruit. Ozark Beauty is a firm good-flavored berry and top producer; Giant Mastodon is one of the first true everbearers, and it still holds its own. Streamliner is medium in firmness and a good producer. Ogallala has good-size fruit, is a fine producer, but has just fair flavor. There are other good ones, but these are the ones we've tried and like.

What's the best way to grow them? Plant in spring for best results. You can also plant them in fall, but keep them watered if soil is dry. They may be grown in a matted row, or in the hill system. We prefer the hill system. With this the plants are spaced 1 foot apart and all runners are pinched or cut off as they develop. Then they are mulched with crushed corncob, sawdust, straw, or whatever material you have available, to conserve soil moisture, keep berries clean, keep weeds down, and help make the planting attractive. Black polyethelene plastic is even used. If you use sawdust, straw, buckwheat, etc., add a little extra nitrogen. Feed plants after blooming and bearing. During dry periods it's a good idea to irrigate, otherwise fall production will be disappointing. In November, mulch with straw to prevent winter injury. In severe winters, plants mulched with plastic only may be injured or killed, so put straw right over the plastic.

Should blossoms be removed? Yes, best results will be obtained if all blooms are removed up until early July. This means first fruit will ripen about mid-August. We're speaking of spring-planted plants. If you transplant or plant in spring, they should bear their heaviest crop in fall. And remember, 1 planting will produce only 1 spring crop and 1 fall crop. They won't bear from year to year. Fruit produced in cool fall months tastes better than fruit produced in midsummer. First-year production is best.

Do they need spraying? Normally, the home gardener doesn't have to spray. However, if your fruit has hardened ends (nubbins or "cat-facing") this is the work of the tarnished plant bug (not spring frosts!) and you should spray the plants after blooming is over, using Malathion, Sevin, or methoxychlor.

Remember, set a new bed of everbearers in each spring, rather than try to rejuvenate the old one. Most of the varieties mentioned previously will do well in a barrel or a pyramid. But make sure the plants are watered constantly. Purplish spots on leaves may be due either to leaf spot or leaf scorch, although they usually are not serious. If buds are cut off from plants before bloom, trouble is due to work of the strawberry bud weevil. Spray with Sevin or Malathion as soon as trouble starts.

Climbing Strawberries: A gardener writes: "As far as I'm concerned I wouldn't recommend climbing strawberries. I planted 4 plants in early spring and tied them to a trellis. They grew fairly well, but I only got 4 berries from the 4 plants. This spring they grew very well, but not a single berry! This summer I tore them out and replaced the space with a 3-tier strawberry pyramid and it's a lot more satisfactory."

Many growers of the "climbing strawberry" tell me the same thing. No one I know has been happy with this novelty!

The climbing strawberry needs winter protection. Take the runners down and protect with straw, as you would with regular strawberries. Actually, there's no such thing as a climbing strawberry. All the runners have to be trained to "climb," or grow up a trellis.

How to Make a Strawberry Barrel: If you want to have a barrel of fun, try raising strawberries in a wooden barrel. It's profitable too, especially if you don't have space to raise a regular patch.

Use any wooden barrel you may have, or buy one from your garden-supply store. Choose a warm, sunny spot for it. We set ours on 3 or 4

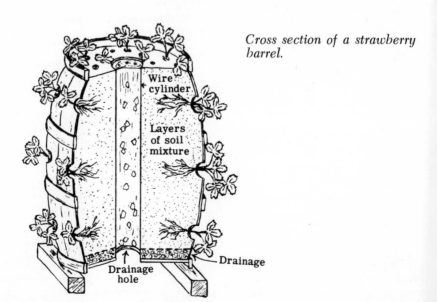

Cross section of a strawberry barrel.

bricks, laid flat, but some folks place it on a sturdy platform equipped with castors to permit turning of the barrel—once a week—to allow all sides to receive the advantage of the sunniest exposure.

The barrel needs a drainage core. For this, form a 4-inch diameter cylinder from screen or hardware cloth, obtainable from your local hardware. This cylinder is placed in the center of the barrel, and surrounded by soil. Starting 1 foot from the bottom, bore a lot of holes in the barrel at irregular intervals, 9 inches apart and large enough to hold a plant without cramping.

You need drainage, so put 6 inches of coarse gravel, cinders, broken clay pots, etc., in bottom, topped with finer material. As for soil, you can use any good garden loam. Mix 2 bushels of topsoil with 1 bushel of manure. To every bushel of mixture, add 3 pounds of 5–10–5 fertilizer.

Planting and filling can be done at the same time. Start by covering the drainage with soil to level of first holes in bottom. Push the roots of a plant through each hole in the bottom row, spread them out, and firm soil over them. Water sparingly. Repeat this planting and filling operation to the top of the barrel, each layer being tamped firmly to eliminate settling of the soil by rain and watering. Water the barrel as needed. In hot weather you may have to water 2 times a day; in cool weather, less often.

Use any everbearing variety that will grow in your locality. After the plants finish bearing, remove the old plants and replace in spring with new plants; or you can root the newly formed runner plants in pots and use them for replacement.

You can cover the barrel with straw or cornstalks if left outside in the winter. These can be held on by means of rope or chicken wire. Some gardeners move their strawberry barrel into the garage, barn, or cool cellar. If you do that, no protection is needed.

TROUBLES

Red Spider Mites: Cause webbing, yellowing of leaves. Use Kelthane on foliage after harvest.

White Grub: Around roots. Apply Chlordane or Sevin, dust or liquid. Do not get any on fruit.

Tarnished Plant Bug: Causes catfacing (see accompanying chart). Malathion or Sevin will lick this pest.

Frog-split or Spittlebug: Frothy deposits on stems and leaves. Dust with methoxychlor, handpick.

Any leaf-chewing pests, use methoxychlor, lindane, or Sevin.

Summer Dying of Strawberries: Home gardeners often ask why their strawberry plants die in midsummer. This is usually due to verticillium wilt, worse on lands where tomatoes, potatoes, peppers, or eggplants have been grown. Strawberries should not be planted in soil where these crops have recently been grown, or where wilt has been observed. Wilt is not easily told from "wet feet," winter injury, red stele disease (see chart). Usually the first symptom is drooping of older leaves at the time fruit begins to ripen. Older leaves take on a reddish-yellow cast, younger leaves are small and chlorotic (yellow). Control: none.

Leaf scorch of strawberry leaves. Spots are dark purple.
(USDA Photo)

STRAWBERRY TROUBLE CHART

Here is a guide for growing better berries by detecting and eliminating certain diseases. This guide is easy to use. For example, suppose your strawberry leaves have spots, and the centers of the spots are gray. Just look at the symptom column, and keep moving down until you find the section mentioning leaf spot disease. A little practice and you'll catch on to it quickly.

I. LEAF SYMPTOMS	DISEASE	CONTROL
A. Leaf yellowing		
1. Yellowing of margins, leaflets cupped upward	Yellows	Burn diseased plants Plant yellows-free stock
2. Yellowing in pinpoint spots, leaflets crinkled	Crinkle	Same as above
3. Yellowing mostly in streaks between veins	June Yellows	Same as above
4. Yellowing more diffuse through leaf	(see symptoms of root troubles)	Plant resistant varieties
B. Leaves with definite spots		
1. Center of spots reddish-brown	Leaf Blight	Spray plants with Bordeaux mixture or zineb in early spring as soon as growth starts
2. Center of spots gray	Leaf Spot	
3. Spots dark-purplish throughout	Leaf Scorch	Due to dry weather
4. Yellow pinpoint spots becoming brown	Crinkle	Pull out plants and burn
C. Leaves distinctly malformed (misshaped)		
1. Leaves contorted, contain galls	Leaf Stem Gall	Soil fumigation, pulling up of diseased plants, and planting disease-free stock
2. Leaves greatly narrowed, glossy	Spring Dwarf	Pull up plants and burn
D. Leaflets cupped upward, undersurface gray to brown	Powdery Mildew	Dust with Mildex or Karathane

(cont.)

STRAWBERRY TROUBLE CHART   (cont.)

	Disease	Control
II. Fruit Symptoms		
A. Mold or mildew on surface of fruit		
1. Fruit decayed or decaying	Gray Mold	Dust with Mildex, sulfur, or Captan
2. Fruits not decaying	Powdery Mildew	Dust with Mildex, sulfur, or Captan
B. Fruit malformed, portions undeveloped, "nubbins" or hard seedy ends	"Catfacing"	Dust or spray with Sevin or Malathion. Some may be due to spring frosts
III. Root Symptoms		
A. Normal number of new roots		
1. New roots with external cankers	Root Rot	Plant in new soil
2. New roots with reddish core	Red Stele	Plant resistant varieties, such as Pathfinder, Temple, Sparkle, and Fairland
3. Roots with definite enlargements or knots	Root Knot	Fumigate soil or plant resistant types
B. Abnormally few new roots	Dud, Grubs	Apply Sevin, Malathion, or Chlordane around roots. Do not get any on fruit. May be due to plants getting too dry before planting. Winter may injure roots. Use straw mulch for protection.

Strawberry Parfait Ring: Spoon strawberry sherbet and soft vanilla ice cream in alternating layers in chilled ring mold. Freeze. When frozen, unmold on serving plate and return to freezer. To serve, fill center with fresh berries.

Strawberry Sherbet: It's smoother and better made with milk—but you can use water instead . . . 4 quarts fresh strawberries, sliced, 4 cups sugar, 2⅔ cups milk, ⅔ cup orange juice, ⅛ teaspoon cinnamon. Mix strawberries and sugar, let stand until juicy (about 1½ hours). Mash or puree in blender. Strain seeds (optional). Add milk, orange juice, and cinnamon. Mix well. Freeze in crank-type freezer (or pour mixture into freezer trays or loaf pans and freeze about 3 hours, stirring 2 or 3 times). Makes about 1 gallon. Pack in plastic containers for freezer.

Strawberry Waffle: 1½ cups flour, 3 teaspoons baking powder, 1 teaspoon salt, 3 tablespoons sugar, 4 eggs, separated, 1½ cups very cold water, 4 tablespoons melted butter or salad oil. Sift flour, measure and resift with other dry ingredients. Beat egg yolks and whites separately. Combine beaten yolks with melted butter or salad oil, add water, add liquid to dry ingredients and beat well. Gradually fold in beaten egg white. Bake on a very hot waffle iron.

Allow waffle to cool, break into 2 pieces, place 2 scoops of ice cream on the bottom half and place other half over ice cream. Cover the waffle with fresh or frozen strawberries.

CHAPTER III

Nut Growing in
Your Backyard

When we were boys it was a common thing to go nutting on someone else's property. In those days farmers didn't care if you climbed their trees and shook down a bushel of nuts, or if you picked them up off the ground. Today, it's different. The population has increased so much no modern farmer cares to have a gang trespassing on his land in search of nuts. One way to get around this nutty situation is to grow and harvest your own nuts.

There's no reason why you can't grow edible nuts right in your backyard. Although the American chestnut has been doomed we're fortunate in having hickories, walnuts, butternuts, Chinese chestnuts, filberts, even almonds to grow. You'll not only enjoy growing and harvesting your own crops for candy, cakes, and eating "as is," but the trees serve admirably for shade and ornament, as well.

Nearly all nut trees have the same cultural requirements, the most important being a well-drained, slightly acid soil and the presence of a nearby rooster tree for cross-pollination. At planting time, dig holes 2 feet across and 2 or more feet deep, so roots will rest in a natural position. Fill around the roots firmly with good topsoil and water well to drive out air pockets from the root area. Prune back the tree before planting to balance the loss of fine roots when trees were dug. Nut trees need little or no spraying for a good crop.

For quick handy guide to nut trees for your backyard, see pp. 102–03.

ALMONDS (*Persica communis*)

If you live in an area where you can grow peaches, then you can grow almonds. While the almond is as hardy as the peach, it's production in cooler areas is more limited because it blooms a month earlier. However, you should be able to have a crop of nuts by the law of chance. Nuts ripen from peachlike, fuzzy fruits into the ripe almond, ready for gathering in August or September. We've had good luck with the new Hall's Almond, which not only produces high-quality nuts but pretty pink flowers in spring, and is a good shade tree for summer. Trees reach height of 15 feet. For best results, plant 2 trees for cross-pollination. You can propagate the almond by budding named varieties onto peach or almond seedlings in spring. Trees bear in 3 years and are in full production in about 12 years.

TROUBLES

Lack of Nuts: Due to improper pollination, or spring frosts killing blossoms.

AMERICAN CHESTNUT (*Castanea dentata*) AND
CHINESE CHESTNUT (*C. mollissima*)

American chestnuts coming back? Many gardeners know where there are some American chestnuts growing in the wild and bearing fruit. Does that mean the tree is shaking off the disease and making a comeback? Unfortunately not. There are no healthy American chestnut trees, as they used to be known. The trees you see are offshoots of the original trees which were blighted. The roots of the chestnuts are highly resistant to the blight, so that new sprouts have in many cases grown from the stumps of blighted trees. There are many such trees in the Northeast, and they are relatively small in size. Because most of the chestnut tree population has disappeared, the fungus which causes the blight is also in short supply. So these new trees escape the blight for several years; but eventually, because they do not become totally resistant to the disease, they succumb.

The U. S. Forest Service and other public agencies have developed a group of hybrid trees (hybrid or native Chinese or Japanese chestnut stock) that may either be timber trees similar to the old American chestnut, or they may produce nuts like the old trees. But no tree has yet been developed that does both, as did the old American chestnut. We're hoping that by a natural process we can soon have trees that are resistant to the blight.

Chestnuts you find in stores are usually the European chestnut (*C. sativa*), and are grown in Europe. Seedlings from these seeds could be successfully kept alive for a few years if they did NOT get the blight. Unfortunately, they are not blight-resistant. Furthermore, they are not hardy in cold regions and probably would be winter-killed after a few years.

Chinese Chestnut: If you go to all that trouble, you might better grow the Chinese chestnut, (*C. mollissima*), since it is hardy and blight-resistant. The quality is just as good. Be sure to plant 2 trees, because a single tree cannot pollinate itself and will produce a crop of "false" nuts each year.

The chinquapin (*C. pumila*) is closely related to the chestnut and resembles it strikingly in most of the important characteristics. Each may be grafted or budded upon the other without difficulty. Chinquapin is highly resistant to blight. Although this nut is not edible, there are some gardeners who will want to grow the tree for shade.

Starting Chinese Chestnuts from Seed: Your best bet is to start with budded or grafted trees from a reliable nursery. However, if you have the patience, and wish to, there is no reason why you can't start your own from seed. Be sure to start with fresh seed. Gather nuts in the fall and "stratify" them; that is, pack the hulled nuts between alternate layers of sand in a box (covered with wire to keep out rodents) and sink the container in the ground or in a cold frame for the winter. In spring plant the nuts in a well-drained spot in the garden and watch them grow! They have to have the cold-winter treatment before they'll germinate. Stratification causes a change to take place inside the seed so it will germinate in spring.

Why is it often so difficult to start new plants from Chinese chestnut seed? It took me a long time to find out the answer to this question. Chinese chestnuts are starchy, and very different from other nuts. They contain about 45% starch, 5% oil, and 50% moisture. This means they are highly perishable, more so than apples, and must be harvested properly if you want to start them for new plants. Unless properly handled, and quickly placed in cold storage, they dry out and become hard and bony.

Nut growers feel that Chinese chestnuts should be harvested at least every other day so that they will not be on the ground more than 2 days at a time. This is especially so where there is a lot of bright sunshine. Hot weather causes rapid deterioration of the "meat," or kernel. A temperature of 32° with 85% relative humidity is fine for storing chestnuts. I find they keep for months in a plastic bag placed in the crisper drawer of the refrigerator.

Grafting and Budding: This is tricky but you can try your hand at it. Budding can be done in spring or in summer. You take a single bud from the variety you want to propagate and unite it to a "mother" tree in such a way that the growing tissue (called cambium layer) of both come in contact. The bud is tied in place with raffia string and covered with wax. Some use plastic tape. The secret is to keep the bud tissue from drying out during the uniting process. When the buds are set, the binding material can be slit to relieve growth pressure.

Home gardeners may find grafting a bit more successful, but don't be discouraged if your attempts fail. Nut trees are harder to graft or bud than other fruit trees. Grafting consists of taking pieces of twigs ("scions") and fastening these on to mother trees (see Fruit Propagation for details).

TROUBLES

Spring frosts and winter injury may cause shrunken kernels, or more often, nuts are killed outright.

Small Nuts: Due to dry weather in summer.

False or Blank Nuts: Lack of cross-pollination. Plant a rooster tree about 50 feet away, or closer.

Wormy Nuts: Due to chestnut maggot or chestnut weevil. Spray with Sevin in June and July.

Moldy Meats: Due to high humidity. Store chestnuts in refrigerator.

Broken Limbs: Ice and snow damage. Chestnut holds leaves all winter, and being weak-wooded, often breaks from snow load.

HAZELNUTS (*Corylus*)

Hazelnuts are worth growing! The hazelnut (also called filbert) is worth some space in the backyard. Plants are quite hardy (same as peach) and very prolific. They make small attractive bushes up to 12 feet in height. The native American filbert (*Corylus americana*) is hardier than the European sort and we recommend it. The varieties usually grown are hybrids with European types. Barcelona and DuChilly are 2 good European varieties. Bixby, Reed, and Rush are good hybrids to grow.

Cross-pollination: Filberts are monoecious, which means the male (staminate) flowers and female (pistillate) flowers are borne separately on the same plant. Nuts will not set when the flowers are pollinated with their own pollen. So 2 varieties must be planted for cross-pollination—any 2 varieties will pollinate each other.

Plant in spring. Trees bear in second or third year. Nuts mature in early September and drop free from the husk. They are easy to crack, high in food value, and very tasty.

Pruning: Prune a little each year in spring to stimulate a moderate amount of new growth, since nuts are formed on 1-year-old wood. Filberts send up a lot of suckers and if you want a filbert "tree" these suckers should be removed. If you want a bush effect, leave the suckers alone.

Propagation: Filbert is the only nut that is propagated by layering the suckers which spring up close to the trunk. Just lay a branch on the ground, pack it down, and cover it with 3 inches of soil, allowing 1 or 2 buds of the top to project beyond the soil. Do this in summer and they'll be rooted by November.

Sometimes suckers have enough roots so they can be dug up and planted. Cutting the bark of the layered shoot hastens rooting. (See illustration in Raspberry section.)

TROUBLES

Lack of Nuts: Means a lack of pollination. Plant 2 different kinds for a big crop.

Filbert Blight: Shrivels leaves, serious in some areas. Spray the tree with zineb or Captan to check it.

Nut Weevil: Not serious. Gather and destroy infected nuts.

There is also a bud mite on filberts which may be troublesome. No good control is known.

HICKORIES AND PECANS (*Carya*)

Hickories for Home Grounds: Hickories are hardy trees and well worth growing. They grow best on well-drained upland soil. As shade trees they have a high ranking. The shagbark hickory (*Carya ovata*) is one of the best because of its resistance to disease and frost. Like other nuts, it may fail to fruit because of short seasons or lack of summer heat.

Other hickory trees include the pecan; also the shellbark or king nut (*C. laciniosa*), the mockernut (*C. alba*), and the bitternut (not the butternut, *C. cordiformis*), good for timber and ornament, though nuts are not edible. Most hickory trees are hard to transplant because of their long taproots, and the shagbark needs particular care in transplanting.

Unnamed or "wild" hickory nut fruits have the kernel locked inside the convolutions of the shell, making it impossible to recover the kernel except in small pieces. However, nuts from a variety known as Wilcox have kernels that may be recovered in halves.

Tip for Hickory Nut Growers: One gardener told me, "After we have cracked the shells on hickory or walnuts, we place them in a pan and put them in the oven at slow heat. This keeps them from molding, brings out the flavor and makes it much easier to pick the meats out.

Pecan: (*C. pecan*) is a hickory nut that will withstand winter cold, but the nuts do not often mature in northern areas because of the relatively short, cool seasons. They make beautiful lawn specimens, but the catch is that they mature a crop of nuts only occasionally in the north. In general, the southern or "papershell" varieties need from 240 to 250 days to mature their nuts, while the northern varieties usually form nuts of smaller size and thicker shells, and need 180 to 200 days to mature.

Pecans like a fertile soil. If you would like to try your skill at grafting, try converting hickory tree into a pecan tree. You might have good luck grafting your hickory with pecan. If your soil is good, growth will be vigorous and you'll find that the hickory may prove to be a satisfactory parent plant for growing pecans. But the operation is a difficult one, so don't be disappointed if it doesn't succeed. (See Fruit Propagation for details of nut budding and grafting.)

Hicans: Natural hybrids of the pecan and hickory are called Hicans. While they bear very large nuts, usually of top flavor, the yield is small. For that reason, grow them as ornamentals. They make beautiful trees and grow as fast as maples.

WALNUT (*Juglans*)

Black walnuts are just about the tastiest of all nuts. Homeowners with spare land should plant all the walnuts they can, for nuts and for timber. Our supply of walnut timber, one of the finest of furniture woods, is decreasing. Trees are being harvested faster than new ones are growing, so we suggest more homeowners set out walnut trees if we're to continue the warmth and beauty of walnut lumber and veneer in our homes. Walnuts make an excellent shade and ornamental tree as well. Plant in fall or spring.

The black walnut (*Juglans nigra*), produces valuable nuts in a growing season of about 150 days or longer. The variety Thomas is very dependable, has same growth rate as an apple tree and will bear in 4 to 6 years. One tree is all you need, as cross-pollination is usually not necessary.

Black Walnut for Lumber: Homeowners with some spare land can plant it profitably with black walnut. Mature walnut trees are now selling for

$50.00 to $1,000 each. Even if you can't be around to harvest the timber, it's good business to plant for another generation. Black walnut can be grown on practically any land that's loose and well-drained. Extreme sand and swamp are not desirable, nor dense woods. Walnut will grow well in pine stands. A cheap way to get a lot of trees started is by planting stratified seed nuts (nuts which have been kept cold through fall and winter). Started nuts cost around $30.00 for 1,000 and they can be planted late in the spring or early summer when the ground has warmed up. Plant 2 inches deep. You can also plant seedlings.

Grass and weed competition the first 2 years may be a problem, but a mulch around each tree will help keep these down. If you have a lot of nut trees planted, Simazine granules do a good job killing weeds.

Walnut Varieties: The English or Persian walnut (*J. regia*) likes a slightly alkaline soil. Most famous strain is the Carpathian, hardy, but susceptible to some frost damage. This tree can produce nuts without a nearby rooster tree, although another one planted within 50 feet will insure a better crop of nuts. The Japanese or Siebold walnut (*J. sieboldiana*) is ideal for shade, fast grower. About as hardy as the Persian walnut. Heartnut (*J. sieboldiana*, var. *cordiformis*) is a sport of the Japanese walnut, and nuts have better shelling quality. Butternut (*J. cinerea*) is a hardy native walnut, rather short-lived. Needs good drainage. Has same problem and care as walnut.

Planting: All nut trees like ample drainage. Walnut trees have a long taproot which should have been pruned in the nursery. To encourage fibrous roots to develop, take clippers and cut the tip end of the taproot back slightly. This will also hasten bearing. A must in starting young nut trees (and all fruit trees) is to protect the trunks from sunscald. In fall, wrap the trunks with aluminum foil. This need not be removed for 2 or 3 years. It reflects heat and protects the trunk from rodents.

Little pruning is needed, except to lower the top branch tips a few inches. The lower buds on the trunk should be removed to prevent too-low branching and to force growth into the central leader.

Cracking Nuts: Did you know that dry black walnuts or hickory nuts will shell a lot easier if you wet them before cracking? Soak them for 15 to 20 minutes and store overnight in a damp burlap sack. Is there any easy way to crack nuts? Black walnuts are easily cracked by pressure from the ends, rather than on the side. If you have just a few nuts, the hammer is the best tool for cracking. If you have a lot of nuts, you might want to look into either a power or mechanical walnut-cracker on the market.

We use a vise to crack nuts. One hand turns the handle and the other holds the nut from flying. Place the black walnut, butternut, etc., in a bench vise, end to end. This usually cracks them open in 4 pieces. Sometimes quarters of nuts drop right out (black walnuts), or halves (butternuts). To finish getting the nutmeats use wire-cutting pliers. Saves a few fingers and thumbs from misguided hammer blows.

For best-quality walnut kernels, husks should be removed as soon as possible after gathering and the hulled nuts washed. One way to remove the husks is to lay the nuts in a driveway and run car over them a few times. Another trick is to pound each nut through a hole in a board, to remove the husks. Some people store walnuts on a cellar floor and crack husks as the nuts are needed, but we feel this is somewhat messy.

One gardener tells me she uses baking soda to remove black walnut stains from her hands. If you don't want to stain your hands, wear rubber gloves when handling black walnuts. Stain rinses off the gloves in cold water. Your hands stay nice and clean.

Nuts can be planted outdoors in fall, cover with can to keep rodents out, remove in spring after seed sprouts.

TROUBLES

Shortage of Nuts: Due to frost injury in spring or insect damage. Inferior nuts may be caused by anything which causes leaves to shed prematurely, such as insects.

Blank or "False" Nuts: Due to lack of adequate cross-pollination. This can be due to bad weather at flowering time, or to a lack of a rooster tree. Many nuts are self-sterile. A safe practice with all nut trees is to plant at least 2 varieties together, with the exception of the butternut, which can pollinate itself. Or you can resort to bouqueting, putting flowering twigs from another tree in a can of water close by your tree.

Walnut Kernels Black in Color: May be due to high temperatures in August, but more likely due to leaving hulls on too long.

Moldy Nuts: Due to rain, or not being picked up soon enough after falling. Husks of nuts long neglected on ground become moldy, may spread to the meat.

To prevent mold, remove husks as soon as the nuts drop to the ground. If left in a bag they may mold. Some growers use artificial heat. Tree fertilization has no effect on kernel mold.

Wormy Nuts: Chestnut weevils or grubs eat their way out of the nut after having been in a warm room for a few days. Next year when the nuts are about $\frac{3}{16}$ inch in diameter, spray with Sevin or methoxychlor, 2 tablespoons to a gallon of water. In mid-August give another spraying to prevent the pest from gaining a foothold. Hickory weevil may cause some damage. Treatment is same as for chestnut weevil.

Wormy nuts may also be due to moth larvae. Spray in mid-August with Sevin.

Walnut Husk Maggot: If you're willing to go to the trouble of spraying, then mix up some Sevin, 2 tablespoons to a gallon of water, and spray the entire tree. Be sure to spray when the nuts are about $\frac{3}{16}$ inch in diameter, which will be around late July.

Leaf Worms (Tent Caterpillars, Webworm and Other Leaf-chewing Insects): Spray with Sevin or methoxychlor in mid-August, 2 tablespoons to a gallon of water.

QUICK REFERENCE CHART OF COMMON NUT TREES

Growing nuts in the backyard is a matter of selecting the right type for your climate and conditions. Nut trees can be grown in practically all parts of the U.S. This chart, prepared with the assistance of my former

KIND OF NUT	MATURE SIZE	PLANTING DISTANCE	FROST DAMAGE	SOIL	LIFE-SPAN	DISEASE RESISTANCE
ALMOND						
(*Persica communus*)	Small (15 ft.)	20 ft.	Yes, blooms	Well-drained	Med. long	Good
BEECH						
(*Fagus*)	Very large	80 ft.	Rarely	Well-drained	Very long	Good
WALNUT						
(*Juglans*)						
Black						
(*J. nigra*)	Very large	80 ft.	Rarely	Neutral	Very long	Good
Butternut						
(*J. cinerea*)	Med. spreading	40 ft.	Very rarely	Neutral or slightly acid	Short	Poor
Japanese						
(*J. sieboldiana*)	Large spreading	60 ft.	Rarely	Neutral	Long	Good
Heartnut						
(*J. sieboldiana cordiformis*)	Med. spreading	35 ft.	Rarely	Neutral	Long	Good
Persian						
(*J. regia*)	Large, round head	50 ft.	Often	Slightly alkaline	Very long	Good
HICKORY						
(*Carya*)						
Shagbark						
(*C. ovata*)	Large, upright	40 ft.	Rarely	Neutral	Med. long	Good
Shellbark						
(*C. laciniosa*)	Large, upright	50 ft.	Rarely	Neutral	Med. long	Good
Mockernut						
(*C. alba*)	Large, upright	50 ft.	Rarely	Neutral	Med. long	Good
Hybrids	Large	50 ft.	Rarely	Neutral	Long	Good
CHESTNUT						
(*Castanea*)						
Chinese					Med. long	
(*C. molissima*)	Med. spreading	35 ft.	Very rarely	Acid		Resists chestnut blight
Japanese						
(*C. crenata*)	Med. round head	40 ft.	Very rarely	Acid	Med. long	Resists blight
HAZELNUT OR FILBERT						
(*Corylus*)						
Filbert						
(*C. avellana*) hybrids	Bush or small tree to 15 ft.	20–25 ft.	Occasional	Neutral	Short, 20 yrs.	Medium
American						
(*C. americana*)	Bush to 8 ft.	10 ft.	Rarely	Neutral	Short, 20 yrs.	Good

Bacterial Leaf Spot: Causes leaves to turn brown with black spots. Worse in wet seasons and in regions with a very humid climate. As the trees grow older and increase in height they seem to develop a resistance to this disease.

Anthracnose: Causes no meat in kernels. Worse in wet years, causes many trees to lose their leaves early in the summer. Loss of foliage results in poorly filled nuts. The variety Thomas is very susceptible to anthracnose, as are most of the trees growing in the wild. The Ohio variety is resistant to anthracnose and usually holds its foliage late in the season.

professor of Pomology, Dr. L. H. MacDaniels of Cornell University, will help you select the tree for your backyard.

INSECT DAMAGE	CROSS-POLLINATION OR CLONES	VARIETIES OR CLONES	REMARKS
None	Yes	New Hall's	Blooms early and often killed by frost in north
None	No		Very hardy
Many pests	No	Sparrow, Elmer Myers, Thomas, Stambaugh	Varieties differ in hardiness and pest resistance
Fair	No	Craxezy, Buckley	Very hardy
Fair	No	Seedlings only	Fast-growing, spreading, of tropical appearance
Fair	No	Gettatly, Stranger, Wright, Walters	Nuts crack easily
Huck maggots troublesome	Yes	Metcalfe, Hansen, Littlepage, Broadview	Carpathian strain hardy Some frost damage
Usually not troublesome	Yes	Wilcox, Abscoda, Glober, Weschke	Difficult to transplant, needs extra care
Some	Yes	Stanley	Nuts thick-shelled
Some	Some varieties	Northern varieties: Major, Greenriver, Peruque	Hardy, but needs long growing season
Some	Uncertain	Burton, Gerardi, Rockville	Attractive trees
Weevils	Yes	Nanking, Kuling, Abundance	Seedlings preferred in north
Weevils	Yes	Stein seedlings	Quality poor
None serious	Yes	Bixby, Buchanan, Reed, Potomac, Rush	Bud mites in some areas
None serious	Yes	Winkler	Very hardy

CHAPTER IV

Outdoor Fruit Trees for
Southern Homes

Homeowners who live in cold regions often have good luck growing indoors southern fruit trees which normally grow outdoors. (See Tropical Fruits for Indoor Culture.) However, for those gardeners fortunate enough to live where they can grow southern fruits in their backyards, I'll list some of the most common types northerners can't grow. In general, "southern" fruits cannot tolerate temperatures freezing or below.

There are a number of especially tender species which cannot be raised successfully in the United States outside of Florida. In addition, culture of some common fruit crops may be different or impossible in the warm climate of the more southern areas. (My thanks to Alice Smart, Director of Public Relations for Florida Nurserymen, for her help.)

Avocado (*Persea americana*)

(For indoor culture, see Tropical Fruits for Indoor Culture.) Grown as far back as 1519 in Florida. Also called "alligator pear." Attractive foliage, evergreen in nature, and a shapely tree. Fruit is rich and popular for salads and other dishes. There are 3 races of avocados: (1) Mexican. Leaves anise-scented when crushed, fruit small, ripens late spring to early fall. (2) West Indian. Fruit summer and fall ripening. (3) Guatemalan. Fruit winter and spring ripening. Start new plants from seed planted 3 to 4 inches deep in well-drained soil, full sun.

TROUBLES

No Fruit: Plant 2 for cross-pollination. In every avocado flower, the stigma (female part) matures before the stamens (male elements) are ready to shed pollen. Thus 2 varieties are necessary for cross-pollination. Some avocado varieties first open their bloom in the morning, whereas others open first in the afternoon. For complete pollination and heavy fruit crops, on both, plant 1 of each type. Mrs. Smart tells me that for a self-pollinating tree, the afternoon-blooming types which open late would prove best, for the female parts of the flower may still be receptive to the pollen next morning when it reopens, since they have had little exposure during the late afternoon to the drying effects of sun and wind. Plant a morning-blooming variety such as Taylor or Lulu, and an afternoon-blooming variety such as Hall.

White Fly: Principal pest. Control with Malathion, which also controls other pests of avocado.

BANANA (*Musa*)

(For indoor culture, see Tropical Fruits for Indoor Culture.) Outdoors, bananas have huge, fleshy, treelike stems and it takes about a year for the plant to reach maturity. Cold winters will damage plants even in central Florida. Bananas have large rhizomes from which grows the single stalklike stem, which flowers only once. After the fruit is mature the old stalk dies and is replaced by suckers. Bananas like a sandy, fertile soil with ample humus.

Varieties: *Musa cavendishii*, grows 6 to 8 feet. Good fruit and attractive leaves. *M paradisiaca* (horse banana); fast grower, grows to 15 feet. Fruit attractive, not edible. Hardiest of all bananas, and grows as far north as Savannah, Georgia. *M. sapientum*, the attractive ladyfinger banana. Small fruits with thin skin. Another species produces small edible red fruit.

TROUBLES

Almost insect- and disease-free. Black spot can be checked with Captan.

COCONUT PALM (*Cocos nucifera*)

Ornamental and beautiful, tree is planted more for ornamental use than for commercial production. Grows 60 to 80 feet. Fruit is large, single-seeded, interior cavity contains liquid coconut "milk." It is the largest seed in the world. Coconuts are eaten both green and ripe. Green portion is spooned out similar to a custard. Coconuts are available almost all year, as trees bear continuously. Salt sprays or an occasional inundation will not kill them.

Fruit production starts when trees are 4 or 5 years old. A tree in good health on fertile soil should yield 75 or more nuts a year, while the average from a neglected tree is about ⅓ this amount.

Propagation: Seed is ordinarily planted in a shaded seedbed, with about ½ of the shell protruding. Some gardeners bury them partially in sawdust, kept moist. It's a good idea to transplant several times before planting out where they are to grow. Plant while seed is a bit soft and they will come up within a few weeks. Hardened ones may take as much as 3 or 4 years. Soaking or sandpapering seed hastens germination.

FIG (*Ficus carica*)

(For indoor culture, see Tropical Fruits for Indoor Culture.) The fig's history goes back to the Garden of Eden. There are many mentions of this fruit in the Bible. Fruit is eaten fresh, preserved (dried), and the juice of the fig is one of the oldest laxatives known.

Makes an ideal small tree, producing edible fruits from June to November. In the south trees require little care. Because the flowers are borne within the fruit, the only successful method of cross-pollination for the Smyrna fig is by means of the unusual insect known as *Blastophaga*, the fig wasp. Trees are heavy feeders, and long-lived. Roots grow close to surface, longer than the tree is tall, so a good mulch is valuable in keeping roots moist; surface cultivation should be avoided. The fig grows in any well-drained soil, abhors wet feet. Likes abundance of organic matter or plant food. Takes 6 to 8 years for a fig tree to reach maturity.

Figs require little pruning. If branches grow low to the ground it's fine, as they help shade the shallow root system. Figs will not ripen after they are picked from the tree, so only ripe fruit should be picked. Caution: wood is brittle and easily skinned, so use a ladder for picking.

Propagation: Figs are not grown from seed. They are readily started by cuttings, buddings, grafting, or layering (see Fruit Propagation). To make cuttings, take a WHOLE branch off, rather than just the tip from the branch. When a branch is cut back it causes numerous shoots to sprout and this makes too thick a foliage, smothering out some of the lower branches.

Cuttings are about 1 to 2 feet long. Take them in the winter after leaves have dropped, from ripened wood of the previous season's growth. Insert them in the spot where you want them to grow permanently, as this saves a setback when transplanting is needed. Place ½ of the cutting into the ground for rooting.

TROUBLES

Nematodes: Use grafted plants on root-knot resistant understock. If figs are planted on virgin soil, you can use tree grown from cuttings.

GRAPE (*Vitis vinifera*)

(See Grape in main fruit section for grape culture in northern areas.) While it's not possible to grow northern grapes successfully in the south, you may be surprised to know you can grow muscadine hybrids and certain bunch grapes. Scuppernong is an old favorite, producing large bronze-colored fruit with juice and flesh musky in flavor. Largest of the muscadines is a variety called James, bearing August to October.

Soil and Care: Plant in well-drained soil. In Florida, grapes produce heavier and better when the rows run north and south. This allows sun to get to the berries. Prune in November and December when the vines are mostly dormant, and they will bleed less. Muscadines are pruned back to 5 or 6 buds (eyes) on the previous year's growth. A mulch around the vines keeps ground moist and cool. Feed vines a complete plant food at rate of 1 pound for each vine of bearing size. Apply in February.

Propagation: Cuttings rooted in ground.

TROUBLES

Aphids, Leafhopper, Leaf Folder: Spray with Malathion.
Fungus Diseases: Black rot, downy mildew, and anthracnose are prevalent in hot weather when summer rains bring a drop in night temperature. Control: Cover leaves with Captan or Bordeaux mixture once a week.

GUAVA (*Psidium*)

Sometimes called Florida's "peach," guava blooms and fruits almost all year. Strong odor of fruit is distasteful to some, but you can get used to the odor and enjoy the fruit. Jelly is a choice delicacy. Fruit varies from size of a walnut to an apple or pear.

Soil and Care: Grows anywhere except in marshy location. Needs good drainage. Feed about mid-March and again about June 15, with balanced plant food. Give plenty of water during the time fruit is being produced and during blooming time when fruit is being set, for heavier crop.

Propagation: By seed easily. Reseeds itself as fruits ripen and fall, or as birds carry pieces of fruit here and there and drop seed along the way.

TROUBLES

Very few.
White Fly: Tiny white insect that can be troublesome. Spray with Malathion.

LIME (*Citrus aurantifolia*)

The lime has long been valued for preventing scurvy, as the fruit is a fine source of antiscorbutic vitamin C. In Florida, limes are a must for pies, sherbets, garnishes, as well as other uses. Limes make an attractive ornamental tree, 10 to 15 feet high, dark-green foliage. Main fruit crop is harvested in late spring, others ripen all year long, providing fruit for the table. While it is a seedless variety of citrus, you occasionally find a few seeds in a fruit.

Lime likes a loose, well-drained soil. Trees are injured by temperatures as low as 28°. Persian lime is one of the most hardy limes.

Propagation: Started by seed, and by budding on good rootstock, such as rough or "wild" lemon seedlings (see Fruit Propagation). This assures a good grade of fruit in a much shorter time. Limes start to bear in third or fourth year after budding. Be sure you select good strains of a known tree for budding.

TROUBLES

Not many.
Aphids, Scale: spray with Malathion.

LITCHI, LICHEE, OR LYCHEE (*Litchi chinensis*)

This is the dried litchi nut of the Chinese, but it is also valued as a rough-skinned fruit, raspberry-red in color. Grown in southern California and Florida.

Soil and Care: The litchi will grow in any fertile, loamy soil with acid (sour) reaction. Trees bear in 4 years, and since they are such vigorous growers, the crop increases each year. Feed in early spring with any well-balanced plant food. Male and female flowers are on same plant. Transplant any time of year, although winter is best.

Propagation: Seed, air layers, grafting, or cuttings rooted in sand. Propagation most often by air layers because this gives larger plants much quicker. Tree is nematode-resistant and is often planted in groves to replace citrus removed due to spreading decline.

TROUBLES

Practically insect- and disease-free.

LOQUAT (*Eriobotrya japonica*)

A handsome dual-purpose evergreen tree with delicious fruit in winter months. Damaged by temperatures slightly below 32°.

Soil and Planting: Needs good drainage, will grow in almost any type of soil. Detests wet feet. You can plant "canned" or balled specimens. Feed about March 15 and again about June 15 with a good balanced plant food.

TROUBLES

Red Spider Mites: Occasionally troublesome. Kelthane clears them up.

MAMMEA (*Mammea americana*)

This item has handsome evergreen foliage similar to magnolia, successfully grown in southern Florida. More tender than mango, needs protection.

Fruit is 4 to 8 inches in diameter, hard until fully ripe, when it softens. Beneath the brown skin is an often bitter membrane which sticks to the flesh. Ripe flesh is fragrant and in some varieties resembles the apricot or red raspberry in flavor.

Propagation: Start plants from seed planted 3 inches deep in sandy soil. Takes about 2 months to germinate. Seedlings bear in 6 to 8 years. You can start new plants from half-ripe cuttings also, perhaps a better way, since a percentage of seedlings will be non-fruiting male trees.

Mango (*Mangifera indica*)

Called "Apple of the Tropics," mango is an ornamental as well as popular fruit, eaten fresh or made into chutney, ice cream, custard, etc. Tree has stout trunk, dense foliage. Grown in southern California and Florida.

Soil and Feeding: Prefers deep, moderately rich soil, well drained. Keep young trees amply fed and watered, and after bearing starts, withhold water and confine feeding to a few definite applications. For bearing trees 5 to 10 years old, feed a balanced food such as 2–8–10 at rate of 2 pounds for each inch of trunk diameter, applied right after fruit has been picked. Apply a second dose at same rate not later than the first part of October. If a heavy crop of fruit has set a third application of balanced plant food is needed, but is never applied until the fruit is definitely set and well developed.

Pruning: Very little pruning is needed. Snip out dead or diseased wood, as well as weak spindly growth in center of tree to let light and air to enter into the tree canopy. Trees with weak growth should be headed back to encourage a low-spreading, symmetrically formed tree. As the tree increases in size, lower branches may be removed to prevent the fruit from touching the ground.

Harvesting: The Florida Department of Agriculture reminds us that care must be exercised in harvesting mangoes. Do NOT pick when green, for they will never ripen properly. Pick just before they begin to soften, or when the fruit takes on a yellow color at the lower end. Takes 120 days for fruit to mature. Crop will hold on the trees fully 3 weeks. Picked at the turning stage and kept in a room at average temperature of 80°, the fruit keeps from 4 to 5 days before becoming overripe.

TROUBLES

White Fly and Scale Insects: Spray oil emulsion or nicotine sulfate soon after fruit is harvested. Spray again just before the first bloom appears.

Anthracnose: Bordeaux mixture or Captan will check anthracnose and other fungus troubles, applied as soon as the blooms start to open, and again after blossoms drop and fruit begins to develop.

ORANGE (*Culture is same as Lime, which see.*)

PAPAYA (*Carica papaya*)

Newcomers to Florida and other southern states have to develop a taste for papaya, since the fruit is unusual in taste and flavor. This most important tropical American fruit tree has a straight, palmlike stalk with milky juice.

The fruit resembles yellow or orange melon, with black seed in the cavity. The flesh is aromatic and delicious. Milky juice and black seed are rich in papain (active ingredient in meat tenderizers) and the juice is often used to make tough meats more palatable. While soldiering in Africa during World War II, I saw Africans use papaya leaves with meats being cooked over a fire. Commercially, papain is obtained by collecting the gum which oozes from cuts on green fruits.

A papaya tree grows about 15 feet high, producing 12 to 30 fruits per year, and the life-span is about 4 to 6 years. Trees bear 12 months or earlier after being transplanted. One good frost will kill it back, so grow it as far south as possible. Too much near-frost will prevent fruiting.

Cross-pollination: On most varieties male and female flowers are produced on different trees, and only the female flowers produce fruit. Cross-pollination is needed, so 1 male tree should be planned to at least every female tree. A group of 3 papayas—2 female and 1 male tree—will make an attractive clump planting. Some bisexual varieties have been developed which bear heavily without cross-pollination.

Propagation: No practical way to propagate these vegetatively. Start seed from hand-pollinated fruits.

PEACH (*Prunus persica*)

(See Peach in main fruit section for culture of northern peaches.) Growing peaches in Florida must be considered a tricky business. Florida winters are too mild to grow peaches (peach trees need a certain amount of cold weather during the year to fruit successfully), though it is possible to grow certain types. One variety, Early Amber, is especially suited to Florida conditions.

Hybridizers have been working to develop peaches that will produce fruit with minimum hours of below-freezing temperatures and some good varieties have been added. In north and central Florida, Floridahome, Early Amber, Sun Red Nectarine, and Jewel do well with minimum of cold. Red Ceylon is the only variety that has produced fruit in southern Florida.

Planting and Care: Peach culture in Florida is different from that of other states. Trees need good drainage. Plant tree in a hole with plenty of peat moss. Feed tree in March with a balanced plant food. Little pruning is needed, just enough to shape tree and remove dead wood, and to thin out branches so sun can get into the middle of the tree.

TROUBLES

Aphid, Scale, Borers, Leaf Rollers: Spray with Malathion during the season. In early spring, spray with Captan or Bordeaux mixture to prevent mildew and various rusts.

Caution: Because the peach is susceptible to nematode damage, all peach trees should be grafted either on wild plum or Nemaguard rootstock to make them root-knot resistant.

Pear (*Pyrus*)

(See Pear culture in main fruit section for information on northern-grown pears.) Pears are not grown in southern Florida and not all pears thrive in north Florida.

Soil and Care: Prefers a well-drained soil, ample moisture. Plant young trees from nursery. Prune before growth starts in spring. Remove narrow-angled crotches. Feed with balanced plant food in March and again in June. Some varieties, such as Carnes, need cross-pollination. Pineapple variety is a good one for interplanting for better pollination.

TROUBLES

Aphids, Blister Mites, San Jose Scale: Spray with Malathion in April.
Fungus Diseases: Include rust, bacterial leaf blight, scab, and sooty blotch. Spray with Captan.
Pear is susceptible to nematodes, so stock should be grafted. (See Pear culture for more details.)

Pecan (*Carya pecan*)

Pecan culture is described elsewhere for northern gardeners. In southern areas it is a valuable tree for nuts and for ornament. Varieties recommended for home plantings in north and central Florida are Stuart and Curtis, both scab-resistant.

Soil and Care: Likes any well-drained location, ample water, and occasional feeding. Pecans have long taproot (even young trees have 3 to 4 feet of taproot), so at planting time do not cramp the root. Once the tree is established, it sends out long lateral roots, almost all of which are in the upper layers of the soil. Surface cultivation may injure roots. No pruning is needed with established tree. Just keep the lower branches pruned off about 5 feet above the ground. Mulch the roots as the heat of summer can affect the pecan root system.

TROUBLES

None serious.

Scale, Aphids, Caterpillars, Leaf Rollers: Can be kept in check with Malathion. Fungus Diseases: Spray with Captan or Bordeaux mixture at time of bloom and every 3 weeks thereafter until 4 applications have been reached. Will prevent loss of bloom and young nuts.

PERSIMMON (*Diospyros*)

(See elsewhere for persimmon culture in north.) The Oriental or Japanese persimmon (*D. kaki*) is a favorite southern fruit. Sugar content is higher than that of peaches, apricots, or oranges. Most varieties are astringent until ripe, although the darker-fleshed types do not have this characteristic.

Soil and Care: Persimmon grows on any well-drained soil. Transplanting is done during dormant season, December to February. Feed about ½ pound of balanced plant food for each year of the tree's age in spring when tree begins to leaf out and a second application about July 1. Prune young trees back to 2½ to 3 feet in height when planted; 5 or 6 shoots should be left spaced over a foot or more of trunk, arranged to avoid bad crotches and produce a well-balanced head. After the framework is formed, no major pruning is needed.

Cross-pollination: Since some trees bear only pistillate (female) flowers, and some only staminate (male) flowers, and still others have both male and female flowers, it's a good idea to plant 2 varieties for pollination and fruit set. A good variety for "rooster" effect is Gailey, which is not good for fruit quality, but excellent for pollination. Some varieties produce fruit even when not pollinated and these fruits are seedless. When pollinated the flesh is dark-colored, and when unpollinated it is light-colored.

PLUM (*Prunus*)

(For culture of plums in north, see Plum.) Ideal for ornamental leaves and blooms and fruit. Japanese-type plum (*P. salicinas*) is better suited to southern areas.

Soil and Care: Plums prefer a light loam or sand. Good drainage is important. Most varieties need cross-pollination, so plant at least 2 varieties for rooster effect. After tree is established little pruning is needed except to keep limbs from crisscrossing. Thin out center so light can get in for fruit production. Feed in March and again in June with a balanced plant food. Keep tree watered for heavy fruit crop, especially during the bloom season and while fruit is developing.

TROUBLES

Scales, Aphids, Thrips, and Leafhoppers: Spray with Malathion as needed.

Powdery Mildew: Add Captan to the spray, or apply separately.

POMEGRANATE (*Punica granatum*)

Grows on diverse soil types in southern areas and is not too affected by extremes of temperature throughout the state of Florida. Fruit, 2 to 4 inches in diameter, is one of nature's neatest package jobs. The tiny red globules of pomegranate flesh are enclosed in a pulpy sac and rind. Pomegranate is eaten fresh, or the juice may be used in preparation of drinks or syrup. Ripens in July and August, extending over a period of several weeks.

Propagation: Seed sown in sand-peat, cuttings or layers in the ground.

LESSER-KNOWN FRUITS WORTH TRYING IN THE SOUTH

Cashew (*Anarcardium occidentale*)
Dovyalis abyssinica
Feijoa (*Feijoa sellowiana*)
Jaboticaba (*Eugenia cauliflora*)
Jambolan (*Syzygium cumini*)

Longan (*Euphoria longana*)
Otaheite gooseberry (*Phyllanthus acidus*)
Sapodilla (*Sapota achras*)
Sugar apple (*Annona squamosa*)

Most of these are started from seed, like a steady supply of food and moisture. If you're interested in more information about tropical fruits, write to the University of Florida, Gainesville, Florida.

CHAPTER V

Tropical Fruits for
Indoor Culture

In recent years interest in growing fruited plants indoors has increased, not so much for the attractive fruit as for the aromatic flowers and handsome glossy foliage. (For outdoor culture of tropical fruits in south see Outdoor Fruit Trees for Southern Homes.)

AVOCADO (*Persea americana*)

Most "alligator pears" we get in the market come from Florida and California. Some also come from Santo Domingo and Puerto Rico. Judge ripeness this way: If fruit "gives" or feels soft to the touch, it's ready to eat. Pinching or poking will bruise it, cause dark spots. If it feels like a stone, take it home to ripen. Put fruit in brown paper bag and it'll ripen inside bag. Don't put it in refrigerator. Flesh will darken when exposed to air. If you use it in salad, a bit of lemon in the dressing will prevent the flesh from darkening. Store pieces in waxed paper. Try mashing chunks of avocado into hot soup before serving. Adds flavor.

How to Start Seed: There are 2 ways, in water or in soil. Some have good luck with seed in plain tap water and glass. Water Method: After you remove the flesh, wash the pit (seed) with warm water, NOT COLD WATER. Sometimes the halves have started to split. It's OK, but they shouldn't be entirely separated because there's a vital thread between them and if it's broken, the seed's germinating power may be hurt. Thrust toothpicks in middle of seed and suspend seed over glass of water, base downward in the water. Top can be differentiated from bottom of seed easily. Base has a dimple in it, and usually the top is tapered.

116

DO NOT PUT ENTIRE SEED IN A GLASS OF WATER as it causes a scum to form, just the base. Place glass in warm spot. Keep water at constant level, making sure base of seed is always immersed. Soon you'll see a split and a long taproot coming from base, and a shoot will start from top. If stem grows too fast, cut it back about ½, even while seed is still in glass. Sometimes a seed will make several shoots or stems. Don't cut them until you've repotted the rooted seedling. Sometimes shoots will fall off, one by one, leaving a tall shoot. This can be cut back to make a bushy plant.

When a thick set of roots is formed, enough to reach the bottom of glass, you can pot it up, using ⅓ sand, loam, and peat mix.

To me a better method is to start seed in a pot of soil. Set seed in soil so that upper half of seed is exposed. Water with warm water. Don't keep soil soggy wet. After germination keep in bright window at room temperature.

Keep leaves washed off, if plant gets too tall, cut it back to ½ so new stems will form at base of old stem. Don't be afraid to trim the plant for symmetry; it's tough and grows fast. If plant gets large, transplant to larger pot or tub and grow in bright room. You may have to use a bamboo stick for support. Feed with 23–19–17 formula once every 3 or 4 weeks, 1 teaspoon to a quart of water.

The plant has perfect flowers (male and female), and can pollinate itself, but it won't fruit indoors. It's even hard to get it to flower, but the foliage is attractive.

TROUBLES

Red Spider Mites and Aphids: Mites cause webs on tips of shoots. Aphids secrete honeydew material which attracts black sooty mold. Control: Spray with Malathion for aphids, also syringe plants weekly in bathtub. For red spider mites, spray with Kelthane.

What can be done with an avocado which grows on a bare stem with only a few leaves on top? Not much. If you cut the top out you'll have a bare stem for several months, but eventually new buds may come from the stalk and the plant will be bushier. The time to pinch the stem is when the plant is smaller, say about 10 inches tall. At that stage you can snip out the tip, leaving a couple leaves for show.

Brown Spots on Leaves: Can be due to hot, dry air, or dry soil. Provide good drainage by adding pieces of charcoal or pebbles in the bottom of the pot.

BANANA (*Musa*)

They knew about this versatile fruit way back in history. Alexander the Great found the people of India eating bananas in 327 B.C. The genus name of the banana, *Musa*, comes from Antonio Musa, physician to Octavius Augustus, first emperor of Rome.

There are over 60 species of *Musa*. The common cultivated banana is *Musa sapientum*, altogether 15 or 20 varieties are grown for commercial banana production.

Due to their fine foliage, many species of banana plants are used for ornamental purposes. Some have large leaves and some have a coppery color. The fruit of some species must be cooked for it to be edible. All bananas are easy to grow. (For outdoor culture, see Outdoor Fruit Trees for Southern Homes.)

Dwarf Banana: *Musa nana cavendishii* has same indoor needs as pomegranate (which see), except that it should not be allowed to grow dry. Give sunny window, loose, humusy soil and uniform supply of moisture. Grows well in the average home.

Flowering Banana: *M. acuminata* (also listed as *M. cavendishii*) is the dwarf ladyfinger banana. Prefers a well-drained soil, ⅓ sand, peat, and loam. Does best in semi-sunny window. Feed liquid plant food in spring. Grows superbly in peat-like mix. Feed weekly and give plenty of room. Should have 24-inch tub at least. Will produce fruit in 1 year.

Propagation: Seeds or plant suckers formed at base of plant. Cut when not more than 1 foot high and use to start new plants.

TROUBLES

Blackening of Foliage: Due to poor drainage.

CITRUS

The citrus family includes lemons, limes, oranges, grapefruits, tangerines, and the like. Many gardeners successfully raise these in the home for flowers, foliage, and fruit. *C. aurantifolia* bears small edible limes. *C. limonia ponderosa*, so-called Ponderosa lemon, is a houseplant that produces big edible fruit, some weighing over ½ pound.

C. mitis (calamondin or miniature orange) has fragrant white flowers, edible fruits 1 to 1½ inches in diameter. *C. nobilis deliciosa*, the mandarin orange, is another citrus grown indoors. *C. taitensis* or *otaheite* (oh-tuh-hee-tee) orange produces golf-ball-sized fruit which is attractive, though not edible.

Soil and Care: All citrus prefer a loose, well-drained soil, loam, sand, and peat mixed together, fortified with ½ cup bone meal to each peck.

Soil should be uniformly moist and preferably watered from beneath. A good soaking in sink twice a week is good. Also syringe to wash away dust and to keep insects down. Spring or early summer is a good time to give citrus plants a light pruning, cutting out any extra-long shoots for symmetry, and trimming tips back to size and shape desired. If plants have not been repotted in past 4 years, do so, using soil formula described. When summer comes, set plants outdoors in partially shaded spot, plunging pots up to rim. This summer treatment helps ripen the wood and prepares fruits for late fall and winter display. Bring indoors before frost and grow in sunniest window available.

Citrus plants like cool temperatures, from 40° to 50°, at night during winter. They also need full sun and an airy location. Temperature and sunlight are important in bringing the plants into flower and fruit.

Hand-pollination Necessary: Hand-pollination is essential for decorative lemons or oranges to adorn your small tree. The operation is very simple. The female blossom is easily distinguished by the long stigma protruding from inside the flower. It is a simple trick to place some of the pollen from another blossom on this stigma. Most citrus need pollination indoors, and you can help this along by taking your cat's tail (don't chop it off!) or camel's-hair brush or the tip of your finger and tickling each bloom, spreading pollen from 1 flower to another.

Propagation: Seeds or cuttings taken in spring or early summer. Take 4-inch cuttings from tips and root in sand. Or you can sow seed in 4-inch pots of soil any time of year. Plants grown from seed produce nice foliage and blooms but cannot be depended upon for edible fruit. If you do start plants from seed of a store orange, don't be disappointed if you don't get lots of fruit, since these come from large outdoor trees and should not be expected to bear indoors. In the home they are capricious as to blooming and bearing. Citrus started from seed can be whip-grafted (see Grafting) in spring and made to bear. For edible fruit, best results will be obtained by buying grafted or budded plants from nursery.

TROUBLES

Failure to Flower: Can be due to lack of summer ripening period, high room temperature, or lack of light. Normally citrus are large outdoor trees, taking years to bear, so don't expect the impossible. Grafted types bear and flower indoors. Those started from seed may take years to flower and bear fruit, and even then you cannot count on them to flower or to fruit. Seedlings of all citrus are capricious as to time of blooming. Some are 10 years or older and have had no fruit or flowers.

Dropping of Buds, Flowers, and Small Fruits: Can be due to a lack of light, improper watering (too much or too little), or high room temperature.

Black Coating on Leaves: Sooty blotch or mold gathering on secretions from aphids or scale. Wash off with soapy water and syringe plants regularly. Spray with Malathion to check pests.

Yellowing of Leaves: Due to poor drainage, too much water, poor light, or pests in the soil.

Coffee Tree (*Coffea arabica*)

Coffee trees for indoor growing are started in Florida from coffee seed gathered in Central America. Plant is a real conversation piece for the home. Hardy, with dark-green, shiny leaves, it will grow as much as 8 feet in height. You won't get many berries but the foliage is well worth the effort.

Soil and Care: Coffee tree should have bright window, well-drained soil. Seedlings grow best at 70° to 75°. Later on, plants need 55° to 58° night temperature for flowering and producing beans. Can be topped at desired height. Encourage bushy horizontal growth by keeping all terminal growth cut off. Flowers and beans are produced on horizontal growth.

Propagation: Start from seed in sand-peat mixture. Once seedlings are up, transplant to 4-inch pots and grow in a semi-shaded or sunny window.

TROUBLES

Brown Leaves: Too much water or pot size too small. Use soil mixture of ⅓ sand, peat, and loam. Do not overwater.

Date Palm (*Phoenix longreiri*)

These are harder to start and grow than most tropical plants, since the hard seed coating keeps out moisture. Filing seed lightly often helps to hasten germination. Plant seed in loose soil and don't be impatient, as it may take 6 months for germination. A temperature of 80° to 85° is necessary for sprouting.

The date is a plant of desert regions, and that means it likes lots of heat. Grow in warm room, bright window, and use a ⅓ sand, loam, and peat mixture. Your pygmy date palm won't bear in the home because you must have a male and female tree. Male and female flowers are on different trees. Plant outdoors in summer, and keep foliage covered with Malathion to prevent red spider mites or scale insects.

Fig (*Ficus carica*)

(For outdoor culture, see elsewhere.) In the home figs may be grown in a number of ways.

In Greenhouse: In a small greenhouse figs can be harvested over a long period. Start new plants from 10-inch cuttings taken during dormant period (winter). Place them in a box of sand and keep in a cool place all winter. During this time they will callous over and get ready for rooting in spring when they are planted out in the garden. They sometimes bear second year. Avoid seed, unless you want plant only for foliage effect. Since they fruit on new wood, the plants should be pruned considerably at end of each growing season. This also makes them easier to handle.

In Pots: For planting indoors in pots, the greenhouse plants are set into 4-inch pots. When roots fill these pots, shift to 6-inch pots. The dormant, field-grown plants are set in 8-inch pots or small tubs. Cramping roots a little will keep the plants smaller and hasten production of flowers and fruit. You can buy dwarf fig trees from nurseries. These are grown in tubs so plants can be taken inside and stored for winter. Plants will winter safely in ordinary cellar. Or you can wrap and bury the top in ground for winter protection. The common fig matures fruit without cross-pollination, so you don't need a second plant. The dried fig of commerce, Smyrna, needs a Capri fig tree and a fig wasp for pollination.

TROUBLES

Figs are relatively free of insects and diseases. Scale, Aphids, Red Spider Mites: Apt to be troublesome. Spraying with Malathion and syringing the foliage regularly while the bush is growing outside will help to keep these pests down.

Failure to Bear: Due to bad weather, age of plant, or lack of light.

Kumquat (*Fortunella*)

There are 2 varieties of dwarf kumquat which can be grown in the home. *Fortunella margarita* seldom bears flowers or fruit. When it does flower, blooms are white and fragrant, followed by orange-yellow fruit about 1 inch in diameter. Grown mostly for foliage. *F. hindsii* is a free-fruiting variety which is almost always covered with fruit. It has small (½ inch), nearly round, orange-colored fruits with almost no juice. Highly ornamental. The care for all kumquats is similar to that of citrus. Fruits can be eaten fresh or pickled.

Mango (*Mangifera indica*)

Here's an interesting item to add to your collection of tropical fruits which can be raised indoors. It may not bear because the mango is a tropical tree that is sometimes 100 feet in height. Start the seed in a pot of sand and peat moss. Don't overwater. After the seed has germinated, you can add a bit more water. If you apply too much before germination starts, rotting instead of rooting sets in. Grow in sun or semi-shade. Keep top trimmed back.

Olive (*Olea europaea*)

You can plant olive "pits" (seeds) in a pot of loose soil and get good foliage plants. Use those of the black olive, since they are ripe. Bulk olives, if available, are best for starting seed. Put 2 or 3 seeds in a 5-inch pot with ⅓ sand, peat, and loam mix. It will take up to 3 months for germination as the seed coat is a hard shell. After they start to grow, transplant to another pot. Give lots of light, ample moisture, and a warm room. Keep foliage cleaned off by syringing from time to time. In summer, place plant outdoors in tubs. *Olea europaea* or manzanillo bears edible fruit and is an excellent decorative tree.

One of my readers, a native of an olive tree country (Portugal), wrote: "Over there anytime a farmer wishes to grow a new olive tree, he just cuts off a branch and sticks it into the ground. Within a short time (and without fail) he has a new olive tree growing."

With this in mind, you might attempt rooting olive trees from cuttings off your friend's plant. Starting olives from seed takes patience, so don't be discouraged. If every trick fails, then try a suggestion sent to me by another reader. She claims she gets olive seeds to sprout by first freezing them in ice-cube trays for 3 weeks. Then she plants them in a pot of sand and peat moss and gets good germination.

Pineapple (*Ananas comosus*)

Usually, the pineapple will not fruit in the home, but it makes a fine bromeliad or foliage plant. Plant needs full sun and ample water.

Make sure soil is well drained. If heavy, add peat moss or broken charcoal. If sandy or light, add only peat moss.

To Start a Pineapple Indoors: First cut the top off with 1 or 2 inches of fruit attached and place in a soup bowl with small amount of water in the bottom. Rooting will take place within a few weeks. You can also start the top directly in a pot of soil. A good mixture is ⅓ sand, ⅓ loam, and ⅓ peat. You can bake it in the oven (200° F. for ½ hour) to sterilize before using it. Let it cool before you put the top in. The top will root fast in a good soil mixture.

You can also take a pineapple top and scoop out the meaty part, being careful not to injure the tough little stem in the center. Then air-dry the top until it's partially dry. Line the bottom of a clay pot with chipped rock, gravel, or sand, for drainage, and over this place a thin layer of sphagnum moss. Place the top in the pot and add just enough soil to cover the skin. Place in a draft-free, sunny spot. Groom by nipping off any damaged leaves. Water sparingly from the bottom each day. Grow in full sun and pinch back from time to time to induce bushiness.

Now that the top is potted and growing, you simply wait for the "red bud," which consists of more than 100 very tiny flowers, to open into blue-velvet blooms. Each flower lasts but a day and each remaining flower brace develops into 1 segment of the fruit.

Forcing a Pineapple Plant to Flower: Many gardeners get their plant to fruit by placing a plastic bag over the plant (mature one) so no air will reach it for 4 or 5 days. An apple is enclosed inside the tent, to gas the plant. Apples give off ethylene fumes which will force the pineapple to flower and form fruit. The plastic bag confines the fumes. After 4 days, remove the plastic tent, and you'll see new leaves starting from the center of the plant. Finally, you'll see rows of pineapple fruit appearing on the bottom of the new leaves. The edible fruit that follows is golden yellow and will grow about 6 inches above the old plant, on a stalk about ¼ inch thick.

How to Judge for Ripeness of Pineapples in Stores: For tangy flavor, eat fruit when the entire shell is green. For full sweetness, allow fruit to remain at room temperature until lower ¼ to ½ of shell turns orange. DO NOT OVERRIPEN. The ripening process may be slowed by refrigerating at temperatures from 45° to 60°.

How to Freeze Pineapples: Peel and cut into desired shapes, pack into freezer cartons. Cover with cold syrup made of equal measure of sugar and water. Dissolve sugar in tap water by stirring. Then chill. It's not necessary to heat the syrup. Seal cartons and freeze at 0°. Will keep 8 to 12 months.

USES*

Mixed Fruits on the Half Shell: Halve pineapple lengthwise. With grapefruit or paring knife, cut around entire half, ¼ inch from outer peel. Remove pineapple from shell and cut into chunks. Mix with other fruits and pile into shells. Place on serving plate and garnish. For seafood or chicken salads, line shell with salad greens of your choice. Add some fresh pineapple to your favorite salad and pile into shell. Garnish with radish roses, carissa plums, or cherries. Serve each person ½ shell.

Pineapple Sour Cream Salad: 1½ cups mandarin oranges, 1½ cups diced fresh pineapple, 1½ cups diced marshmallows (or miniature marshmallows), 1 cup shredded coconut, dash salt, ½ pint sour cream. Combine first 5 ingredients and blend in sour cream.

Shredded Fresh Pineapple and Cream: 2 cups fresh, shredded pineapple, 1 tablespoon fresh lemon juice, ½ cup sugar, 1 cup heavy cream, whipped, ¼ teaspoon nutmeg. Combine pineapple, lemon juice, and sugar. Fold in whipped cream and nutmeg. Chill and serve as dessert. Makes 3½ cups.

Whole Pineapple Fruit Tray: Wash pineapple. With sharp knife, cut around each section or "square" of pineapple. Be sure to cut deeply enough to reach core. Leave row of uncut squares or sections at top and bottom. Guests pull out in sections as they serve themselves. Place on fruit tray and surround with other fruits and cheese. Serve as dessert or party refreshment.

POMEGRANATE (*Punica granatum*)

Pomegranate is grown indoors for its flowers and foliage, as well as small edible orange-red fruit. The dwarf double varieties have flowers that are a bit more frilled and double, but they do not produce fruit.

Soil and Care: Likes sunny window, 72°, ⅓ sand, peat, and loam mixture. Keep soil uniformly moist. Place plant outdoors in summer and water regularly. Trim back any extra-long shoots, bring in before frost. Goes through a semi-rest period in winter and sheds leaves.

Propagation: Sow seed in sand-peat mix or root cuttings. If you want to increase your supply of pomegranates or start a plant for a friend, there are 2 methods of propagation you can use. A great many basal

*Thanks to Knapp-Sherriff Koell, Inc., Donna, Texas, for recipes.

shoots appear at all times of the year. These may be gently pried out of the pot and potted individually. As they begin to grow, nip the top to make the plant have a more rounded contour. During the summer months, when the wood is in a soft state, cuttings can be taken and rooted in a pot of damp sand.

TROUBLES

Aphids and Red Spider Mites: Syringe plant regularly, spray with Kelthane.

CHAPTER VI

Fruit
Propagation

All fruit plants, including nut trees, may be propagated by seeds, layering, budding, or grafting. Except for use as stocks for grafting, planting of seedling trees is not recommended for the home gardener. Buy your trees from a nurseryman.

Layering: Layering simply means bringing a branch or shoot into contact with the soil for the purpose of having it form a new set of roots. While layering is a method for propagating many ornamental plants, it is also useful in propagating some fruits (including filbert nut). Bush fruits, raspberries, gooseberries, etc., and grapes are often successfully propagated this way.

Cuttings: Small fruits, such as black and red raspberries, grapes, etc., can be started from cuttings taken in fall. These are placed in bundles in moist sawdust and kept in the basement. Others place them outdoors in small trench and leave them covered all winter.

TRICKS TO GRAFTING AND BUDDING

Imagine having a tree in your backyard with 15 or 20 kinds of apples growing on it! You can have such a tree and you can do it yourself. A friend of mine has a Rhode Island Greening mother tree, on which is grafted Red and Black Jonathans, Red Delicious, Golden Delicious, Banana, Yellow Transparent, Early Red Bird, Early Red June, Winter Pearmain, Red Rome, Green Porter, and a few pioneer varieties of which he does not know the name. He even has the Golden Blush crab apple growing on this remarkable tree.

This is just one of the many striking effects and helpful transformations made possible by the techniques of grafting and budding. Budding and grafting are usually done to place fine-fruited domestic varieties on hardy, "wild" rootstocks.

For the average home planting, it's better to go to a nursery and buy budded or grafted fruit trees. These are "true-to-name" and you'll be sure of getting cultivated or "tame" fruit. However, for those who like to try their skill, grafting and budding are tricks which bring a lot of satisfaction.

It is important to remember that buds and grafts will only be successful between varieties of the same species, or closely related species of a genus. This means you can't graft or bud a stone fruit such as a peach onto a seed fruit such as an apple.

While most amateurs find budding easier than grafting, they also will find that grafting is a more successful propagation method for nut trees. We find that both budding and grafting are a lot more difficult with nut trees than with other fruit trees such as apples. The best commercial growers will tell you that you can expect many failures from both grafting and budding of nuts, so don't become discouraged. Nut grafting takes skill, although the principles involved are same as for apple grafting. It takes skill to fit the scion (see discussion of grafting) to the stock and to match the cambium layers so they'll knit. But you can do it.

GRAFTING

Almost every gardener has a hankering to practice the art of grafting in some of its forms. To graft, you take a stem with leaf buds (called scion, or cion, and pronounced "cy-un") and insert it into a part (limb or trunk) of another (closely related) plant, called the stock. Several different procedures are used in grafting techniques but the secret of making a bud or a graft take is to remember one important point: Growth takes place in a single layer of cells lying just between the inner bark and the wood. You must bring this layer of cells (called the cambium tissue) of scion and stock in contact with each other as perfectly as possible so they will unite and grow.

How to Graft: First, study the illustrations. When it comes to explaining budding or grafting, 1 picture is worth 1,000 words.

To make a graft, you select a limb or sucker from last year's growth. Cut it back to about 6 inches in length. Peel back a narrow strip of bark about ⅛ inch wide and 2 inches long. Take the young shoot (scion) of a different variety and cut the bark to fit the 6-inch limb on the tree. Place the 2 exposed limbs together and bind firmly with plastic tape so it will be airtight. Leave the tape on for 3 months. Many old-timers still use grafting wax but the plastic tape is just as effective.

Grafting Wax: Here's a formula for a soft grafting wax: resin (crushed), 4 parts, beeswax or paraffin (finely cut), 2 parts, tallow (rendered), 1 part, or raw linseed oil, ½ part. Melt these together, pour mixture into a pail of cold water. With greased hands, flatten out this spongy mass so it'll cool evenly. Wax may be kept in oiled paper or aluminum foil. Soften it by heat of your hands, or heat and apply with a brush. Heat until just warm enough to flow fairly freely. Overheating may cause some of the ingredients to separate out. Wax keeps in moisture and hastens union. You can also buy water-soluble asphalt grafting compounds which are simpler to use.

How to Make Waxed Tape and String: Although you can buy these materials they are sometimes difficult to locate. Waxed tape may be made by tearing cotton cloth into strips about ½ inch wide, making the strips into rolls, and then soaking in hot grafting wax. When the cloth is thoroughly saturated with the wax, remove and cool. Store for future use. Waxed string is made by soaking balls of twine in hot grafting wax. When the twine is completely saturated with the wax, the balls should be removed and handled like the waxed tape.

Time to Graft: Spring is the time to graft. It's important that you gather grafting scions with care. Twigs that have made growth of from 1 to 2 feet during the preceding season usually furnish the best scion wood. Buds should be plump and mature. The midportion of the 1-year growth furnishes the best scions; top and bottom portions of

Cleft Grafting: (1) Cut scions, with bud at base. (2) Scions ready for insertion. (3) Scions inserted in the cleft. (4) Completed graft with all cut surfaces waxed. (New York State College of Agriculture)

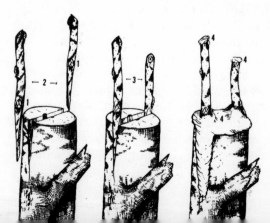

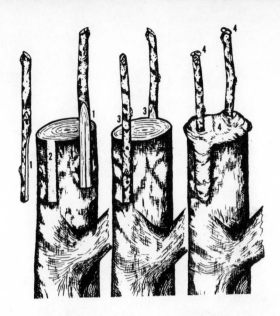

Inlay Grafting: (1) Cut scions ready for nailing. (2) Bark on stock removed. (3) Scions nailed in place. (4) Cut surfaces thoroughly waxed. (New York State College of Agriculture)

most 1-year growth contain underdeveloped and weak buds. Scions may be cut during the winter while dormant; keep them cool and dormant until time for using. Wrapped in cloth or covered with sawdust in the cellar, they keep well. Do your grafting in spring, just before, or as buds are starting up.

Types of Grafting: There are many types of grafting. Following are some of the more common kinds.

Cleft Graft: Twigs (scions) are cut to a wedge and inserted into the stock (see illustration). Wax the cuts and cut surfaces, and all parts of the scions, after wrapping with raffia or plastic tape.

Side Graft: A form of cleft graft in which the cleft is cut on the side of the stock and the top of stock left on. After the scions have started to grow, or show signs of uniting with the stock, you cut off the top of the stock.

Inlay Graft: Take a scion or scions 3 or 4 inches long with about 3 buds. Beginning about 2 inches from the lower end of the scion, take a sharp knife and make a slanting cut—right into the center or heart and straight to the lower end—leaving a smooth surface. Place the cut surface against a smooth portion of the stub of the stock, to mark an outline. Cut and remove bark of the stock to match outline. If you do the grafting on a warm day, about the time some growth has started, the small portion or plug of bark will slip off readily and leave a clean surface of green cambium cells exposed. If it does not remove easily, delay inlay grafting until the bark does slip easily. Tack (small wire

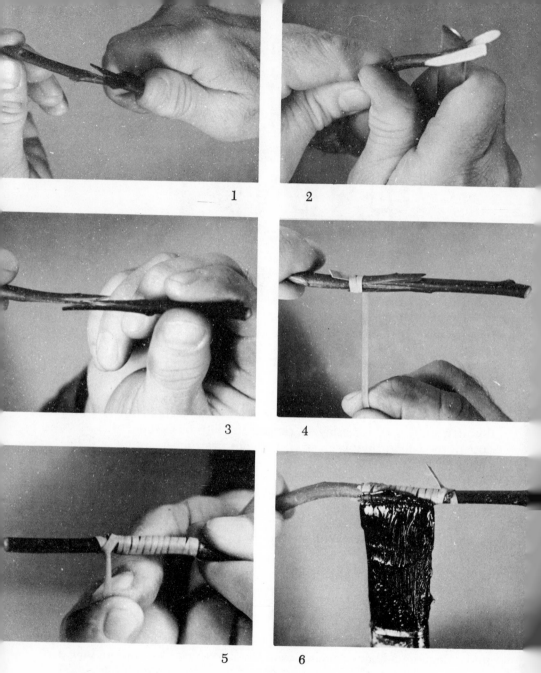

1. In whip grafting, the scion is cut so that it contains 2 good leaf buds. The lower cut is sloping with a surface 1 to 1½ inches long. **2.** The upper end of the rootstock is cut and shaped in the same way as the lower end of the scion. **3.** The scion (right) is slipped on the rootstock in tongue-and-groove fashion. **4.** Rubber budding strip used to wrap the graft union. **5.** Graft union completely wrapped with rubber band, to hold scion in place until growth knits. **6.** Grafting wax applied to scion and tissues to prevent drying out. (E. S. Banta)

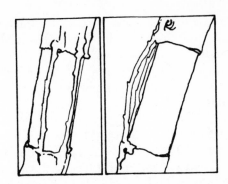

Left, bridge grafts in place. Right shows proper outward bowing of scions. (New York State Agricultural Experiment Station)

nails, ¾ inch long) scions in place, then wax cut surfaces thoroughly with wax.

Tongue or Whip Graft: Select a smooth place on the stock, sever it with a slanting cut about 1½ inches long. Make a similar cut on the bottom end of a scion. The scion should have about 3 buds on it. You then make a tongue on the slanting end of both stock and scion, then the 2 tongues fit into each other. Bind the union with string or a budding band and cover with wax. Strong cord must be cut soon after growth starts. (See illustration.)

Bridge Graft: Many home gardeners have noticed that mice and rabbits have ruined fruit trees by chewing on the bark. Will such trees survive? If the girdling has been completely around the tree, it's gone. The tree will survive if up to ¾ of it has been girdled.

You can save a girdled tree by resorting to bridge grafting. As the name implies, this consists of bridging over the wound by taking twigs (scions) of same variety and tacking (1-inch wire nails #18) each end onto the live wood above and below the girdled area. Sap rises (bypasses) the damaged area and keeps the tree alive.

Make the scions about 4 inches longer than the space to be bridged. The secret is to get good contact, with the scions bowed outward (see illustration); to do this about 2½ inches of the ends of the scions must be whittled into a wedge shape. Cover the entire graft with wax, applied with a brush. Some gardeners wrap the graft with a plastic bag to keep the moisture in, which is the purpose of the grafting wax.

BUDDING

Budding is a form of grafting and consists of taking a bud from a desirable fruit tree and starting it to grow on an undesirable tree or another good tree. When the bud grows out, it will bear the same variety of fruit as the tree from which it came. For example, if you take a bud from a Northern Spy apple and start it on a wild apple tree, or even a cultivated one such as McIntosh, you would get Northern Spy apples, regardless of the variety the bud is growing on.

Budding is done mainly on fruit trees such as the apple, peach, plum, and cherry. It is also done on ornamentals. As with grafting, the important thing to remember is to bud the right (closely related) varieties.

Shield or "T" Budding: The most common type of budding (see illustrations). With this you make a cut in the stock in the shape of a "T." Then you cut a bud from a desirable tree, in the shape of a shield, starting the knife blade about ½ inch below the bud and cutting deep enough into the twig so as not to injure the bud. You may get a small piece of wood with the bark—this can be removed or left on. Now the bud is inserted in the cut in the stock. The bud is then wrapped with rubber strips or strips of cloth. It isn't necessary to wax the buds. If the budding has been successful, the bud will have united with the stock at the end of 2 weeks. If the wrapping material hasn't loosened by that time, it should be cut. The bud will remain dormant the rest of the year but will start growth in spring.

The stock can be cut off just above the bud in the spring. And remove all sprouts arising from the stock around or below the bud, to allow the strength of the tree to go into the growth of the bud.

Time to Bud: Budding can be done in July or August or September, when the sap is running—and that's the time when the bark lifts easily from the wood. Sometimes the bark sticks, but often it will slip off easily after a rain. If you have a fruit tree that's bearing poor quality of fruit, you can make it bear top-quality fruit by budding. Find buds in the axils of the leaves on current season's growth of a good variety. Select nice healthy buds. Vigorous shoots that have formed their terminal buds generally contain good mature buds. Buds taken from the central ⅔ of the growth are better than buds taken from the tip or bottom ends of the growth. Bud growths are cut from the tree and the leaves trimmed off, leaving about ½ inch of the leaf to act as a handle when inserting the bud. Buds are more successful when placed on current season's wood, or 1-year wood. The thicker the bark, the less likely the buds are to succeed.

FRUITS AND NUTS FROM SEED

Starting Nut Trees from Seed: Many ask about the possibility of starting nut trees from seed. If you're interested in growing finest quality nuts my advice is to buy budded or grafted trees from your nursery, especially if only a few trees are to be planted. However, if you'd like

1. *Cutting the shield bud from the bud stick begins about ½ inch below the bud. Cut through the bark into the wood. The thin section of bark and wood is called the shield.* **2.** *A shield bud cut from the bud stick.* **3.** *The shield bud is pushed gently into place beneath the bark flaps.* **4.** *Shield bud is in place and ready for wrapping with rubber band.* **5.** *A rubber budding strip is used to wrap around the bud to hold it firmly in place.* **6.** *About a month after budding, rubber band starts to check and rot. It breaks up before causing restriction of tree. (E. S. Banta)*

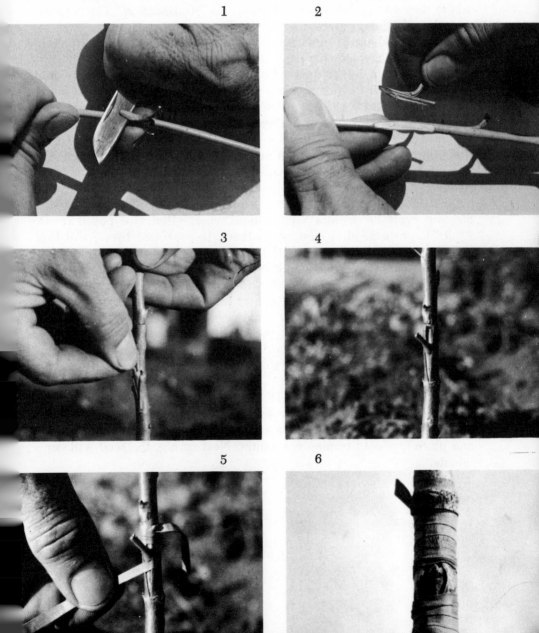

to try your hand and take a chance, you can grow seedlings from selected strains. Keep in mind trees started from seed show great variation in hardiness, vigor, yield, and quality.

Many who try to start trees from nuts find that the seed never germinates. The biggest reason for this is that the home gardener forgets that nuts are highly perishable. Kept in an attic or basement, the kernels dry out, or mold. The secret is to plant the nuts immediately after harvest. You can do this in a cold frame or directly in the ground, where they get a cold treatment known as "stratification." During this period a physiological change takes place in the seed, if exposed to temperatures about 3° or 4° above freezing. If the seeds freeze during winter the same change happens, without harm to seed.

If you have a lot of nuts to plant, pack them (hulled) between alternate layers of sand in a box covered with wire screen (to keep out rodents) and leave them there all winter. In spring, plant the stratified nuts where you want them to grow. Or, you can use an empty beer can as a protector and plant right outside. In fall, put the nut in the ground, place an empty can over the nut, leave it there all winter. In spring the nut will germinate, send a shoot up through a hole punched in the top of the can.

Starting Fruit Trees from Seed: Homeowners often save peach seeds ("pits"), prune seed, apples, and others. If you plant these, will the fruit be as good as that from the parent tree? Sometimes fruit from trees started from seed is good, but in most cases it is "common" or almost wild and hardly fit to eat. Unless you want to experiment and find out just what kind of fruit comes from trees started from seed, I wouldn't take the time to grow such trees. A better idea would be to graft or bud "tame" stock onto the seedlings you get from seeds. It's still more sensible to plant a budded tree from a nursery, because you can be sure the fruit will be true to name.

Seeds Need Cold Treatment: If you're willing to try starting seeds from fruit trees, remember they need a cold treatment before germination. You can plant the seed in a sand-peat mixture, cover with screen, and place in a cold frame over winter. Next spring, the seed will germinate.

INTRODUCTION
TO
VEGETABLE GARDENING

CHAPTER VII

Planning and Maintaining

the Garden

GARDENING IS PROFITABLE

Few enterprises about the home give as much satisfaction and as big a boost to the budget as the vegetable garden. Studies show that for the time you spend in the garden, you get a net return of from $2.00 to $5.00 an hour.

One state college figures that the average home garden in its state will be worth $165. The average gardener will spend $34.50 on his garden, and that means he'll be getting back about $4.75 in produce for every $1.00 he spends. So you can figure that it pays to plan and plant a garden!

How to Read Seed Catalogs

Home gardeners have a choice of starting their own plants from seed, or buying them. Quite often plants sold at roadside stands are mislabeled and are not true to name. Good seed is cheap and a good investment.

A seed or nursery catalog is a storehouse of useful information. Here are a few tips for getting the most from it: (1) Don't go overboard on brand-new items. Some may not be as good as your old favorites. (2) Don't hesitate to experiment and try new ones. (3) Look for varieties marked "Disease-resistant," especially with vegetables. Disease-resistant does not mean the plants won't get any disease. It means they will resist certain diseases. For example, Delicious melon is fusarium-wilt re-

136

sistant, but it can get a dozen other diseases which plague melons. Likewise Heinz 1350 is a tomato which resists both verticillium and fusarium wilts, both bad troubles in most home gardens, but it can get anthracnose and various blights. The point to keep in mind is that some of the resistant types should be grown because there is no other way to fight the disease. Blights can be licked by sprays, but soil-borne diseases cannot. (4) Save yourself a few cents by ordering the larger amounts. For example, if the catalog prices hybrid watermelon seeds at the rate of 10 for 40 cents, or 50 for $1.50, get the larger amount and make a 25% saving, or a cent a seed. This may sound like small peanuts, but it all adds up when you make out a big seed order. Good seed is a bargain, regardless of what it is priced at in a catalog.

For example, a packet of carrot seed, properly planted and cared for, can produce over 2,000 carrots—enough to supply a family of 8 for a year. With new hybrid varieties, yields can be about 25% higher.

What is a hybrid? A hybrid is a cross between two stable varieties or "inbred lines." For purposes of illustration, assume we take the pollen from the Earliana tomato and place it on the pistil of the Rutgers variety. The seed obtained from this cross is called a hybrid. It is often referred to as F_1. In many instances, the tomato plants produced from such a cross show remarkable vigor, increased yield, and perhaps other desirable characteristics which we all look for in a tomato variety. This accounts for the popularity of hybrid vegetables. The cost of producing hybrid seed is very high. Each flower on the mother plant must be emasculated (have pollen sacs removed by hand) and then hand-pollinated with pollen taken from the selected male line. This requires a lot of careful hand labor and results in your paying as much as a penny apiece for the seed. Usually the extra cost is worth it, although this doesn't mean that hybrids are always better than regular or "open-pollinated" varieties.

There is no perfect variety of any vegetable. You must compromise between earliness, disease resistance, eating quality, and the like. New and better disease-resistant strains come out every year. Don't give up your regular varieties until you've given the new ones a good trial.

Ordering Vegetable Seeds or Plants: Home gardeners who order vegetable seeds or plants should buy them by variety name. Don't ask for just any tomato or melon. You buy cars, dogs, pianos, by name so buy your plants by variety name. If you can't get the variety you want, buy the seed and start it yourself. (See section on Starting Seed Indoors.)

Coated or Pelleted Seed: The so-called "coated" seed is known in the trade as pelleted seed. The idea of coating small seed was to make it larger, more uniform in shape, making it possible to sow the seed more evenly. Pelleting received a lot of publicity a few years ago, but each year you hear less and less about it. Tests show that pelleting delays sprouting, due to the fact that it takes longer for the soil water to penetrate to the germ of the seed, thus, a slower emergence of the plant. Also, pelleted seed costs more.

You'll see a lot of claims made for pelleted seed but I don't think they are justifiable. If you buy well-grown, well-cleaned seed with high germination, and are careful in sowing it, you'll get your money's worth without resorting to pelleted seed.

Testing Seed: Saving seed of your favorite vegetables is sometimes desirable, but never save hybrid seed as it will not come true. Test your seed before planting. It's simple. Place a known number on a piece of moist blotter or paper towel, and keep them moist between 2 plates, at room temperature. Check daily to be sure blotter is moist. The germination of most seeds can be checked in 5 to 7 days, and it should be at least 80%. If you put 100 seeds in the blotting paper or paper towel and 10 of them sprout, that means 10% germination, which is very low.

Seedsmen have so much better facilities for selection and keeping strains true that unless you have something special of your own, or prefer some old-time variety that isn't readily available now, it's just as well in most cases to buy your seed, rather than try to save your own.

PLANNING THE GARDEN

A garden plot 50'x50' (that's 2,500 square feet) will be sufficient for a small family, but if you have a larger family, say 5 or more members, then you'll need a space 50'x100', or even larger, especially if you want to have vegetables to can or freeze, besides all the fresh ones you want to eat.

If you have only a limited space available, the least you will want to grow is your salad greens, lettuce, tomatoes (so expensive in stores), radishes. Fresh herbs, so important in cookery, can be grown in very little space. Beets, carrots, onions, and snap beans are good, dependable yielders. If you have a good-size space, summer squash and sweet corn will provide a lot of good eating.

In choosing your garden space, keep in mind that crops should get at least 4 to 6 hours of sunlight daily. It makes little difference which way the rows run, although running them lengthwise of the garden makes cultivation easier. If they run east and west, plant your large crops on the north side of the garden so that they will not shade the small crops. Get your garden in shape as soon as the ground permits and select the best plants and seeds.

Stretch your Vegetables into Fall: Many home gardeners do not know the joy of planting crops so they can harvest them throughout the fall season. Frequently, the fall garden is more productive, and fall-grown vegetables are usually of higher canning quality than those which mature during the hot dry periods of midsummer. This is called "succession" planting—planting vegetables at weekly intervals during the summer to stretch out the harvest period. You can make 3 or 4 plantings of corn, snap beans, radishes, etc., until July. Carrots and beets for winter storage can be sown in late June.

Summer drought and early killing frost are the 2 factors you have to consider in planning the late garden. You can beat the midsummer drought by watering and mulching (which see). As for beating Jack Frost, concentrate on hardy vegetables like spinach, kale, turnips, and broccoli, since they are not injured by freezing temperatures.

Cool-season crops like lettuce, spinach, radishes, turnips, and kohlrabi can be sown again around August 1, so they will mature during the cool fall weather.

Make the right selection for your fall plantings. Most vegetables can be planted as late as July 1, and still produce a fair crop. Long-season crops such as tomatoes, peppers, eggplants, will bear until frost, if started early. Sweet potatoes and vine crops (watermelons, cantaloupes, pumpkins, and winter squash) will make normal growth in midsummer, and will not grow and mature in cool fall months. Lima beans and okra will produce a partial crop when planted as late as the first of July. Garden peas (Wando) are a dependable fall crop, and so is cauliflower. Onion sets may be planted any time during summer for green bunching onions. Top sets from winter onions can be planted for fall use. Those not used may be left in row for spring use.

How to Treat Your Seed

Many seed houses treat their seed, although I don't know of any that treats all its seed. It's a costly and messy proposition. In addition, there are many gardeners who will not use any treated seed for fear of the chemical coating being poisonous. Quick-growing crops like lettuce and radishes need no treatment, but beans, corn, peas, need treatment, since they are often planted in cold, wet ground and sprout more slowly. Seed of such vegetables are usually treated by reliable seed houses.

Overcoat method: Dusting a chemical on (overcoat method) is simplest way to protect seed. Some materials to use include Semesan, Thiram, Captan, or Spergon.

The simplest way for a home gardener to treat his seed is by dusting with Captan. Just scoop up some Captan on the tip of a knife blade, dump it into the packet, and shake vigorously until the seed is coated. Don't bother measuring the amount as only a very light coating is needed for protection.

Hot-water Treatment: Hot-water treatment protects against seed-borne diseases and has no effect against soil organisms. The hot-water treatment is exacting and should be done by experienced persons. The usual recommendation is to soak seed in hot water (122° F.) for 25 minutes, then cool and dry the seed. Some even apply a dust (such as Captan or Semesan) as further precaution.

Mercuric Chloride Method: Useful on pepper, squash, cucumber, for killing organisms on seed surface. Chemical can be bought in drugstore as a blue powder or in coffin-shaped tablets. VERY POISONOUS, SO KEEP IT AWAY FROM CHILDREN. One tablet in a pint of water, or an ounce of powder in 7½ gallons of water makes a 1:1000 solution. After 5 minutes, remove and wash seed in running water.

Never use treated seed to feed birds or livestock, or for human consumption. Avoid breathing dust while treating seed.

STARTING SEED INDOORS

Soil Mixture: Seeds do not need a rich soil for germination. The lighter the soil, the better. If you have access to muck soil, use it for starting seeds. It's light and seeds push up through it easily. If not available, use 1 part garden loam, 1 part peat moss or leaf mold, and 1 part coarse sand. Be sure to sow seed very lightly for husky plants. If seeds are sown too thickly you get spindly plants. Plan to sow about 7 to 10 small seed or 4 to 7 large seed per inch of row, and don't cover too heavily. Using a flour sifter, shake a very light coat of peat moss or muck over the seed.

Soil Sterilization: In the home, damping-off disease causes seed to decay before they sprout, and often kills the young seedlings. If your soil or seed is covered with furry white substance, that's damping-off, caused by several fungi which live in the soil. It likes wet soil conditions. So be safe and sterilize your soil before planting. Otherwise the seedlings will lop over and die.

Formaldehyde is good. Add 2½ tablespoons of formaldehyde (also called formalin) to one cup of water. Sprinkle this on a bushel of soil and mix well. Cover with blanket, and wait 2 or 3 days before sowing. Better still, wait until the smell of formaldehyde has left.

Another method consists of baking the soil in a moderate oven (250° F.) for 30 minutes or so. Allow soil to cool before sowing. Or you can pressure-cook your soil at 5 pounds pressure for 20 minutes.

Vermiculite: If you've been having trouble getting small seeds to germinate, you can try any of the new materials in the market. One such material is vermiculite, a mica-like ore heated to a temperature of 2000° F. until it pops. This makes an ideal growing material because it is sterile, eliminating damping-off. It has no plant food, so seedlings must be transplanted to a soil mixture as soon as they are about 1½ inches tall. Perlite is a volcanic ash used for starting seeds and cuttings. It's sterile, too.

Another material you can use is sphagnum moss, obtainable from florists, or swamps. Dry the moss and run it through a ⅛-inch screen. Fill your seed flat with soil, about 1 inch below top edge of flat. A ½-inch layer of screened sphagnum moss is put over the surface of the soil. Then you sow the seed and cover it with the sifted moss.

Sowing Seed: Do not sow seed too thickly, especially fine seed. They should be at least ⅛ inch apart. DO NOT COVER SEED TOO DEEPLY. Fine seed such as petunias, snapdragons etc., has little pushing power and

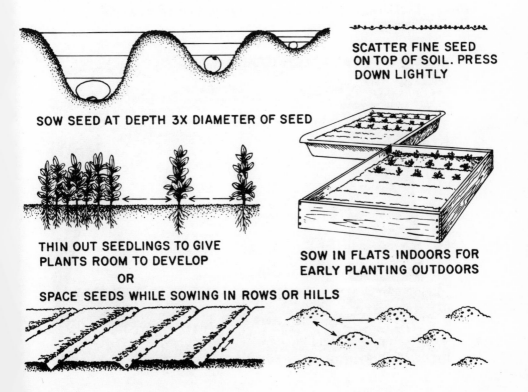

SOW SEED AT DEPTH 3X DIAMETER OF SEED

SCATTER FINE SEED ON TOP OF SOIL. PRESS DOWN LIGHTLY

THIN OUT SEEDLINGS TO GIVE PLANTS ROOM TO DEVELOP
OR

SOW IN FLATS INDOORS FOR EARLY PLANTING OUTDOORS

SPACE SEEDS WHILE SOWING IN ROWS OR HILLS

will rot before it can germinate, if covered too deep. Sow thinly, either broadcast, or in rows, omit covering, if seed is fine. Just press it into the soil. Coarser seed can be covered with vermiculite, sifted muck, pulverized peat moss, or "rubbed" sphagnum moss. After the seed has been sown, and watered from below, cover the seed flats or boxes with a pane of glass or newspapers to save moisture. The seed flat can also be put inside a plastic bag, using a couple of small stakes to hold it off the surface of the planting mixture (see illustration). Check seed boxes every day to see if any mold has formed, or if the soil is dry. If a mold has formed it means not enough air circulation, or too much moisture. In such cases, place the seed box in a light, airy place until mold disappears. Dust with Fermate or Captan.

Light: Light is not necessary for germinating seed, so you can put seed box in a dark place, but once seeds have started to sprout, move it to a full light. Attic windows are fine, if the temperature does not drop too low at night. You don't need greenhouse facilities for getting a good catch of seedlings, since a sunny window or sun porch is adequate if the temperature is around 65° to 75°.

Using polyethylene bag to keep seedlings from drying out. (Joseph Harris Company)

Transplanting young tomato plants, loosening roots with pencil point to minimize plant shock. (Joseph Harris Company)

Temperature: A temperature of about 68° during germination period is good, and about 60° after the seedlings appear is ideal. Too high a temperature causes spindly soft growth.

Seedling Care: Just as soon as seedlings pop up, remove the glass or paper or plastic, and place the seeds in full light. Seedling plants are 90 to 95% water. Seeds need air as well as water. Soak your seed flats in a pan of water (called subirrigation) until the soil is automatically watered by capillary action from beneath. DO NOT WATER FROM THE TOP UNLESS EXTREMELY CAREFUL. AVOID GETTING WATER DIRECTLY ON THE SEEDLINGS.

Transplanting Seedlings: As soon as the seedlings are about 1½ inches high, move them to other boxes or pots (see illustration). Gardeners use clay pots or peat pots, and a newer wrinkle consists of using "Jiffy-7 Pellets," for starting seeds. These look like a wafer or a checker, about ¼ inch thick. Each pellet consists of a growing medium (sterile sphagnum peat with plant food added) enclosed by a plastic mesh. When you add water, each pellet swells in minutes into a cylinder nearly 2 inches across and over 2 inches high, all ready to sow seeds or set transplants. No pot is needed, since the plastic net holds the cylindrical shape of the peat moss. All you do is line the pellets in a flat tray or pan so that the edges are touching, then add water to the trays, to a depth of an inch. When pellets have completely expanded, sow the seed or set seedling plants. This is done after the first true leaves have appeared and root systems are well branched. Cut out blocks of seedlings and transplant each young plant separately, without breaking roots.

Many gardeners move or "prick" the seedlings into small pots (peat pots or clay pots) and allow to become established. In a greenhouse or in a home, growth is apt to be soft and "leggy," so your job is to toughen or "harden" off the plants in a cold frame before planting outdoors. They can also be hardened by moving outdoors to a sunny spot on favorable days and bringing back in each night. Subjecting seedlings to a cooler temperature and giving them less water slows down growth and makes them better able to withstand the shock of transplanting into the garden.

A slightly richer soil mixture of compost, sand, loam is good for transplanted seedlings. Nearly all seedlings can be grown in these pots or boxes for 3 or 4 weeks—after which they can be set outdoors. If seedlings get a bit tall, pinch them back to make them nice and bushy. Pinching simply means nipping out the growing tip with your thumb and forefinger. This makes plants stockier and you get more blooms per plant. If you don't pinch your plants, they'll be spindly and weak.

Use of Cold Frames and Hotbeds: If you don't have good indoor facilities for starting seed you can do the job by sowing directly in the hotbed, or a little later in cold frames. These structures come in handy because they can be used to toughen up plants before planting outdoors (see Cold Frames and Hotbeds).

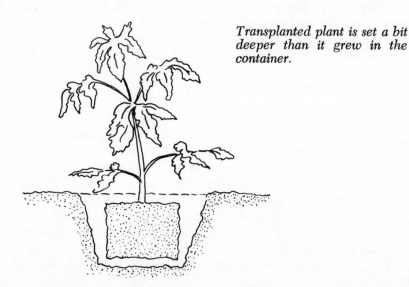

Transplanted plant is set a bit deeper than it grew in the container.

WHEN TO START SEEDS IN YOUR WINDOW, HOTBED, OR GREENHOUSE

February	March 1 to 15	March 16 to 31	April 1 to 15	April 16 to 30	May 1 to 15
Celery	Broccoli	Broccoli	Broccoli	Celery, late	Cabbage, late
Onions,	Brussels sprouts	Brussels sprouts	Brussels sprouts	Muskmelons	(in outdoor beds)
Sweet Spanish	Cabbage, early	Cabbage, early	Cabbage, early	Watermelons	Cauliflower, late
	Cauliflower, early	Cauliflower, early	Cauliflower, early		(in outdoor beds)
	Celery	Kohlrabi			Muskmelons
	Eggplant	Lettuce			Watermelons
	Kohlrabi	Peppers			
	Lettuce	Tomatoes			
	Onions,				
	Sweet Spanish				
	Peppers				
	Tomatoes				

This chart is adapted to climatic conditions of central New York State. For warmer sections, advance the dates about 2 weeks. In colder sections use the latest dates possible. Check with your state college or "green thumb" neighbor to find out exactly when you can set out plants without danger of them getting frosted.

In any locality, the rate of growth will depend upon the temperature in the window, hotbed, or greenhouse. Low temperatures, dry soils will retard growth. Try to time your plants so they'll be nice and stocky when it is time to transplant them to the garden. For example, a 5- or 7-week-old pepper or cabbage plant will generally grow better than a 10- to 12-week-old plant. A common mistake is to start plants too early indoors. As a result, you often get tall, leggy transplants, which do not yield earlier than shorter ones.

FITTING THE SOIL

Workability: Anyone who works with soil likes to scoop up a handful and let it dribble through his fingers. This way you can tell if your soil has good working quality, or "tilth." If a soil is nice and "loomy" it means it's just right for plants. Loam (called "loom" by old-timers) is simply a well-balanced mixture of large, medium, and small particles—known as sand, silt, and clay.

Nature breaks down soils into loams. Sun, with its drying action, assisted by dry winds and by plants, helps produce a loam. Temperature works for the gardener, too. When it drops low enough to freeze the ground the soils tend to break up later in good working condition. Earthworms help by leaving aeration channels, ideal for heavy soils. Well-fed plants have good root systems, and on dying leave large amounts of residues in the soil. Organic matter is the best soil conditioner there is. If your soil isn't a natural loam, you can juggle it around and convert it into a workable loam.

The cheapest and best way to do this is by adding organic matter, such as compost, peat moss, sawdust, leaves, dead weeds and plants removed in cleaning up the garden, lawn clippings, wood chips, kitchen scraps, muck, barnyard manures, and green manures—crops such as winter rye and buckwheat, and legumes such as clover and vetch, which are turned under (see Cover Crops).

How to Handle Clay Soils: A clay soil is heavy because it has finer particles in it than a sandy or light soil; this type of soil can be most discouraging at times. If you have a clay soil, your job is to make it "breathe," because a soil not well aerated is unproductive.

Many tricks are used to loosen up a tight clayey soil. One is to use various homemade soil conditioners such as lawn clippings, corncobs, leaves, garbage, compost, coal and wood ashes, sawdust, peat moss, wood chips, muck, and any other form of organic matter. Humus opens the clay, encourages earthworms to be more active helpers. The earthworms in a single acre may pass more than 10 tons of dry earth through their bodies annually; they mix organic matter thoroughly with the subsoil in the process. They also build up topsoil and their burrows aerate the soil.

Adding sand to a claylike soil will not loosen it, and may result in a concrete-like mixture harder than the original clay. Limestone has a loosening effect on a heavy clay soil, coagulating the fine particles into larger ones, allowing air and water to pass freely. Limestone does not have the same beneficial effect on sand. There is little or no danger of applying too much limestone to heavy soils because it breaks down slowly, and the clay has a buffer effect, preventing the calcium in limestone from making the soil alkaline, even when large quantities are used.

Another way to keep a clay soil in top condition is to avoid working it when it's wet. One day's work in a wet clay soil can make it hard the rest of the year. If you're one of those gardeners who likes to whip up a garden soil with a rotary power tiller before planting you'll be surprised to know this working-over is poor for plants and makes a clay soil even worse. Fluffing up a soil breaks down the structure, plugs the soil pores, and as a result the earth will turn to a sticky gumbo after the first rain. Millions of dollars are lost each year by farmers who try to make a lettuce bed out of their fields by overworking the soil.

Nature improves clay soils each time you have a drought. Drying destroys the water film that normally surrounds soil particles, causing them to form granules. This in turn gives soils larger pore spaces which means better aeration, a more workable and productive soil.

Sandy Soils: Easier to work but dry out faster and lose plant foods quicker than clay soils. Fortunately, practices which help loosen up a heavy soil will also tighten a sandy soil. The correct way to handle a sandy soil is to apply organic matter in any form available. These materials act like a blotter, holding moisture and nutrients. Sandy soils, unlike clayey soils, may be worked early in spring, and even while wet, without danger of puddling or caking.

Spading the Garden: Spading should be done as soon as the soil is dry enough. Here's a simple green thumb test for soil fitness. Grab a handful of earth and squeeze it tightly for 10 seconds. If the soil breaks in several places when dropped from a 3-foot height, it's workable. Soil that forms a mudball is too wet to work. Heavy soils (clay types) are slow to dry out in spring and should not be worked when wet. Sandy loam soils are ready to work earlier in the year because they are better drained.

When spading or plowing the garden soil, go to a depth of 8 inches. Over that brings up undesirable subsoil. Rake to break up large clods or clumps. For most crops there is no advantage to over-raking, or reducing the soil to fine crumbs. Removing small stones from the garden each year is hardly worth the effort, as more keep coming to the surface.

Facts about Your Garden Soil: The soil around your home is full of life! If you went out and scooped up a teaspoonful of it, you'd have as many as 5 billion living organisms in your hand. Keep these helpful workers happy through sound soil management.

I'm often asked if earthworms are helpful in the home garden. I believe they are valuable, especially in clay soils. They help build up topsoil, aerate soil, allow rainwater to seep down where it's helpful. Earthworms take organic matter down, and as part of their digestive process, mix it with subsoil. Dead earthworms release about 40 to 50 pounds of nitrogen to an acre.

Should you "plant" earthworms? No, they are already there. Add humus to the soil and they'll multiply. Soil mulched in winter helps build up the worm population, but it is not absolutely essential.

Do sprays or chemical fertilizers kill earthworms? Not in the amounts customarily used in gardens. Fertilizers and earthworms team up to improve the soil.

Sowing Seed Outdoors

Never sow seed in cold, wet soil. Wet soil dries to a crust that will be difficult or impossible for seedlings to break through. Avoid planting seed deeply. There is greater danger of planting seed too deep than too shallow.

Hills and Drills: Vegetable gardeners plant seeds in either drills or hills. A drill is a single row of plants spaced more or less evenly. A hill is a cluster of plants, not a mound of soil. Do not plant in mounds as the soil in them dries out faster than if kept level. Seeds most often planted in hills include melons, cucumbers, squash, pumpkins, and sometimes corn.

During late June or early July, plant root crops such as carrots, beets, parsnips, rutabagas. Cucumbers planted as late as first of July will produce a good crop, and early varieties of sweet corn, planted as late as July 20, should give you fall corn, barring heavy frosts. Bush snap beans can be planted at 2-week intervals until middle of August. Late cabbage, broccoli, and celery set in first of July will produce good fall crops. Chinese cabbage seed sown at the same time will make sound heads by early fall.

Thinning Your Plants: Thinning seedlings in the row is one of the most important (and neglected) garden operations. Thinning is hand work but it is necessary because it is difficult to sow small seeds far enough apart to allow plants to grow best. If you don't thin plants, they become weeds to themselves, competing for moisture and nutrients. Thin while plants are small (about 1 inch high) and when soil is moist, so they can be pulled out easily without injuring remaining plants.

Onions from seeds can be left in the ground until those that are thinned out are large enough to eat. Carrots should be thinned when they are 2 or 3 inches tall, so as to stand about 1 inch apart. Pull surplus beet plants when they are 4 or 5 inches tall and use the greens. Plants thinned from the turnip row can also be used for greens.

Feeding: Nutrients removed from the soil by early crops should be replenished by a feeding of complete fertilizer (such as 5–10–5) at rate of 1 pound per 25 feet of row, or use liquid foliage food such as 23–19–17, poured from a sprinkling can on top of seedlings. Or use a hose-type applicator.

Weed Control and Cultivation: The best weed killer you have is the hoe or cultivator. A 50'x50' garden plot has about 170 pounds of weed seeds in it and the best way to lick these future bandits is to get them while they are small. In hoeing, you don't gain a bit from deep cultivating. Just enough to break the crust is all you need. Never hoe or cultivate too close to the plants, especially in a season of plenty of rain.

Deep cultivation destroys necessary roots. Shallow cultivation is better.

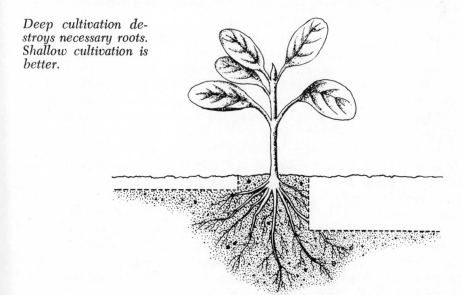

When there's a lot of moisture in the soil, roots are likely to be near the soil surface. Deep cultivation near the plant may cut off as many as half of the feeder roots. A good rule of thumb: cultivate shallow, just deep enough to cut off the weeds below the surface of the ground, then apply a mulch.

Many gardeners prefer to use a mulch of straw, old hay, shredded cane, wood shavings or chips, or plastic sheets. These keep the soil warm, weeds down, and water in. (For detailed discussion, see Mulches.)

WATERING THE GARDEN

In some areas, there's been a water shortage for the past several summers. That means home gardeners must conserve ground moisture in every way possible. During dry spells a shortage of water can be as damaging to plants as insects or diseases. Soil is a storage place for water, and every drop of water must be carefully used to make sure that the ground moisture isn't wasted. Let's see where our water comes from: All the fresh water in the world adds up to only about $\frac{1}{30}$th of the water there is in the salty ocean. And $\frac{1}{5}$ of that fresh water is locked up in snow and ice. Much of the rest is too far underground, or too loaded with minerals to be usable. So all the fresh water needed by man and life on earth must come from the rest.

Water is supplied by the "water cycle." Every year about 30 inches of water rise as vapor into the sky, and this falls back to earth as snow, rain, etc., and runs to the sea. It then evaporates again into the sky. It is a process that is a cycle, repeating itself. Nature distributes water very unevenly; you might get plenty but a neighbor a few miles away might not. The average person in the U.S. uses from 100 to 150 gallons of water a day, and a family of 4 uses over 400 gallons, without any allowance for use on plants. Incidentally, did you ever wonder how vegetables come through dry spells? They are helped by dew. Dew can often total as much as 10 inches of water a year, so even if your soil seems bone-dry, the plants may still be getting some moisture in the form of dew.

Watering the Vegetable Garden: All growing plants need water, and most vegetables are about 90% water. That means they must have an even supply of moisture—1 to 2 inches of water per week. Throughout the hottest part of the season most garden crops benefit by at least 1 inch of water a week. To apply the equivalent of 1 inch of rainfall requires about $\frac{2}{3}$ of a gallon of water to each square foot of soil. This can be supplied by perforated hose or sprinklers. Water anytime during the day or night. Time of day is not important, although you lose some water to sun in the heat of the day.

If you must ration water, here is preference: first, water fruit trees and shrubs, then gardens, then lawns. All of these can be mulched with your favorite material after watering. We use straw, pine needles, buckwheat hulls, cocoa bean shells, muck, peat moss, black plastic sheets, compost, sawdust, or wood chips. If you can get sawdust or wood chips free of charge, by all means use them to conserve moisture. Water the mulch with a liquid plant food (23–19–17), 1 handful to a sprinkling can. Just drench it over the mulch, and this will fortify it, adding nitrogen and other nutrients. (See Mulches.)

You CAN overwater your plants. Too much water around the base of tomatoes will cause cracking of fruit, yellowing of many flowers, or even death. Excess water, especially around roots of plants in clay soils, shuts off oxygen, suffocates the plants, and they die. Heavy soakings in sandy soils washes out the nitrogen, causes pale color of foliage. Most garden plants will be well satisfied with soil moistened to a depth of a foot. Sandy soils dry out faster than clay, and you can tell by looking at your plants how often you should apply the water. Any water that runs off is wasted, not absorbed by the plants.

What You Should Know About Garden Hoses: These come in plastic and rubber, and different sizes, based on inside diameter. NOT ALL HOSES DELIVER THE SAME AMOUNT OF WATER. The larger the diameter the more volume a hose can deliver per minute. For example: A hose with ⅜-inch diameter delivers 4.3 gallons of water a minute (based on 50 pounds of water pressure), a ½-inch hose 8.8 gallons per minute, and a hose with ¾-inch diameter, 15.3 gallons per minute. You get more volume with a shorter length of hose, a longer hose gives you less. If you use 100 feet or more of hose, use a hose of the larger diameter. If you have high water pressure and only need a short length, the smaller diameter will suffice.

Perforated hose is best for your garden watering because the water soaks right into the soil, without wetting foliage and spreading plant diseases.

Sprinklers: Sprinkling is good but not necessarily the best possible way to irrigate the garden. If sprinkling does not wet down at least 3 or more inches, it's likely to do little good, and may be even harmful. There are many good types of sprinklers on the market. We do not like overhead sprinklers because they tend to increase leaf spot and other diseases by splashing spores. Water from sprinklers goes straight down, with little side-to-side movement. That's why you should water in the vicinity of the plant.

Hot Weather Tips: Unnecessary deep hoeing or heavy cultivation in dry weather will waste precious soil moisture. Pull out moisture-rob-bing weeds. A packed soil also wastes water, by runoff. A soil with a heavy crust can be improved by shallow cultivation. This lets water enter, instead of run off. The secret is to save moisture by trapping it in.

A mulch of sawdust, etc., will control weeds and reduce surface loss of moisture. Mulches keep roots cool, prevent leaf curl, blossom-end rot, and cracking of tomatoes and other vegetables (see Mulches). Water your plants well and apply mulch to trap moisture in. Also, just because you use a mulch, this does not mean you won't need additional moisture. Your plants will grow vigorously under a mulch and will pull lots of moisture from the soil.

Black plastic, as discussed in the section on mulches, makes an especially fine mulch for saving water.

Let Plants Dry Out: Allow your plants to go a bit dry between waterings. It doesn't harm most plants to get a bit dry. Outdoors it toughens them up by hardening the cells, enabling them to withstand drought better. If water is allowed to remain at the roots constantly, it keeps oxygen out and the plants suffocate. Too much water causes a peculiar odor and that's when you say your soil is "sour." Actually, a wet soil is no more likely to be sour than a dry one. The odor is due to gases (mostly methane) produced by soil organisms working in the absence of oxygen. A fair rule of green thumb: Give plants a good soaking when you do water, then allow them to go a bit dry between waterings. This works fine for vegetables, flowers, trees, shrubs, or lawns, as well as houseplants.

Types of Water: Use water from ponds, streams, wells, cisterns, or city water. Don't worry about chlorine in city water. It's harmless. If your water contains iron, calcium, magnesium, and other salts, it's harmless. Water from softener is O.K., but it's not a good policy to use since it's cheaper to bypass it.

Is cold well water harmful? A reader wrote me: "I have a well 65 feet deep near our country home, and temperature of the water is 40° to 45°. It is so hard that lime or calcium from it makes the blacktop drive turn white. During dry spells, we watered our corn, peas, carrots, and other crops. They were all slow-growing and stunted. Was it the cold water or the hard water?"

We get this question often from folks who have a well in hard-water areas, and I think that the excess of lime in the water does affect growth. It's like adding lime in powder form, and no one would do that every few days. Too much hard water will change the acidity to the other side and make the soil so much more alkaline (sweet) that some plants cannot grow. The only way to counteract this is to add an acidifying material, or avoid using well water that's so "hard." Temperature of the water has nothing to do with poor growth.

Empty coffee or fruit can makes a good reservoir for growing tomatoes and other vegetables. Punch holes in bottom of can and sink can in ground. Mix liquid plant food and pour into can to feed and water your plants. (Borden Chemical Company)

The Truth About Laundry Water: In some areas water is so scarce some gardeners use wash water, dishwater, or laundry water. These may contain detergents, soaps, ammonia, borax, and other household chemicals. Will this harm plants? The answer is no. The ammonia supplies nitrogen, soaps are harmless, and the detergents actually make the water wetter, more able to penetrate. So if water is scarce, use wash water on fruit trees, shrubs, evergreen flowers, vegetables, and even lawns. Add a handful of liquid plant food (23–19–17) to each 4 gallons.

During dry spells, one way to save moisture for your garden and fruits is to fix leaky faucets. If you don't stop that drip you'll lose money, because leaky faucets and water pipes waste water. Under average pressure a slow drip will lose from 15 to 400 gallons per day! You might better use this water in your vegetable or fruit garden.

Miscellaneous Notes on Watering: There's no truth to the idea that watering while the sun is out will burn plants. YOU CAN WATER DURING THE HEAT OF THE DAY. There are periods during the life of any plant when shortages of water seem to be more critical: generally at pollination and fruit-setting time. Most plants can survive prolonged dry spells if they have ample water during these periods. Plants use more water in July and August than at any other time because the days are longer and temperatures higher. A 20-day drought in May or October is equal to only 10 days of drought in July or August. Recharging the root zone of plants takes a lot of water. Sandy soils hold ½ inch of water per foot; loams with sands, 1 inch per foot; loams and clays, about 2 inches. In other words, a loamy soil can go 4 times as long without water, but requires 4 times as much to recharge it as a sandy soil. It will take 350 gallons of water to recharge 1,000 square feet of sandy soil to 1 foot deep, and 1,400 gallons for the same amount of loam soil. Dry soils (sandy or clay) will not absorb water as fast as soil that is slightly moist. Add organic matter to soil to increase water-holding capacity.

HOME GARDEN SOIL BANK

Building up the home garden soil bank is a good investment for any homeowner. If your soil seems heavy, drains poorly, bakes in summer or seems just plain fagged out, or your crops do poorly each year, then you need a soil bank program of your own.

If there are no other factors involved, such as shade or robber roots from nearby trees, insufficient drainage, or too much acidity, then organic (coming from living things) matter is the heart of your soil improvement plan. To date, nothing has been discovered that is superior, on a cost basis, to organic matter as a soil builder and conditioner. When organic matter rots in the soil, slimy materials are formed by millions of soil microbes. These materials bind the soil particles together into loose crumbs, leaving much pore space through which air and water can penetrate easily. Soils well supplied with organic matter remain in good condition to absorb rain throughout the season, and plant roots grow and breathe readily in such soils.

On sandy soils, organic matter has additional benefits that other conditioners can't duplicate. Moisture stored by the soil for plant use increases as the humus content goes up, and fertilizer elements are also retained by the humus instead of being washed out by the first rain.

But how does the home gardener get this organic matter which is to be added to the soil? There are 3 ways: (1) save it, (2) haul it in, or (3) grow it.

1) Save all crop residues such as cornstalks, tomato and pea vines, etc., as well as leaves, lawn clippings, sawdust, wood shavings, and leafy garbage for use in a compost pile, as described elsewhere.

2) Obtain organic matter such as peat, manure, straw, sawdust, leaves, or similar materials and mix in the soil or use as a mulch (see Mulches).

3) Grow organic matter in the form of a cover crop and let plant roots work on your soil. Later plow it under for humus.

Cover Crops

What is a cover crop? The term "cover crop" comes up in garden publications quite often, but not all gardeners know what it really means. A cover crop is merely a temporary planting made to add organic matter to the soil and help keep it in good physical condition. Cover crops also hold nitrogen and other plant foods that might be leached away during the winter. Their tremendous root systems loosen heavy soils, whereas the added humus will help hold the particles of sandy soils together. The use of a commercial fertilizer to produce a heavier cover crop will usually benefit the garden crops which follow.

If you have plenty of garden space, a good plan is to put ⅓ to ½ of your garden into a cover crop each year, then alternate or rotate the cover crop with your vegetable planting. This method plus the addition of fertilizer and lime should produce a garden soil that's hard to beat. Cover crops are often called "green manure" crops, a good substitute for barnyard manure. Oats, buckwheat, clover, and ryegrass are a few common cover crops.

Annual ryegrass is a fine cover crop and soil builder because it develops heavy tops and large root systems which add many pounds of humus to the soil. Sow the seed in among corn, tomatoes, or other crops at the rate of 2 pounds per 1,000 square feet. Loosen the soil up first with hoe or cultivator, then sow seed. We sow it at time of last cultivation, thus doing 2 jobs at once. DO NOT COVER THE SEED. Just sow it on freshly cultivated soil, and rake it in very lightly. Ryegrass is a cool-weather grass and makes most of its growth late in fall after your corn and other crops are harvested. Sown in July or August, domestic ryegrass does not go to seed that year and it is plowed under before it seeds the following year. Hence, no danger of it becoming a weed.

If you want to plant sweet clover, first add about 50 pounds of limestone per 1,000 square feet, unless the soil is already above pH of 6.5 (see Liming and Soil Acidity). Sow seed in spring, and this will give you a green manure crop, roots and tops, which can be plowed under in fall or next spring.

Alfalfa, another legume, can also be used as a green manure crop, if the soil is sweet (has enough lime). The advantage of alfalfa over sweet clover is that you can make 2 or 3 cuttings during the growing season. This would allow you to mulch your early vegetables from your first cutting and use later cuttings on crops such as tomatoes, strawberries, and others.

Keep in mind that the different kinds of roots do different kinds of jobs. Fine grass and clover roots are ideal for developing soil crumbs in the upper 6 to 12 inches of your garden. Alfalfa and sweet clover taproots extend deeper, and when they die and rot, leave channels for air and water movement.

Buckwheat can be sown in July. It dies down in fall and is plowed under in spring or fall.

How to Make a Compost Pile

The backbone of any soil is humus, the dark substance derived from organic sources such as leaves, lawn clippings, sawdust, evergreen needles, garbage, manures, coffee grounds, and dozens of similar materials. Organic materials should not be discarded but placed on the compost pile, which is similar to putting money into the bank.

How to Start a Pile: As materials become available, start piling them in a spot away from the house, where it can be screened off by plants. Add materials in such a way that the center is depressed to catch rainwater. Try to alternate ingredients in thin layers. From time to time add a layer of balanced fertilizer, 1 pound over a 6-inch layer, where the compost is 10 feet long and 5 feet wide. Apply a liquid plant food such as 23–19–17, using a handful in a sprinkler can for a 10-square-foot area. This fortifies the compost and hastens decay. A liberal sprinkling of lime from time to time is helpful. Stirring "ripens" the pile (hastens decay) and aids in destroying insect pests, but it is not essential.

One of the best materials for the compost is leaves. A ton of them is worth $10 in nutrients alone. Owners of sandy or clayey soils should save all the leaves they can rake up, for leaf mold has a miraculous ability to hold moisture. Subsoil can hold a mere 20% of its weight, good topsoil will hold 60%, but leaf mold can retain 300 to 500% of its weight in water. Leaf mold from non-evergreens is richer in nutrients than that from conifers. They are all good property, so don't believe the story that leaves are harmful to crops. Oak leaves are acid and are recommended for acid-loving plants. Yet, they are still usable for non-acid plants.

Plastic for the Compost Pile: The latest wrinkle in composting is to cover the pile with polyethylene plastic film. You make the compost in the regular manner, alternating leaves, clippings, sawdust, soil, garbage, and other materials with a scattering of lime and plant foods. Then the pile is watered down thoroughly and a sheet of black polyethylene is spread over the pile. Use a piece large enough to allow about 18 to 20 inches of flap on each side. Cover the flaps with soil so the pile is completely enveloped. The beauty of plastic is that you do not have to fork or turn over the compost. Leave it alone for 8 months and you'll find the plastic hastens decay by trapping heat inside and preventing loss of moisture. There's no magical material which converts raw organic matter into humus overnight in a compost.

Diseases and Insects: Are they a problem to compost gardeners? Because of danger of infecting the pile with plant diseases and insect pests there are some materials to be avoided. These include iris leaves, if borers have been a problem and peony tops if botrytis blight blasted the buds. Also avoid refuse from cabbage and other crucifers (cabbage family), and cornstalks if borers or smut were present. If a compost is allowed to stand for 2 seasons with occasional forking over, it is doubtful if diseases and insects will persist any more than they do in the garden where plants have been grown for years. Flies may congregate but a plastic sheet keeps them out, as it will a stray dog or 2.

How to Use Compost Soil: For potting, screen through ½-inch mesh wire to remove coarse material, then mix with sand or garden loam or both. If used in the garden or as a mulch, no screening is necessary. Compost doesn't replace fertilizer. You still should fortify it with a light scattering of plant food to achieve maximum use from it.

MULCHES SAVE WORK!

Summer and Winter Mulches: Few garden practices are less understood than mulching. When you mulch you take a tip from nature and cover the soil to keep soil moisture in and temperatures from fluctuating. The purpose of a summer mulch is to save moisture and choke out weeds. Summer mulches will cut down weeding as much as 90%. A winter mulch is not designed to keep out cold, but rather to prevent a phenomenon known as "heaving," due to freezing and thawing, which forces plants upward and out of the ground. You might say that summer and winter mulches act like a thermostat in the soil, maintaining a more constant temperature.

Newly planted trees, shrubs, and evergreens respond to a mulch because it traps moisture in the soil, favoring the growth of roots.

It's only fair to point out that mulches have several disadvantages when used in the garden. On poorly drained soils in wet seasons mulches may help contribute to the holding of excessive soil moisture, which may prove harmful to the root systems of many vegetable crops. Mulches can't be used on soft crops, as they trap moisture and may result in rot. Mulches also attract snails, and some mulches (such as grass clippings) may attract mice.

When to Apply: A summer mulch is put on the garden between May 15 and June 15. It takes about 6 inches of straw or hay or 2 to 3 inches of sawdust to make a good mulch. Use a nitrogen fertilizer, such as ammonium nitrate, at the rate of ½ pound per bushel of sawdust or ½ bale of straw.

Winter mulches are placed on the garden *after* the ground is frozen, to prevent changes in temperature which might produce thawing and heaving. A winter mulch is applied about 2 inches thick; any material usable for summer mulching may be used for winter mulch. Do not apply a winter mulch if your soil is heavy clay.

Mulch Materials: There are many mulch materials available, and there's no danger of using too much of any one of them. Here are some of the most common mulches used for the vegetable garden, flower beds, lawns, trees, and shrubs:

Buckwheat Hulls: These are light, clean, do not mat or freeze. May be dug into the soil where they decay slowly to build up a supply of humus. Apply 3 inches thick.

Cocoa Bean Shells: Contain 92% organic matter, 3.2% mitrogen, 2% phosphorus and 2% potash. This mulch has a chocolate odor which disappears in a week. Ideal around trees and shrubs, for new lawns, rose beds, in composts. There is little danger from fire. Apply 1 to 3 inches thick.

Coffee Grounds: Valuable as soil conditioner and mulch, although low in nutrients (2% nitrogen, .4% phosphoric acid, and .5% potassium). Nontoxic to soils, coffee grounds are acid, making them valuable around blueberries, azaleas, rhododendrons, and other acid-lovers.

Corncobs: Excellent in the vegetable garden, as well as for rose beds, flower borders. Have your farmer-neighbor grind some extra cobs for you, and apply about 2 inches thick.

Dust Mulch: Created by shallow surface cultivation, a layer of dust (pulverized earth) prevents upward movement of water, reduces evaporation. When the moisture hits the broken soil surface it stops, to be absorbed by plant roots.

Evergreen Boughs: All kinds are suitable. Since they allow air to enter and prevent smothering, evergreens are ideal winter mulch for soft perennials. Needles are useful as summer mulch, although they present a fire hazard.

Excelsior: Free from weed seed, insects, and disease, but more difficult to apply than most materials. However, it does last for years, and if you have access to it, by all means use it. Apply 2 inches thick.

Glass Wool: Makes a good mulch, applied in 2-inch thickness, but tends to tear or blow away. Use chicken wire to cover it.

Gravel Mulch: Gravel stone comes in various colors, is easy to weed and maintain around trees or shrubs. Applied 2 inches thick, makes a fine lawn substitute under shaded trees, and in spots where eaves drip and splash mud against the foundation. My objection is that children like to scatter it around the house and lawn, making it a problem for lawn mowers. Also, some folks feel it is difficult to remove debris from gravel mulch.

Leaves: Makes a poor mulch because they tend to pack down and prevent the escape of moisture. They are excellent on the compost pile, however, and can be useful around trees and shrubs.

Newspaper: Place 4 or 5 thicknesses around the plants and cover with peat moss to hide the papers. Paper ashes can be used as a mulch and on the garden. Being alkaline, they should not be used around acid-loving plants such as blueberry, blackberry, raspberry, azalea, rhododendron, holly, and others.

Plastic Film (polyethylene): Makes a fine summer mulch for hastening maturity and controlling weeds. The plastic material used has a thickness of .0015 inch. With it you can increase the yield of warm-season crops such as melons, peppers, eggplants, tomatoes, and sweet potatoes. Black plastic is preferred to the light because it shuts out sun, hence weeds cannot grow under it. During the day it absorbs the sun's heat more so than do organic mulches (such as sawdust) and at night radiates the heat back faster. Thus plants mulched with plastics are somewhat less liable to frost injury than those mulched with organic mulches.

Make sure the soil is well soaked a few days before the plastic is laid. Apply on a windless day and immediately after planting. For most transplanted crops it's easier to apply it first and plant through it.

Cover edges with soil or stones or it is even better to bury about 6 inches of each edge in a furrow. Don't stretch the plastic tightly, because it will shrink upon cooling. If plastic is applied directly over a row of seeds, anchor it on all sides, then cut the plastic down the middle. Water gets under the mulch by running into the hole around the plants. In very dry seasons you can run a shallow furrow around edge of plastic to help water seep around the plants. Also, additional holes could be cut in the plastic along the furrow. Increase in soil temperature is about 3° to 6°, and the climate around the plant (air between soil and plastic and air above the plastic) is generally warmer. Use the plastic year after year, if you can get it up intact at the end of growing season.

Peat Moss: The common brown moss sold in bales. There are many different size bales, but you can figure that 1 cubic foot of compressed baled peat will fluff out to 2½ cubic feet, and about 5 cubic feet will equal 4 or more bushels. Most peats are acid, and are ideal around acid-loving plants, and just about all other plants. Use a 3- or 4-inch thickness as a mulch. During dry weather peat moss tends to form a crust which is more or less waterproof. Stir up this crust from time to time so rainwater will enter more readily. Since baled peat is compressed, it sometimes gets lumpy and is slow to take up moisture at first. Once you wet it, the material becomes soft, loose, and absorbent.

Salt Marsh Hay: A clean, highly sought-after material because it does not contain grass and weed seed, does not mat down or become soggy. It can be gathered up in the spring and used year after year. Salt marsh hay does not break down readily, hence it cannot be used as a cover crop or source of humus.

Sawdust: Good gardeners will tell you that sawdust is not the "debbil" many think it is. Contrary to belief, sawdust is not acid, nor is it toxic to plants or soils. Sawdust is organic matter, and is beneficial both as a mulch and a soil conditioner. Sawdust can be either weathered or unweathered, and from hardwood or softwood. Used 3 inches thick, it's ideal for fruit trees, shrubs, perennials, around evergreens, and in border plantings. It has no value on lawns.

Sawdust sometimes turns plants yellow, as will manure, leaf mold, and other carbonaceous materials. This is because soil fungi and bacteria that decompose sawdust consume so much nitrogen that temporarily none is left for the plants, and leaves turn yellow, a hunger sign. This can be prevented and controlled by adding extra nitrogen, such as a cupful of nitrate of soda for each bushel, or by watering the mulch with a liquid plant food such as 23–19–17, mixed at the rate of ¼ pound to 11 gallons of water.

Shredded Bark: Tree bark, formerly a waste product, is used for mulch purposes. Upon decomposition it has a rich, dark appearance.

The bark retains moisture and has little tendency to dry up and blow away. Apply 2 inches thick.

Snow: "Poor Man's Manure," snow is good if you can get it, having small amounts of ammonia, nitric acid, and other compounds.

Straws: Wheat, oat, and buckwheat straw are good mulches, but have some disadvantages, especially as weed-seed carriers and a fire hazard. Use straw 4 to 6 inches thick. An investment of $5 or more in straw will provide mulch for a lot of ground and may produce $100 worth of vegetables—and this with no weeding problem.

Sugar Cane: Shredded sugar cane ("bagasse"), commonly sold as chicken litter, is coarse-textured, stays in place, remains loose and springy, admits passage of rain and melting snow, and thus makes a fine mulch. It has excellent insulation value. Apply 2 inches thick.

Wood Chips: Several manufacturers are putting out a portable wood chipper which chews up logs and limbs into chips. These chips may be used 3 inches thick, but be sure to add some nitrogen, as you would for sawdust.

LIMING AND SOIL ACIDITY

Use of Lime: Gardeners often use either too much lime or not enough. Cornell University analyzed several hundred home-garden samples and found that ⅓ needed lime, ⅓ were just right, and ⅓ had too much lime. Most fruits and vegetables are happy with a slightly acid soil, so if your garden is in that condition, don't change matters. The majority of surface soils in eastern U.S. are naturally acid, however, and require some liming for best production.

Here's what liming acid soil does: reduces soil acidity, supplies calcium and magnesium, speeds the decay of organic matter and the liberation of nitrogen. It increases the efficiency of plant foods like phosphorus that may be otherwise unavailable to plants, promotes the growth of legumes such as clover, controls certain diseases like blackleg of cabbage, and to a limited extent helps loosen up heavy clay soils. A WORD OF CAUTION: Do not lime a soil that doesn't need it. Excess lime is apt to "lock up" plant nutrients chemically so plants can't use them.

The natural acidity of a soil is determined by the type of rocks from which the soil was originally derived. For example, quartz, granite, sandstone, and shale usually produce acid soils. Marble and limestone produce alkaline soils. Often the lower subsoil is much less acid than the surface soil, unless lime materials have been added.

Rainfall and removal of plant material from the soil tends to make surface soils more acid. On the other hand, soils around our houses sometimes have become alkaline because grading may have uncovered limey subsoils, or lime-rich fill may have been added. Continuous watering with water that is "hard" because of calcium and magnesium adds to the alkalinity of a soil. These are factors to keep in mind, especially when acid-loving plants such as blueberries, rhododendrons, azaleas, mountain laurel, trailing arbutus, trilliums, and most lilies are to be grown. These must have acid soils. When planted on alkaline or neutral soils, they quickly become chlorotic (yellowed) and die. If you want to plant these in a limey soil, you will have to convert it to an acid condition by adding sulfur or aluminum sulfate (see Making Soils More Acid).

Chemical Tests Tell if Soil Is Sweet or Sour: What's pH? Gardeners often come across a 2-letter term, pH, before a number and it baffles them. pH is a term used to measure soil reaction—whether it is "sweet" (alkaline) or "sour" (acid).

The pH scale (see illustration) is used to measure soil acidity. A pH reading of 7 is neutral; that is, neither acid nor alkaline. The smaller the number the stronger the acidity; soils with pH above 7 are alkaline.

It's a simple matter to test your soil to see if it is acid or alkaline. There are kits on the market which are simple to operate and fairly accurate.

The pH scale for soil reaction.

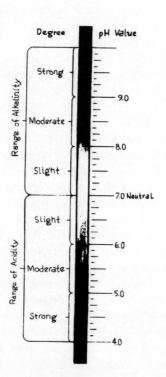

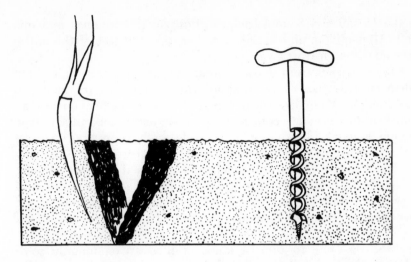

There's a correct way to take a sample of soil for testing. Run spade down to plow depth (about 8 inches), using a shovel, spade, or soil auger (right).

Tests for Major Elements: A pH test alone is not the answer to all your garden problems. Actually there are two types of useful soil tests: (1) soil acidity, and (2) major elements. To me, the first is the most important, but if your lawn or garden is producing well, you won't need a test. Carrots and beets are good indicators. If they grow well, you don't need lime.

The test for major elements is best made through your county agent or state college of agriculture testing service (which will perform this service for a nominal fee), but keep in mind that a soil test can do no better than the soil sample you take. For this reason, in many cases a soil test can be a waste of time. If the soil sample is not representative of the soil in the garden, the results are meaningless. To illustrate this: The plow layer of soil on each acre weighs about 2 million pounds. The average soil sample weighs about 1 pound. This means that if a sample is taken from 5 acres, that 1 pound of sample sent for testing must represent some 10 million pounds of soil in the field! You just can't go out, scoop up a can of soil, and send it in for a test!

How to Take a Soil Sample: Soil samples must be gathered in a clean container, and taken with a proper sampling tool. A garden spade or auger is fine. If you use a spade, first dig a V-shaped hole to plow depth (about 8 inches). Second, cut a ½-inch slice of soil from face of hole. Third, trim away soil from both sides of spade, leaving a 1-inch strip of soil down the middle of the spade. Fourth, place this in a clean pail. Take 15 samples from various sections in this manner and mix in a pail. After mixing all samples together, select 1 pint of the entire mixture and throw the rest away.

Don't take samples from unusual areas. Avoid wet spots, lime piles, areas near trees, burned areas, or spots where fertilizer, etc., has been lying in piles. Your fertilizer store has soil-test cartons for you to mail the sample in to your state college. Or you can use a clean plastic bag. Send along as much information as possible, such as crops grown last year, plant foods used, and troubles involved with crops. State colleges determine plant-food deficiencies by chemical analysis of soils, plant-tissue testing, and some use "quick" soil tests. If you plan to have a soil test made, talk to your local fertilizer dealer, your county agent, or a successful neighboring farmer.

Which Kind of Lime to Buy: 4 kinds of lime are commonly sold: burned lime, hydrated lime, ground limestone, and dolomitic limestone. (1) "Quicklime" is another term for burned lime (calcium oxide). In general, it should not be used in the garden because of its caustic action on the skin. (2) Hydrated lime is a fluffy white powder formed from burned lime and water. It is faster-acting than ground limestone, but more expensive for the same end result. (3) Ground limestone (calcium carbonate) is a grayish, gritty, very finely ground lime rock. This is the material most commonly used for counteracting acidity. It is slower to dissolve than hydrated lime and takes longer to work. Supply stores sometimes sell a mixture of hydrated lime and limestone combining benefits of both. Ground limestone is less expensive, keeps better, is easy to apply. (4) Dolomitic lime has 20 to 30% magnesium, plus 30 to 50% calcium, and is available in both hydrated and ground stone types. Because magnesium is another element needed for plant growth, we recommend dolomitic limestone, which is just about as inexpensive as the older forms. You may not be able to get it from your dealer—if not, use the others.

Actually, any form of lime can be used, but keep in mind that the more concentrated forms such as the hydrated or burned-lime forms should be used in lesser amounts. The big problem most gardeners run into is using the 3 forms in equivalent amounts. Roughly speaking, 100 pounds of ground limestone is equal in action to about 74 pounds of hydrated lime, or 56 pounds of burned lime.

We want to remind gardeners who use the burned or slaked lime to be careful not to allow it to sift inside your shoes, since the moisture of perspiration is enough to blister tender skin. And wash immediately if it gets in your eyes.

How Much Lime to Use and When: A fair rule of thumb is: If no lime has been added during the past 4 years, then your garden (or lawn) probably needs it. An application of 50 pounds of lime per 1,000 square feet is a good rough-and-ready treatment. Then for regular applications, use 25 to 30 pounds per 1,000 square feet every 4 years. Apply either hydrated or ground limestone in fall or spring before plowing. I like fall application because it enables you to take advantage of the weather. Winter rains and snow will help carry the lime down into the soil where it can go to work quickly. In the spring, when this ground is plowed, the lime will be turned under close to the subsoil and will help roots grow better.

If you have had your soil tested and the soil test shows a pH reading between 6 and 6.8, don't add lime. If pH is between 5.5 and 6, use 3 pounds of ground limestone to each 100 square feet on sandy soils, 5 pounds on heavier soils. If pH reading is between 5 and 5.5, use double amounts.

Dangers of Over-liming: Some minor but necessary elements such as boron, iron, manganese, and zinc become less available to plants when soils are heavily limed. Excess liming may result in chlorosis (yellowing of leaves) and poor growth. Correct this by acidifying (see following). Never put lime in contact with manure because it causes loss of nitrogen. Don't mix lime and fertilizer in a single application, as lime may cause loss of nitrogen and reduction in available phosphate.

Making Soils More Acid: As previously mentioned, soils may be too sweet for acid-loving plants such as azaleas, rhododendrons, laurel, lilies, blueberries, and others. Then the soil must be acidified with sulfur, ammonium sulfate, manganese sulfate, aluminum sulfate, or even iron sulfate (ferrous sulfate). Sulfur is by far the cheapest way, but also the slowest, whereas the sulfates have full action in the first season. Apply sulfur at the rate of 1 to 2 pounds per 100 square feet, depending on the acidity at the beginning. Use sulfates according to the following table:

Acidity of Soil at Start (as determined by pH test)	Ammonium or Aluminum	Sulfate/Sq. Yd.
Medium acid (pH 5 to 6)		¼ lb.
Slightly acid (pH 6.5 to 7)		½ lb.
Neutral to strongly alkaline (pH 7 to 8)		¾ lb.

Spread the sulfur or sulfates uniformly and mix thoroughly with the soil. Acid soil in our acid-loving plant beds does not always remain that way, because the water in the soil is apt to become limey and rise from below. Also, angleworms are likely to mix the soil near the plants. On acidified soils, avoid use of all alkalizing materials, such as wood ashes, hard water, and composts made with lime.

High-lime soils are impossible to acidify, or nearly so. If you must grow acid-loving plants, consider other methods, such as replacing soil in beds, growing plants in sunken tubs or drums, or building raised beds with surface layers of acid soil or peat.

PLANT FOODS AND FERTILIZERS

Liquid Plant Foods: Liquid plant foods have come a long way and many predict that soon half of all the fertilizer used in America will be applied in liquid form. Foliar or foliage feeding ("non-root") was pioneered by a nurseryman, the late Tom Reilly of Dansville, New York. (Ra-Pid-Gro.)

In my garden and greenhouse, I use a liquid foliage plant food (23–19–17) on all crops, mixed with pesticides, and it never burns. First a stock solution is made of 1 cup of the concentrated 23–19–17 to 2 gallons of water. A hose-type applicator (found in any garden store) is inserted into this and attached to the water faucet. As I water the crops it automatically feeds them. To foliage-feed, always buy a plant food made especially for spraying on the leaves. What isn't absorbed will fall to the ground and be absorbed through the roots. Apply every 3 or 4 weeks.

Starter Solutions: Liquid plant foods make ideal "starter" or "booster" solutions, helping young transplants get off to a better start. Simply place 1 teaspoon of the concentrated fertilizer (23–19–17) in 2 quarts of water, and as you set out the cabbage, tomato, pepper, or other vegetable, dip the roots and plant while wet. Word of caution: If you make a homemade booster solution, try it first on a few plants because it may burn. You can make one from a common grade of fertilizer such as 5–10–5 (or something similar) by dissolving 1 pound in 5 gallons of water. This liquid is applied in the row at the rate of 1 gallon to 20 feet of row, before planting or later.

Band Method: This consists of applying dry fertilizer such as 8–24–8 at the rate of 1 pound per 50 feet of row, in a band to one side of the seed. Or after plants are up, apply it in a row *without* touching the plants or seeds.

Broadcast Method: This consists of applying dry fertilizer over the plot after it has been plowed and disked, and just before you make the final seed bed preparation with a harrow or rake. Use about 1 pound per 100 square feet of area. Rake it into the upper 3 inches of soil.

Organic vs. "Commercial" Plant Foods: Will we get better crops, more nutritious food, and do a better job of conserving our soils by fertiliz-

ing with organic composts rather than commercial fertilizers? I'll answer this controversial question by saying we grow crops by both organic composts and commercial fertilizers. I feel that good points about
each method should be briefly mentioned.

Organic plant foods are of plant or animal origin. Examples include
bone meal, cottonseed meal, and dried blood, as well as composts and
manures. The inorganics or "chemical" fertilizers are either mined or
made chemically, sometimes as a by-product from industrial processes.
Both organic and inorganic forms supply the essential elements required for plant growth: nitrogen, phosphorus, potassium, and others.

Inorganic fertilizers are much more concentrated and often are
much cheaper sources of these plant nutrients. Humus from organic
matter is vital to good soil conditions, and we do all we can to incorporate all organic materials available. We use chemical plant foods
along with organics to get the best results. There is no evidence that
there would be less trouble with insects or diseases if commercial
plant foods were not used. This is one of the main arguments of the
"organic folks." Some hold that commercial fertilizers, having been
made through the use of strong acids like sulfuric, are corrosive to soil
bacteria and earthworms, or even give rise to crops of inferior food
value, causing disease in animals and humans. There is no scientific
data to support this. In fact, commercial fertilizers tend to increase the
number of beneficial bacteria and earthworms in soils. But why ar-
gue? If you believe in commercial fertilizers, then use them. If you
don't, then grow your plants the organic way (see chart on pp.
168–69).

SOME ORGANIC FERTILIZERS FOR HOME GARDENERS*

Fertilizer	What's In It			Amt. to Use	Remarks
	% Nitrogen	% Phosphorus	% Potassium	Pounds per 100 Sq. Ft.	
Dried Blood	13	1.5	0	3	A very rapidly available organic fertilizer.
Fish Scrap	9	7	0	3 to 4	Not to be confused with fish emulsives, which generally are quite low in fertilizer content.
Guano, Bat	6	9	3	3 to 4	Partially decomposed bat manure from caves in southwestern U. S.
Guano, Bird	13	11	2	2 to 3	Partially decomposed bird manure from islands off coast.
Kelp (seaweed)	1	0.5	9	5	Not always readily available.
Leather (processed)	8	0	0	3 to 4	Unless steamed under pressure, leather is valueless as a fertilizer. See process tankage.
Bone meal, Raw	4	22	0	5	Main value is nitrogen since most of the phosphorus is not soluble.
Bone, Steamed	2	27	0	5	As a result of steaming under pressure, some nitrogen is lost but more phosphorus is soluble (available for use by plants).
Cocoa Shell	2.5	1	3	5	Primarily a conditioner for complete fertilizers, mulch.
Cotton Seed	6	2.5	2	3 to 4	Generally very acid. Quite useful for bed-grown azaleas and other acid-loving plants.
Rice Hulls (ground)	0.5	0.2	0.5	5	Do not use raw! See discussion under Sludge.
Sewage Sludge	2	1	1	5	

Material					Remarks
Sewage, Activated (special micro-organisms added)	6	5	0	3 to 4	Examples of activated sludge are Milorganite (Milwaukee, Wis.), Hu-Actinite (Houston, Tex.), Chicagrow (Chicago, Ill.), and Nitroganic (Pasadena, Calif.)
Tankage, Cocoa	4	1.5	2	5	
Garbage	3	3	1	5	
Process (leather, hair, wool, felt, feathers, etc.)	8	1	0	3 to 4	
Tobacco Stems	2	1	6	5	An excellent organic material, high in potash. Has an alkaline reaction.
Wood Ashes	0	2	6	5	Quite alkaline (see Ashes). The steam-treated and ground material is a rather quickly available source of nitrogen.
Hoof & Horn	14	0	0	2	
Linseed	6	2	1	3	Surprisingly low in nitrogen considering the plant is a legume.
Peanut Hulls	1	0	1	5	
Soybean Meal	7	2	2	3 to 4	Manures in general are low in fertilizer, used in relatively large amounts to improve soil structure. Damage may occur if fresh or "hot."
Tung Nut	4	2	1	5	
Manure, Cattle	0.5	0.3	0.5		
Manure, Chicken	0.9	0.5	0.8		
Manure, Horse	0.6	0.3	0.6		
Manure, Sheep	0.9	0.5	0.8		
Manure, Swine	0.6	0.5	0.4		
Mushroom Manure (spent)	1	1	1		
Oyster Shells	0.2	0.3	0	5	Because of their alkalinity these are best used for raising pH rather than as a fertilizer.
Peat (reed or sedge)	2	0.3	0.3	5	Best used as a soil conditioner rather than as a fertilizer. Breaks down rapidly. (See Peat Moss.)

*Courtesy Ohio Agricultural Experiment Station

What Commercial Plant Foods Do: The most important plant foods in a commercially mixed fertilizer are nitrogen, phosphorus, and potassium (potash). These elements are essential to plant growth, and likely to be deficient in the average garden soil. Nitrogen gives dark green color to plants, promotes increased leaf, stem, and fruit growth, and improves the quality of leafy crops as well as hastening growth. Phosphorus stimulates early root formation and growth, gives rapid and vigorous start to plants, hastens maturity, stimulates blooming, and aids in seed formation. Potassium or potash imparts increased vigor and disease resistance to plants, producing strong, stiff stalks. This reduces lodging (falling over) of plants.

What's in the Fertilizer Bag?: Home gardeners are often baffled when they find a recommendation calling for 5–10–5 or 5–10–10 grade of fertilizer, or a similar analysis. Every mixed fertilizer sold has a guaranteed analysis, stating the nitrogen (N), phosphorus (P), and potassium (K), the "Big 3" elements required by state laws to be on the label. This analysis tells the buyer what he's getting in terms of N–P–K. So let us take a 100-pound bag of 5–10–10 fertilizer and see what it contains. Such an analysis contains 5% nitrogen, 10% phosphorus, and 10% potash, or 25 pounds of the 3 primary nutrients. The question you'll ask is, what constitutes the other 75 pounds of fertilizer you bought?

The 75 pounds remaining is inert material known as "filler." It is necessary for manufacturers to add filler to dry fertilizers because pure forms of nitrogen, phosphorus, and potassium cannot be used as plant foods. Nitrogen is a gas, and phosphorus and potassium are 2 of the most active chemicals known and wouldn't be safe to use in pure form. Fertilizers must therefore contain their nutrients in diluted forms that are safe to plants and man, economical, and easily assimilated by plants. (See Liquid Fertilizers elsewhere in this chapter.)

Manure Good or Bad; Value of Manure: Several years ago some readers of my garden column told of a fight they had over a pile of elephant manure deposited along a railroad track near Buffalo, New York. This is an indication of what some folks will do to get manure.

In this age of horseless carriages, sputniks, and mechanization, manure has become a thing of the past for many home gardeners, and even if available it is low in fertilizing value. A ton of barnyard manure has about $3.00 worth of plant food if bought in the form of commercial fertilizer. But much of this may be lost by the time you get it from a farmer. The liquid part of the manure contains 45% of the total nitrogen and 65% of the potassium, and most of this has been lost by drying and leaching by the time you get that "well-rotted" stuff from Farmer Jones' stockpile. Yet, gardeners still clamor for it.

There's another unfavorable side to manure. It may carry plant disease as well as weed seed. Only if you're equipped to sterilize your soil can the use of manure create no problems.

For the home gardener, the value of manure is not for plant food, but for the organic matter. Organic matter is the backbone of soils, promoting good structure and aeration.

The organic material supplied by manure can easily be provided by a compost pile (which see), peat moss, sawdust, ground cornstalks, leaves, or other organic substances, fortified with additions of commercial fertilizer.

So, if you cannot get farmyard manure, don't worry about it. With fertilizers you can make composted material which is disease and weed-seed free, and will do the same things manure will do.

Manuring the Garden: If you can get cheap manure, use it liberally on your vegetable garden. A coat of manure adds humus to the soil and increases its water-holding ability even though it is a rather poor fertilizer. Manure is particularly low in phosphorus. To correct this, gardens should receive about 30 pounds of a 5–10–10 fertilizer for each 1,000 square feet of area, in addition to the manure. Or, you could add superphosphate, about 100 pounds of the 20% grade to each ton of manure. Superphosphate and 5–10–10 are available at your feed and seed store.

Never put fresh strawy manure to a garden that's ready to plow and seed. Broadcast fresh manure over the soil at least 6 or 8 weeks before plowing. Then add a high-nitrogen fertilizer over the manure at the rate of 300 pounds per acre to help decompose the straw. Manure, as with commercial plant foods, is gradually consumed and should be replenished.

Some Manures Gardeners Ask About:

Hen Manure: Hen manure is higher in nitrogen, phosphorus, and potash than barnyard manure and should be used whenever possible. Fresh poultry manure can burn plants, but can be used safely if spread in the fall. About 2 tons of poultry manure can be applied to a 50'x100' garden. Like other manures, this is unbalanced in plant food content and needs additional phosphate. This can be supplied by 100 pounds of 20% superphosphate to each ton of manure.

Rabbit Manure: Rabbit manure is valuable, being high in nitrogen and humus. You can mix it with peat moss or straw, or put it in compost. Leave it exposed for a month or so, then apply to soil at the rate of 8 pounds per 100 square feet. Well-rotted and mixed with peat, rabbit manure becomes a safe material. If fresh, apply as a light covering between the rows, but make sure it doesn't touch plants, as it is one of the strongest animal manures.

Sheep and Cow Manure: These are fairly quick-acting organic ferti-lizers, good for houseplants. Sheep manure has about 2% nitrogen, 1% phosphorus, and 2% potash. Cow manure has lower plant-food content. Both are ideal for mixing with the soil to add humus.

Horse Manure: This has roughly the same composition as cow ma-nure and those gardeners who live near riding stables or racetracks should take advantage of it as a soil conditioner.

Coal Ashes: Coal ashes have little or no plant-food value, although in sufficient amounts they do improve the mechanical condition of a soil which packs hard. They can be used with manure without harm. Scat-ter them over the garden and plow in.

They are dry and more or less antiseptic and discourage snails, snakes, and worms. Hence, screened coal ashes are good for greenhouse aisles, benches, and under potted plants, or you can use them in the bottom of borders or beds to protect roses and other plants which do not like wet feet.

Soot: Coal soot is a limited source of nitrogen and some potash and phosphorus. It repels wireworms, maggots, cutworms, and snails. Do not use soot and lime together, otherwise the nitrogen will be lost.

Incinerator Ashes: Ashes from burned papers and garbage vary greatly in composition according to the amount of vegetable refuse and paper. They are not harmful and can be spread on the garden or lawn. They'll be alkaline, due to the calcium, magnesium, and sodium from the original materials. Their nutritive value will be chiefly in the phosphorus and potassium, with traces of many additional ele-ments. There are some toxic metal compounds that might get into the ashes, such as zinc from batteries, metal polishes, waste borax, etc., but ordinarily these are not abundant and can be kept out of the home gardener's incinerator. Roughly speaking, incinerator ashes should be more or less equivalent to wood ashes and can be used wherever lim-ing would not be objectionable.

Wood Ashes: Wood ashes, unleached, contain all the mineral elements that were in the original wood. The most abundant elements are lime and potash. At one time wood ashes were the chief source of potash, the plant food that gives stiff stems and imparts increased vigor and disease resistance to plants. Besides potash, wood contains about 2% phosphorus, the plant food that stimulates growth and root formation.

Ashes from various woods differ greatly in value as a plant food. Twigs are richer than mature wood. Both hardwood and softwood ashes are all right to use in the vegetable or flower garden. If you have a stubborn peony or iris bed, sometimes wood ashes scattered on them will force flowers to bloom.

Don't use wood ashes with manure, unless it is well rotted. They can be used in the compost pile with leaves to hasten decomposition.

Since wood ashes contain lime, don't use on soils for potatoes—and keep them away from acid-loving plants such as blueberries, azaleas, and rhododendrons. If you use ashes year after year, the soil should be tested to make sure it's not overly sweet, or so saturated with ashes as to cause drying out of the soil.

Generally speaking, scattering ashes on the garden is satisfactory to a certain extent, although a rather meager way of building up fertility. An 80-pound sack of lime, where needed, and one bag of 10–10–10 fertilizer will do more for the home garden than several bushels of ashes. But, if you've got them, use them.

Bone Meal: Some gardeners still prefer bone meal as a plant fertilizer. Because it is so slow-acting, there is no danger of its burning plants. It penetrates the soil so slowly, about an inch per season, that it's best to work it into the soil rather than sprinkle it on. Steamed bone meal, which contains about 1 to 2% nitrogen and about 22 to 30% phosphoric acid, is more quickly available to plants. Raw bone meal takes longer to break down so plants can absorb it. Bone meal is good for bulbs of all sorts, and vegetables, but an objection is that it often induces dogs to dig around plants in search of phantom bones. Superphosphate is generally used instead of bone meal in modern gardening, since the phosphorus in superphosphate is more readily available and the cost is less. Bone meal has little humus value.

Sewage Sludge: Sludges make good soil improvers. They are equal to low-analysis fertilizers containing from 1 to 3% nitrogen, phosphorus, potash. The important thing is that the nitrogen is in the long-lasting organic form and the organic-matter content is high enough to warrant use as a mulch or a substitute for farm manure.

As for the sanitary status of sludge, there are many widely different opinions regarding its safety. If you use the heat-treated sludges there is nothing to worry about from a sanitary standpoint. Such treatment is normally provided for material that is marketed. These sludges are useful as mulches around certain kinds of flowers, shrubs, and in vegetable gardens.

Digested Sludge: Not heat-treated, this should be used with some caution. One way is to incorporate it in the soil several months before vegetables to be eaten raw are grown. According to the USDA all danger is thought to be removed after the sludge has been in the soil for 3 months of a growing season. It's reasonable to assume that digested sludges are satisfactory for lawns, shrubs, flowers, and ornamental crops.

Raw sewage sludge is not sterile, and has undergone no process to kill any harmful organisms that might be in it. We'd like to warn against growing vegetables in septic-tank drainage fields. There are many human communicable diseases—virus, bacterial, and parasitic—which can be transferred by vegetables contaminated with human waste. A septic tank in no way renders this waste less dangerous. So the effluent in the disposal field found in many backyards can be dangerous, particularly with vegetables that are eaten raw. In many ways this situation is quite similar to those foreign countries where "night soil" is used as fertilizer for vegetable gardens.

My former teacher at Cornell University, Dr. L. H. McDaniels, a fine gardener, assisted me with this chart for feeding the garden.

RATE OF APPLICATION OF FERTILIZERS AND SOIL AMENDMENTS

MATERIAL	METHOD OF APPLICATION	RATE OF APPLICATION
Leaf Mold	Incorporate in topsoil	Same as for peat
Lime	Dry	Apply to correct acidity (see Liming and Soil Acidity)
Liquid Plant Food (23–19–17)	Solution only	1 tsp. to a qt. of water for root or foliage feeding, every 2 or 3 weeks
Manure (rotted: cow or horse)	As fertilizer	From 10 to 50 tons per acre, or 4 bu. per 100 sq. ft. of soil
	As mulch	1 in. deep on top of soil
Manure (poultry, rabbit, or hog)		5 tons per acre, or 1 bu. per 100 sq. ft. of soil
Mixed Fertilizer (5–10–5, 5–10–10)	Dry	2 to 3 lbs. per 100 sq. ft. of soil, or 3-in. pot to 3 bu. of soil, or 1 tsp. to a 5-in. pot of soil
Mixed Fertilizer (10–20–10, 15–30–15)	Dry	1 lb. or less per 100 sq. ft. of soil, or 2-in. pot to 3 bu. of soil, or ½ tp. to a 5-in. pot of soil
	Solution	1 oz. to 2 gals. of water
Muriate of Potash	Dry	300 lbs. per acre, or ½ lb. per 100 sq. ft. of soil
	Solution	½ lb. in 10 gals. water applied to 100 sq. ft. of soil, or ½ cup of solution to 5-in. pot of soil
Nitrate of Soda	Solution	Same as sulfate of ammonia

Material	Method of Application	Rate of Application
Peat or Compost	Incorporated in topsoil Mulch	5 bu. to 100 sq. ft. of soil for garden 1-in. layer
Sulfate of Ammonia	Dry Solution	1 lb. to 100 sq. ft. of soil 1 lb. in 30 gals. of water applied to 100 sq. ft., or 1 cup of solution to 5-in. pot of soil;
Sulfate of Potash		same as for muriate of potash
Superphosphate (16 or 20%)	Dry	1,000 lbs. per acre, 5 lbs. per 100 sq. ft., 3-in. pot to a bu. of soil
Tankage or Sewage	Dry	4-in. pot to 3 bu. of soil, 5 lbs. per 100 sq. ft.
Urea	Solution only	5 oz. to 35 gals. of water applied to 100 sq. ft. of soil, or 1 cup solution to 5-in. pot of soil

Green Thumb Tips on Soils and Fertilizers: You can make a good flower or vegetable garden wherever weeds will grow. Good soils are usually made, not born. You can tame the wildest soil into a productive one by following the tips in the preceding chapters.

Don't be discouraged if you have a heavy soil. It can be as productive as a sandy loam. Crops on sandy soils suffer quicker from dry spells than do those on heavier soils.

Don't be afraid to use lime, fertilizers, and compost to fortify your soils.

Organic gardeners need not fear that plant foods are harmful to themselves or to their crops.

High-potency fertilizer mixtures, soluble in water, do a lot to get young plants off to a fast start and increase the survival rate.

Watch out for advertisements about wonder-growth stimulants. They are not a substitute for good cultural practices such as feeding, spraying, and cultivation.

GARDEN DISEASES AND PESTS

How to Avoid Garden Troubles

Reduce losses by using these accepted tips.

ROTATE LOCATION OF VEGETABLES: Why rotate? The soil builds up certain disease organisms, such as root knot, clubroot, fusarium wilt, cabbage yellows, if plants are planted in the same place year after year. These organisms can survive in the soil for many years. Tomatoes, melons, cucumbers, and other crops should not be on the same land oftener than once in 3 years, unless the soil is disinfected (see How to Disinfect Your Soil). Even a small garden may be divided into thirds, with fast-growing vegetables that are susceptible to root diseases grown in a different third each year.

PRACTICE CROP SANITATION: Many plant parasites overwinter in refuse from last year's crop. Burning vines, stalks, etc., is an effective way to control plant-disease fungi and bacteria.

USE GOOD SEED: Certified seed or treated seed is good crop insurance.

PLANT TREATED SEED: If your seedsman does not sell treated seed treat your own (see How to Treat Your Seed). Treatment protects seed and seedlings against fungi on seed or in the soil. Treated seed gives better stand. WARNING: Chemicals used for treating seed are poisonous. Any seed you buy from a seed house should be assumed treated and never used for birds, livestock, or human consumption.

USE DISEASE-FREE PLANTS: Buy from a trustworthy grower (some of them switch labels)—or raise your own (see Starting Seed Indoors). Reject any plants with root swellings or lumps, to avoid introducing root knot into the soil.

GROW DISEASE-RESISTANT VARIETIES: Your seed catalog lists resistant types—the only effective means of controlling many common and destructive diseases of vegetable and fruit crops.

RECOGNIZE HUNGER SIGNS: Garden vegetables express their need for fertilizer through hunger signs which are specific for various nutrients. These hunger signs can be detected by careful, experienced observation, but usually plant growth has slowed down even before symptoms become apparent.

A disadvantage of this method of diagnosis lies in the fact that the deficiencies are usually revealed too late for effective treatment of current crops. The information can be used, however, in preparing for the following season.

Common hunger signs:

Nitrogen Deficiency: (1) Foliage a sickly yellowish-green color. (2) Distinctly slow and dwarfed growth. (3) Drying up or "firing" of leaves, which starts at the bottom of the plant and proceeds upward.

In plants like corn, grains, and grasses, the firing starts at the tip of the bottom leaves and proceeds down the center or along the midrib.

Phosphorus Deficiency: (1) Purplish leaves, stems, and branches. Tomatoes are particularly sensitive. (Plants exposed to prolonged cold weather also turn purple.) (2) Slow growth and maturity. (3) Small, slender stalk in case of corn. (4) Low yields of grain, fruit, and seed.

Potash Deficiency: (1) Mottling, spotting, streaking, or curling of leaves, starting on the lower levels. (2) Lower leaves scorched (browned) or burned on margins and tips. These dead areas may fall out, leaving ragged edges. (3) In corn, firing starting at the tip of the leaf proceeding down from the edge, usually leaving the midrib green. (4) Premature loss of leaves and small, knotty, poorly opened bolls on plants like cotton. (5) Plants falling down prior to maturity due to lack of root development of plants like corn.

Minor Elements: The typical hunger signs for most minor elements differ among vegetables. Boron deficiency causes cracked stalks of celery and discolored areas on cauliflower heads. A lack of manganese in most vegetables is associated with a between-the-veins yellowing of young leaves. Insufficient magnesium causes a similar pattern on older leaves. Check with your county agent for information on specific minor element deficiencies.

How to Diagnose Your Vegetable Troubles

Garden crops, like other living things, often suffer from diseases caused by bacteria, fungi, deficiencies, microscopic parasites—and human beings. Plant troubles such as wilt, root rots, dying of young seedlings, poor stands, rusts, mildews, and spotting of leaves and fruits are usually caused by plant diseases. Here are a few general tips to help you track down your problems.

SEEDLINGS FAIL TO COME UP: Due to damping-off, a fungus problem found in soil. Control: Use sterile starting mixture (see Starting Seed Indoors).

PLANTS WILT, TURN YELLOW, AND DIE: Could be due to root knot, caused by nematodes, tiny worms which infest the soil. Control: Rotate crop. Plant resistant varieties when possible. (See How to Disinfect Your Soil.)

If roots appear sound, but tissue just under bark of stems is discolored, this is a wilt disease, caused by fungi or bacteria in soil. Control: Use wilt-resistant varieties, as with tomatoes. Also rotate land. Always plant treated seed.

If roots are dead and decayed, this is root rot disease, usually accompanied by foul-smelling odor. Control: Improve drainage. "Wet feet" (water at roots) causes death and foul smell by excluding oxygen.

LEAVES, STEMS, FRUITS SHOW ROUND OR IRREGULAR-
SHAPED DEAD SPOTS:
Called "spot diseases" and caused by fungi and bacteria. Control: Don't work in garden when leaves are wet. Keep foliage covered with a good fungicide such as Captan, Zineb, or Bordeaux mixture.

WHITE FUZZY MOLD ON LEAVES: Powdery mildew, causes yellowing, drying up, and falling of leaves or buds. Control: Dust or spray with Karathane, Captan, or Phaltan (also called Folpet). Improve air drainage. Avoid wetting foliage.

LEAVES MOTTLED WITH LIGHT AND DARK AREAS: Mosaic virus, also causes curling or twisting, stunting, poor yield, but not death of plants. Control: Pull weeds nearby and burn. Use mosaic-resistant varieties.

HOLES IN LEAVES: Due to insects and other leaf-chewing pests. Spray or dust with Sevin, covering both top and bottom surfaces. Slugs work at night. Scatter metaldehyde bait (see section on Animal Control).

POOR GROWTH: Too much fertilizer, or not enough, clay soil, or lack of moisture. Check and correct. If excess fertilizer, loosen soil and water it to wash fertilizer salts into the soil.

PLANTS CUT OFF AT BASE: Due to cutworm, a greasy caterpillar which hides under stones in day, works at night. Control: Chlordane around base of plants. Use paper collars at planting time. If plant is cut off with a sharp angle left on stub, it's work of rabbit. Control: Fence (see section on Animal Control).

TOPS NIPPED OUT: Due to blackbirds. Cover new plants with netting or bushel basket until established.

BURNED FOLIAGE: Too much sprays or dusts, overdose of chemicals, may burn foliage. Herbicides cause twisting, yellowing of foliage, followed by death. "Household" fly and mosquito sprays containing oil may burn foliage of vegetables. They weren't made for such crops. Use garden sprays and dusts.

LOW TEMPERATURES: Cold summers raise havoc with "warm" crops such as melons, squash, tomatoes, and corn, delay ripening, cause flat-flavored melons.

EXCESS RAINS: Delays ripening, affects yield, and may cause yellowing due to washing nitrogen from soil.

INSUFFICIENT LIGHT: Nearly all vegetables need full sun. Keep tall-growing crops like corn away from small crops—beets and carrots—to avoid shading. Don't plant near shade trees, or in shade of buildings. Plants which receive insufficient light have spindly growth and poor fruit set.

How to Disinfect Your Soil

Treating Your Soil: Your garden soil is teeming with beneficial and not-so-beneficial organisms. For those who have a small space and find it difficult to rotate crops, try treating the soil before planting. Use a mixture of Terraclor and Captan, tilled dry into the top 4 inches. One cup each of Terraclor and Captan are mixed and spread over 100 square feet of ground. Then till the soil in the usual manner and plant.

Or, Terraclor and Captan may be watered into the soil after planting, instead of treating soil before planting. One half-pound each of Terraclor 75 and Captan 50 are added to 100 gallons of water and 5 gallons of this suspension are added to each 100 square feet of bed. A sprinkling can is useful for this.

If you've been plagued with soil pests such as wireworms, centipedes, white grubs, and other pests, treat the soil before you plant. For small areas, use dieldrin, Chlordane or aldrin, following manufacturer's directions. Labels now must give recommended rates to use. I mix ½ cup of the emulsifiable concentrate to 2 gallons of water and spray it on each 1,000 square feet after plowing, but before it's worked the final time prior to planting. There's no danger of vegetables absorbing the chemicals if the materials are worked into the top 3 or 4 inches of soil.

Nematodes: The previously mentioned materials will not check nematodes (eelworms, so small that 50 of them span an inch) in the soil. Control of nematodes is difficult for the home gardener. Use nematocides. Chloropicrin (tear gas, larvicide, picfume) is a heavy liquid effective against nematodes, weed seeds, soil insects, and soil fungi. Apply with special soil injector, and soil must be sealed with moist papers or burlap for 48 hours. Wait 14 days before planting. Ethylene dibromide (EDB, Dowfume W85, Soilfume 85) or dichloropropene (D-D) may also be used. Vapam (VPM) is good for nematodes, weeds, and disease. Usual rate is 1 quart in 15 to 20 gallons of water, sprinkled on 100 square feet, either broadcast or in marked rows. Wait 14 to 21 days before planting. Be sure to follow manufacturer's directions when using all nematocides.

Mercuric chloride (bichloride of mercury, corrosive sublimate) is an old soil drench useful on cabbage family. One ounce is dissolved in a little hot water, then diluted to 15 gallons. One pint is applied to each square foot of seedbed or ground. Mercuric chloride is poisonous. Be careful about using any chemical. Always follow instructions and keep them locked up!

CHEMICAL CONTROL OF INSECTS AND DISEASES OF FRUITS AND VEGETABLES

Most insects and diseases are mentioned, with controls, under TROUBLES of each subject. General information is added here, however, for those interested in pursuing the matter further.

Pesticides: It is estimated that about 90% of our insect problems are solved by natural controls such as weather, other forms of plant and animal life, diseases, and other insects. To deal with the remaining 10%, or to speed nature, man uses other controls such as good house-keeping and garden practices, crop rotation, mechanical control (flyswatters), biological controls, laws and regulations, and chemicals.

Chemical control is often the quickest and most dependable method. In many instances, we have no alternative. Chemicals to kill pests (living things) are pesticides. Pesticides are applied in a number of forms. They may be grouped according to the organisms they are used to control.

Insecticides: for insects causing annoyance, damage, and destruction.
Fungicides: for fungus organisms causing disease.
Miticides or Acaricides: for tiny spider-like animals called mites.
Herbicides: for unwanted vegetation, either selectively or generally.
Rodenticides: for rats, mice, other rodent pests.
Nematocides: for nematodes, minute worms.
Molluscides: for snails and slugs.

Are Pesticides Dangerous to Humans?: There are 2 groups of gardeners: those who use pesticides and those who don't. I never try to influence either group. Frankly, it would be nice if we take all the pesticides and dump them into the bottom of the ocean. But we can't. Insects and disease present a threat to food production, necessitating man's reliance on these chemical weapons.

If you use pesticides, use them with care. Materials poisonous to one form of life are usually poisonous to other forms if the dose is large enough. Pesticides are poisons and should be treated as deadly weapons. Used improperly, pesticides can be harmful to human beings, pets, fish, and wildlife. Used properly, they benefit all.

The newspaper account of 58 persons being hospitalized after eating a vegetable salad in Venezuela brings home a good point. Be sure to wash all fruits and vegetables found in stores and grown in your own garden. Processors try to do a good job in our own country although quite often you see chemical residues on produce. For example, when you pull celery stalks apart, you often notice a green residue. This is from copper pesticides and it's almost impossible for processors to get it out. However, it's an easy matter for the homeowner to clean it properly with a brush and running water. When you eat an apple, wash it. I like to cut out the stem end as well as the calyx end (bottom) because these depressed areas are often coated with pesticides.

I wouldn't worry about pesticides because their residues can be washed off. Without their use, our fruits and vegetables would be higher in cost and much of the crop wouldn't be fit to eat. The Irish famine which took the lives of so many thousands in the 1840's would never have occurred if each farmer had had as much as a pound of copper fungicide.

Simple rules for the safe use of any pesticide are common sense and extra caution. Never forget that pesticides are poisons.

We're hoping the day will come when plant pesticides will not be necessary. We may be able to kill diseases and insects by using parasites, microbial diseases, interference with insect reproduction, sex attractants (attracting males), resistant plants, and by planting plants which ward off pests. Meanwhile we must continue to rely on chemicals.

GOOD BUGS AND BAD BUGS?

A garden club member once wrote me: "I've had many discussions concerning our local insects and worms. One person says that earwigs are beneficial and harmless. Some say white larvae or grubs turn into June bugs and are good, others say those shield-shaped stinkbugs are helpful. Could you compose an article which tells how to identify insects (good ones and bad ones) so we won't be guilty of poisoning the ones we need? Most books tell us what to spray for, but do not describe the bug, so we need help in identifying insects."

With nearly a million species of insects (and many not yet classified), it'd be impossible to describe all the pests which plague the home gardener. Also, insects do not fall into 2 simple groups, such as harmful and beneficial. Some bugs feed on bugs and these same ones sometimes feed on vegetable matter as well.

The important thing for the home gardener to know is *not* what an insect looks like, but the type of damage it causes. Entomology (bug study) is a complicated subject. If we tried to describe an insect it'd be necessary to use jawbreaking terms such as mandibular, scutellum, and embolium.

So you should not concern yourself with identifying an insect, or finding out "what kind of bug it is." More important is to know what *kind* of damage it causes to plants. If it's a leaf-chewing pest, a stomach poison (such as Chlordane or Sevin) will kill the pest. If it's a leaf-sucking type, or one that "rasps" the foliage, use a type which kills on contact with the body. If you still aren't sure, use an almost all-purpose insecticide such as Malathion. It kills a wide variety of bugs, good and bad, and there's no way to separate the 2. Diazinon is an excellent wide-spectrum insecticide too, meaning it will kill many kinds of insects.

NATURAL OR BIOLOGICAL CONTROL

The possibilities of controlling insect pests by making use of their natural enemies are illustrated in a letter I received from an amateur fruit grower who used to grow wormy fruit until he switched to biological insect control:

"I lacked the apparatus and didn't want to use poison sprays on fruit to be eaten. I ordered some trichogramma, the microscopic natural enemy of the apple worm and all other members of the Lepidoptera order of insects. The trichogramma destroys the eggs (which hatch into harmful worms). The natural enemy will not feed on or harm vegetation, and is perfectly harmless to everything except the undesirable lepidopterous eggs. You should tell your readers about this safe approach to insect control."

Trichogramma is an efficient egg parasite on many lepidopterous insects (moths and butterflies). This parasite is being used with considerable success in citrus groves and cotton fields in California. Ladybird beetles (ladybugs) have also been used for aphid control, particularly in melon fields in some areas. Theoretically, it will someday be possible to control many types of crop pests with well-timed releases of parasites. Also experimental are programs of male pest sterilization.

As yet such programs are not completely adequate, but they are worth trying.

SPRAYING OR DUSTING?

Dusting vs. Spraying: Should the home gardener dust or spray his plants? Since a duster and a sprayer are inexpensive, you should have both. Dusting is an older practice than spraying and is preferred by many. Dusting is favored for many reasons: No water is needed to add to chemicals, also less time and labor are involved. A small garden can be maintained by using a general-purpose dust, but a larger garden should have sprays.

If you use a duster, apply between showers, or while dew is on foliage (except when using sulfur). Plants wet with dew may burn or deface if sulfur-dusted. Dust lightly and thoroughly, coating the entire plant—top and bottom sides of leaves. A heavy dose is not needed. Apply a thin, inconspicuous layer, and repeat weekly, if necessary, rather than apply heavy coat of dust to "last all summer." You want to repeat often enough to keep the new growth covered.

I like spraying in many instances because usually spray materials are cheaper, and sprays are easier to apply if there's a slight breeze. When large puffs of dust drift in the wind, it's money wasted. Spraying is more adaptable. For example, you can mix fertilizers and insecticides in the spray and do 2 jobs at once. This isn't possible with dust. Spray nozzles enable you to spray trees and bushes 15 to 30 feet, but you can't do this with a duster.

If you spray your garden, start as soon as foliage growth begins. Keep a spray residue on at all times with 7- to 10-day interval applications. Spray after rains. Don't spray flowers when in full bloom as injury may result and pollinating insects may be killed.

Buy a good duster or sprayer. Cheap equipment is short-lived, less efficient, expensive in the long run.

Use Fresh Chemicals: Most insecticides will last for 2 or more years in containers. Malathion will last for a year or longer, if kept stored in a tightly closed, dry, cool place. Insecticides kept in containers that cannot be tightly closed after they have been opened lose Malathion continuously. The aerosol bombs keep their original quality because the containers have vapor-proof walls. Store your pesticides in tight containers, in a dry, cool place, and make sure they're fresh when you buy them from the dealer. Do not burn aerosol containers when finished as they are explosive.

How to Dust or Spray Properly: Cover all parts of plants, especially undersides of leaves. Do not dust or spray when plant is wilted. Any time of day is fine, but morning is preferred while wet with dew. Do not dust or spray when temperature is over 85°. Measure all amounts accurately—and don't work on the theory that if a little will do some good, a lot will do better. KEEP ALL PESTICIDES OUT OF REACH OF CHILDREN AND ANIMALS. Burn all containers (except aerosol). Don't keep pesticides next to foods, and don't smoke while you spray.

Spray or dust *before* insect and disease set in. Preventing is easier than eradicating a disease.

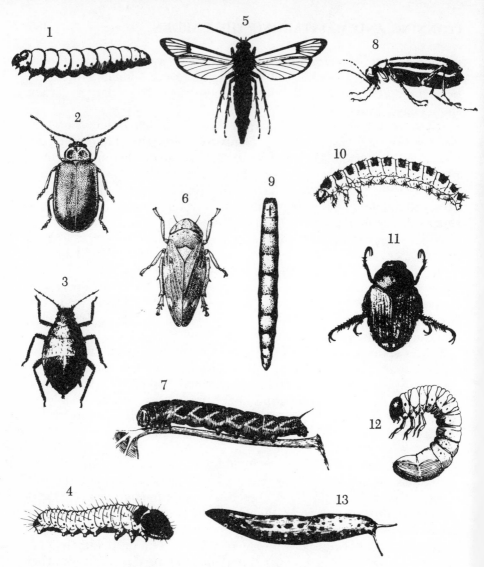

SOME COMMON PESTS AFFECTING FRUITS AND VEGETABLES

1. Squash Vine Borer: bores in vines, causing wilting. 2. Cherry Beetle: feeds on leaves of cherry, peach, plum apple trees. 3. Corn Leaf Aphid: causes reddish-yellow patches on leaves, coats tassels and silk with honey-dew, may transmit virus diseases. 4. Codling Moth (larva): enters fruit at blossom end, tunnels to center and eventually out. 5. Peach Tree Borer: larva tunnels in trunk of fruit trees, tree shows gummy mass at point of entry. 6. Spittlebug: young secrete frothy mass about selves, suck plant juices. 7. Hornworm: eats foliage and fruit of eggplant, pepper, tomato, other plants. 8. Blister Beetle: feeds on leaves of beets, chard. 9. Carrot Rust Fly (larva): tunnels into fleshy roots, destroys fibrous roots. 10. Raspberry Fruit Worm: adults make long slits in leaves, larvae feed on roots. 11. Japanese Beetle: adults feed on leaves, larvae feed on roots. 12. White Grub: larva of May beetle, feeds on roots and tubers. 13. Slug: chews holes in leaves and soft plant parts. 14. Flea Beetle: tiny beetle that feeds on young

plants in swarms, chewing small holes in a "shot-hole" effect.   15. Pill Bug: feeds on roots and tender growth, especially in greenhouses and lathhouses. 16. Wireworm: punctures and tunnels in stems, roots, and tubers.   17. Harlequin Bug: sucks plant juices, causing wilting of plants, browning of leaves. 18. Corn Earworm (adult and larva): serious pest of corn ears, tassels and leaves, also attacks beans, tomatoes, okra, other garden plants.   19. Cutworm: cuts off plants at, above, or below soil surface.   20. Strawberry Weevil: pest on many berries, larvae feed on buds.   21. Beet Webworm: eats leaves and buds of young plants, rolls and folds leaves.   22. Rose Chafer: feeds on foilage, buds, flowers, and fruits of blackberry, raspberry, cabbage, beans, beets, and peppers.   23. Potato Leafhopper: feeds on many garden plants. Leaves turn whitish, stippled, plants are stunted, yields reduced, leaf tips and edges scorched.   24. Spider Mite: tiny pest that causes stippling, browning, yellow specks on leaves, stunting of plant.   25. Spotted Cucumber Beetle: feeds on leaves and fruits of cucumbers.   26. Green Peach Aphid (wingless form): sucks juice from leaves.   27. European earwig: feeds on

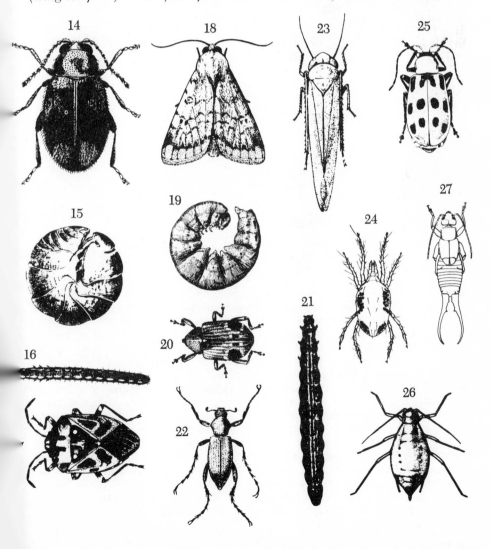

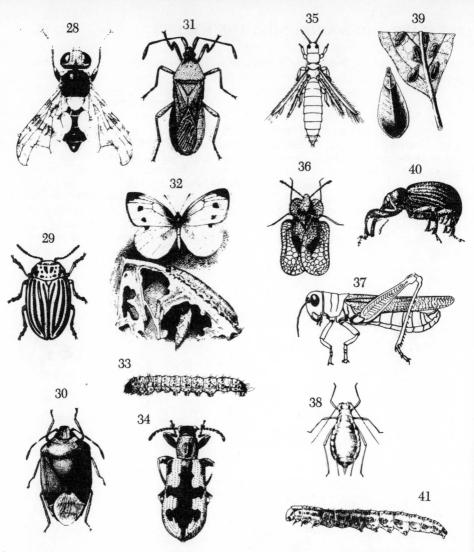

shoots, blossoms and fruits, may invade homes and become a nuisance.
28. *Cherry Fruit Fly:* adults feed on leaves and fruit, larvae feed inside
fruit, causing misshapen, undersized cherries, often with one side shrunken.
29. *Colorado Potato Beetle:* adults and larvae feed on leaves of eggplant,
potato, and tomato.   30. *Green Soldier Bug:* one of the so-called stinkbugs,
feeds on many types of plants, a special pest on beans and peaches.   31.
Squash Bug: feeds on squash and pumpkins, plants wilt and die.   32. *Imported Cabbage Worm (adult and larva):* larva feeds on undersides of leaves,
bores into heads.   33. *European Corn Borer:* feeds in stalks and ears of corn.
34. *Asparagus Beetle:* eats foliage, disfigures shoots.   35. *Thrip:* sucks plant
juices, disfigures blooms and buds, causing dropping.   36. *Lace Bug:* feeds
on undersides of leaves, leaves turn yellow and brown, plants die.   37. *Grass-
hopper:* feeds on all types of vegetation, may destroy entire plantings.   38.
Pea Aphid (wingless form): sucks juices, wilting and deforming growth,
vines die.   39. *Japanese Citrus Scale:* attaches to plant and sucks juices.
40. *Pepper Weevil:* feeds on foliage, buds, and pods of peppers.   41. *Stalk
Borer:* tunnels in tomato stem, causing plant to wither and die.

Make Your Own All-purpose Pesticide: You can buy multipurpose garden sprays or dusts, or mix your own. Use the following insecticides and fungicides in 1 gallon of water for a good all-purpose spray: Sevin or methoxychlor (50% wettable powder), 2 tbsp., Malathion (25% wettable powder), 4 tbsp., and Maneb (80% wettable powder), 2 tbsp. Captan may be substituted for Maneb. Use level tablespoons. A heaping tablespoon may be equivalent to 2 level tablespoons. Agitate the spray from time to time to keep the chemicals in suspension.

If you buy your own all-purpose pesticide, read the label and make sure it has ingredients such as Sevin or methoxychlor and Malathion, plus a fungicide such as zineb, Captan, or Maneb.

MEASURING CHART FOR PESTICIDES

Few things are more exasperating to the home gardener than to read a label calling for "100 gallons per acre," or "2 pounds per 100 gallons of water." These large amounts are OK for a farmer, but of little help to the small grower. I've put together a measuring table which helps you break down big amounts into little amounts. Study the chart and you'll see how it works.

HANDY MEASURING TABLE

ITEM	CUPS	FLUID OUNCES	TABLESPOONS
1 gallon	16	128	256
1 quart	4	32	64
1 pint (1 lb.)	2	16	32
1 cup (½ pt.)	1	8	16
½ cup (¼ pt.)	½	4	8
⅓ cup (⅙ pt.)	⅓	2⅔	5⅓
¼ cup (⅛ pt.)	¼	2	4

Use level tablespoons
1 tablespoonful (tbsp.) equals ½ fluid ounce
3 teaspoonfuls (tsp.) equal 1 tablespoon

Suppose the recommendations call for 2 pounds per 100 gallons of water. We convert 2 pounds into 32 ounces. You put 32 over 100, and get .32 oz., or about ⅓ of an ounce per gallon. To find out how many tablespoons that is, refer to the table and you will find that 1 ounce equals 2 tablespoons. Since you have ⅓ of an ounce, you take ⅓ of 2 (tablespoons) and you get ⅔ of a tablespoonful, the amount needed per gallon of water. The amounts you get by this method are close enough for practical purposes.

CHARTS OF CONVERSION FOR FRUIT AND VEGETABLE GARDENERS

Here are some additional tables which help the home gardener get amounts down to usable size. These tables will be helpful if you spray fruits and vegetables or grow corn.

TABLE A: DRY INSECTICIDES

For 100 Gallons of Water	For 50 Gallons of Water	For 25 Gallons of Water	For 6¼ Gallons of Water	For 3⅛ Gallons of Water
1 lb.	8 oz.	4 oz.	1 oz.	1 tbsp.
2 lbs.	1 lb.	8 oz.	2 oz.	2 tbsp.
4 lbs.	2 lbs.	1 lb.	4 oz.	4 tbsp.

If manufacturer's instructions call for 1 pint of liquid (abbreviated EC for Emulsion Concentrate) per 100 gallons of water, then use Table B to reduce the proportions to a workable amount.

TABLE B: LIQUID INSECTICIDES

For 100 Gallons of Water	For 50 Gallons of Water	For 25 Gallons of Water	For 6¼ Gallons of Water	For 3⅛ Gallons of Water
½ pint	¼ pint (4 fl. oz.)	4 tbsp. (2 fl. oz.)	1 tbsp. (½ fl. oz.)	½ tbsp. (¼ fl. oz.)
1 pint	½ pint (8 fl. oz.)	¼ pint (4 fl. oz.)	2 tbsp. (1 fl. oz.)	1 tbsp. (½ fl. oz.)
1 quart	1 pint (16 fl. oz.)	½ pint (8 fl. oz.)	4 tbsp. (2 fl. oz.)	2 tbsp. (1 fl. oz.)

WORKABLE CONVERSIONS FOR SOIL AREAS

1 oz. per sq. ft. equals 2,722.5 lbs. per acre
1 oz. per sq. yd. equals 302.5 lbs. per acre
1 oz. per 100 sq. ft. equals 27.2 lbs. per acre
1 lb. per 100 sq. ft. equals 435.6 lbs. per acre
1 lb. per 1,000 sq. ft. equals 43.6 lbs. per acre
1 lb. per acre equals 1/3 oz. per 1,000 sq. ft.
5 gals. per acre equals 1 pt. per 1,000 sq. ft.
100 gals. per acre equals 2.5 gals. per 1,000 sq. ft.
100 gals. per acre equals 1 qt. per 100 sq. ft.
100 gals. per acre equals 2.5 lbs. per 1,000 sq. ft.

AMERICAN DRY MEASURES

3 level teaspoons equal 1 tablespoon
16 level tablespoons equal 1 cup
2 cups equal 1 pint
2 pints equal 1 quart
8 quarts equal 1 peck
4 pecks equal 1 bushel

Note: A liquid pint is 28.875 cubic inches; a dry pint is 33.6 cubic inches, but for all practical purposes in measuring fertilizers, don't worry about the difference.

AMERICAN FLUID MEASURES

80 drops equal 1 teaspoon (tsp.)
3 teaspoons equal 1 tablespoon (tbsp.)
2 tablespoons equal 1 fluid ounce (fl. oz.)
8 fluid ounces equal 1 cup
2 cups equal 1 pint (pt.)
2 pints equal 1 quart (qt.)
4 quarts equal 1 gallon (gal.)
1 gal. equals 4 qts., or 8 pts., or 128 fl. oz., or 256 tbsp., or 768 tsp., or 61,440 drops.
1 qt. equals 2 pts., or 32 fl. oz., or 64 tbsp., or 192 tsp., or 15,360 drops
1 pt. equals 16 fl. oz., or 32 tbsp., or 96 tsp., or 7,680 drops
1 tbsp. equals 3 tsp., or 240 drops

Note: The apothecaries' measures have 60 drops, or 1 fluid dram (medicine teaspoon); 4 fluid drams equal 1 tablespoon; 2 tablespoons equal 1 fluid ounce. The standard teaspoon is ⅓ larger than the fluid dram or medicine teaspoon.

MISCELLANEOUS MEASURES

1 acre equals 43,560 sq. ft., or 4,840 sq. yds., or 160 sq. rods
1 U. S. gallon equals 231 cu. in. or 8.34 lbs. of water
1 imperial gallon equals 277.4 cu. in. or 10 lbs. of water

EMULSIONS OR WETTABLE POWDERS

Emulsions may be substituted for wettable powders and they leave less visible residue.

> 4 lbs. 50% Malathion wettable powder equal 3 pts. 50% Malathion emulsifiable solution
>
> 1 lb. 25% Lindane wettable powder equals 1 pt. 25% Lindane emulsifiable solution
>
> 2 lbs. 50% Ovotran wettable powder equal 2½ qts. 20% Ovotran emulsifiable solution
>
> 2 lbs. 15% Aramite wettable powder equal ½ pt. 50% Aramite emulsifiable solution

DILUTION TABLE

Here's a helpful table of equivalents for mixing items that come in liquid form:

> 1 to 1,000 . . . ¼ tbsp. per gal. water
> 1 to   750 . . . ⅓ tbsp. per gal. water
> 1 to   500 . . . ½ tbsp. per gal. water
> 1 to   250 . . . 1 tbsp. per gal. water
> 1 to   200 . . . 1¼ tbsp. per gal. water
> 1 to   150 . . . 1⅔ tbsp. per gal. water
> 1 to   100 (about 1%) . . . 2½ tbsp. per gal. water
> 1 to   50 (about 2%) . . . 5 tbsp. per gal. water
> 1 to   33 (about 3%) . . . 7½ tbsp. per gal. water
> 1 to   25 (about 4%) . . . 10 tbsp. per gal. water
> 1 to   20 (about 5%) . . . 12½ tbsp. or ¾ cups per gal.
> 1 to   10 (about 10%) . . . 25 tbsp. or 1½ cups per gal.

FERTILIZER MEASURES FOR POTTED PLANTS

Superphosphate (20%): 1 to 2 tablespoons to an 8-qt. pail soil
Wood ashes (4% potash): 1 cup to 8-qt. pail soil
Dried blood (12% nitrogen): 3 tablespoons to 8-qt. pail soil
Bone meal (20% phosphorus): 2 tablespoons to 8-qt. pail soil
Complete fertilizer (such as 5–10–5): 4 tablespoons to 8-qt. pail soil
Ground limestone: 4 tablespoons to 8-qt. pail soil
Muriate of potash (50–60% potash): 1 teaspoon to 8-qt. pail soil
Nitrate of soda: 1 tablespoon to a gallon

CLAY POTS ARE HANDY FOR MEASURING

2-in. clay pot equals ⅓ cup
2½-in. clay pot equals ⅔ cup
3-in. clay pot equals 1 cup
4-in. clay pot equals 2½ cups
5-in. clay pot equals 4½ cups
6-in. clay pot equals 8 cups or 2 qts.

CONVERTING LIQUID MEASURES

Here are some figures you might want to use to convert liquid measures: 1 gal. equals 4 qts., or 8 pts., or 16 cups, or 128 oz., or 256 tbsp. or 768 tsp., or 3,840 grams. 30 grams equal 1 oz. or 6 tsp.; 1 tsp. equals 5 grams.

From any of these equivalents we can find out the "parts per million" (p.p.m.) usually recommended by manufacturer—for instance:

10 p.p.m. .... 4 grams or ⅘ tsp. per 100 gals. water
20 p.p.m. ....8 grams or 1⅗ tsp. per 100 gals. water
40 p.p.m. .... 16 grams or 3⅕ tsp. per 100 gals. water, or
¼ tsp. per 8 gals. water
60 p.p.m. .... 24 grams or 5 tsp. per 100 gals. water, or ½
tsp. per 10 gals.
80 p.p.m. .... 32 grams or 6 tsp. per 100 gals. water, or ⅗
tsp. per 10 gals.
100 p.p.m. .... 40 grams or 8 tsp. per 100 gals. water, or ⅘
tsp. per 10 gals.
200 p.p.m. .... 80 grams or 16 tsp. per 10 gals. water, or 1⅗
tsp. per 10 gals.

"Parts per million" appeared in newspapers during a nationwide pre-Thanksgiving cranberry scare. Frequently mentioned was the 1/10 of a part per million parts of cranberries that represented the alleged contamination of the fruit. Roughly, 10 parts per million equal 4 grams per 100 gals. or 4 to 5 tsp. per 100 gals. of water. Some analogies might help to illustrate this scientific measuring unit.

For example, 1/10 of a part per million equals:
1 crystal of granulated sugar in 5 pounds, or
1 drop of water in 160 gallons, or
1 penny in $100,000, or
1 inch in 158 miles, or
the thickness of a strip of cellophane compared to the height of the Washington Monument.

Poisonous Plants

Without attempting to be an alarmist, I'd like to point out that there are hundreds of plants around us whose parts are poisonous to man. Since the beginning of time, man has lived close to plants which can cause irritation, illness, or death. Some of these plants are seriously toxic, others are moderately poisonous, some causing dermatitis, hay fever. It's the duty of parents to teach their children not to eat leaves, seeds, or flowers of strange plants, just as you'd teach them not to drink or eat medicines, cleaning solvents, shoe polish, etc.

The castor bean which many of us grow in our gardens has attractive seeds which are highly poisonous. If you clip the seed heads off before they mature, this plant may be grown with safety for its quick shade and as a garden ornamental. Some folks who handle castor pomace as a fertilizer develop severe allergic reactions.

In spite of precautions, accidents will happen, so it's a good idea to be prepared. The first thing to do if someone has eaten a poisonous plant part is to induce vomiting by giving a tablespoon of salt in a glass of warm water, if the patient is conscious. Keep the patient quiet and warm. Apply artificial respiration if he is not breathing. Try to get the patient to a doctor or to the closest medical facility as quickly as possible.

If you eat weed plants, wild fruits, or wild vegetables, be sure you know exactly what they are. Unless you happen to be an expert, it's best to leave wild mushrooms strictly alone. The list of cultivated fruits and vegetables is long, and unless you've become lost in the woods or fields, I'd stick to them.

Controlling Small Animals in the Vegetable and Fruit Garden

Vegetables are good not only for bugs, birds, and people, but also many small animal pests. When it's all boiled down, fencing is the easiest way to keep animals out. Here are a few pests and their control:

BYE BYE BAD BIRDS! Our feathered friends can be fiends in the fruit and garden patch. They snip off tips of tomatoes and peppers, tear off ears of corn, eat holes in tomatoes, rob cherries, grapes, strawberries, blueberries, and other fruits.

In vegetable garden, cover transplants with bushel baskets, crates, etc. In fruit garden, best control consists of covering strawberries, blueberries, cherries, etc., with one of the netting materials (anti-bird netting) made of plastic or nylon. These are draped over the vegetables or fruits. These materials can be taken down and used year after year. (See illustration.)

Lightweight and easy to handle, nylon bird screen lets rain and sun in and keeps birds out. (Conwed Products)

Scare Devices: Try a scarecrow made of Grandpa's plug hat, Dad's old coat, and Junior's worn-out pants. A change of scares every few days is a must. Otherwise the birds will get used to them.

Stuffed "snakes," owls, rags, fur pieces, etc., used in tree or garden must be changed frequently also.

Noisemakers: Firecrackers are woven in a fuse rope at intervals of ½ foot. You light the rope, and it burns slowly at the rate of ½ foot every 55 minutes, igniting a fuse and touching off a cherry bomb. You must get a permit to use this.

Some folks use tin cans on strings suspended between posts. Commercial fruit growers use automatic acetylene exploders.

If tree is near kitchen, put a bell in tree, pull string every time you see robins snitching cherries. Radio in strawberry patch playing rock 'n' roll music scares away the birds.

Flashy Devices: Tin-can tops on string, shiny foil-backed paper that winds and unwinds (you see this at gas stations).

Firearms: Some folks in the country use firearms' discharge, especially .22 rifles to scare off birds, but THIS TYPE OF AMMUNITION IS DANGEROUS WITHIN DISTANCE OF A MILE. Far better to use firecracker ropes, or other noisemaking devices.

DEER INJURY: Deer do a lot of damage to young fruit trees and ornamental plants. The male deer (buck) has a covering of "velvet" on the horns, and in an effort to remove this, will select young springy plantings. Their small size and great flexibility aid the deer in rubbing off the velvet. The result is a badly skinned or broken tree.

Control: Place stakes so they project 3 or 4 feet above the ground, and in a triangular fashion around the tree. Hardware cloth around the trunk is helpful, but does not protect the branches above. The Conservation Department recommends a rosin-alcohol mixture for repelling both rabbits and deer. Mix 7 pounds of powdered rosin in a gallon of denatured alcohol, set in a warm place for a day or 2 till rosin is dissolved. Spray or paint mixture on bark of trees or shrubs from ground level to safely above the height of expected damage. Rosin mixture will last all winter and turns whitish on hardening. Use a fence.

DOGS AND CATS: These pets can be a nuisance sometimes. Spray shrubs with nicotine sulfate, 1 teaspoon to 2 quarts of soapy water, every 5 days. These animals do not like the smell. If dogs constantly dig up your tulip bulbs, use superphosphate instead of bone meal fertilizer.

MOLES: Not harmful to crops. Cause tunnels, burrows. Moles do a lot of good by eating grubs and insects. As far as we know, they do not eat plant roots, but do leave unsightly ridges and mounds in lawns.

Control: Buy harpoon-type traps from hardware. Very good for catching moles. Mothballs, Chlordane in runways discourage moles. Flooding runways with hose water in spring will drown young moles and mice.

MOSQUITOES: Spray edge of garden shrubs with Malathion. Spray stagnant areas.

OPOSSUMS: Will eat mushrooms, berries, vegetables, corn. Trap with box traps.

RABBITS: Will eat vegetables, shrubs, and flowers in summer or winter. Trees can be protected by wrapping trunks with newspapers, building paper, aluminum foil, aluminum mesh, or hardware cloth. Multiple-stemmed shrubs can't be wrapped, so use chemical repellents. Chemical repellents sold at various seed and supply stores are the only practical treatment for small seedlings, tulips, shrubs, etc., so you might want to try some. They will also repel deer. Rabbits do not like creosote. Dip strips of roofing felt in creosote and place along edge of garden.

Trapping: Trapping rabbits with the old familiar box trap is humane. Rabbits are active in late evening and early morning. Set the box trap where they enter, catch them alive and transport them some distance away to release. Wire fences help keep rabbits out of gardens if carefully erected and if the mesh is not greater than 1½ inches.

Fruit growers, nurserymen, householders may want to try the Ringwood Repellent. Fall is a good time to apply any repellent. We've had good success repelling deer and rabbits by applying repellent after leaves have fallen, and before snow has fallen. The coating makes leaves so bad-tasting to animals, they leave it alone. Contains an adhesive so it sticks better.

RATS, MICE, AND VOLES: Field mice aren't nice. Every year field mice damage fruit trees, hedges, and ornamental shrubs and the innocent mole gets the blame. Moles seldom attack plants—95% of their diet consists of worms, grubs, and bugs. However, there are molelike mice which have ravaging teeth and these are the real villains.

Field mice swarm in salt marshes, slopes, lush meadows, neglected fields and even vacant suburban lots, overgrown to tall weeds. They like areas where dead grasses shield them from the telescopic eyes of soaring hawks. Newborn mice can shift for themselves when 12 days old, and females become mature at the ripe old age of 4 weeks. A female can bear 17 litters in a year, and a litter can be anywhere from 3 to 8. No other mammal is more fertile than the mouse.

Field mice come in cycles, about every 4 years. You get them in between so be prepared for these pests. They work during the winter and their damage is not revealed until the snow disappears.

Voles, another rodent species, do damage to fruit trees and crops.

Prevention: Wrap the trunks of your fruit trees with screen. Make sure it is sunk into the ground an inch or 2 and held together by wire. Some use aluminum foil as a temporary guard. Commercial growers use poisoned baits such as zinc phosphide, finely powdered arsenic compounds, and other materials. The U.S. Fish and Wildlife Service prepares poisoned baits for mouse control. ALL RAT AND MOUSE BAITS ARE POISONOUS SO HANDLE THEM WITH CARE. Around young fruit trees, a pile of ashes or cinders is good to discourage mice. Trim sod away from trunk, to discourage nesting. You can also use snap back mouse traps baited with oat flakes or peanut butter. Place the traps under spreading evergreens.

Mice aren't altogether useless! Birds, snakes, skunks, bears, and other animals use them for food. Even fish will eat mice when they venture into the water.

SKUNKS: Often dig up lawns and gardens looking for grubs to eat. Scatter Chlordane in lawn to kill the grubs and skunks won't bother. Under buildings skunks can be trapped.

SNAILS AND SLUGS: Slugs may be defined as snails without shells. A snail is capable of withdrawing its body inside a hard shell. Slugs and snails lay eggs in masses of from a few to 40 or more, in a moist location, and one pest alone can lay as many as 100 eggs. Snails do heavy damage because of the many teeth they have to satisfy their hungry appetites. One common slug in a garden or greenhouse has 85 teeth in a single row, and there are 100 rows, making a total of 8,500 teeth in a single critter!

Slugs live where there is dampness, since these night marauders like it moist during the day, when they hide under boards, leafy trash, or stones. At night they do their dirty work. Slugs and snails travel along with a sliding movement on their "foot," exuding a slimy mucus to lubricate their trail. That silvery track you see on the ground or on plants is the mucus secreted by these gruesome pests.

Control: They don't like dry materials, such as lime, wood ashes, etc. Scatter these over the affected areas. Control has been outstanding using a 10% methaldehyde and 5% Chlordane dust scattered in infected areas. In the garden or strawberry patch, place dampened shingles, boards, etc. between the rows so these slimy pests will hide under them during the day, then go out and scrape them off and destroy. Some of our friends put orange and grapefruit halves in the rows; a poison such as arsenate of lead or metaldehyde is put inside the "cup." Snails have a sweet tooth for citrus rinds and once they crawl underneath to eat it they're finished.

Beer Is a Good Snail Killer!: A reader wrote: "Sometime ago you said that a gardener put beer in pie tins around his tomato vines and he never had a bit of trouble with slugs or snails. I want to tell you it works! About the 15th of August when the first of the tomatoes were getting ripe, slugs or snails started to come around (they never touch green tomatoes). I put some beer in pie plates around the tomatoes at night. The next day the plates were loaded with the snails, either dead or dead drunk or both! Snails and slugs would rather drink the beer than eat the tomatoes. Beer is cheaper and safer to use than poisonous baits and it sure did the trick."

SNAKES: You can discourage snakes from staying around grounds and buildings by removing boards, rock piles, etc. Closely mowed lawns are less favorable to snakes than areas of tall grass. If a snake enters the home, it may be looking for hibernating quarters, or mice. You can trap a snake by putting wet cloths on the floor near where the snake is thought to be. Cover wet cloths with dry cloths or burlap bags. Snake will crawl under or between the cloths.

Methoxychlor may be scattered heavily in snake area. Turkeys make good alarm-bells, gobbling noisily if snake is around, while geese, ducks, and chickens will also kill and eat snakes they can manage. Some dogs and cats are good snake-killers. Hogs will eat snakes. If you kill a snake, crush its head, because snakes often play dead if stunned. A snake's head can inflict a bite even when cut off the body. Do not destroy snakes indiscriminately because only a small percentage are poisonous and a great many feed on home and garden pests.

SQUIRRELS, CHIPMUNKS, RACOONS: Difficult to check. Try wire guards or shooting where permitted.

WASPS AND HORNETS: These are beneficial, but unwelcome. Find nests and remove at night, then burn (see Grapes).

WOODCHUCKS: Shooting is effective, also trapping. Run automobile exhaust pipe into the hole in spring to kill entire brood. Attach a hose to the exhaust pipe and seal around the hose where it enters the burrow. Twenty minutes or ½ hour should be effective.

GARDEN SUPERSTITIONS DEBUNKED

Home gardeners shouldn't be bogged down with a lot of scare rules for growing crops. Here are a few rules which don't hold water.

1. Rows must Run North and South. False. Garden rows can run east and west or north and south. If they run east and west, plant the tall-growing crops on the north side of garden so they don't shade the shorter ones.

2. Should Seeds and Plants Be Planted by Signs of the Moon? Not necessarily. There is no scientific proof that vegetables should be planted according to phases of the moon. Nor are there records to substantiate the theory that frosts are more likely to occur when the moon is full. *Note*: I can see how moonlight might affect plant growth, and I feel that it does provide some benefit.

3. Cross-pollination Between Vegetables: Don't worry about your vegetable plants crossing, since you probably won't save your seed. It is true that many closely related vegetables will cross-pollinate. For example, hot peppers with sweet peppers, summer squash with winter pumpkins, watermelons with citron, to name a few. But the effect is only on the seed, and not the fruits. Thus, you can safely plant melons with cucumbers, red tomatoes next to yellow ones. In fact, any vegetable may be mixed in every possible combination without influencing the edible portion. *Note*: One exception. Sweet corn planted near field corn, popcorn, or ornamental (Indian corn) might get pollen from these and take on a different color, shape, and flavor of the kernels. Another fallacy: Vegetables don't do well unless there's a male and a female plant nearby.

4. Plant in Spring According to Flowering Trees: It's often recommended to plant certain vegetables to coincide with flowering of certain trees and shrubs. This is OK as it reflects the advancement of spring. But it's safer to plant when old-timers near you say "all danger of frost has gone," with the exception of cool-weather crops such as lettuce, peas, and radishes.

5. Chemical Fertilizers are Poisonous: I never like to take issue with organic gardeners because we practice organic gardening to a point in our garden. Animal manure, decaying leaves, kitchen refuse, grass clippings, compost are all fine, but there's no reason why you can't also add some commercial fertilizer, particularly nitrogen, phosphorus, and potash. Chemical fertilizers will not injure plants, kill earthworms, or harm people. Pesticides used with caution are also safe. Be sure to wash your crops after using pesticides.

UNUSUAL USES FOR VEGETABLES

Vegetables in Outdoor Flower Borders: No room for growing vegetables, you say? Then try this trick: Combine them with annuals in the flower border. Vegetable plants can serve a dual purpose here, providing food as well as making an attractive display. The only caution: Plant vegetables and flowers of the same height together, choose those whose colors blend well, and select vegetables which give an interesting appearance even after the fruits are harvested. As an example, the University of Minnesota suggests the purple and red pigment in the tassels and stalks of midget sweet corn as a colorful accent to the back of a border.

Vegetables may be used in the foreground, middle, or background of the flower border. But be sure to use a number of plants, half a dozen, 8 or 9—not just one.

The following are some dual-purpose vegetables the University recommends as possibilities for combining with appropriate annuals. For the background: pole beans (could be used on a trellis as screen), sweet corn (midget types), and staked hybrid tomatoes.

Middle of the border: Use vegetables of medium height—Royal Purple bush beans, Ruby Queen or King Red beets, eggplants, purple and green kale, Jade or Catskill Brussels sprouts, Nantes carrots, purple cauliflower, Savoy King or Emerald Cross cabbage, Peter Piper pepper, Rhubarb or Burgundy chard, zucchini or Patty Pan squash.

Edging plants: parsley, leaf lettuce, Bibb lettuce, purple and green kohlrabi, endive, herbs of various kinds.

City gardeners short of space should use planters to add beauty to the patio or rooftop. Dwarf vegetable plants like tomatoes (Tiny Tim) with their small fruits lend themselves especially well to planting in combination with flowers in tubs and special containers. Other appropriate vegetable plants are Ruby Queen beets for their colorful foliage, the very ornamental Nosegay and Pinocchio peppers, and parsley interplanted with Salad Trim lettuce and purple kohlrabi.

Growing Vegetables on a Roof: With land shrinking, many city dwellers may be growing vegetables and flowers on the roof. An 80 square foot plot of soil can produce substantial crops. You'll need drainage holes in the bottom of any soil container used in "sky farming." You can make containers out of wood or cinder blocks. A container or box 10 to 12 inches deep is satisfactory, though depth of soil can vary according to the crop you intend to grow. For example radishes and lettuce can be grown in shallower containers, requiring less soil to fill, than can carrots.

Tomatoes, radishes, carrots, beets, kale, lettuce, kohlrabi, spinach, bush beans are a few easy-to-grow vegetables for a rooftop garden.

Apartment dwellers and homeowners with access to roofs can derive untold pleasure and satisfaction from raising a good crop of vegetables—and it might be possible that many thousands of acres of rooftops might be used for growing vegetables in the "farms of the future."

Vegetables for Indoor "Flower" Arrangements: Many readers tell us that vegetables are useful in "flower" arrangements. For a pretty table decoration, cut a beef in half and place the upper part in a black bowl with some colored stones. A little water is added. Green and red leaves appear and last a long time. Very attractive.

Regular kale makes a beautiful foliage in bouquets and then there's ornamental kale, with soft cream, pink, lavender, and green shading, plus crinkled and frilled edges. Dark opal basil is a fine herb with reddish-purple leaves and spikes of blue flowers. Rhubarb chard has crimson stalks and veins, with artistically "crumpled" leaves. Good for summer arrangements. Bronzed lettuce is a fine border for a flower bed, and the leaves can be used at the bases of arrangements. A friend of mine made an unusual arrangement of forced rhubarb leaves with potatoes at the base.

Vegetable flowers are also attractive in arrangements. Try sprays of yellow broccoli flowers, or the cream-yellow blooms of okra (a real "orphan" in today's gardens). And don't forget the heads of Purple Head cauliflower.

Gourd and pumpkin centerpieces: Ever try arranging chrysanthemums and autumn leaves in a colored pumpkin or gourd? Scoop out the insides of the pumpkin (use "meat" for pies) or gourd, clean the outside, and insert a vase of water that cannot be seen (a small jelly jar is fine). Then arrange your flowers. You'll have an unusual and eye-catching decoration which is very "Octobery."

TIPS FOR USING VEGETABLES

Home Storage of Vegetables: The old-fashioned root cellar went out when the freezer and improved preserving methods came in. If you're interested in storing your crops remember this rule: Fruits and vegetables are still living parts of plants, and the cooler you can keep them the better. An orchardist-friend recommends sinking a clean garbage can in the garden for storing crops. The can is fitted with a tight cover and covered with a pile of straw to a depth of 2 feet. Heat from the ground will keep the fruits and vegetables in fine condition. Another trick is to use an old refrigerator buried backside down in the garden. BE SURE TO KNOCK THE LOCK OFF so no curious child could possibly lock himself in. My neighbor's 8-cubic-foot refrigerator, stripped, holds 5 bushels of produce and has kept apples and vegetables in 20-below-zero weather, although he still covers it with straw for extra protection.

Cooking Tips: Be sure to wash all fresh vegetables thoroughly to remove chemical residues, soil or sand, and insects. A vegetable brush is the best way to reach all those little crevices.

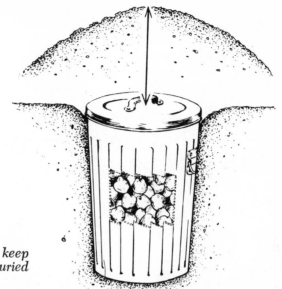

Fruits and vegetables keep well in galvanized can buried in garden in winter.

Cook vegetables like carrots, beets, turnips, potatoes, etc., with the skins on, for full flavor and health value. Use as little water as possible in cooking vegetables, and cook tightly covered. Better yet, use a pressure cooker, if you have one.

Save Vegetable Cooking Waters: Cooking waters contain large amounts of valuable vitamins and minerals. For example, from 9 to 54% of the thiamine and riboflavin in vegetables are dissolved in the cooking water. If this water is thrown away, these food values are lost, even from frozen vegetables. The cooking water includes the frost of frozen vegetables, and should be saved and used. Cooking water can be used in juice cocktails, soups, sauces, gravies, stews, pot roasts, and casserole dishes.

You can also shred, sliver, slice, make into sizeable sticks, or julienne such old-timers as squash, beets, carrots, eggplant, cucumbers, celery, parsnips, turnips, and broccoli stems. Some may be cooked first, then cut into small balls with a melon baller.

See specific vegetables for many appetizing uses of your garden crops.

Vegetables With Fruits: Flavor and prettify certain vegetables by teaming them up with fruits. After cooking the vegetable just enough, butter and heat with these suggested fruits, fresh or canned.

Take carrots, beets, or winter squash—add drained, crushed pineapple chunks or bits, orange segments, mandarin oranges, thin, thin lemon half-slices, diced apricots, pears, or nectarines, peaches, seeded black or red grape quarters.

CHAPTER VIII

The Most Important
Vegetables

ARTICHOKE

The familiar globe artichoke (*Cyanara cardunculus*) is a variation of the thistle-like cardoon, and just one of several unrelated types of plants referred to as artichokes. The part of the globe artichoke used for food is the bud of the flower, which is picked before it is open. Of the large outer leaves only the small fleshy base is useful but the center leaves are tender almost to the tip. The spiny center called the "choke" is not edible.

The globe artichoke is not recommended in areas where the season is short. In fact, the California coastline is one of the few places they grow well. They are vigorous growers and need at least 18 square feet for each plant.

The Jerusalem artichoke (*Helianthus tuberosus*) is not an artichoke at all, nor has it anything to do with Jerusalem. The name is a corruption of "girasole"—turning to the sun. Girasole was perverted to Jerusalem (how?) and then someone added the artichoke tag to confuse matters even worse. Actually, it is an American sunflower, known by its Indian name of Sun-root. American Indians originally ate the white tuberous root which contains a starchlike material which can be safely eaten by diabetics. Roots sold in health food stores are inferior in flavor to the homegrown crop.

The Jerusalem artichoke is started from tubers. Grows 6 to 8 feet tall. This is a vigorous grower and may spread. The Jerusalem or American artichoke is simple to grow, and produces a heavy crop. Freezing improves flavor, so dig them as late as possible in fall, or in

202

a winter thaw, or in spring before they sprout. Boil and serve with cream, or dice raw, chill, and mix with salads.

TROUBLES

Aphids: Spray with Malathion.

Asparagus (*Asparagus officinalis*)

Every home should have a small asparagus patch. It's a high-priced item in stores. According to records asparagus has been growing in gardens for a little over 2,000 years. We know of some plantings that are over 50 years old and still producing good crops. Before asparagus was used as a food, it had quite a reputation as a medicine for almost anything—from the treatment of beestings to curing a toothache.

The Greeks apparently collected asparagus only from the wild but the Romans, as early as 200 B.C., gave detailed instructions for the cultivation of this plant. Asparagus has been grown in the gardens of America since the earliest settlements were established.

Soil: Asparagus will grow in any well-drained soil. Soil should be neutral or almost alkaline. If acid, add some lime to sweeten it. Add all the humus you can before planting. Enrich with manure, compost, or bone meal.

Sex of Asparagus: Asparagus is unique among our vegetable crops in that it has both male and female plants. That is why you find seed pods only on about half of the plants. These are the pistillate or female plants. The others are male plants.

Male plants yield about 25% higher than female plants. One gardener asked me if it wouldn't pay to plant a patch entirely with male plants and in that way obtain a higher yield. On the surface, this sounds quite sensible, but there's a hitch to it. Higher yields of male plants are usually offset by a decrease in the size of spears. In other words, male plants yield more, but female plants have larger stalks. Male plants have 3 to 5 times as many stalks as the female plants, but the individual spears are smaller.

Also, young asparagus plants are like baby chicks—it's nearly impossible to tell males from females. You don't have to pay much attention to sex of these plants because you'll get a mixture of both when you buy them.

Buying Plants: Allow 15 plants for each member of the family. If you plan to freeze also, allow 25 plants for each member of the family.

To start a new bed it's probably best to buy new plants from your seedsman. Large 1-year-old crowns are best. Many 1-year-old crowns have larger and more vigorous roots than do lots of the 2-year-old crowns. A good crown should have 10 or more roots at least 6 inches long.

If you want to sow asparagus seed, you can grow your own plants. There are about 1,500 seeds to an ounce. Soak seed 24 hours before planting. After they come up be sure to thin them out to 2 inches apart in the row.

Setting the Crowns: Spring is best time to plant. In sandy soils, set plants 6 inches below ground level. In heavy soils, shallower planting is suggested, but it may be wise to winter-protect in areas of severe temperatures. Some use a trench, others don't. Spread roots out flat, keeping the buds so they point upward. A couple of inches of topsoil is firmed around them. Don't fill the trench until later on. Too much soil may keep weak plants from starting, too little may allow the roots to dry out. Commercial growers set the crowns 18 to 24 inches apart, in rows 3 to 6 feet apart, but in the small home garden you can plant as close as 12"x30". As the plants get good strong shoots several inches tall, and danger of frost is over, the trench is gradually filled. Just add soil to those roots that have sent out top growth.

I never like to transplant old roots. You might better start all over again, using 1-year shoots, obtainable from your own patch or from a qualified seed house. Some folks divide their crowns in the spring and they have fair success, especially if the roots are in good shape.

Asparagus was formerly grown with the soil ridged high over the roots so the shoots would develop white. We have now learned that green shoots are more colorful and nutritious, and ridging is no longer practiced.

Annual Care: Work in some 5–10–10 or 5–10–5 fertilizer each spring before the spears start, at rate of 5 pounds for each 100 square feet or for each 25 linear feet of asparagus row. Manure is good for asparagus, but it encourages weed growth. If asparagus plants are set out in spring, don't harvest any shoots until the second spring. At that time you can cut a few spears, but it is better to wait until the third spring. It's a good idea to wait until the bed is established fully before cutting heavily. The third year after setting you can cut for 4 weeks, older plantings until about July 1, unless the spears become spindly before that date. For an established bed, 8 weeks of cutting is enough. After the harvest season, the tops should be allowed to grow until winter.

Salt: The old and still persistent idea that salt is particularly good for asparagus has been pretty much discredited. Recent experiments have indicated that salt is of little value as long as there is adequate potash in the regular fertilizer. Salt is still used as a weed killer (which see).

Weed Killers: Fine ground salt is used for killing weeds on asparagus. Use a solution of 2 pounds per gallon of water when weeds are 3 inches high. That's the only value salt has in asparagus plantings. You can also use calcium cyanamid. A single application (1 pound to 40 feet of row) should nearly eliminate hoeing during cutting season. After cutting has stopped, give another dose. Cyanamid has 22% nitrogen, so has fertilizer value. OVERDOSE MAY KILL THE ROOTS AS WELL AS WEEDS. Apply while weeds are less than 1 inch tall.

Sesone is good on asparagus. If top layer of soil is dry, moisten by sprinkling with water, after applying. Here's how to figure the rate of application (always following instructions on labels):

AREA TO BE TREATED	AMOUNT TO USE	AMOUNT OF WATER NEEDED	
		For sprayer	*For sprinkling can*
200 sq. ft.	1 level tbsp.	1 gal.	3 gals.
400 sq. ft.	2 level tbsp.	2 gals.	6 gals.

Sesone will not kill weeds that are up. It kills the germinating seeds and seeds resting in the ground. Apply it before seeds start to grow. The hoe is still the best weed killer for the home gardener!

Winter Care: Some gardeners like to cut the plants down in fall to prevent seeds from scattering. Others like to leave the plants on until spring, since the plants hold the snow as mulch. This is desirable. If you want to cut the plants back because they look unsightly in fall or winter, leave 8- or 10-inch stubs so they'll hold the mulch of snow.

Harvesting: Spears should be allowed to grow at least 8 inches above the ground, unless the heads begin to bud out. Harvesting at much shorter growth reduces the yield. Tests show that you can increase yield by snapping the spears off, instead of cutting them. To snap asparagus you grasp the stalk just below the head, and give it a push or slight bend. The stalk will snap off at its tenderest point, and you'll have a stalk that is 100% tender, without the least bit of toughness or fiber. Cutting or breaking the spears slightly above ground saves all that is usable and prevents the destruction of any young invisible spears. Cutting below the surface unknowingly destroys many oncoming spears and thereby reduces the harvests.

Cooking: To be sure asparagus will keep its best flavor, the proper cooking procedure must be followed. If it is to be boiled, the asparagus should be tied in bunches and placed upright, with tips protruding 1 inch above the surface of the boiling water. It should be left in this position until the butts begin to be tender. Then the bunches should be untied and the entire spears immersed in the boiling water and cooked for 5 or 10 minutes, until tender.

TROUBLES

If your asparagus was tough and pithy you can blame it on either lack of fertility, an acid soil, or allowing spears to get too old before cutting.

Black Spots and Chewed Tips: This is the work of the asparagus beetle (see illustration p. 186), a pest that feeds on the stalks for a few days, and then starts laying eggs. The small black eggs are laid separately, and one end is stuck to the tips. When the infestation is heavy, the tips appear black, due to the many eggs laid. These eggs hatch into small, sluglike larvae which feed on the spears.

Control: Dust the tips with 1% rotenone dust or Sevin or spray with rotenone, all during the cutting season. Material should be applied as soon as the tips appear and every week thereafter. You can use Malathion spray or dust AFTER the cutting season is over, or on new beds not being cut. For spears you're going to eat, use Sevin or rotenone only, and wash spears before eating. Never use DDT on the spears.

Rust on Stems: Rust disease of asparagus. Rust can often be prevented by planting rust-resistant varieties, although I don't believe there is a 100% rust-resistant strain of asparagus. Try Mary or Martha Washington, or any of the selections carrying the Washington name. Waltham Washington and Viking (Mary Washington Improved) are especially rust-resistant.

BEAN (*Phaseolus vulgaris*)

Snap Beans: Snap beans are eaten fresh, pod and all, and come in "bush" and "pole," or climbing, types. Few garden vegetables yield so much. If picked frequently, beans will continue to produce over a long season.

Planting: The dwarf or bush varieties can be planted in rows 2 or 3 feet apart. Drop the beans (eyes down) about every 2 inches, cover with 1 inch of soil. If planted 3 inches apart, no thinning will be required. Do not plant until the soil is warm, or the beans will rot in the ground. It's not safe to plant the main supply of beans until after the ground has been warmed. After that, you can plant them at intervals of 2 or 3 weeks, if a constant supply of green beans is wanted. Beans are a warm-weather crop and will not germinate if the ground is cold and wet.

Pole beans do best if vines are supported on poles or a trellis of some sort. I take rough poles from the woods and sink them firmly into the ground. Then about 5 or 6 beans are planted around each stake, and thinned to 3 strongest plants. You can also tie poles together at the top, tepee-fashion. Or you can plant pole beans in a row along a fence or trellis, thinning to about 8 inches apart.

Lima Beans: A light sandy soil will produce the best set of lima bean pods, although limas will tolerate a workable clay soil. A good baby lima is Thaxter, having bush vines. Fordhook U.S. 242 is another good bush lima, good fresh, canned, or frozen. If you want a good pole lima, try King of the Garden.

Planting: Lima beans are not as hardy as snap beans and shouldn't be planted as early. They like to be planted when the ground is good and warm, otherwise the seed will rot. Plant them 1 inch deep, 3 beans to every 15 inches of row, in rows 3 feet apart. Make sure you place the eyes downward (makes a difference in yield for all beans). Thin to 8 to 12 inches apart.

Give the plants plenty of room and you'll have larger yields. A good point to keep in mind about lima beans is that they resent deep cultivation. Stirring the soil will cause the buds and blossoms to drop. So will a soil too rich in nitrogen. Bud drop may also be caused by hot, dry weather, overfertilization, or cloudy, wet weather. Prevent dropping of flowers and increase yields considerably by mulching your plants with grass clippings or black plastic film. Hormone sprays, available in aerosol cans at your garden-supply store, may also help hold blossoms.

Fava or Horse Beans Are Good!: Bean lovers are in for a real treat if they are willing to try the fava or broad bean, sometimes called horse bean, a misnomer. Fava plants are upright, contain 6 or 8 flat oblong beans in each 7-inch pod. Fava beans can be cooked fresh or as a winter shell bean with an unusually good flavor. Plant seed early in spring, as soon as soil can be worked, since they don't like hot weather. Set seed about 8 inches apart in rows 3 feet apart. Takes 80 to 85 days to mature a crop.

Dried beans for home use are grown in much the same way as garden beans except that the beans are allowed to ripen fully. Shell out the beans, dry thoroughly in a warm place, and then treat for weevils by placing the seed in an oven at about 130° F. for 30 minutes (see Bean Weevil).

TROUBLES

To avoid bean troubles: 1) Start out with disease-resistant varieties; 2) use disease-free seed; 3) plant your beans in a new spot each year; 4) never weed, dust, cultivate, or pick beans when they are wet, as this spreads diseases; 5) pull up plants and put them on the compost pile or burn as soon as crop is harvested.

Bean Beetle: Feeds on undersides of leaves. Control: Dust with Sevin or rotenone. Be sure to cover undersides of leaves. Also handpick those orange-colored egg masses underneath, as this will reduce beetle population before it gets started.

Bean Weevil: Many gardeners raise good beans in the garden, only to have them turn "buggy" or full of weevils during storage. Bean weevils can ruin a jar of dry or shell beans, making them unfit for food or seed. The weevil begins its work by attacking the growing pods in the garden. When the dry beans are hulled and stored they are already infested with the small white grubs. When beans are stored in a warm place the grubs mature and eat their way out of the dry beans, leaving small holes in the bean.

When you eat fresh green beans from the garden you unknowingly eat the tiny grubs. But the buggy dried beans are not appetizing. Here's how to lick them: (1) Store beans in cans in an unheated out-building or porch (beans won't freeze). (2) Or you can dip the beans in boiling water for 1 minute and then spread them out to dry (not usable for beans to be used as seed). (3) Or, heat the beans in a shallow open container in an oven for 30 minutes at 130° F.

Seeds may be heated to a temperature of from 130° to 145° F. with-

Bean anthracnose. Masses of light-colored spores of the anthracnose fungus are produced in the centers of the spots. (USDA Photo)

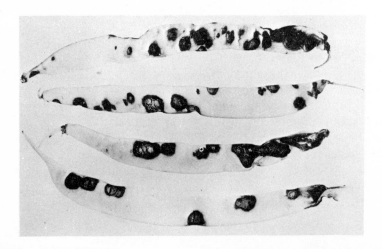

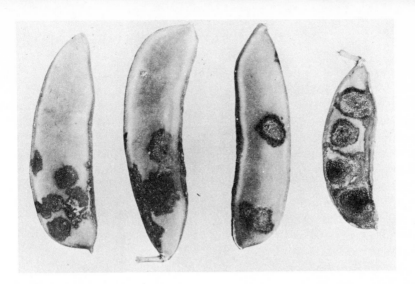

Lima beans shown here are damaged by common blight, a bacterial disease. (USDA Photo)

out affecting their germination. A temperature of 135° F. for 1 hour will kill almost any type of weevil which may be encountered. In heating the seed, it is necessary to spread it thinly so that the interior will reach the proper temperature.

Some folks mix the beans with hydrated lime, using 1 pint of lime to each quart of beans. Some gardeners use carbon disulphide (inflammable!), 3 tablespoons for each 10 cubic feet of space, a clean garbage can being ideal for this treatment. Keep cover on for 24 to 36 hours.

Storage After Treating: After seed has been fumigated or heated, it is possible for it to become reinfested with weevil if it is not stored properly. Small quantities should be placed in tin containers or boxes, while larger quantities are reasonably safe when stored in tight cotton bags. Weevils are able to penetrate burlap bags, so they should not be used.

Anthracnose: (see illustration) Causes black sunken cankers on pods, stems rot off as they emerge from the ground. Control: Grow resistant varieties. Use well-drained soil and practice 3- to 6-year rotation with other crops.

Halo, "Rust," or Bacterial Blight: (see illustration) Similar to anthracnose. Whole leaf becomes spotted, then dies, drops off. Large brown patches develop from small spots on pods. Pods develop greasy wet spots and ooze. Beans inside pods are shriveled, misshapen, and unfit to eat. Bean patches near lilacs, flowering balsam, pear, sweet cherry are apt to get bacterial spot. Blight is worse in wet seasons, one reason why you should stay out of the bean patch when the leaves are wet. Manure from sheep or cattle fed on contaminated plants will also spread the disease to the soil.

Control: Insist on certified bean seed, and plant in ground not used for beans for at least 2 years. Sprays or dusts are not effective or practical as yet, and so far as I know there is no resistant snap bean variety. Researchers are said to have a new resistant kidney bean, but we haven't seen it or tried it.

Mosaic: (see illustration) Light-yellow leaves, caused by virus. Infection favored by high temperature and high humidity. No control. Do not grow beans in areas near gladiolus, or where tomatoes, peppers, eggplants, or potatoes have been growing.

Dry Root Rot: Plant parts above ground rot or turn yellow. Control: Clean up bean refuse in fall and burn. Practice crop rotation. Avoid close cultivation.

Aphids, Leafhoppers: Check with Malathion.

White Mold Mildew: Causes infected pods to turn into soft watery masses, may girdle the stem. White cottony growth ("snow patches"). Worse in rich, wet soils. Control: Dust or spray with Terraclor (PCNB) at time of first bloom, preferably after last cultivation.

Powdery Mildew: (see illustration) White patches on leaves. Dust with zineb or Copper.

Aphids spread the mosaic virus by feeding on infected and then on healthy plants. Yellow mosaic (shown here) is identified by the striking contrast between yellow and green areas of the affected leaves. (USDA Photo)

Powdery mildew, a fungus disease that develops very rapidly. The crop could still be saved by dusting with finely ground sulfur. If not dusted, the plants will lose all their leaves. (USDA Photo)

Pod Blight: Worse on pole limas than on bush varieties. Spread by splashing rain or washing dirt. Spray or dust with Captan.

Leafhopper: Partial cause of bud drop. Dust with Sevin after beans start blooming. Leafhoppers must be controlled for high yields of straight pods.

Yellow Leaves: Due to old age. If on young productive plants blame it on leafhoppers, pests with piercing and sucking mouthparts. After you pick a leaf to look at it, the hopper skips off quickly, and that's why the untrained eye sees no insect on the troubled leaf. Control: Dust or spray leaves with Malathion or Sevin as soon as the plants begin to show this injury. Severely yellowed and stunted plants might not be benefited. Gardeners who make successive plantings of beans should plan to protect the new seedlings and plantings with Sevin or Malathion at weekly intervals, particularly during the early growth.

USES

Green beans can be frenched, diced, cut diagonally, or left whole if small. Bunch together a handful and slice off ¼-inch "dices," or cut on the bias.

Green Beans Cape Cod Style: 4 cups diced green beans or wax beans, 1 teaspoon sugar, 2 tablespoons butter, 3 tablespoons heavy cream, salt and white pepper. Cook beans in as little water as possible in a covered saucepan for a few minutes, until crisp-tender. Drain and stir in sugar, butter, and cream. Season to taste with salt and pepper. Heat thoroughly. Serves 4.

Mustard Sauce for Cold Beans: ½ cup mayonnaise, 2 tablespoons prepared mustard, ½ teaspoon horseradish, 1 tablespoon vinegar, 1 tablespoon chopped onion, salt, cooked string beans, lettuce leaves. Blend first 6 ingredients well. Mix with cold cooked string beans. Serve on crisp lettuce leaves.

Salting Down Beans: A gardener wrote: "I'd like to tell you how to salt down snap beans as I've done it for years. In a crock I place layers of uncooked beans, cut into strips, and handfuls of pure table salt. After you build up a crock of beans, some water will accumulate, then you place some grape leaves on, and place a plate over them. A stone is placed over the plate until it forms a brine. Diced bacon and a bit of vinegar help to freshen up the beans when you're ready to eat them. With this method of keeping beans, one can have them practically fresh all winter."

BEETS (*Beta vulgaris*)

Beets are easy to grow, yield heavily, and are rich in iron and vitamins, especially when the tops are included for greens. This has been called a "double-header" vegetable in that both the fleshy roots and tops are edible. Young plants from thinning the row make ideal beet greens.

Planting: Beets are so hardy the seed can be sown in the ground very early. Sow seed in rows 14 to 18 inches apart, dropping 1 or 2 seeds to an inch of row. Cover with ½ inch of soil. Don't plant too thickly. Each "seed" has 1 to 4 seeds in it. When plants are quite small thin to 4 or 5 plants per foot of row.

A second planting in early July will give nice tender beets for fall use and winter storing. If you want to raise beets for greens only, just sow the seed thickly in rows 1 foot apart. Feed and water to promote quick growth. The tops may be used when about 5 to 8 inches tall. Some gardeners who like beet greens sow the seed thick in a broad row, 4 to 6 inches wide, and when the tops are 3 to 5 inches tall, they are thinned out and used as tender greens. This method of sowing takes 1 ounce of seed for 20 feet of row. Harvest when roots are 1 to 1½ inches across for tops, but roots can be harvested up to 3 inches. Small beets are better to eat than large ones, so you should make several sowings to keep new crops coming in to be harvested in their prime. Store beets in cool cellar.

Beets are lime-lovers, so if yours look yellowed, stunted, and off-color as if they're dying, then look to the soil for trouble. If your garden hasn't been limed in the past 4 or 5 years, scatter 35 pounds of lime on 1,000 square feet. But don't forget you can over-lime your beet soil.

TROUBLES

Black Spots and Dry Rot: Condition due to a lack of boron in the soil. In severe cases, a boron deficiency may turn the beets black as if they were struck by a dry rot. You often see this trouble in sweet (alkaline) soils, or soils heavily limed. Boron is less available in sweet soils.

Over-liming makes the soil too sweet. If your test shows this (see Liming and Soil Acidity), use ½ pound of manganese sulfate and 1½ tablespoons household borax to each 100 square feet of garden. Or you can use sulfur at the rate of 1 pound for each 100 square feet. You can have a well-drained and fertilized soil but still get poor growth, if the soil is too sweet. A simple soil test will help a lot.

All Tops No Bottoms: Due to close planting, lack of thinning, or lack of boron.

CABBAGE AND RELATED CROPS (*Brassica*)

All members of the Brassica tribe, including cabbage, cauliflower, Brussels sprouts, broccoli, savoy cabbage, and kale, are easy to grow in the home garden.

BROCCOLI (*Brassica oleracea*, var. *botrytis*)

There are 2 types of broccoli, the cauliflower-type broccoli and the green sprouting or calabrese. The green sprouting type is what gardeners commonly know as broccoli.

For early crops sow Spartan Early indoors, transplant to open ground in late April or early May, spacing the plants to 2½ feet apart each way. For later crops, sow Waltham 29 in early June in rows where they remain. Thin to 2 feet apart, using some extras for transplanting.

Harvesting: The dandy, edible heads should be picked while the tiny buds are still tight. Plants will produce green flower buds way into fall. Center heads develop first and after these are cut, numerous side shoots are produced, providing a continuous supply for freezing.

TROUBLES

Cabbage Worms and Aphids: Control with Sevin or Malathion. Do not use Malathion within 7 days of harvest.

USES

Bonus Broccoli Coins: Broccoli often has long edible stalks which require far more cooking than the tops. Cut the tops off about 1 inch from top and cook as usual. Peel the stalks and cut into really thin slices. Serve these raw as a dip scooper, in tossed salad, or as a different raw relish. Or cook in a little water until tender-crisp, then butter or sauce to suit your taste.

BRUSSELS SPROUTS (*Brassica oleracea*, var. *gemmifera*)

Not as easy to grow as cabbage, but will be productive if plants are

Brussels sprout plant Jade Cross, which formed sprouts as leaves were removed. (All-America Selections)

started early indoors or in hotbed. Jade Cross is a good hybrid to grow. When plants are 5 or 6 inches high, transplant 2 feet apart in rows 3 feet apart. Treat same as cabbage (which see).

When the sprouts are formed break off lower leaves and stems. The largest sprouts on bottom should be picked off and eaten and the plants will continue to produce more sprouts until stopped by cold weather. Dust plants with Malathion or Sevin in early stages to prevent aphids from getting into sprouts. Discontinue 7 days before harvest.

Here's a good tip for better sprouts: In mid-September, or when the lower sprouts are beginning to make size, pinch out the growing points in top of plant. The sprouts on the upper part of the plant promptly start to develop more quickly and get larger.

Plants may be left in open ground until very cold weather. Moderate freezing will not injure the sprouts and is much better than too much warmth. Flavor is improved by light frost.

Storing Sprouts: If you want to keep the sprouts into winter, take up the plants with some soil on roots and stand them up together in a cool cellar or pit, where they will not freeze hard. Earth can be packed around roots to keep the plants fresh so the sprouts will be crisp and tender.

TROUBLES

Same as cabbage (which see). Worst pest is green and white plant lice (aphids).

CABBAGE (*Brassica oleracea*)

Cabbage is another vegetable which has come a long way. It was once believed to have great medicinal value. The leaves were used as a poultice for bruises and to prevent bald heads. Cabbage leaves were also crushed in vinegar to cure dog bites. The juice, mixed with honey, was a remedy for coughs and hoarseness and today it is believed that cabbage juice is good for ulcers.

Varieties: There is early, midseason, and late cabbage. All are easy to grow. A wise selection of varieties planted at the right time should give you fresh cabbage for several months and the time can even be lengthened by cold storage. Select disease-resistant varities to avoid yellows, a fungus disease which causes yellowing and dwarfing. Some yellows-resistant varieties are Golden Acre, Marion Market, Jersey Queen, Copenhagen, and Improved Wisconsin.

Planting and Care: Start your plants indoors, or sow seed directly out-doors. Plants should stand 20 inches apart in rows 2½ to 3 feet apart. Early cabbage should be planted in May, whereas the late can be set out in July. The only requirements are ample moisture and plant food, plus a nonacid soil. Water your cabbage plants every 6 or 8 days in dry weather since the plants have a fairly large root system. Cabbage roots run shallow, a good reason why cultivation should be light.

Savoy Cabbage: This is the one with curled or savoyed head and worth growing in your garden. Try Savoy King or Vanguard II, a favorite for coleslaw and salads. And don't forget the red cabbages—Red Acre and Red Danish. Both excellent for salads, pickling, or coleslaw. Deep red color adds color to salads.

Chinese Cabbage: Chinese or celery cabbage is more delicate than regular cabbage, and you'll like the tender crisp heads, which resemble celery. Leaves may be cooked like spinach or used fresh for salads or coleslaw. A good strain is Michihli.

Sow seed in the open ground where the crop is to grow, in rows 2 or 3 feet apart, and thin out the plants to 18 to 20 inches apart in the row. Do not sow until the first of July or later; if sown early it quickly runs to seed and is useless. Chinese cabbage matures in 8 to 10 weeks and will succeed on any good soil. Dust the young seedlings with Sevin or rotenone to keep flea beetles off.

Storage of Cabbage: All cabbage will keep well if buried in the garden in a pit or clean garbage can, or kept in a cool cellar.

TROUBLES

Split Heads: Due to a soaking rain following several weeks of late-summer drought. Excess fertilizer and insects may also be responsible. All varieties are susceptible, although the early types split easier than late ones. You can prevent bursting by seizing the stalk of the plant and giving it a slight pull, until you feel the roots tearing out of the soil. Checking the growth in this way will help the cabbage resist bursting.

Clubroot: Cabbage and members of the family—cauliflower, broccoli, Brussels sprouts, kohlrabi—are susceptible to clubroot ("finger and toe" disease), a fungus that persists for many years in acid soils. If you look on the roots of sickly or yellowed plants you will find ugly lumps, which give rise to the name of clubroot or clubfoot. The slime mold fungus can live in the soil for at least 6 or 7 years. Control: Grow seedlings in virgin soil. Never set out plants having small swellings on roots, and rotate your crops. Chemical control consists of using Terraclor at planting time. Mix 6 tablespoons of Terraclor to a gallon of

Clubroot of cabbage. (Dr. Arden Sherf, College of Agriculture, Cornell University)

water and use ½ pint of the solution to each hole you set a plant in. Terraclor also goes under the shortened name of PCNB and is sold in garden centers. Also add hydrated lime to your soil so that the alkalinity (sweetness) is around pH 7.

Black Leaf Spot Disease: (see illustration) Dust plants with Captan to prevent spreading.

Cabbage Maggot: Feeds on roots and stems. Control by mixing 1 teaspoon of dieldrin, Chlordane, or methoxychlor to a gallon of water and wet the soil of newly set plants in spring.

Cutworms: Destroy young plants. Place paper collars around stems and dust soil with Malathion after plants are set in.

Imported Cabbage Worm and Cabbage Looper: Caterpillars that feed on cabbage, broccoli, Brussels sprouts, cauliflower. If you see a sulfur butterfly, you'll soon have green caterpillars. The first sight of a butterfly should mean you start dusting plants immediately.

Aphids (Plant Lice): A serious pest but can be controlled by spraying with Malathion. ALWAYS WASH THE EDIBLE PARTS OF VEGETABLES BEFORE EATING THEM. Sevin is a good insecticide for most cabbage pests. Do not use Malathion within 7 days of harvest.

USES

Kitchen Tip: Cabbage, broccoli, and Brussels sprouts can drive you out of the kitchen with cooking odor. To eliminate this, place a heel of bread on top of the vegetable. Then put the lid on, and voilà, no odor.

Black leaf spot on cabbage. (USDA Photo)

CAULIFLOWER (*Brassica oleracea,* var. *botrytis*)

This member of the cabbage family has been defined as a variety of cabbage in which the head consists of the condensed and thickened flower cluster instead of the leaves. The oldest record of cauliflower dates back to the sixth century B.C. Cauliflower was found on the London vegetable market as early as 1619 and has been grown for about 200 years in America.

Like broccoli, cauliflower did not become popular in the United States until the past 25 or 30 years. During this time, it has become increasingly popular because of its fine appearance and delicate flavor. Cauliflower, along with broccoli, has been called the "true aristocrat of the cabbage family." Mark Twain once defined cauliflower as "cabbage with a college education."

Planting and Care: For early crop sow seed indoors in March and set plants out 18 to 24 inches apart in rows 3 feet apart. Cauliflower is hard to raise for an early crop as it does not head well during the hot summer months. We have better luck sowing the seed outdoors in late May and transplanting in June or July, so that the crop will head in September or October. Cauliflower grows best in cool moist weather and unlike cabbage, will not withstand severe freezing or extreme heat. IT IS VERY IMPORTANT THAT THE PLANTS ARE NOT CHECKED IN GROWTH AT ANY TIME. They must be kept growing steadily and vigorously or the heads will be small and poor. When the heads start to form, and have reached a diameter of 2 or 3 inches, gather the large outside leaves together and pull them over the head, then tie together with rubber band or string. This protects them from weather and light and blanches the edible curds. Harvest the curds when they are still compact, not open and ricey.

TROUBLES

Heading When Plant Is Only 2 or 3 Inches Tall: This is due to hot weather, regardless of soil moisture. Cauliflower likes the cool moist months of fall.

Maggots: Dust stems with Sevin.

KALE (*Brassica oleracea,* var. *acephala*)

A good "green" for late fall is kale or borecole. Kale is in the cabbage family but does not form head. It's good for winter and early spring use, ideal for garnishing, and even in flower arrangements. Young, tender shoots are delicious greens, and the quality is improved by a touch of frost.

Planting and Care: Start like cabbage and thin plants to 16 inches apart. You can plant directly into the garden. Flavor is improved by light frosts, and best kale is produced when plants are set out in June or July. With a little protection it will live in garden and furnish delicious greens in winter. Use Sevin or Malathion for insect control.

USES

Kale is recommended for its high food value and vitamin content. It can be chopped, boiled as a green, and served buttered. Or you can cook it with ham or bacon.

Scalloped Kale: boil chopped kale until tender. Drain, mix with chopped hard-boiled egg. Place in baking dish. Moisten with soup stock or bouillon. Cover surface with slices of cheese and sprinkle with seasoned bread crumbs. Bake in oven about 15 minutes until heated through and crumbs and cheese are browned.

KOHLRABI (*Brassica oleracea* var. *caulorapa*)

This is one of the forgotten vegetables that needs discovering. Kohlrabi is a cabbage-family member of which the swollen stem is the edible part. Kohlrabi is easy to grow, can be eaten raw or boiled. There is a new variety available that grows to about the size of a radish, is lovely as a decoration.

Early White Vienna is the most important variety grown. The interior of this variety is white, with a light green exterior. There is also a Purple Vienna variety but it is not as popular as the white.

Planting and Care: The seed may be sown at any time from May to July in rows 18 inches to 2 feet apart. The young plants should be transplanted or thinned to stand about 6 inches apart in the row. Kohlrabi may also be started early in hotbeds and set out like early cabbage. It is at its best when grown in the cool days of spring or autumn and should be used while young and tender, not larger than a baseball.

TROUBLES

Same as cabbage (which see). Use Sevin or Malathion for control of flea beetles and other insects.

USES

Small, tender kohlrabi are best steamed without peeling, but as they get more mature it is best to strip off the tough fibrous skin, cut into quarters or slices or dices, and boil in a very little salted water. Kohlrabi is also excellent peeled and sliced and eaten raw.

CANTALOUPE (See Muskmelon)

CARROT (*Daucus carota*)

The carrot is believed to have originated in Afghanistan and adjacent Asiatic areas. When carrots were first brought to England from Holland, stylish ladies used the feathery leaves to decorate their hair. At one time the carrot was chopped, dried, and used as a coffee substitute in Germany. In some parts of Europe, sugar was extracted from the carrot but its manufacture was found not profitable.

Carrots are a great source of Vitamin A, thiamine, riboflavin, and sugar, low in calories.

The carrot is a cool-season vegetable. It is best adapted to regions or seasons with relatively long periods of mild weather that are free from extremes of temperature. Prolonged hot weather may retard growth, depress yield, and cause strong flavor.

Soil and Planting: The land for carrots should be light, moist, and deeply worked, and should be made rich with manure or fertilizers. Plow or spade the soil as deeply as possible and work into fine condition. Do not let the soil become compacted as carrots are generally short, rough, and of inferior quality if grown in hard soil. If possible plant them on raised beds or ridges and keep the soil as loose as possible. Carrots grown in this way are of fine quality.

Seeds are slow to germinate, and can be sown from late spring until late June. In dry weather sprinkle the rows in evening for a couple of weeks to insure quick come-up and a good stand. Make successive sowings every 2 or 3 weeks if you want a continuous supply of tender young carrots throughout the season. Do not cover with more than ½ inch of soil. Prevent a crust from forming by breaking the soil with a rake a few days after sowing. Sow a little radish seed with the carrots to mark the rows for cultivating and to help break the crust barrier.

Thinning: Thin the early varieties to 2 inches and the large later varieties to 3 or 4 inches. If grown on a loose soil such as muck or sand, leave them thicker than on heavy soils. Thin the carrots just as soon as they come up or they'll compete with each other for water and nutrients. However, if you want young tender carrots for table use in the fall or winter, sow the seed thinly in mid-July and do not thin. You'll get small, finger-size carrots that are excellent raw or cooked. Keep weeds down, as carrots cannot compete with them.

Storage: The worst way to keep carrots over winter is to store them in dry sand. The best way to keep them fresh is in a crock. Here's how one reader keeps his carrots: "After digging them, the roots are hosed off, allowed to partially dry, then packed in sawdust, in tin cans (the foothigh kind frozen cherries come in), with NO cover. The sawdust is dampened from time to time during the winter. Our vegetable cellar averages 40° to 50° during winter. I do place a newspaper over the cans, but never tin lids. The carrots are as crisp as when we dug them."

Another reader writes: "For the past 10 years, I've been using the following method with great success. I wash the carrots thoroughly, then let them dry (usually all day in a warm room), then I pack them in a crisping pan and put it in the bottom shelf in the refrigerator. I cooked some today and they were as fresh and crisp as the day I dug them. The main thing is to have them dry when you pack them in the pan."

Here's another reader's suggestion: "I have good luck storing carrots in crocks. Wash them, then dry off, then cut a thin slice off the top. Place these into crocks and put earthenware lids on top. I still have some, fresh as when dug last fall."

Another trick is to leave them in the ground over winter, but be sure they are covered with a tarpaulin and enough straw to keep them from freezing. Or try burying carrots in a galvanized garbage can in the garden (see How to Store Apples over Winter). The can should have a lid on, plus ample protection such as straw or evergreen boughs.

TROUBLES

Carrot Rust Fly (see illustration p. 184): Resembles a housefly except that it is quite frail and long-legged. Rust flies come into the garden twice during the year and lay eggs which develop into tiny maggots. The first-generation maggots cause deformation of the carrots or forked carrots, and the injury may be very similar to that caused by microscopic nematodes.

The second generation attacks the carrots when they are making fair-sized growth toward the end of the season. This brood tunnels under the outside skin of the carrot, leaving unsightly trails. Sometimes disease infection gets in the trail, causing rot.

Yellows: Causes purpling and twisting of the tops and the development of numerous hairy roots on the carrot (see illustration). This virus is spread by leafhoppers from asters, lettuce, and certain weeds. Control: Spray the tops with Sevin or Malathion and eliminate perennial weeds near the garden. Dust the seed with Diazinon or Chlordane and cover with soil. If you sow after the first of June in most areas, you can bypass the first brood of maggots. Harvesting early in September, before the second-brood maggots have a chance to burrow into the carrots, is also helpful. Treating the soil in early spring at planting time with Diazinon or Chlordane will control both broods of the carrot rust fly.

Carrot yellows. (Dr. Arden Sherf, College of Agriculture, Cornell University)

Bitterness: Ethylene gas causes bitterness. Ethylene is produced by apples and other fruit. Even exhaust gases from gasoline engines contain enough ethylene to affect the quality of carrots. About the only method I know to keep out bitterness is to store your carrots in old-fashioned ways, using a hole in the earth, or a barrel sunk in the garden and covered with straw. This keeps carrots firm, sweet, and fresh.

USES

Savory Carrot Sticks: Scrape or peel 2 fair-sized carrots for each diner. Cut into sticks about 2 inches long and ⅛ inch thick. Put into the top of a double boiler, add 2 tablespoons chopped onion, 1 tablespoon butter or margarine, add 1 pinch dried thyme, rosemary, or marjoram. Cover and cook over boiling water for about ½ hour or until crunchy. Do not overcook. Season with salt and pepper. Sprinkle with minced parsley.

CAULIFLOWER (See Cabbage and Related Crops)

CELERIAC (*Apium graveolens*)

Ever raise any celeriac, the so-called "turnip-rooted" or "knob" celery? Easy to grow, this celery-like vegetable produces large thick roots with a nutlike celery flavor. Celeriac is raised in the same manner as unblanched celery (see Celery culture). A 25-cent package of seed started indoors might introduce you to a brand-new vegetable.

Harvesting: Use the roots when about 2 inches across. They can be stored by simply cutting off the tops and storing the roots in sand in the cellar. Very tasty in fall or winter.

TROUBLES

Leaf Blights and Spots: Spray with Bordeaux mixture, starting early.

Yellows, Stem Rots: Spray with Bordeaux mixture and Malathion.

Mosaic: Destroy infected plants. Keep down weeds. Spray with Malathion to control aphids.

USES

Try celeriac cubed, boiled, served with cream sauce, or in soups and stews.

CELERY (*Apium graveolens*)

It isn't generally known that this popular salad vegetable can be grown in most home gardens. A rich moist soil is best, although excellent results can be obtained on any deep loamy soil that is well supplied with organic matter.

Planting: Seed can be sown indoors in a window box, or you can buy the started plants from a greenhouse. Sphagnum moss and other artificial growing media have made it much easier to start good celery plants indoors or in cold frames. Cover the seed very lightly if at all, and keep moist and cool.

To raise celery plants in the open ground, sow as early as the land can be properly worked. A fine soil is needed, well fertilized and if possible manured. As it requires about 3 weeks for the plants to come up, scatter a little radish seed with the celery to mark the rows for cultivation.

Moist muck land is the best for celery, but good crops can be grown on upland soil if it is rich and kept watered. Well-rotted manure is almost essential to this crop; together with commercial fertilizer, it should be mixed in large quantities with the soil and may also be used later as a side dressing between the rows.

Space the rows about 2 feet apart if not blanched, and 3 or 3½ feet apart if you wish to blanch with boards or by banking up the soil. Celery plants should stand 8 to 10 inches apart in the row. Be sure not to let the fine roots dry out in transplanting and water thoroughly immediately after setting out. Side-dressing with nitrate fertilizer every few weeks is very helpful.

Celery is slow-growing, has small root system, which means frequent shallow cultivation is needed as the plants cannot compete with weeds. By early September the plants should be well hilled up. This encourages the development of compact plants with straight, crisp leaf stalks. Watering is essential for a good celery crop. The soil around the roots should be soaked once every 10 to 14 days during July or August, and watering several days before harvesting is desirable since it produces a crisp and well-flavored product.

Blanching Celery: Gardeners may be baffled by the term "blanching" as applied to celery. Blanching is nothing more than growing celery in subdued light to whiten the stalks. Any way you can keep the light off the growing stalks, but not the leaves, will blanch them. Some feel this gives the celery a nutty flavor, and makes it tender. Close planting or the use of boards, paper, or soil around the plants are ways to induce blanching. Banking the soil is not safe in hot weather, but it is the most economical method for fall blanching and it protects the plants from freezing weather. In summer, a period of 12 to 15 days is needed for blanching, but a longer period is needed in fall.

"Why is it that all the celery you buy in stores has green instead of yellow stalks? Green celery is bitter," I'm often told.

There's no truth to the idea that green celery is bitter. Green celery dominates the markets now. In fact, it's quite a problem finding blanched celery these days. The reason is simple. The cost (mainly labor) of having this extra job done makes it more expensive to grow blanched celery. Actually, there's little need for blanching celery, since the green celery is just as tasty, and probably more nutritious.

TROUBLES

Yellows: If celery plants are bitter, dwarfed, and yellowed, it's due to yellows disease, a soil-borne trouble. Plant resistant varieties.

Blight: Celery gets early and late blights which spot and yellow the foliage. These blights are seed-borne and live over refuse or in the soil as well. Rotate the planting site, and stay out of the celery patch when plants are wet. Spray or dust the plants with Bordeaux mixture at 10-day intervals. Use Captan, Maneb, or zineb, applied every week to 10 days all season, starting with 1 or 2 applications in the plant bed.

Tarnished Plant Bug: Control with Sevin.

CHARD, SWISS (*Beta vulgaris*, var. *cicla*)

This "unknown" vegetable is one of the easiest of all to grow. You might say it's a beet grown for its leaves. Takes hot and cold weather. Produces all season. There is a brilliantly colored red variety, called Rhubarb Chard.

Swiss chard is raised the same way as ordinary garden beets except that the rows should be 18 to 24 inches apart and the plants thinned to 8 inches apart. This can be done by first thinning to 4 inches and pulling out every other plant for use when they are 10 to 12 inches high. Keep old leaves picked off to encourage younger ones. In early August cut off all the old leaves, give the ground a light dressing of nitrate of soda, or a complete fertilizer with readily available nitrogen, and you will have fine greens right up to freezing weather.

TROUBLES

Brown Spots with Reddish-purple Borders: Spots on leaves become dry, brittle, and drop out. Control: Bordeaux mixture.

USES

Ann Wanda's Chicken Chard: 1 bunch Swiss chard, 2 cups flour, 1 teaspoon salt, ½ cup milk, ½ cup water, 2 eggs. Wash chard and cook in lightly salted water for 20 minutes. Cut off leaves (leaves can be chopped and used as a green vegetable with salt, pepper, and butter to taste). Cut stems in 2 or 3 pieces, drain well. Heat 1 inch of cooking oil in a heavy frying pan. Dip stem pieces in batter made from remaining ingredients and fry until golden brown on both sides. Drain and serve sprinkled with garlic salt, if desired. Delicious—tastes just like fried chicken!

CHICORY (*Cichorium intybus*)

Chicory (*Cichorium intybus*) and endive (*C. endivia*) are closely related, and belong to the same family as lettuce and dandelion. The terms chicory and endive are frequently interchanged because a forced type of chicory (witloof) has been erroneously named "French endive." Chicory is also known as succory. In the U.S. it is grown principally as a salad crop and for its roots, which when dried and ground serve as an adulterant for coffee.

Planting and Care: Start seed 110 to 130 days before average date of killing frosts in fall. Too early planting results in plants going to seed, or oversized, multiple-hearted roots. Chicory likes plenty of plant food and water.

Forcing Chicory: Home greenhouse owners can force witloof chicory under benches (or in cellars) where temperature is steady 50° to 60°. Force anytime from late fall to early spring. Place chicory roots in box with soil. Any old box, about 18 inches deep, will do to hold the roots and sand. Put a little soil in the bottom of the box and then place the roots, crown up, in rows almost touching each other. Put a little soil or sand about the roots to hold them in place. When the box is full, put enough soil over the roots to cover them. Water thoroughly so the soil is wet to the bottom and then cover with 6 or 7 inches of dry sandy soil.

Examine in 3 weeks and if the heads or sprouts are coming through the surface, they are ready to use and may be cut as wanted. The best heads are 4 to 5 inches long and weigh 2 or 3 ounces. In the meantime other boxes should be filled so as to give a constant supply during the winter months. The fertility of the sand or soil used is of no importance, and the roots do not require anything except water. No light is needed.

It may be necessary to water the roots a second time. This is best done by making a hole down through the top soil or sand and pouring the water in without wetting the surface.

TROUBLES: None.

Chives (*Allium schoenoprasum*)

Chives grow successfully indoors and outdoors. You can bring a clump from the outdoors in fall and pot it up, or grow in the indoor window box. Fresh tender shoots will continue growing for use all winter. Or you can plant the seed in pots. Germination is slow.

A clump or 2 in the vegetable garden will grow like a weed and supply the needs of the average family. Keep watered. It's a good idea to separate clumps every 3 years and keep flower heads cut off.

Indoor Culture: If you bring in a clump of tiny bulbs, set them in a pan of light, sweet soil. Chives like a sunny window at low temperature if possible, and don't overwater. Indoors they seem to do best if grown on the dry side. When a clump is brought in from the outdoors, cut the leaves back to allow new growth to start.

TROUBLES: None.

USES

The fresh leaves of chives are a most popular seasoning in appetizers, cheeses, eggs, sauces, soups, and salad dressings. Many gardeners pickle the tiny bulbs, just as you'd pickle small onions. (For other tasty herbs, see section on Herbs.)

Corn (*Zea mays*)

Sweet Corn: You can't beat corn from your own garden! Fresh-picked corn has far more sweetness and flavor than any you can buy. Corn will grow well on many types of soil, but usually the richer the ground, the sweeter and more tender the corn will be. Corn is a warm-weather crop, so try to get the seed in the ground as soon as possible so it can grow through the hot summer weather.

Varieties: Hybrid sweet corn is rapidly replacing the open-pollinated varieties in home gardens. A hybrid corn is a first-generation progeny produced by crossing 2 inbred lines: This doesn't mean that just any hybrid is superior because it happens to be a hybrid. There are poor hybrids as well as dandy ones. Try different varieties and when you find a good one, stick with it. If you have a pocket-sized garden, try the midget varieties of sweet corn.

A reader sends information about black sweet corn, "the sweetest sugar corn ever!" She writes: "The variety is Black Mexican and the kernels turn color as they mature, hence the name 'red, white, and blue' sweet corn." Personally, the blue kernels do not appeal to me but gardeners who have tasted and grown the corn say the quality is hard to beat.

Planting: Sweet corn is best planted in blocks of at least 3 rows side by side rather than in a single row, to insure pollination and development of a full set of kernels. Space the rows 2 to 3 feet apart and drop the seed 4 to 6 inches apart, for later thinning to 8 or 10 inches apart for the early varieties and 12 to 18 inches apart for the later kinds. To grow corn in hills or groups, use 5 or 6 seeds per hill, 2 or 3 feet apart, to be thinned to 3 plants of early kinds and 2 of the later. "Hill" means a group of seeds planted together, not a mound of soil. Seedsmen will tell you that even on high-germination seed, you can expect a loss of about 15% on the final stand. Just what happens to this 15% no one knows. Poor stands can be due to seed rot in cold, wet soils.

Make 3 successive plantings about 10 days apart to enjoy a long season of sweet corn. Or try planting an early, midseason, and late variety at the same time, and your corn won't mature all at once. An additional planting of a midseason variety about a month later will yield fine corn in early fall.

Usually early corn is more wormy than late corn, especially in areas where there is only 1 brood of the corn borer, and that accounts for the fewer worms on the later varieties. The moth is done laying eggs by the time much of the late corn is along.

Feeding: Corn is a heavy feeder. Side-dress in summer with a balanced plant food or use liquid feeding at the base. Give another feeding when ears begin to silk. When corn leaves show a sickly, yellowish-green color, with some plants dwarfed, or leaves have a purplish hue, chances are these are hunger signs. Yellow leaves mean lack of nitrogen (or poor drainage), and purplish color means lack of phosphorus. If you want top-notch flavor, apply water to your corn plants, especially when the silks appear and the ears are developing.

Suckering Corn: Removing suckers from base of the plants is not sensible. Removing tassels from corn plants DOES NOT GIVE YOU EARLIER CORN, nor worm-free ears. You get more ears if you leave the suckers on and leave the tassels on too!

Picking Tips: Sweet corn is at maximum sweetness when the kernels have filled out, but still spurt "milk" when punctured with thumbnail. In picking corn, don't rip open each ear to check color. You can tell more about quality by looking at the outside. Look for dark-green husks. Corn with yellow or whitish husks is old or overmature. Dark-brown moist silks indicate well-filled kernels. Old, poor quality corn has dry or matted silks that crumble at the slightest touch.

Corn loses its flavor fast after picking. Loss of flavor starts at the instant corn is picked. For best results, have the water boiling when you set out to pick. Don't boil corn too much when cooking; 3 or 4 minutes is plenty.

Freezing Corn: Did you ever freeze corn on the cob? Take a variety with a small cob. Ears should be blanched in boiling water for 5 minutes and cooled immediately in ice water. Ears can then be placed in cellophane bags and placed in the freezer. Later, to prepare frozen corn for table use, remove it from the plastic bags, place it in a shallow tin and heat in a 350° oven for 30 to 45 minutes, until the ears are thoroughly warmed through to the center of the cob. Some folks freeze the ears with some of the inner husks left on. Then, when they prepare it, they just drop the ears in boiling water until done. Frozen corn will keep in the freezer for a year.

Storing Corn: Regardless of how you prepare corn, keep it in a refrigerator or ice water until you're ready to use it. Tests show that sweet corn loses 50% of its sugar when stored 24 hours at 86°, and only 8% when stored at 32°. The longer you allow corn to sit around in husks the more flavor it will lose.

If you buy sweet corn, give it a drink. Immerse the ears, husks and all, in cold water for 10 minutes, then wrap in a damp cloth to keep moist.

Popcorn: Popcorn requires the same care as sweet corn. Popcorn is classified into 2 main groups: the rice corns (which have sharply pointed kernels), and the pearl corns (which have smooth, rounded kernels). White Rice has an ear about 7 inches long, with 16 to 20 rows of kernels, while Japanese Hulless has smaller ears, about 4 inches long, with 30 to 40 rows.

For a novelty, try growing black-kerneled popcorn. It's white inside. Strawberry corn is a popcorn only 2 inches long and 1½ inches thick, well worth trying. Also try White Cloud, Golden Pearl, or Hybrid Hulless. All are easy to grow.

Hang harvested ears up to dry for 2 or 3 months. Shell and seal tightly in glass jars. Popcorn keeps for ages, and pops better, if kept in jars in refrigerator.

Indian ("Ornamental") Corn: Indian corn is ideal for fall decorations. Kernels have a variety of colors: red, yellow, white, with some blue and purple. Culture is same as sweet corn.

Note: Sweet corn should not be planted next to popcorn or ornamental corn, if both have the same ripening date. In other words, if you plant sweet corn next to ornamental corn, be sure to use an early or mid-season sweet corn to avoid contamination. You will get ears with purple, orange, or yellow kernels if a late variety of table corn is used. With early corn, it makes no difference, since ornamental corn is late and won't shed pollen at the time early corn will. So if you're going to plant ornamental corn along with edible sweet corn be sure to select an early-maturing variety.

TROUBLES

Corn Borer and Corn Earworm: Serious corn pests. The corn borer enters the ear from the stalk or side, whereas the corn earworm (see illustration p. 186) is larger and enters the ear only through the silks.

Corn borer is probably the worst single pest of corn. It attacks early plantings mostly but will get late ones also. On early corn, the newly hatched grubs feed for a short while at the tip, then tunnel downward through the tassel and stalk. Borers that hatch when corn is silking often enter the ear along the silk, as does the earworm.

The corn earworm hits mid- and late-season sweet corn, reaching peak numbers in September or late August.

Control: The most important single application is when the tassels are first visible. Dust them with Sevin. Starting in early August be sure to apply pesticide at first silking, and repeat at 3- or 4-day intervals. A safer bet is to start dusting when corn is about 18 inches high. Drive the dust or spray down into the crown and the axils of the leaves. When the silks begin to come out well, dust them lightly but thoroughly. Cover silk on which eggs of the earworm moth are laid.

Army Worm: Strips leaves. Handpicking is best means of control. Use Sevin.

Corn Smut: Causes black patches or boils on ears and stalks, worse in hot, dry weather. When soil is dry, the dust blows more readily and it is by means of airborne dust that the powdery fungus spores are carried from one garden to another. Control: pick the boils and burn them. Get your neighbor to do the same.

Ants and Aphids: Ants on corn tassels means aphids are present. In hot years, aphids may be plentiful enough to cause incomplete pollination. Ants do no harm. Control: Spray tassels with Malathion to kill aphids and ants will go away.

Corn smut. (Dr. Arden Sherf, College of Agriculture, Cornell University)

Bacterial Wilt: Sudden wilting or scorching of leaves is due to bacterial wilt or Stewart's disease, spread by flea beetles. Control: Use resistant varieties. Spray with Sevin.

Corn Root Maggot: Stalk appears withered and brown. Dust soil with methoxychlor, Diazinon, or Sevin before planting.

Bird Damage: Treat seed with crow repellent, available in most garden-supply centers. It keeps birds from eating seed. There's no control for birds which eat the ears. Use old fashioned scarecrows made from Grandpa's plug hat, Dad's old coat or Junior's worn-out pants—all arranged on a post (see section on Animal Control). Don't leave scarecrows in the same spot because birds and animals get used to them.

There's a bird-proof corn on the market. Bird-proof means it has a tough husk cover, especially at the tip where the birds attack the ear. One variety we tried has such a tight husk cover that in dry years the corn has a tough time getting the tassel to get through it far enough to allow proper pollination. If we can get our sweet corn to have this tough husk cover, we won't be raising corn for the birds anymore!

Animal Damage: Coons are also destructive. Use electric fence to prevent stripping of ears. Firecrackers on a fuse rope keep these pests out.

Woodchucks and squirrels also are troublesome. Put a wire fence around your garden to keep woodchucks out!

Plastic Covers for Corn: Suggested by a reader, here's a good use for plastic bags. "I decided not to raise corn for the birds this year, so I placed plastic bags over each ear of corn. They do a fine job of keeping out birds and coons. Even cheesecloth works for me." Several readers have told me about this fine tip. Some have wondered if there is any harm from the heat and moisture which accumulates inside the bag. My answer is no. Don't worry about it.

SOME QUESTIONS I'M OFTEN ASKED REGARDING CORN

Q. Right after we cultivated our corn, the lower leaves turned yellow and dried. Why?

A. Sounds like you damaged the roots by deep cultivating. Hill corn when 10 inches high and practice light cultivation only.

Q. Why were kernels on our corn poorly developed on one side and O.K. on the other?

A. Due to poor pollination from hot, dry summer, or during period of steady rain. High temperatures during drought dry up the silks (female) and pollen (male) does not have a chance to grow through the silk and produce kernels. High temperature sometimes has a depressing effect on pollen.

Q. Last year our corn was full of earworms. Any help?

A. Use Sevin and apply to silks of ears only, beginning when silks are first noticeable, and repeating every 3 to 4 days for 5 or 6 doses. A way to reduce earworm damage without spraying is to make about 4 plantings of sweet corn at 2-week intervals. You'll usually find that the first planting is pretty riddled by the earworm, the second planting is likely to be free or nearly free of worms. The other 2 plantings may have worms feeding on the upper inch or 2 of the ear, but a quick chop with a butcher knife and you'll have a pretty good-sized ear of corn left that's worm-free.

Q. Our sweet corn has good vigorous stalks but no signs of any ears, even though we used hybrid seed. Why?

A. Sounds like you used a later variety and planted too close for the weather conditions you had. Early varieties can be planted closer than the later ones that produce a taller, heavier, more leafy stalk. Where seed of high germination is planted, we recommend not less than 1 foot spacing in the row. In hybrid sweet corn trials, we find that 3 kernels planted every 15 inches and later thinned to 1 plant every 15 inches in rows 3 feet apart produce the most perfect ears.

Since gardeners are more interested in yields than in perfect ears, try planting 2 kernels every 12 inches and later thinning to a uniform stand of 12 inches apart in rows 3 feet apart. If you want to plant in hills, put in 3 kernels every 30 inches and eliminate the thinning.

Q. Can corn be started in pots indoors and transferred to a garden later?

A. Yes, provided you do not start too early, or they are not kept too warm, or planted out too soon. You will get earlier corn this way.

Q. My corn was a failure—few ears, in spite of fertilizer and ample water. Why?

A. Maybe due to close planting. See previous discussion of spacing.

Q. Why did my corn grow 2 feet high and tassel out?

A. Dry weather, lack of nitrogen, too acid a soil (corn likes slightly acid soil).

For other possible causes of corn trouble, see section on Hunger Signs in Plants.

CRESS

Watercress and curled cress, or peppergrass, are worth space in any home garden. Both are appetizing and mildly pungent herbs used in sandwiches and popular for salads and garnishings.

Peppergrass (*Lepidium sativum*) is a very quick-growing crop of pleasing pungent taste, exceptionally easy to grow. Plant in rows about 1 foot apart in early spring and again 2 or 3 weeks later if a continual supply is desired. It will be ready to cut in 4 or 5 weeks. It does not do well in midsummer, but is excellent for spring or fall.

Watercress (*Nasturtium officinale*) is a slow-growing perennial and thrives only where there is running water or very moist soil. The seed can be simply scattered on the muddy banks of a stream in summer or spring. A small stream fed by springs and running through low land is the ideal place to raise watercress. If a large amount is wanted, dam up the stream so as to overflow the land a few inches deep and scatter the seed all over the flooded land. Watercress can also be successfully grown in greenhouses and gardens by the liberal use of water.

Grow a little upland cress (*Barbarea vernapraecox*) on the window-sill to add a fresh note to salads and sandwiches. Upland cress is a weedy little plant in the mustard family which grows in ordinary garden soil but tastes almost exactly like watercress. In England it is sprouted over water, and the sprouted seedlings are sold in bulk to be used in making thin bread and butter sandwiches. One of the simplest ways to grow it in the home is to fill a soup bowl half-full of sphagnum moss or shredded paper towel or some such material, soak it with water, and then scatter the seed on top. In 10 days the bright green little seedlings will be 2 or 3 inches high and ready to harvest.

Clubroot, Damping-off, Mosaic, Mildew: None serious. Plant in new spot, avoid overcrowding. Chemical control not worth it.

USES

One joy of an early spring day—a walk through the woods to the spring to see if the watercress is up—is one of our traditions. If we have heavy spring rains the rush of water carries away the early plants. More often they get a good start and we harvest enough to mix in our first salad of greens.

Cream of Watercress Soup: Chop finely 3 bunches of watercress. Sauté in 1 tablespoon of butter with 1 minced onion, 4 minced shallots, salt, freshly ground pepper, and a few drops of lemon juice. Cream 1 tablespoon of flour in ¾ cup of chicken broth and add to watercress mixture, stirring until smooth. Simmer and add enough cream to make desired consistency. Serve hot.

CUCUMBER (*Cucumis saturis*)

Cucumbers are a warm-season crop, and should be planted when all danger of frost has passed. They can be raised either in evenly spaced rows or hills (groups of plants together, not mounds of soil). Cucumbers can even be trained on a trellis or wire fence, if the home gardener doesn't have too much space. The greatest yields are obtained when the soil has been made rich with manure or fertilizer.

Varieties: There are many fine varieties to select from. The long varieties are used primarily for slicing; the pickling varieties, being blunt-ended when small, are preferred for pickles by many.

There are many good pickling varieties on the market, ideal for "bread and butter" pickles, pickle chunks, and pickle slices. Pickling cucumbers are a good item for the home gardener. They also make a good cash crop for anyone with extra land. Little investment is needed and they bring quick cash returns. You should get about 85 bushels an acre. It takes about 55 days to get a crop.

Can you use slicing varieties of cucumbers for pickling? Yes, if the fruits are removed when they are small enough, but the quality of the pickled product will not be as good as if you had used pickling varieties. The reverse holds true also—pickling varieties usually do not make the best-tasting slicing cucumbers.

If you're one who can't eat cucumbers, try raising the "Burpless" cucumber. It's good!

We have grown the Burpless variety several seasons. The cukes are slender and often crooked. Some actually grew over 30 inches long! They are deliciously crisp and mild in taste, but so large we ate only a few. These cucumbers are actually burpless and are recommended to anyone who cannot eat the regular kind. Just don't plant too many, as they are mighty heavy bearers.

Planting: Avoid planting until night temperatures are above 40°, or seed will rot. In our area (western New York State) seed may be planted about the first of June for large cucumbers, and up to July 15th for pickles. In other areas they may be planted earlier. Use 8 or 10 seeds to a hill, and cover ½ inch deep. Hills are spaced 3½ to 4 feet apart each way, thinned to 3 or 4 strong plants in each hill when plants get their second leaves. If continuous rows are preferred, the seeds can be drilled in with a garden drill in rows 5 feet apart and the plants thinned out to 1 or 2 feet apart.

One of my friends sows cucumber seed in the 4 corners of his tiny garden, then puts a pot of fertilizer in the center, buried part of the way. At night when he waters the garden he fills the pot and it carries plant food down to the roots where it does some good. Another friend uses a half barrel with the end removed, for this trick: The barrel is filled with well-rotted manure and tamped down. Then soil is heaped around the barrel and 4 hills of cucumbers are spaced equally in the ground around the barrel. The hills are thinned to 2 plants. Our gardener friend then douses the barrel of manure with several buckets of water, several times a week. The plant nutrients are leached from the manure into the soil at the base of the plants. Cucumber roots quickly catch onto this supply of free moisture and plant food and respond with fast growth.

You might also want to try this trick: While your cucumbers are small, put 1 of the fruits inside a glass milk bottle (quart or pint) and let it grow inside. By midsummer the cucumber will fill the inside of the bottle and you can cut it off the vine. Pour vinegar in and seal if off. Your friends will wonder how you got such a large cucumber inside the bottle.

Cross-Pollination: Cucumbers do not cross with muskmelons, watermelons, pumpkins, or squash, as many believe. Different cucumber varieties will cross-pollinate, however. Even if they do, the edible portion will not be affected.

Nubbins and crooks are the result of improper pollination. That's why you shouldn't move the vines any more than necessary while cultivating or picking. Moving the vines destroys blossoms, drives away bees, results in kinking and matting of the vines, and tends to increase the number of misshaped fruits. Cucumbers are very shallow-rooted and sometimes the roots will extend beyond the tips of the vines. That means after the vines start to ramble freely you shouldn't do much cultivating. We mulch ours with straw and let them ramble over the straw. When the cukes don't make top-notch growth I boost them along with a shot of liquid fertilizer (such as 23–19–17). Or you can place a handful of nitrate of soda around the plants, keeping 1 foot away from the base of the plants.

Harvesting: If you're after pickles, it's important to remove early fruit, since big-sized fruits reduce the production of new blossoms. The same applies to slicing varieties. The fewer cucumbers that are allowed to become large, the more vines will produce. When the crop is developing rapidly, pick 3 or 4 times a week. Remove all fruits that have become too large as soon as noticed. Never grasp the vines by the tips and lift them high above the ground. This not only slows picking and tears the vines, but also cuts down on yield. Roll vines over and after the fruits are picked, roll them back into place.

TROUBLES

You'll have fewer disease problems if you destroy all milkweed, pokeweed, ground cherry, catnip, and wild cucumber plants near the garden. They are the host plants of the mosaic disease (which see), which causes yellowing of vines.

"Poor Set" of Fruits: Home gardeners are often disturbed by the apparent failure of cucumbers (and melons) to set fruits. Plants are loaded with blooms but no cukes or melons are found. After a few days they are surprised to find that the plants are setting plenty of fruit. Here's what happens: Cucumbers and muskmelons are "monecious" plants—that is, the male and female flower parts are borne on separate flowers on the same plant. Generally, the first 10 to 20 flowers that appear on the cucumber or muskmelon are male flowers, and there are generally 10 to 20 male flowers produced for each female flower. The male flowers are for pollination and naturally do not produce fruit, so when you see the blossoms drop off, don't be alarmed. Nature was overly generous and wanted to make sure pollination takes place.

Bitter Taste: Ever wonder what makes cucumbers taste very bitter some years? A certain amount of bitterness can be expected in most cucumbers, although weather can be a real factor, particularly fluctuations in temperature. Cucumber flavor is best where there's no more than a 20° variation. A sharp drop in temperature following a warm spell causes bitterness. Sawdust mulch has been blamed for bitterness but there is nothing to this. Mosaic (which see) will also give cucumbers a bitter taste.

Cucumber Scab or "Pox": A fungus disease which carries over in the old cucumber refuse. Black sunken spots form on surface of fruit. Control: Use seed that's treated with corrosive sublimate, and plant seed in a different spot each year. Burn the vines each season after harvest. Some varieties are resistant to this trouble. Rotate your crops and spray with zineb. Be sure to cover undersides of leaves. Grow scab-resistant varieties.

Misshapen Fruits: "Nubbins," curved fruit, or fruit with constrictions at the stem end are due to hot weather or rainy weather, bacterial wilt or mosaic (which see). Lack of pollination may also result in culls.

White Cucumbers: If the fruit of all the plants is mottled white and green, then blame the cucumber mosaic virus disease. If the fruit of your plants is entirely white, then disease is not involved. The white color is probably an inherited trait.

White cucumbers are not very common, although they've been known since at least 1778. A single gene determines whether a fruit of a cucumber plant will be green or white. These genes "mutate" (change), so that the one for green fruit could change to produce white fruit, although this doesn't happen too frequently. It could be that the seed of a white-fruited variety was accidentally mixed with the seed of a green-fruited variety. In general, seedsmen are doing an excellent job of keeping vegetable varieties pure and true to type, but once in a great while a mixture of this type occurs.

Cucumber scab. (Dr. Arden Sherf, College of Agriculture, Cornell University)

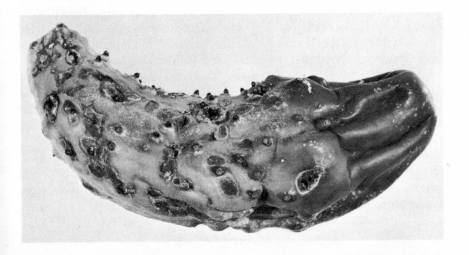

Angular leaf spot on cucumber. The spots are grayish-white and often are beaten out by rain. (USDA Photo)

Angular Leaf Spot (see illustration): Grayish-white spots often beaten out by the rain. Dust or spray with zineb or Mildex.

Bacterial Wilt: Causes complete collapse of young or old vines. A good test is to cut one of the wilted vines. If wilt is present, a white sticky ooze will come out where the vine is cut. This ooze is stringy and may be pulled into strands as much as an inch long. This disease is spread by the striped or 12-spotted cucumber beetle and is carried over in winter in the bodies of cucumber beetles. Control: A combination spray of Bordeaux mixture and Malathion or methoxychlor should kill the beetles and keep the bacterial disease out. Rotate the planting site each year and keep weeds down in or near the garden. Also use varieties that are more resistant to wilt. Gardeners who start their plants under paper caps should treat them as soon as these are opened.

Sometimes mature vines of cucumbers or melons will wilt as if diseased when weeds are pulled out of the patch. Any disturbance of roots of cucurbits will cause the vines to wilt, so don't pull weeds out of a mature patch.

Cucumber Blight: When vines and fruit shrivel or dry up, chances are this is common blight or anthracnose. Control: Treat seed with corrosive sublimate prior to planting. Also have as long a rotation with other crops as the size of your garden permits. Dust the plants with Captan or Bordeaux mixture. Malathion, 1 tablespoon to a gallon of water, will lick most insects, and you can add a fungicide too. Spray plants once a week until the vines are too large to pass through easily.

Mosaic Disease: Leaves take on a yellowish-green color; plants are stunted and wrinkled; fruits are runts instead of nice juicy cukes. Virus is "systemic"—that is, it moves from one part of a plant to another (roots, stems, leaves, and flowers). Mosaic is carried by insects such as aphids and leafhoppers from nearby weeds, flowers, and other vegetables. The virus lives in milkweed, catnip, burdock, wild cucumber, horsenettle, pokeweed, phlox, marigold, petunia, hollyhock, and many other plants. Control: Pull up affected plants and burn. Plant mosaic-resistant varieties.

Wisconsin SMR 12 is an excellent mosaic-resistant pickling variety, and I'd recommend Surecrop Hybrid as a resistant slicing variety. Also try Challenger, Saticoy Hybrid, Triumph, and Tablegreen. Any of these varieties will resist the disease and give excellent quality cucumbers throughout the season.

Some seedsmen feel that the hybrid slicing varieties are a great deal more resistant to mosaic than the open-pollinated varieties. This di-

Cucumber fruits showing dark, warty swellings and mottling caused by the cucumber mosaic virus. Leaves of infected plants also are mottled with yellow-green. (USDA Photo)

sease resistance, together with heavy yields, make the hybrid cucumbers a profitable venture, even though in small quantity the seeds cost about 1 cent each. We recommend planting hybrids.

Wilting Vines: Downy mildew disease, a destructive fungus trouble more prevalent in periods of dew or rain. This disease strikes fast and hits hard, wiping out a cucumber (or cantaloupe) patch in a very short time.

Downy mildew first appears as irregular yellowish to brown lesions on the top sides of leaves. The disease starts at center of the hill and kills leaves rapidly, often leaving green ones at the ends of the vines. The entire patch looks curled and withered, as if scorched. Sometimes when rain or dew is present you can see purplish fungus growth on the underside of the leaves.

Control: Once downy mildew has set in, nothing can be done. If your patch is free and you want to keep it that way, spray and dust with Captan or Bordeaux mixture. Keep the leaves coated until harvest. You can also mix 1 part of dusting sulfur with 4 parts of Bordeaux mixture. Apply lightly, as heavy doses of sulfur will burn the leaves.

Yellow Cucumber: Cucumbers bear nicely but the vines turn yellowish as they get older, and even if watered, fail to bear steadily. Keep all cucumbers picked off before they get too large—certainly before they begin to turn yellow. You might want to make pickles from some of the ripe yellow fruit, so if you do, allow a few vines to go.

Cucumber Borer: Even cucumbers get borers, causing the vines to wilt. Little can be done to control this pest. Treat the stems and main runners with methoxychlor, Malathion, or rotenone, starting about first of June or so.

Striped Cucumber Beetle: Don't let the striped cucumber beetle ruin your vines, spread bacterial wilt disease. Dust with methoxychlor or Malathion at weekly intervals, soon as the plants are up out of the ground. Sevin is also highly effective. DO NOT USE DDT ON CUCURBITS (plants belonging to the gourd, melon, cucumber, or squash family). Also, plant seed under paper caps to keep beetles off until plants are well started. Work Diazinon in the soil before planting. This pest enters the ground at night.

For beetles, aphids, bugs, and borers on cucumbers you can dust your plants with methoxychlor or Malathion. Do not apply during the blooming period when bees are working. Malathion should not be applied when plants are wet as it may burn them. For most diseases of cucurbits, you can dust with Captan and Karathane, at same time you apply the insecticides.

For all insects, use a combination of methoxychlor and Malathion wettable powders. A tablespoon of each per gallon of water should be adequate. Malathion will also control aphids or plant lice that fre-

quently collect on undersides of leaves and cause them to curl downward. You must spray every week for satisfactory control.

USES

Braised Cucumbers: This one is for elderly cucumbers. Allow 1 cucumber for each person. If the seeds have become woody, remove with
a spoon after cutting peeled cucumber in half. Score the outside with
a fork. Dry with a paper towel inside and out. Sauté in a skillet in a
little hot butter or margarine until golden brown on all sides. Add
¼ cup bouillon, or beef or chicken stock. Cover and cook until just
tender.

Iowa Sliced Pickles: 25 small pickling cucumbers (large ones can also
be used), 12 onions, 2 teaspoons celery seed, 2 teaspoons mustard seed,
1 teaspoon tumeric, 1 teaspoon ginger, 1 quart vinegar, 2 cups sugar,
½ cup salt. Soak cucumbers overnight in cold water. Slice cucumbers and
onions ¼ inch thick, cover with ½ cup salt, and let stand for 1 hour.
Add all remaining ingredients and let boil for 3 minutes.

Mustard Pickles: 1 pint each lima beans, string beans, cauliflower,
small onions, pickling cucumbers, celery, green tomatoes, 3 green peppers and 3 sweet red peppers, 1½ pounds sugar, ⅓ cup flour, 3 tablespoons mustard, ¼ tablespoon tumeric, and 1 quart vinegar diluted
with water to taste. Boil beans in salt water until tender. Let cauliflower come just to a boil and drain. Put all other vegetables in brine
overnight. Drain well in the morning. Mix sugar, flour, tumeric, and
mustard with cold vinegar-water mixture and cook until thick and
creamy, then mix with vegetables and cook 10 minutes, fill jars and
seal.

Pickle Chips: 30 cucumbers (3 to 4 inches long), 1 quart white vinegar, 8 cups sugar, 2 tablespoons mixed pickling spice tied in bag, 2
tablespoons salt. Wash cucumbers, drain. Put in crock, and pour in
boiling water to cover. Let stand overnight, drain. Repeat each day
until they have had 4 hot baths. On fifth day drain, rinse, cut in ¼-inch
slices. Heat remaining ingredients, bring to boil, pour over cucumbers.
Let stand overnight. Drain off liquid, bring to boil and pour over cu-
cucumbers again. Let remain overnight and repeat process 3 more days.
Then reheat syrup, put cucumbers in sterilized jars, pour boiling
syrup over them and seal jars tightly.

Pickled Yellow Cucumber: Peel cucumbers, cut in strips, and scrape
out seeds. Soak in cold water overnight or for 8 hours, drain. In each

pint jar put ½ teaspoon salt, 1 bay leaf, piece onion, small piece red pepper, and a pinch of alum. Make a syrup of 2½ cups white pickling vinegar, 5 cups water, 3 cups sugar, 2 tablespoons mustard seed. Bring to a boil, add cucumbers, and boil 3 minutes. Put in jars and seal. Enough syrup for 6 pints and about 6 large cucumbers.

Sun Pickles: Soak large pickles overnight in salt water. Next morning prepare some water by bringing to boil and then adding enough salt so the water will float an egg. Drain the pickles and dry them with a towel. Place pickles in jars, add a piece of dill, 2 or 3 little red peppers, 2 garlic cloves, and other herbs to suit your taste. Fill jar half-full of the salt water that floated the egg and completely fill remaining half of jar with vinegar. Screw shut gently and place jars in the sun for 10 days. Then screw lids tight and age at least 6 months or longer.

Sweet Pickle Chips: 1 gallon sliced cucumbers, ¼-inch thick, or thinner if desired, 2 cups sliced onions (optional), 4 cups sugar, 4 teaspoons salt, 1 teaspoon tumeric, 2 tablespoons mustard seed, 1½ teaspoons celery seed, 1 cup white vinegar. Mix together sugar, salt, tumeric, mustard seed, and celery seed. Add vinegar and mix well. Pour over sliced cucumbers and onions, mix thoroughly and cook slowly over medium high heat, stirring occasionally, to boiling point. Lower heat, simmer 10 minutes, stirring. Pack into jars and seal. Yields approximately 5 pints.

"3-Day Pickles": Wash and slice very thin 1 gallon cucumbers, don't peel. Soak in salt brine (see following) 3 days. Drain cucumbers and rinse. Boil in clear water with 1 heaping tablespoon alum for 10 minutes, then drain. Boil in clear water with 2 teaspoons ginger for 10 minutes, then drain. Cook 10 minutes in syrup, or until they turn light green in color. Pack in hot jars and seal. Salt Brine: 1 cup salt (not iodized), 1 gallon of water. Syrup: 1 teaspoon pickling spice, 1 teaspoon whole cloves, 1 teaspoon salt, 1 teaspoon celery seed, 1 quart white vinegar, 1½ quarts water, 3 pounds granulated sugar. If you desire the pickles to be sweeter add more sugar than the amount specified. Hint: Use cucumbers with small seeds for slicing.

DANDELION (*Taraxacum officinale*)

You can grow a patch of dandelions from seed, although the wild dandelions in your lawn, garden, and backyard are just as good to eat.

Takes no green thumb to grow this one. You can buy seed if you wish, and scatter in a spot in the garden. Leaves are used in salads, or boiled. Flavor can be improved if leaves are tied together and the hearts blanched and eaten like endive.

TROUBLES

Snails: Wash them off!

USES

Dandelions are prized by the gourmet for good eating, while others may regard them as a "sulfur-and-molasses" spring tonic. Besides those found growing by the wayside, dandelions are grown by truck gardeners in surprisingly large quantities to be sold to grocers.

It is easy to find dandelions in spring and cover them with a basket. In a week or so they will be bleached white, crisp, and tender, with no trace of bitterness. The tender bleached leaves are particularly good with cottage cheese and French dressing. The famous French cook Brillat-Savarin says that a taste for bitter flavors is a sign of highest sophistication, but I doubt if that was what our grandmothers had in mind when they dished up a steaming bowl of dandelion greens cooked with bacon. They knew instinctively that they were good and good for us.

Serve the small inside leaves in a salad along with other native greens —shepherd's purse, cowslip, dock, chicory, plantain, and purslane. The following recipe is for a real spring-tonic salad:

Make a basic gelatin aspic using lemon juice and freshly ground white pepper. Chill, and when it begins to thicken add ½ cup of young dandelion leaves, 2 sliced hard-cooked eggs, 3 tablespoons of blue cheese, and ¼ cup of French dressing.

You might also like to try this recipe for dandelion salad: 4 cups dandelion leaves, 4 slices bacon, 1 egg, beaten lightly, 3 tablespoons vinegar, 2 tablespoons sugar, 2 tablespoons water, 4 tablespoons bacon fat, 1 medium chopped onion.

Wash dandelions and place in bowl. Fry bacon until crisp, then crumble. Mix beaten egg, vinegar, sugar, water, hot bacon fat, chopped onion, and bacon, pour over dandelions.

French Fried Dandelion Blossoms: Ever try eating dandelion blossoms? They're good french fried, and here's a recipe you'll want to try. First, gather a batch of blossoms, look them over, and wash thoroughly. Roll in a towel to remove excess moisture. Dip each blossom in flour and fry in deep fat. Sprinkle lightly with salt and you'll find they're delicious!

Dandelion Wine: Quite often I've been asked how to make dandelion wine. Legally, you must get permission from your state Department of Alcoholic Beverage Control to make wine. To qualify as a home brewmaster, you must be the head of a household and can make no more than 200 gallons for your own consumption. According to federal law, it can be served to guests but may not be sold, bartered, or given away. If you meet all these requirements, home wine-making is within the law.

While I'm not wild about dandelion wine, home gardeners with unimpeachable taste buds report its bouquet matches champagne and its overall effect is memorable. Here's a "Closely Guarded" recipe sent me: 15 quarts dandelion blossoms, 3 gallons cold water, 15 pounds sugar, 1 yeast cake, juice and rinds of 12 oranges, juice and rinds of 6 lemons, 2½ pounds of raisins. Place the blossoms in cold water and simmer for 3 hours. Then strain the liquid. Mix it with sugar, let it boil up, then strain through cheesecloth. When lukewarm, add the yeast cake, and let the mixture stand for 2 or 3 days, skimming it each day. Add the juices of the oranges and lemons with the thinly peeled rinds of both which have been simmered for ½ hour in a little water. This should make about 5 gallons. Put it into a cask and add the raisins. Leave the cask open for a day or 2. Then seal it tightly and let stand 6 months before bottling. This makes a lively wine which improves with age.

This is one way to get rid of those yellow dandelion blossoms in your lawn and garden each spring.

EGGPLANT (*Solanum Melongena*)

Eggplants are considered difficult to grow, but actually take the same culture as peppers. Eggplants need a long season to mature fruit.

Varieties: Select earliest varieties for northern culture. The best eggplant for the home garden is Black Magic hybrid, requiring only 72 days to ripen from the time the plants are set out. This hybrid produces crops even where other eggplant varieties fail. Vines are husky.

Sowing: Seed should be started indoors in a sunny window where the temperature is between 70° and 90°. Seed will not come up if temperature is lower. Plants are tender! When seedlings are 2 inches high, transplant singly into pots. Eggplants do not transplant easily. It takes about 8 or 9 weeks to grow the plants to proper size for setting out.

A patch of 6 plants will produce all the fruits that an average family of 5 will need. Set plants 24 to 30 inches apart, and plant in new soil location. Make sure you wash your hands with soap and water if you use tobacco in any form. A rich, sandy, warm soil produces the best eggplants and the most fruit. You may also buy plants already started in flats. Do not plant outdoors until soil is warm. Keep well watered, especially at flowering.

Harvesting: Fruit is ready to eat when about ⅔ grown. Harvest fruits when still glossy and clip close to the fruit. They're too old when the skin becomes dull.

TROUBLES

Blossom Drop: Can be due to low night temperature, hot, dry winds, or a deficiency of nitrogen in a sandy soil.

Verticillium Wilt: The most important disease affecting eggplant is verticillium wilt. Causes wilting, drying out of plants. Never set eggplants close to tomatoes or potatoes. Never work eggplants when foliage is wet with rain or dew. Do not plant more than once every 4 to 5 years on same soil. Rotation is best means of reducing losses of disease. Grow eggplants off tomato ground to avoid disease.

Leaf Spot and Fruit Rot: Avoid overly rich soils or too much nitrogen. Do not feed until fruit starts to set.

Flea Beetle (see illustration p. 185): Causes "shotgun" holes in leaves. Dust or spray with Malathion.

USES

My thanks to our friends who sent me these eggplant recipes.

Eggplant Soufflé: 1 medium eggplant, 2 onions, sliced, ⅓ cup butter, 3 eggs, separated, 1 can mushroom soup, 1 teaspoon monosodium glutamate (Accent), fine bread crumbs. Peel and slice eggplant, cut into 1-inch cubes. Cook in salted boiling water until tender. Drain and cool. Sauté onions in butter. Beat egg yolks, add eggplant, sautéed onions, undiluted mushroom soup, and monosodium glutamate. Beat egg whites stiff and fold into eggplant mixture. Place in buttered 2-quart casserole. Bake 45 minutes at 375°. Serves 4.

English Eggplant (also made from pattypan squash): 2 cups cooked, mashed eggplant pulp, or squash, well drained, 1 egg, beaten, ¾ cup flour, ¼ cup milk, ¾ teaspoon salt, sprinkling pepper, 1 teaspoon baking powder, fat for frying. Peel, slice, or dice eggplant, or squash, boil till tender, then drain and mash. To 2 cups mashed eggplant or squash add the remaining ingredients, drop mixture by tablespoon on hot, greased griddle. Fry like griddle cakes, turning them once. Serve as a vegetable at dinner or with bacon as a breakfast or luncheon dish.

Lebanese Eggplant and Cheese (Baitinjaan wa juban): 1 medium eggplant, 1 egg, beaten, 1 teaspoon salt, ¼ cup oil, ¼ pound sharp cheddar cheese, 1 8-ounce can tomato paste, 4 tablespoons minced onion. Cut eggplant into ¼-inch slices. Dip slices in egg beaten with ½ teaspoon salt. Sauté in hot oil until brown on both sides. Arrange sautéed slices in shallow baking dish. Place slice of cheese between layers of eggplant and top each stack with a slice of cheese. Pour the tomato paste around the stacks. Spread the onion over all and add ½ teaspoon salt. Bake in moderately hot oven (350°) for 25 minutes or until cheese is melted. Serves 6.

Lebanese Eggplant Stew (Yekhinet baitinjaan): 1 pound lamb, cubed, 5 medium eggplants, 1 large onion, chopped, 3 tablespoons butter, 1 No. 2 can (about 1 quart) tomatoes, salt, pepper to taste. Boil meat in water for 30 minutes. Peel eggplants and cut into cubes. Fry onion in butter, then add to meat. Add eggplant, tomatoes, and seasoning. Cook over medium heat for 30 minutes. Serves 6 to 8.

Panfried Eggplant: 1 eggplant (¾ pound), 2 tablespoons flour, ¼ teaspoon salt, 2 tablespoons butter. Wash eggplant and remove stem, do not peel. Cut into round slices about ¼ inch thick. Mix flour and salt on a sheet of waxed paper, dip eggplant slices on both sides in flour mixture. Melt butter in skillet, fry slices slowly until golden brown on both sides and cooked through. As slices get done, stack them at side of skillet and fry remaining slices.

Roman Eggplant: 1 medium eggplant, pared and cut in ½-inch slices, ½ cup butter or margarine, melted, ¾ cup fine dry bread crumbs, ¼ teaspoon salt, 1 cup spaghetti sauce with mushrooms, 1 tablespoon crushed oregano leaves, 1 cup shredded American cheese or mozzarella cheese. Dip eggplant in butter or margarine, then in mixture of bread crumbs and salt. Place on greased cooky sheet. Spoon spaghetti sauce atop each slice, sprinkle with oregano and cheese. Bake in hot oven (450°) 10 to 12 minutes or till done. Serves 4 or 5.

Stuffed Eggplant: 2 small or 1 large eggplant, 2 onions, chopped fine, 2 tablespoons butter, 2 tablespoons chopped parsley, 1 pound ground beef, salt and pepper to taste, 1 egg, beaten, ½ cup grated cheese, 2 tablespoons milk. Cut eggplant lengthwise, and scoop out pulp from the center. Sauté the onions in butter, add the pulp of the eggplant, parsley, and then the meat. Season with salt and pepper and mix well. Simmer about 10 minutes. Stuff the eggplant shells with the mixture, cover, and bake in a moderate oven (350°) for 30 to 35 minutes. Mix beaten egg, cheese, and milk, and season with a dash of salt and pepper. When eggplant is cooked, remove from the oven, and cover each slice with the cheese mixture. Place under the broiler and brown.

ENDIVE (*Cichorium endivia*)

Finely curled or fringed-leaved varieties of endive are grown as salad crop. Broad-leaved varieties are grown as late fall and winter crop in south and shipped in a green or a partly blanched condition to northern markets as "escarole." Similar to lettuce in culture.

Sowing: This hardy plant is used mostly in the fall and early winter and for this purpose the seed should be sown in June or July. For early use, plant outdoors as soon as possible. The seed should be planted shallow, ⅛ row ¼ inch deep, in rows 18 to 24 inches apart. Thin the small plants to 8 to 12 inches apart.

Blanching: Blanching improves the texture of the leaves and removes the bitter flavor. A convenient method is to gather the outer leaves together over the heart and fasten them with a string or large rubber band. A 5-inch board placed over the center of the row and held off the plants by placing bricks or stones underneath will also accomplish this purpose. The leaves will blanch in about 2 weeks in warm weather, 3 weeks in cool weather. As freezing weather approaches, the planting may be protected with a mulch. Examine the plants carefully in warm, moist weather and remove the covering until dry if there are signs of decay.

TROUBLES

Snails: Chew holes in leaves. Scatter lime or wood ashes around each plant.
Bitter Taste: Due to lack of blanching (which see).
Rotted Centers: Due to rain. Avoid overcrowding.
Endive has same troubles as lettuce, chemical control not worth it.

FENNEL (*Foeniculum officinalis*)

The bulb type of fennel, also known as finocchio, is best grown as a spring or fall crop as it tends to develop seed stalks in hot weather. Plant in early May for spring crop and in late June or early July for fall use. When the bulbs begin to form, draw earth up to cover and blanch them. Use in salads, or cooked as a vegetable. Fresh, licorice-like flavor.

GARLIC (*Allium sativum*)

Up until recent years, this hardy perennial plant was not too popular with Americans, but now more and more use it to flavor soups, stews, and other dishes.

Planting: If you've been having trouble raising garlic, try sowing it in the fall. Garlic is grown from seed, just like green onions, or you can plant the cloves (divisions of the bulb). Planting the cloves is more satisfactory. A rich, sandy soil seems to be best. Plant cloves right side up, about 1 inch deep and 4 inches apart. Keep plants watered, especially in a dry summer.

Harvesting: When the tops are ripe and have died down, the bulbs are pulled and left on the ground long enough to completely dry the tops. Some gardeners braid the stalks and hang them in an airy place to dry. Or you can remove the tops and dry the bulbs in a basket, bag, or similar container.

Growing Garlic Indoors: Here's a good tip passed along to me: "My wife sticks a wooden toothpick into a clove of garlic and then puts it into a small glass of water. Soon it starts to grow and when she wants a little fresh garlic, she just snips the green part off. She keeps it in a north window so it won't run out of water. Works like a charm."

USES

Some gardeners use herbs such as garlic, onions, thyme, and basil to keep bugs away from their plants. Some say it works and some say it's useless to use herbs for this purpose.

GOURD (*Cucurbita*)

The hard-shelled fruits commonly known as gourds are not edible, but we have included them here because they belong to the same family as cucumbers, squash, and pumpkins, and are of considerable interest to the home gardener for their ornamental value.

Gourds are of 2 general types: the highly colored small sorts—spoon, pear, apple, orange, egg, warted, etc., in solid orange, yellow, green, white, stripes, and bicolors—and the large sorts, calabash, dipper, Hercules' club, etc., often used as containers and utensils.

Planting and Care: Start from seed planted in May, grow on fence, wire trellis, screen, so you can train vines. GOURDS WILL NOT STAND FROST. They take the same general care as cucumbers and melons. Mix a little dry plant food in the soil, and add some peat moss, or you can feed the vines liquid foliage food (23–19–17) as soon as they start to run. Sow seeds directly in ground, 4 feet apart each way, or start in pots indoors and plant outdoors after danger of frost is over.

Ornamental gourds. (Massachusetts Horticultural Society)

Harvesting: Gourds will not keep well if picked immature. Leave fruit on vines as long as possible before frost threatens. Look for browning and drying of stem, a good indication of maturity. Don't scratch a gourd with your fingernail as it may mar the shell. On a cold, clear afternoon take a sharp knife and cut the gourd, leaving a few inches of stem attached. Usually the stems slough off after drying, although sometimes they remain on the fruit and enhance the value.

Drying and Treating: If gourds are not clean, wash them in soapy water (disinfectants and detergents are O.K.) to remove fungi and bacteria. Then be sure to dry each gourd with soft towel. Gourds will not keep well if treated while shell is moist. It takes about 8 days to fully dry the shell. During this time the outer skin hardens and the color on the surface sets. An attic is good place to dry out gourds. Good ventilation helps the drying and subdued light prevents colors from fading. A garage or well-ventilated room is fine as long as gourds are prevented from freezing.

Next step is to treat your gourds with paste or liquid floor wax for shiny effect. You can also use the aerosol wax sprays florists use, or give the gourds a coat of shellac for hard, glossy finish (shellac will change the color).

Make sure gourds are dry before you apply any type of polish. Sealed-in moisture will hasten rot. Treated gourds will last 6 to 8 months.

Most gourds are frost-touchy, but the large lagenarias may be left outdoors all winter, making for greater hardening of the shells. Any gourd with a thin rind should be protected from the least touch of frost. The pear-shaped, etc., will take a slight touch of frost.

TROUBLES

Powdery Mildew: White coating on leaves. Dust with Mildex.

Squash Borer: Gets in stem and causes sudden wilting. Dust plant with Sevin or take a knife and cut out borer. Cover cut stem with soil and new roots will form.

Squash Bug (see illustration p. 186): Spray with Malathion or Sevin, both control melon aphids as well as squash bug. Pull up gourd vines in fall and burn.

Bacterial Wilt: Vines collapse, no control. Spread by aphids.

USES

You can tint gourds any color you wish with sprays sold in florist shops. For arrangements, use silver, gold, etc., and add bittersweet, seed pods, dried berries found in woods, or use fresh fruits, grapes, lemons, apples, oranges, etc., with gourds. You can save seeds from your gourds, or buy new ones from your seed house.

Dipper-type gourds make good birdhouses. Some people tape the neck, although it's not necessary.

HERBS

The 20th-century cook has discovered the charm of homegrown herbs and we see many herb plots in the garden or pots on the windowsill in the homes of the cooks whose cooking is rated the best in the community. They know the magic that herbs can perform, on even the simplest of dishes.

Herbs take us back beyond the present mechanized, material age, when seasonings are purchased in packaged form at the supermarket, to the days when the homemaker relied on her backyard garden for the seasonings which gave distinction to her meals.

The early settlers in America brought with them cuttings of their favorite herbs and we find herb gardens at such treasured spots of colonial America as Mount Vernon, Wakefield, and Stratford.

If you've ever wondered how to pronounce the word, it's either "herb" or "erb," depending on where you live. Here are the secrets of success for your herb garden:

The ideal location for the herb garden is near the house, where the plants will be easy to gather and easily tended and watered during dry weather. A 10'x12' herb garden will supply the herb needs of the average family. In general, 1 short row or only a few feet of row of each of the annuals or ½ dozen plants of the perennials should be sufficient.

Starting Seed Indoors: Most herb seed can be started indoors in a pot of loose, humusy soil, such as a mixture of ⅓ sand, ⅓ peat, and ⅓ loam. Do not sow too thickly. After seedlings are about 1 inch tall, they can be transplanted into small pots or grown together in a 5-inch pot.

Or you can start your herbs outdoors as shown in the accompanying herb chart, then pot up a clump in the fall and bring indoors for winter use. Trim back extra growth to encourage young shoots.

Herbs like a bright window, ample water, feeding once a month, and that's about all. Wash off foliage occasionally to keep them fresh-looking. Snip off any dead foliage and pinch the tops out so they will be nice and bushy. If insects happen to bother herbs, avoid spraying with anything but soap and water. In the summer, you can put the potted herbs outdoors and bring them indoors again in fall.

The accompanying chart lists some common herbs the home gardener should attempt to grow.

USES

Herbs should be used sparingly. Experiment with them singly and in combinations, but always remember that they should *enhance* the food flavor rather than *disguise* it. The proportions in recipes may be changed to vary the flavor and to suit the tastes of your family.

Herb	Green Thumb Tips	Outdoor Uses	Indoor Uses	Harvesting & Storing
Angelica	Start by seed or plants, grow in light shade. Sow in fall and transplant in spring.	Grows 6 ft. tall, ideal for background plant. Cut flower heads off after blooming for longer life.	Use young leaves with fish, seed for cookies and candies.	Cut seed head before dry and keep in warm, airy place.
Anise	Plant seed in May in well-drained soil, full sun. Sow seed directly without transplanting.	2-ft. annual, sprawling and rather slow-growing.	Fresh leaves in salads, soups, and stews. Seeds in cake, cookies, and fruit pies.	Pick fresh leaves as needed. For seed clip flower clusters when gray-green and dry in attic.
Basil	Sow seed in well-drained soil after frost. Likes full sun and ample water.	Border plant, 2 ft. tall. Attracts bees.	Use fresh or dried leaves in eggs, meats, salads, and vegetables.	Cut 6 in. above ground when plants flower, and dry. Strip leaves and flower tips and store in opaque jars.
Borage	Sow seed in poor, dry soil, full sun. Thin to 12 in. apart.	3-ft. annual, star-shaped blue flowers. Good in rock garden.	Teas and vegetables.	Use fresh. Pick flowers and leaves, dry and store in jars.
Caraway	Sow seed in spring or fall in dry, light soil. Germination is slow.	2-ft. biennial, white flowers, useful in back border.	Seeds in meats, salads, soups, rye bread, and cookies.	Cut seed heads before dry and leave on cloth in attic. Store dried seed after separating.
English Chamomile	Sow seed in spring or late summer in sunny spot, thin to 10 in. apart.	Hardy perennial, 12 in. tall. Useful in border or as ground cover.	Herb tea.	Cut flower heads in full bloom and dry in sun. Store in closed containers.

Chervil	Sow seed in spring, grows best in shaded, moist spot. Thin to 4 in. apart.	Hardy annual, 2 ft. tall, handsome deep green foliage. Ideal in back of border.	Use fresh or dried as aromatic garnish, or use like parsley.	Cut leaves and dry quickly. Keep in tightly sealed glass jars.
Chives	Sow seed in spring or fall, or use divisions. Likes full sun, loamy soil, indoors or outdoors. Divide clumps every 3 or 4 years.	Onion-like perennial, 12-in. clumps with lavender blooms. Good in rock gardens.	Use in omelets, salads, cheese, appetizers, and soups.	Cut leaves as needed.
Coriander	Sow seed in late spring, 1 in. deep in well-drained soil, full sun. Thin to 1 foot apart.	Handsome annual 12 in. tall, do not disturb by cultivating.	Meat, cheese, salads, soups, and pickles.	Snip stalks when seeds are ripe, dry in shade, then separate seeds and store in glass.
Dill	Sow seed in spring or late fall in full sun. Do not transplant.	4-ft. annual which may need fencing for wind protection.	Heads in cheese, eggs, pickles. Seeds in soups, gravies, and vegetables.	Pick whole sprays and hang upside down to dry.
Fennel	Sow in rows in May and thin to 6 in. apart. When plants are half-grown, draw earth up around them to blanch the bulbous stalk.	Grown as an annual. Common sweet fennel grows similarly.	Valued for its anise-like flavor cooked or in salad.	Plants mature in 60 days and are then dug. Seeds of common fennel used in cookies, cheeses, and with vegetables.
Horehound	Plant seeds or root divisions in spring. Takes poor soil, full sun.	Coarse perennial, 2 ft. tall, forms bush for background use.	Cakes, cookies, sauces, and meats.	Cut stems just before flowering, dry in shade, and store in opaque jars.

Herb	Green Thumb Tips	Outdoor Uses	Indoor Uses	Harvesting & Storing
Lemon Balm	Sow seed in summer, in full sun.	Hardy perennial, good border plant, 3 ft. tall. May be a pest if allowed to self-sow.	Valuable in seasoning.	Cut tips 2 or 3 times a season. Store in opaque jars after drying.
Lemon Verbena	Start from cuttings in sand. Full sun and ample water.	Fine perennial, also good houseplant.	Sachets, perfumes, toilet water. Flavors fruit salads, jellies, beverages.	Pick tender leaves and dry.
Sweet Marjoram	Start early and transplant out in spring to dry, well-drained soil.	Annual, 15 in. high, with gray foliage, white flowers. Front border.	Eggs, sauces, soups, stuffings.	Use fresh, or dry leaves and store in opaque jars.
Parsley	Soak seed in warm water for day, plant outdoors in rich soil, full sun.	Neat plant 12 in. tall, used in front border or edge. Bring indoors in fall and keep in bright window. Biennial grown as annual.	Use as garnish in egg dishes, meat sauces, salads. High in vitamins.	Cut as needed, or dry in oven and keep in tight jar.
Peppermint	Plant roots or runners in spring. Shade and wet soils are good.	Spreads fast, keep in bounds with metal strips. Set in back border.	Fresh or dried leaves in jellies, desserts, beverages.	Cut stems in bloom, dry and store in tight jars.
Rosemary	Start seed indoors in spring, or root cuttings. Likes full sun, poor, limy soil.	Perennial 4 ft. high, blue flowers. Needs winter protection.	Fresh or dried leaves in poultry, meats, or seafoods.	Cut leaves just before blooming period, crush and store in tight container.

	Culture	Description	Uses	Harvesting
Sage	Start from seed or cuttings in spring. Full sun and drained soil. Mulch in winter, remove dead wood in spring.	Shrubby 2-ft. perennial, light-blue flowers. Fine addition to border.	Chopped fresh leaves in cheese, pickles, or sausage. Powdered leaves in stuffings.	Cut young tips, dry over stove, pulverize leaves and store in tight jar.
Savory, Summer	Sow seed in spring in loamy soil, full sun. Grows fast. Winter savory has same care and uses.	Annual, 18 in. high, bushy, pinkish flowers.	Fresh leaves in green vegetables. Dried leaves in meats, turnips, or cabbage.	Pull up plant and dry, store leaves in sealed jars.
Shallot	Start from new shoots or cloves in spring. Rich, moist soil.	Bulbous annual without much ornamental value.	Use in same manner as onion.	Pull up when tops are yellow, dry 2 or 3 days. Cut off tops and store cloves in trays.
Spearmint	Same as for peppermint.			
Sweet Cicely	Plant seed in fall or spring, or divide parent plant. Partial shade, any type soil.	Fernlike leaves, fragrant white flowers, 2 to 3 ft. tall.	Seeds have spicy taste, used with other herbs.	Pick seeds when green.
Tarragon	Root cuttings in spring, well-drained soil, full sun or semi-shade. Divide every 2 or 3 years as plants get woody.	Handsome foliage enhances the border.	Flavors sauces, salads, seafoods, stuffings.	Cut anytime and hang in loose bundles.

In each herb there is an essential oil that characterizes the flavor of that herb. Herb plant parts must usually be crushed, pressed, or finely cut to insure release of this aromatic oil.

Fresh herbs may be used (chopped very fine, to extract full flavor) or they may be cut at the right stage, dried, and used throughout the winter.

Since dried herbs are more concentrated in flavor, the quantity of dried herbs should be less than when fresh herbs are used. If a recipe calls for 1 tablespoon of fresh herbs, ½ teaspoon of dried herbs should be adequate. Dried herbs need to be in contact with the food longer than fresh herbs do in order to transmit the full herb flavor to the food.

Herb Bouquets: For soups or stews. Tie together 3 or more sprigs of different kinds of fresh herbs (basil, oregano, parsley, and chives are good), using white thread. Place bouquet in stew or soup for an hour or less toward the end of cooking. Remove herbs before serving food.

Dried Herb Bouquets: Place a small amount of mixed dried herbs in 2-inch-square cheesecloth bag. The following will make 6 soup bags, each will season about 2 quarts of soup: 2 teaspoons each thyme, parsley, and marjoram, ½ teaspoon sage leaves, 1 teaspoon savory, 4 teaspoons celery leaves.

Herb Butter: Mix 2 ounces of butter with 1 tablespoon very finely cut or chopped green herbs or ½ teaspoon dried herbs. The butter should be creamed and a few drops of lemon juice added. If dried herbs are used, before serving add some finely chopped chives, parsley, or even a few raw spinach leaves.

Herb Honey: Bruise fresh herb leaves, flower petals, or dried rosebuds very slightly, and place a layer of the leaves or petals in a small saucepan. Pour honey over this. Warm over low heat for 2 minutes. Pour into jar, seal tightly. Allow to stand in a warm room about a week for the flavors to mingle, then strain.

Cardamom Honey: Pour 1 pint of pure clover or orange-blossom honey into small bowl, stir in 1 teaspoon of ground cardamom. Blend well, and cover. Let mixture stand in warm room for 2 days before using. Honey will absorb the warm, sweet flavor of the cardamom.

Poppy-Seed Clover Honey: This recipe calls for 1 pint of pure clover honey. Let it stand in warm room, and then pour into small bowl and add 1 tablespoon whole poppy seed. Blend well and cover. Let it stand 2 days longer before using. Honey will have poppy-seed flavor. Following these directions you can also make honey from leaves of horsemint, spearmint, peppermint, sage, horehound, thyme, marigold, or borage. I find the leaves of rose geranium give a piquant, exciting flavor to honey. You can use almost any herb or combination of herbs— it's all a matter of taste.

Herb Recipes to Improve Appetites: Someone has said that there is really no such thing as an herb recipe—instead herbs are added to some of the millions of recipes now in existence. As a guide to those cooks who are afraid to rely entirely on their imagination, the following recipes featuring herbs are offered. Thanks to my readers for sending them along.

Broiled Tomatoes: Cut firm unpeeled tomatoes into thick slices. Make a mixture of bread crumbs, salt, powdered dried herbs (basil, savory, marjoram, and parsley), 1 heaping teaspoon per slice. Cover tomato slice with mixture, dot with butter. Put on a baking sheet and broil about 10 minutes.

Chicken Cacciatore: 4 to 6 chicken breasts (or 1 ready-to-cook frying chicken, 3 to 3½ pounds cut in serving pieces), 2 tablespoons olive oil, 1 clove garlic, minced, 1 teaspoon oregano, crumbled, salt and pepper, 1 cup sliced mushrooms, 1-pound can stewed tomatoes. Brown chicken in olive oil with garlic. Before turning chicken, sprinkle with oregano, salt, and pepper. Remove garlic. Add mushrooms, brown lightly. Add stewed tomatoes, cover. Simmer 30 minutes. Uncover and continue cooking till sauce is reduced to consistency desired and chicken is very tender. Garnish with parsley. Serve with hot cooked noodles.

French Dressing with Fine Herbs: 1 tablespoon vinegar, 3 to 4 tablespoons oil, ¼ teaspoon salt, pinch sugar, dash cayenne, dash paprika, black pepper. Place all ingredients together in a stoppered glass bottle or a jar with lid, and shake well. To this mixture add finely chopped herbs, such as summer savory and chives, sweet basil and marjoram, chives and chervil, sweet basil and chives. Other combinations or single herbs can be used. Set dressing aside for ½ hour to develop flavor before serving.

Pepper Steak: 1½ pounds round steak, 1 inch thick, ¼ cup salad oil, ½ clove garlic, minced, 3 small onions, sliced, pinch of basil, ⅓ cup tomato sauce, ½ teaspoon sugar, 1 teaspoon salt, dash of pepper, 1 tablespoon soy sauce, 1½ cups bouillon, ½ cup chopped celery, 3 medium-sized green peppers. Cut meat into 1-inch cubes. Heat oil in heavy skillet, add garlic and meat. Brown slowly, about 20 minutes, stirring often. Add onion last few minutes of browning. Add all of remaining ingredients except green peppers. Cover and simmer until meat is tender, about 1 hour, stirring occasionally. Remove stems, seeds, and cores from peppers and cut into 1-inch squares. Add to mixture in skillet. Cover and cook 15 minutes longer. Serve over rice.

Plymouth Colony Stuffing: 9 cups toasted bread crumbs, 1 teaspoon each of summer savory, sweet marjoram, thyme, celery leaves, parsley, powdered or chopped, 2 large onions, minced, ½ teaspoon grated orange or lemon peel, 2 teaspoons salt, ¼ teaspoon pepper, 2 tablespoons butter, 1 egg. Clean the fowl, rub the inside with 1 teaspoon salt, and leave it while the stuffing is being made. Toast day-old whole or cracked wheat bread, and break into crumbs. Toasting not only prevents the bread from becoming soggy, but gives a delightful nutty flavor, especially to cracked or whole wheat bread.

Potatoes Scalloped with Herbs: Following your favorite recipe for scalloped potatoes. Chop fresh herbs—marjoram, savory, chives, parsley— about ½ cup in all. Sprinkle over each layer of potatoes.

Thousand Island Dressing: 1 cup mayonnaise, 3 tablespoons chili sauce, 1 tablespoon chopped green pepper, 1 teaspoon chopped pimiento, 1 teaspoon chopped chives, lettuce wedges. Blend first 5 ingredients thoroughly and chill. Serve over lettuce wedges. Makes 1¼ cups.

Tomato Sandwiches: Add chopped basil, 2 small leaves to each serving.

Tomatoes with Herbs: Peel and cut tomatoes into thick slices. Sprinkle each slice with a pinch of dried basil. Let stand in refrigerator 2 hours. Serve with French dressing. Sprinkle with chopped chives.

HORSERADISH (*Armoracia rusticana*)

Horseradish is still one of the best ways to pep up a jaded appetite. Grows in any soil, but a deep, rich, moist soil is best. Heavy soils produce short, prongy roots and lots of waste.

Plant roots from your nursery. Maliner Kren is a good variety of Bohemian horseradish. Plant in spring, or anytime you harvest, set tops in ground, and new plants will develop. Harvest in spring or fall.

Propagation: Root cuttings. Does not form seeds.

TROUBLES

Flea Beetle (see illustration p. 185): Dust with Sevin.
Rots: Due to fungus, no control.

Grate the roots after harvesting and peeling. If you keep root and grater under a plastic bag, you won't cry. Mix grated horseradish with white-wine vinegar to desired consistency, bottle quickly. To keep hot, keep it cool in refrigerator.

KALE OR BORECOLE (*See Cabbage and Related Crops*)

KOHLRABI (*See Cabbage and Related Crops*)

LETTUCE (*Lactuca sativa*)

There is no question that lettuce is the most popular salad plant. Used alone, or in combination with other vegetables, with or without dressings, it is a tasty part of many of our meals.

Lettuce has been used for many years. According to early writings, lettuce was served on the tables of the Persian kings of the sixth century B.C. Lettuce was popular among the Romans about the beginning of the Christian era and actually had been brought to a fairly advanced state of cultivation.

Lettuce likes cool weather and a loose, well-drained soil. Boost it along through the growing season with applications of liquid plant food (23–19–17).

Leaf Lettuce: Leaf lettuce is most popular with home gardeners because it is so easy to grow. Good loose-leaf varieties are Salad Bowl and Black Seeded Simpson. Salad Bowl holds its quality despite hot, dry weather and will not "bolt" (go to seed) or become tough and bitter under adverse growing conditions. For years Bibb has been an outstanding salad lettuce, but it's too sensitive to temperature and is difficult to grow in hot summers. Also, goes to seed too easily. Matchless (Deer Tongue) is a lettuce hard to beat. A single planting properly thinned and spaced can furnish leaf lettuce over a considerable period during the growing season. Buttercrunch and Summer Bibb are 2 others that won't bolt in midsummer and remain free from bitterness.

Seed of loose-leaf lettuce is sown anytime from early spring until July, making several plantings for a continuous supply. Plant in rows about 2 feet apart, covering seed very lightly. Some gardeners thin the plants, using the thinnings for salad, and it's a pretty good idea. If you've had trouble getting seed to germinate in hot weather, try putting it in the refrigerator prior to planting. This treatment makes the seed come up faster. Put the seed in a shallow dish (no water) and let it remain in the refrigerator for 24 hours, then sow.

A reader passes along a good tip: "I mix some Bibb lettuce seed with sand and in February when there's a thaw, I scatter the seed on the ground and forget about it. Then in May I have a real privilege—harvesting some fresh lettuce. I hit on this accidentally, and would like to have some of your other readers try this."

Head Lettuce: To get good head lettuce you should sow seed early indoors. Transplant seedlings in pots, and toughen them up (harden them off) in a cold frame before setting outdoors. Or you can sow the seed in open ground, and thin the plants to at least 15 inches apart in the row. This is important, since good heads cannot form unless the plants have plenty of room. White Boston is a popular "Butterhead" lettuce grown for the home garden as well as market. It holds up well under most garden conditions, although it doesn't do well in hot weather so spring sowing should be early. For something different, try the upright-headed Romaine lettuce, with crisp leaves and delicate flavor.

For fall use sow head lettuce seed the last of July or first part of August and treat in the same way as the spring crop. As with all lettuce, you get good crisp leaves when the plants are grown rapidly and well watered and cultivated. If yours do not form heads, chances are they have not had enough room for growth.

TROUBLES

Tipburn: About the most serious problem of lettuce. If the edges of your lettuce leaves turn brown or die back, this is tipburn, caused by unfavorable weather. It may also be brought on by a degeneration of cells due to high temperature, particularly high night temperatures. There is no control. Bitterness may also result from high temperature.

Yellow Leaves or Mosaic: Due to virus spread by aphids and leafhoppers. Control: Destroy nearby weeds such as wild carrot, chicory, dandelion, and wild aster.

Rust Streaks in Center of Leaves or Inside Heads: No one knows exact cause, but we do know it can be aggravating.

Slugs: Worst pest of lettuce. Use metaldehyde baits, or try this trick my readers send along: Fill pie plates with beer, set out among the lettuce rows. Attracts and kills 'em.

USES*

Curried Buffet Cups: Marinate cooked mixed vegetables in Italian

*Courtesy Western Iceberg Lettuce, Inc.

oil and vinegar dressing with a little curry powder added. Fill lettuce cups with marinated mixture.

French Toss: Marinate cooked green beans and sliced fresh mushrooms in an oil and wine vinegar dressing flavored with Dijon mustard, salt, and pepper. At serving time, toss marinated mixture with torn, bite-size pieces of head lettuce, tomato wedges, and garlic croutons.

Ham and Bean Slaw: In a bowl, combine shredded lettuce with cut green beans, slivers of cooked ham, and grated lemon rind. Toss with a sharp fresh lemon juice and salad oil dressing, seasoned to taste.

Hot Cheese-Sauced Lettuce: For a "do-it-again" luncheon or weekend supper: 1 cup grated sharp cheddar cheese, ⅓ cup bottled Thousand Island dressing, ⅓ cup sour cream, ¼ teaspoon salt, 1 head lettuce, 16 slices Italian dry salami, 4 pickled onions, 4 pitted ripe olives. Combine cheese, dressing, sour cream, and salt in saucepan. Heat, stirring, over low heat until cheese is melted. Cut lettuce into 4 wedges, place on serving plate. Spoon hot sauce over wedges and place 2 salami slices on each side of each wedge. Place 1 onion and 1 olive on each of 4 toothpicks, spike into wedges through salami. Serves 4.

Lettuce Basket Salad: (Party-pretty for potluck suppers or festive dinners) 1 large head lettuce, cored, ½ cup mayonnaise, ½ cup sour cream, 1½ cups diced red apples, 1 cup pitted ripe olives, cut into rings, 1 cup thinly sliced carrots, 2 tablespoons chopped red onion, 1 teaspoon grated lemon rind, 2 tablespoons lemon juice, 2 teaspoons sugar, ¾ teaspoon salt, ¼ teaspoon rosemary, crumbled. From the core end, cut out and chop enough lettuce to make about 1 cup. Rinse head, gently separating and spreading leaves at core end to form a basket. Chill all lettuce in a plastic bag. Before serving, mix chopped lettuce with all other ingredients and heap into lettuce basket. To transport, place on small board or plate atop the upside-down lid of plastic container, cover with container and seal. Serves 6.

Lettuce Cooler: Mix bottled Green Goddess dressing with an equal measure of creamed cottage cheese and a little chopped pickle. Spoon over crisp wedges of lettuce and garnish with crumbled corn chips. Serve with chili.

Meatball-Vegetable Salad: ¾ pound ground beef, ½ teaspoon garlic salt, ½ teaspoon seasoned pepper, ¼ cup cooking oil, ½ pound thinly sliced zucchini or crookneck squash (about 1½ cups), ¼ cup cider vinegar, 1 clove garlic, minced, few drops aromatic bitters (optional), 1 head lettuce, 1 large tomato, cut into wedges, ¾ cup onion rings. Combine beef, garlic salt, and seasoned pepper, form into 24 small balls. Heat oil in skillet, add meatballs, and cook until browned and done as you like them. Transfer meatballs into salad bowl. Add zucchini, vinegar, garlic, and bitters to skillet, mixing with drippings from bottom of pan. Heat slightly, then pour over meatballs. Chill, turning occasionally to coat. Just before serving, coarsely chop enough lettuce to measure 6 cups. Add chopped lettuce to meatball mixture along with tomato and onion. Toss gently. Garnish with strips from frilly outer leaves of lettuce if you wish. Serves 10 to12.

Mexicali Crescents: Cut lettuce rafts into halves and place back-to-back on individual salad plates. Allow 1 raft per person. Spoon bottled chili sauce thinned with a little salad oil and vinegar into each. Top with avocado crescents, shrimp or crab, and a lime or lemon fan.

Orange-Iceberg Salad: (An eye-catching centerpiece salad for a bridge luncheon.) 2 large California oranges, 1 tablespoon cornstarch, 1 tablespoon butter or margarine, ¼ teaspoon salt, ⅛ teaspoon marjoram, crumbled, dash onion powder, 1 8-ounce package cream cheese, softened, 1 head lettuce, parsley sprigs. Grate 1 tablespoon rind from orange, halve 1 orange and squeeze juice to make ⅓ cup. Blend cornstarch with orange juice in saucepan, add grated rind, butter, salt, marjoram, and onion powder. Cook, stirring, over medium heat until mixture comes to boil and is thickened and clear. Blend with cream cheese and chill. Just before serving, pare remaining orange and cut crosswise into 8 slices. Cut lettuce lengthwise into wedges. Spread cheese mixture on cut sides of wedges, fit wedges together with orange slices in between to resemble whole head of lettuce. Place on serving plate and garnish with parsley around base. Serves 4.

Roquefort Relish: Combine shredded lettuce with mayonnaise, vinegar, fresh or frozen chives, and crumbled Roquefort cheese. Mound in lettuce cups and garnish with sprigs of watercress as an elegant accompaniment to lamb.

Salad Bonanza for Beef: Spread rafts of lettuce with horseradish-flavored mayonnaise and top with orange slices, Tokay grape halves, and roasted slivered almonds.

Tropical Salad for Ham: Perfect accompaniment for ham is chunks of iceberg lettuce tossed with fresh or canned pineapple tidbits, seedless raisins, and a sprightly dressing of mayonnaise and thinned orange marmalade. Garnish with chopped walnuts.

Wilted Lettuce: 2 slices bacon, 2 tablespoons sugar, 1 teaspoon salt, dash of pepper, 3 tablespoons vinegar, 5 cups chopped lettuce, 1 medium onion, sliced. Cut bacon in small pieces and brown in skillet. Remove crisp bacon, add sugar, salt, and pepper to drippings. While drippings are still hot, add vinegar (but remove from fire so strength of vinegar doesn't boil away) and pour over cleaned and chopped lettuce and onion. Mix well, garnish with bacon, and serve immediately.

Wilted Lettuce Italiano: Tear lettuce into bite-size pieces, mound in shallow bowl. To bottled Italian dressing add some strips of Italian dry salami, ripe olive rings and fresh or frozen chives. Heat and pour over lettuce.

MUSHROOMS

It's possible to raise edible mushrooms in the basement of your home during fall and winter months, but don't expect to raise them for a living. The advertisements might fool you into thinking you can. It takes a real green thumb to grow mushrooms successfully in the cellar. Commercially prepared mushroom trays are available, and they're ready to bear a crop as soon as they're given the right conditions. You can also buy mushroom spawn in "bricks."

Mushrooms for Money?: A reader wrote to ask us if he could successfully grow mushrooms in his basement, using the specially prepared kits. He sent along an ad from a firm which pays $3.50 a pound for mushrooms grown from kits purchased from the firm.

Home growing of mushrooms is all right if you want to experiment but don't fall for that hokum of making money by raising mushrooms in the cellar and selling them to a company. The Federal Trade Commission tells us that in one year the public paid one company $328,000 for mushroom kits in hope of making money, and all the customers sold back to the company was $5,324.76 worth of mushrooms. Money was made on mushrooms, but it was the company that profited, and not the customers.

This shouldn't discourage you from trying to grow a mushroom tray or 2 in the cellar for the fun of it. We've had a lot of fun raising mushrooms in the trays, but it's mighty tricky getting a crop. The trays come complete with compost and topsoil.

They need temperatures between 52° and 65° and darkness, since mushrooms are a fleshy fungus with no chlorophyl. Mushrooms do not manufacture their own food, as do all normal green plants.

The most common failure with mushrooms comes from high cellar temperatures. If temperature is over 75° for as much as a day, failure will result. If the air temperature drops below 50°, the crop will be delayed, if not killed.

The air in many basements is too dry for a successful crop of mush-rooms, so your biggest job is to protect them from dry air. One way to do this is to put a piece of muslin or cloth of some sort over the trays, leaving it on all the time, raising it only to pick mushrooms (if you're lucky enough to get any).

Water right over the cloth, repeating several times until the soil sur-face is damp. After that, watering twice a week should be enough. Never allow the beds to dry out, but they must not be soaked, either. Water the surface of the bed just enough to keep it moist, using rain-water or tepid tap water.

It takes about 3 weeks (with luck) to get small mushrooms the size of pinheads. These increase in size daily until mature. Mold on the sur-face usually precedes the mushrooms, but it's nothing to be alarmed about. If you succeed in getting mushrooms, you'll find they don't all mature at once, so pick the ones that are ready and leave the others to develop. Mushrooms grow in "flushes"—that is, they'll pop up all at the same time and then there'll be a period when there aren't any. Pick as they mature and allow new ones to come along later.

A friend of mine in the Midwest wrote: "May I tell your readers how I grow mushrooms in our cellar? First, we put a barrel of earth and horse manure mixture in the corner of the cellar. The temperature stays about 60° all the time, and the corner is dark. We buy a brick of mushroom spawn from a seed house and break it up into pieces the size of hen's eggs. These are raked into the manure-earth mixture, watered with tepid water by hose or sprinkling can, and kept damp for several weeks. We have a beautiful crop of mushrooms continu-ously for months. They produce all we can use and give away.

"The second year, after a rest, they come back again. One year, we were so tired of them we threw the soil mixture out into the garden and in the following warm, humid weather, the little buttons con-tinued to pop up for years!"

OUTDOOR MUSHROOMS—POISONOUS AND NONPOISONOUS

The common practice of eating mushrooms found growing wild has sent many to their graves. Eating mushrooms growing along the road, in lawns, etc., is tricky business. There is no dependable test to deter-mine whether a mushroom is poisonous or edible. The only way to be sure is to recognize an edible mushroom on sight, as you would a violet, a rose, or a lily. There is no dependable test such as the "silver spoon" test or the "peeling of the cap" that will enable an inexperienced person to differentiate between the harmless and the deadly.

Some general rules for mushroom collectors are: NEVER EAT MUSH-ROOMS UNTIL YOU ARE SURE OF THEIR IDENTITY. Be sure all mushrooms are collected fresh. Never eat brightly colored ones, as they are likely to be loaded with a deadly poison. Reject all forms that have a cup around the base of the stem, and any with white gills or white spore dust. Don't let that white puffball growing in your yard tempt you or your children. It may or may not be poisonous.

Our good friend Charles Wilson of the Harris Seed Company says he heard a mushroom grower say once that the best way for anyone but an expert to tell whether a mushroom was safe to eat or not was by the word MUSHROOMS printed on the box in the grocery store!

Play safe and let the experts pick the outdoor mushrooms. People who eat the wild types say they are out of this world. If they eat the wrong type they too will be out of this world!

USES[*]

Dips and Dunks: For cocktail serving, prepare raw mushrooms by simply wiping with damp paper towel and snipping off the end of stem. Cut through the cap and down through the stem into quarters, bite size. Run toothpick into each piece and place around bowl of good dip. Nothing is better than the well-tried sour cream and onion soup with variations. It is a nice complement to the delicate flavor of mushrooms.

Mushroom Dip 'n' Dunk Sauce: Drain ½ cup (4-ounce can) mushrooms, stems and pieces. Chop finely and add to ¼ cup mayonnaise and ¾ cup sour cream. Stir together and season with few drops hot pepper sauce, or tiny pinch cayenne pepper, ¼ teaspoon salt, plenty of freshly ground black pepper, 1 teaspoon horseradish, drained, and 2 teaspoons grated onion. Chill and sprinkle paprika on top. (1 tablespoon brandy or 2 tablespoons dry wine will add flavor to mixture.)

Nippy Dip 'n' Dunk Sauce: Use ½ cup mayonnaise, and with a fork lightly stir into it ¼ teaspoon dry mustard, 2 or 3 drops hot pepper sauce, ½ teaspoon prepared horseradish, 2 teaspoons lemon juice, and 2 tablespoons chili sauce. Strain all ingredients through sieve. Mix lightly and if a bit too thin add sour cream, or even whipped cream to make it hold up longer. This may be varied to suit your own taste and fancy. Must be really cold for dipping. Keep in refrigerator until serving time.

French Fried Mushrooms: This recipe came from the 1960 Reading, Pennsylvania fair. These crisp delicious bites were made in the Muhl-

[*]My thanks to the American Mushroom Institute for their assistance with these recipes.

enberg Rotary Club booth and the crowds clamored for more and more. Such a simple recipe, but oh, so good!

Drain stems and pieces or sliced mushrooms, then scatter out on paper toweling until quite dry. Transfer to another dry piece of paper toweling and dust with coating of flour. Drop a few at a time into a coarse sieve and shake off excess flour. Heat peanut oil, or any favorite shortening, to 375°. Place floured mushrooms in hot deep oil or fat and fry approximately 2 minutes. Do not overcook. These crisp bites should not be too brown. Drain on absorbent paper, sprinkle lightly with salt. Serve piping hot.

Mushrooms and Green Peas: The French chef wants a lift in every serving. He knows "banquet peas" should be good enough to eat, not just left on the plate. Here's how: In heavy saucepan having tight lid, make a nest of outside lettuce leaves, dipped out of cold water and still dripping. Into this, center 1 pound frozen peas. Add a chunk of butter, a dash of salt and pepper, and a dash of nutmeg, freshly grated if you have it. Cover with more lettuce leaves, cover, and cook gently for about 15 minutes. When ready to serve, remove all lettuce leaves and discard. Stir into the peas 4 to 6 finely diced mushrooms lightly sautéed in butter. Serve from heated bowl. Delicious and different. If you like, use a 4-ounce can sliced mushrooms (drained) in this serving.

Teen-agers' Pizza-Quick: The teen-agers have already been tested on this recipe and "dig" it plenty, because as they say, all they have to do is pick up the makings and put them together, at the moment hunger strikes. This, they say, is important. Split English muffins in half. Add 2 tablespoons tomato paste to each muffin half. On top of this settle sliced well-drained mushrooms and sprinkle plenty Parmesan cheese over all. Dot with chunks of mozzarella cheese and add a pinch oregano. Drizzle olive or peanut oil generously over them and broil slowly, not too close to heat, until cheese melts and pizza is sizzling hot. Serve now or sooner. Note: If you happen to have no tomato paste, use fresh tomato slices, or canned tomato, well drained and seasoned.

MUSKMELON (*Cucumis melo*)

Muskmelons are so named because of the delightful odor of the ripe fruits, musk being a Persian word for a kind of perfume. The varieties known as cantaloupe, honeydew, casaba, and Persian melon are all muskmelons.

The muskmelon is native to Persia, Iran, and adjacent areas on the west and east. The oldest record of muskmelon goes back to an Egyptian painting of around 2400 B.C. The Greeks appear to have known the fruit in the third century B.C., and in the first century after Christ it was definitely described by the Roman naturalist Pliny, who said it was something new in Campania.

Culture of muskmelons spread westward over the Mediterranean area in the Middle Ages and was apparently common in Spain by the 15th century. Columbus carried muskmelon seeds on his second voyage and had them planted on Isabella Island in 1494. This was doubtless their first culture in the New World.

In the United States, the small, oval, netted shipping type of muskmelon is commonly called a cantaloupe. In Europe, however, the type of muskmelon referred to as cantaloupe is a long-keeping type with a hard, ridged, or warty rind. So we might say that all cantaloupes are muskmelons but many varieties and types of muskmelons are not cantaloupes.

The dual name of this fruit, which is an important truck and garden crop in the United States, has been a matter of considerable puzzlement to many folks. The American usage of cantaloupe is strongly established and generally accepted in this country.

Cantaloupes are not only one of the most tasty of our garden fruits but are also one of the most nutritious. Deeply colored cantaloupes are very high in vitamin A and all cantaloupes are excellent sources of vitamin C.

Soil and Planting: Muskmelons (and most melons) like a well-drained soil, dislike "wet feet." They need a long growing season and hot, dry weather. Melons are likely to be of inferior quality in cool, cloudy seasons.

For best results start them indoors in a light, rich, sterilized soil. Sow in a flat or box and transplant to individual pots about 5 days after they come up. Or seed direct in peat pots or similar containers, 2 or 3 seeds per pot, thinning to the 1 or 2 stronger plants. Be sure to keep the soil very warm, 70° to 80°, during germination. The plants will be ready for setting out in 3 or 4 weeks.

If possible, plant melons on sunny, sandy, well-drained soil where melons and similar crops have not been grown in recent years. Delay planting until the soil is warm. Melons do not succeed on poorly drained soils and they are less subject to disease on new ground.

Soil should not be too acid, about pH 6.0. If soil is too acid, leaves turn yellow, curl, or show dying at the edges. This acid-yellow shows up more during dry seasons than during seasons of ample rainfall. To add lime once the yellowing has set in is usually too late.

Well-rotted manure is excellent for melons, worked into the soil under the row before planting. Fertilize well and side-dress with extra fertilizer along the row when the plants begin to run. Disturb the vines as little as possible. Avoid injuring or moving vines when cultivating or hoeing. Do not cultivate deeply as the melon root system is shallow. Irrigate in dry spells.

Paper caps, "paper greenhouses," and similar plant protectors are ideal for melons, which are injured by cool nights and cold winds. The plants can actually be killed by temperatures below 40° and must have protection. Ventilate the protectors well when the sun is out.

Melons respond well to growing on plastic mulches. They will mature more quickly and yield more, and a great proportion of the yield will be top-grade fruit. Black plastic discourages weeds and so is preferable to clear plastic. Simply set the plants through holes or slits in the plastic, but be sure the soil is watered well before laying the plastic. Straw mulch may also be used.

In warm areas, melons may be seeded direct in the field, through slits in the plastic mulch or in open ground, but the crop will be later than when started indoors. Sow in 6-foot rows, covering the seed ½ to 1 inch deep, and thin plants to stand about 1 foot apart.

When to Pick: The time to pick cantaloupes is when the body color turns to a yellowish-green and the netting on the skin becomes rounded. Don't test the skin with your fingernail, as rot may set in. Rather, try the "half-slip" method, which is quite reliable. Press lightly on the stem with your thumb at the point where the stem joins the fruit. If the disc slides off with just a little resistance, the melon is ready. Cantaloupes don't develop additional sugar after they are picked. If taken from the vine too green they will never get sweet, though they will soften.

Honeydew melons have a sweet odor when ripe, and a yellowish color to the skin.

Sweeter Melons: If your melons are flat and tasteless, it may be due to a lack of magnesium or boron in the soil. Specialists have found that such plants can be sweetened up by giving them a dose of Epsom salts and borax. When mixed and applied with an insecticide, you get bigger fruits and more of them. The ideal time to spray your melons is when the vines start to run, and again when the fruits are between 1 and 2 inches in diameter. Field recommendations are to add 4 pounds of magnesium sulfate (Epsom salts) and 2 pounds of borax to 100 gallons of fungicide spray. For the home garden this figures out to 6½ tablespoons of Epsom salts and 3⅓ tablespoons of borax (household type) to 5 gallons of spray water.

How to Buy a Ripe Melon: Melons are perhaps one of the most difficult fruits to select, as their internal quality cannot be seen. Many a food shopper is observed shaking a melon held to the ear and listening intently to determine quality. This technique actually tells you little, for the noise you hear is not necessarily quality, but rather loose seeds.

The wisest guide to quality in buying, as in picking, is the condition of the netting on the cantaloupe, the color of the skin, and the resilience of the fruit. For a mature cantaloupe, the netting should be coarse and the rind showing through should be grayish-yellow.

A ready-to-eat cantaloupe will feel springy when general, slight pressure is applied. The trick of pressing the thumb against the stem end is not a very fair one. The pressure can damage the fruit.

Color is also the shopping cue to quality in honeydew melons. A ripe honeydew has a creamy-yellow surface color, coupled with a light, pleasant odor. Melons can be ripened at room temperature, but they will not have the sugar content that gives flavor.

TROUBLES

Don't be disappointed if not all your blossoms set fruit. The first blossoms on muskmelons are male, thus cannot produce fruits. They are for rooster effect. A combination of male and female flowers comes later, and it's the female flowers that produce.

Wilt: If your melons make fine growth, then all of a sudden the vines wilt and die, this is the work of a wilt organism spread by aphids or the striped cucumber beetle, pests of all melon vines. The cucumber beetle chews leaves of young plants, also transmits diseases from one plant to another.

Control: Spray melons and cukes with Malathion, 1 tablespoon to a gallon of water. Do not apply later than 10 days before harvest, and do not apply unless plants are dry. Destroy disease-carrying weed hosts such as wild cucumber, catnip, pokeberry, ground cherry, plantain, etc. Also, it's a good idea to keep your melon patch away from such flowers as petunia, gladiolus, phlox, hollyhock. Always plant wilt-resistant varieties such as Delicious 51 or Iroquois.

Mosaic: Foliage mottled, yellowed. Destroy weed and insect carriers as for wilt disease, plant mosaic-resistant varieties.

Other diseases of melons include damping-off, bacterial wilt, downy mildew, and blossom-end rot. Include some Captan or ferbam in your spray, or you can dust these on your plants. Apply as soon as the plants break through the ground, or are 3 inches high. Make a second application 4 days later, then once a week as long as they need protection.

USES

If you get carried away and plant more muskmelons than your family can eat, you can always find a ready market for the extra ones. I've found that melon balls freeze very well and offer a rare treat in winter when served as a dessert. Simply cut the firm, well-ripened flesh into balls or cubes. Cover with a thin sugar syrup and place in freezer.

MUSTARD GREENS (*Brassica*)

Easy to grow, ideal for greens because of the ease of preparing the broad, smooth leaves. Can be used in salads or cooked.

Sow early in spring, broadcast or plant 2 to 3 inches apart, and make successive plantings. For fall use, plant seed in August. Burpee's Fordhook Fancy is recommended for its green leaves that curve backward like ostrich plumes.

There's a Chinese mustard (Bok Toi) with thick stems and green leaves that are chopped and added to meat dishes before serving. Or they can be lightly steamed with butter or a touch of bacon. The tender young leaves are fine in salads. Plant outdoors in early spring or late summer, matures in 60 days.

OKRA (*Hibiscus esculentus*)

Either you like okra (also known as gumbo) or you don't. Those who don't like it probably never tried it. Southerners rely on it because okra, butter beans, and cowpeas will continue to bear in spite of summer heat. Okra is great for soups and as a thickening agent and is easily prepared for freezing. You can grow it as far north as New York State. Okra likes full sun.

Planting and Care: Soak seeds in warm water for 12 hours prior to planting in warm soil. Sow the seed in the open ground as soon as the soil becomes warm. Rows should be 2½ to 3 feet apart and the plants should be thinned out to 1 foot apart in the rows. The seed should be sown not more than 1 inch apart to get an even stand of plants. The pods should be picked while they are still small and tender, 2 or 3 inches is ideal, never over 4 inches. All mature pods should be kept picked off so the plants will continue to bear.

TROUBLES

Fusarium Wilt: Rotate crops.

Yellowing of Leaves: Due to chlorosis (soil too acid or alkaline). Test soil and see if pH reading is around 5.6 or so (slightly acid), best for okra.

Bud Drop: Due to hot, dry weather, drop in temperature, or poor soil drainage.

Woody Okra: Failure to pick regularly. Pick plants clean of any okra over 1 inch.

USES

Okra is prepared by steaming and dipping in batter for quick-frying. Southerners also steam whole pods lightly and serve buttered.

Onion (*Allium cepa*)

This vegetable, in 1 or more of its many forms, is found in practically every home garden. Its pungent odor may be a source of distress to some persons and situations, but it would be hard to name another vegetable that does so much for such a wide range of recipes.

Onions are grown from seed, sets (bulblets), or plants, depending on the purpose and the variety. They like a rich sandy loam with plenty of humus or muck. If soil is full of clay, be sure to add plenty of peat and plant food in early spring. During dry spells in summer, give them LOTS OF WATER, or the onions will be hot to taste. Keep onions weeded and cultivated for best growth.

Onions from Seed: To raise them from seed, sow thickly in rows 2 inches apart, covering about ½ inch, and dropping 8 seeds per inch to allow for maggot damage (see Troubles of Onions). Thin out to 1 or 1½ inches apart for small green onions and 3 or 4 inches for large mature bulbs. The thinnings can be used for green onions or boiling onions.

Onion Sets: Both early green bunching onions and large dry onions are very easily raised from sets. "Sets" are small onion bulbs, ½ to ¾ inches across, produced from seed the previous year. Sets larger than ¾ inch are unsatisfactory because they are apt to bolt and set seed quickly.

Sets should be planted early in spring in rows 18 to 20 inches apart, and about 3 inches apart in the row. If you want small early green onions, plant thicker. I dig a trench and put the onions in it, close enough so they touch one another. Cover sets completely with soil, and in a few weeks you can pull them for green onions, or let them mature into large onions by July.

Some gardeners make successive plantings of sets for green onions during the spring and early summer. Although these plants can be allowed to mature to dry bulbs, they are not as good for storage as these grown from seed or plants.

Onion Plants: If you like the big "hamburger" onions (Bermuda and Spanish onions) set out seedling onion plants early in spring. These plants are grown in the South, and you buy them in bunches ready to plant. If you want to raise your own, start seed indoors in January. Use light, rich soil. When plants are 6 inches high, trim them back to 4 inches with shears. Set out in open ground as early as possible, 4 to 5 inches apart in rows. Spread roots out well when planting. Hamburger onion plants are cheap. A bunch is a handful as pulled in the field in the South, running 55 to 110 plants per bunch. A couple of bunches might cost you $1.50 or so, well worth it.

As soon as you get your bunch of onion plants from the seed house, open them and give air. If you can't plant immediately, spread out in cool dry place. DO NOT WATER or heel in. Don't worry if the roots on plants are dry, as the bulb will make a new set of roots when planted. Set plants 4 to 5 inches apart in rows 1½ to 2 feet apart, or set somewhat closer, and pull every other one for green onions in spring and early summer.

Spanish Onions: The large, sweet Spanish onions are ideal for the home garden and roadside stands. And don't forget the hybrids, such as Early Harvest. The Sweet Spanish is not a long-storage onion like the hard commercial onions. It will keep quite well under good storage conditions, but it is not likely to last all winter as some of the real storage onions do. Some people freeze these onions. Grown from plants.

Red Onions: There's a Burgundy and a Southport Red Globe red onion. Bulbs are large, round, small-necked, with thick, deep, purplish-red skin, white flesh tinged with pink. Good keeper, heavy yielder. The flavor is quite mild. However, some red onions are hot. Those you see in stores are often raised in Italy, at the base of Mt. Vesuvius, although you can grow your own at home, from plants.

All these relatives of the onion are easy to grow.

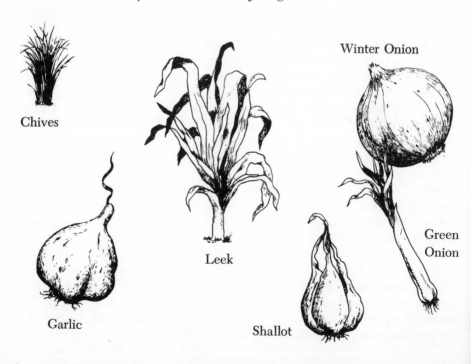

Chives

Winter Onion

Garlic

Leek

Shallot

Green Onion

Bunching Onions: These are onions which do not make a bulb, but make long slim "scallions." There's a white Spanish bunching type and White Portugal, ideal for bunching. Make excellent pickling onions, snow-white and very firm. White Ebenezer sets are good for bunching, and make fine little onions early; if allowed to mature, produce flattened bulbs in midsummer.

Multiplier Onions: These are hardy perennials planted in fall for early green onions. They are grown from top sets, sets that develop on top of plant in July. May also be grown from divisions of clumps that develop.

Small bulbs of Yellow Multipliers and White Multipliers (potato onions) grow into large ones which break up into smaller onions and thus are propagated. Small bulbs O.K. for pickling. Onions are hardy and can be left in ground during winter, but it's better to take up when mature and separate and reset 3 to 4 inches apart in spring. Multiplier onions are sometimes erroneously referred to as "shallots" (which see).

Perennial or "Tree" or "Top" Onion (Egyptian): This is a common winter onion on which clusters of small onions (bulblets) are produced on top of the onion stalk. Grown for green onions and more common than multipliers. May be set in late summer, fall, or spring.

Shallots: Related to onions, perennial, seldom produce seed. Here's a little-used vegetable with a delicate flavor. Ideal for flavoring mushrooms, salads, scrambled eggs. This onion is started from sets planted in spring. Shallots mature in September, when they are harvested and stored in a cool, dry place. Good keepers and will last until the new shallots are mature the following spring. Small bulbs are compound and grow and break up into smaller ones. These small bulbs are the sets used for planting.

Leeks: Look like green onions, except leaves are flat, plants are thicker, and do not form bulbs. Use for flavoring, or boil and serve with white sauce. Grow from seed sown 2 inches deep in a trench. Thin to 3 inches apart in row. As they grow, hill soil around stems to blanch them. Seed can be sown indoors in March and plants set in garden in April for early crop.

Non-edible Onions—Ornamental Only: The Pregnant onion (sea onion) and the alliums are not edible. You grow these like you do regular onions. (Sea onion is not hardy, but alliums are.) Sea onion is used for poultice, burns, etc., but alliums have large flowering heads florists use in decorative arrangements.

Harvesting and Storing: In late summer or early fall, onion tops die down naturally. One common mistake is to attempt to hasten maturity by rolling down tops with a lawn roller or a cart of some sort. This practice is not recommended in light of new evidence, because it leads to lower yields, poor storage quality, and increased losses due to neck rot. LET THE BULBS COMPLETE THEIR GROWTH AND HAVE THE TOPS DROP OVER NATURALLY (as the root system on the onion plant begins to die.) You can help by bending over the top lightly with a rake, but do not bruise the neck as it shortens storage life. When tops have died down pull up onions and bring in garage to dry. Tops should be cut off, leaving 1 inch of stem on bulb, and they should be placed in slatted crates or coarse mesh bags and stored in a dry, dark storage at around 40° for a couple of weeks. Some people put a fan on them to hasten drying. Eat thick-necked bulbs first!

TROUBLES

All onions have same troubles.

Onion Maggot: Worst pest of onions. It bores into stem and bulb. Control: Use Diazinon or add 3 level tablespoons of 5% Chlordane dust over the seed of a 25-foot row before the furrow is closed. If large numbers of adult flies are present around your onions, apply Malathion or Sevin over your rows every 3 to 7 days. Applying Chlordane or Sevin to seed will also kill or check wireworms.

Onion Thrip: Incorrectly called "thrip" and "onion louse," is a microscopic pest, causes "white blast," "white blight," and "silver top." Responsible for "thicknecks" and "scallions"—undeveloped bulbs. Adults and larvae of thrips rasp the leaves, sucking juices, leaving tops with whitened appearance. Whitened leaves begin to curl, crinkle, and die. Tips wither and brown.

Control: Spray with Malathion or nicotine sulfate. Do not apply within a week of harvest.

Downy Mildew: Causes leaves to suddenly collapse. Keep plants covered with Captan or Bordeaux mixture. Blast: A brown wilt caused by a fungus, and downy mildew can be helped by using zineb. Neck Rot: A storage problem. Mature, well-dried, well-stored onions do not get it.

Tipburn: This can be due to ozone accumulating during weather storms. Air in an electrical storm contains a lot of ozone gas, toxic to onions. Control: Use ozone-resistant onions.

General Rot: Spray with Maneb or zineb, 1½ tablespoons per gallon, beginning in early June and applying 6 doses at weekly intervals.

Brown Insides: Bacterial soft rot, a common cause of "slipperyness" of onions. Not much you can do about it, but next year delay harvest until the tops are completely died down. Also apply several sprays of Maneb during the latter half of the growing season.

Onions can be used to pep up any flat-tasting dish, except maybe ice cream. Great in stews, sauces, soups, gravies, salads, cheese dishes, breads and rolls, mixed with other vegetables—just about anything.

Egyptian Onion may be used as scallions, to be munched raw, or whenever you wish onion flavor in a recipe. Snip the tender green shoots into potato salads. A good sandwich is Egyptian onion chopped fine and combined with mayonnaise. For a taste of spring in January, dig up a clump of 2 or 3 dozen onions. Parboil for 1 minute (cooked longer, they get mushy), drain well, and chill. Arrange a bundle of stalks (they look like young leeks) and serve with French dressing.

PARSLEY (*Petroselinum crispum*)

Parsley will succeed in any good garden soil and will also do well in partial shade. It takes little room and is worth the space. Leaves may be dried and kept in airtight bottles for seasoning use in winter. Good variety is Paramount, noted for its extra-fine curled leaves. You might like the parsnip-rooted parsley (Hamburg). Roots are used, boiled and served like parsnips. Fine for soups and stews.

Sow in rows 15 to 18 inches apart in the spring. Thin out the plants to 6 to 8 inches apart. The seed germinates very slowly and care should be taken that weeds do not smother the young plants before they get well started. A little radish sown with the parsley will mark the rows. For winter use the plants can be taken up and planted in boxes of earth or pots which may be kept in a window in the house or cellar.

TROUBLES

Slow Germination: Start seed indoors in peat pots and plant pot and all in garden.

Yellow Leaves: Due to dry soils.

Woody Growth: Cut tops regularly to encourage young growth.

PARSNIP (*Pastinaca sativa*)

Here's a welcome addition to the list of so-called winter vegetables. Anyone who's had french fried parsnips will agree this fine vegetable should be in every home garden.

Soil and sowing: Parsnips do best on a rich, loamy soil which should be plowed or spaded deep to get roots of good shape. Sow seed in April or May in a rich, loamy soil. This highly nutritious vegetable does poorly in heavy clay soils. Sow seed in rows 24 to 30 inches apart, dropping 3 or 4 seeds to the inch. Do not cover seed too deeply as it has little "pushing" power and will not come up. ¼ inch covering is plenty, or sprinkle lightly with sand or vermiculite. Deep covering causes more failures with parsnips than any other cause. Sow radish seed with parsnip to break the crust. When plants are small, thin them to 3 inches apart.

Harvesting: Leave parsnips in the ground all winter for early spring harvest. Place a light mulch of hay or straw over the row and they'll keep wonderfully. Some gardeners don't even do this, and get good parsnips. Contrary to popular belief, parsnips do not become poisonous if allowed to start growth again the following spring. Their flavor will decline after growth starts since sugars from the roots are used up when top growth is resumed. Leaving them in the ground all winter improves the flavor of parsnips by changing the starch to sugar. If you harvest in fall store them in an earth pit or cool cellar. You'll find that nature's own deepfreeze in the ground keeps them best.

Parsnip Poisoning: There's no such thing as poisoning due to eating the edible roots. But there is a poisoning from parsnips. This poisoning comes not from eating the plants, but from contact with the leaves.

Parsnip, like many of our other root crops, is a biennial—a plant which requires 2 seasons to come to maturity. The first year the parsnip makes top growth and a fleshy root which is eaten. The second year it produces flowers and seeds, after roots have been stored over winter and set out again the following spring, a practice followed by seedsmen only.

The first year, there's no poisonous effect from coming in contact with the leaves, but in the second year great care must be taken in harvesting the seed, because at the seed stage, the plants are poisonous to the touch. Hands and arms must be covered. In fact, there is danger of infection on any part of the uncovered body, seedsmen warn us. Meanwhile, don't worry about being poisoned from eating cultivated parsnips. No one ever has been poisoned.

TROUBLES

Parsnips fall heir to the same troubles as do celery and carrots (which see).

Celery Blight: Tops show mottling, browning, can be checked by spraying with Bordeaux mixture.

Carrot Rust Fly (see illustration p. 185): Roughens up the roots, making them hardly edible. Control by applying Chlordane or Diazinon to the soil.

Canker: Another serious disease, especially in cool, wet seasons. Rust spots are a sure sign of canker, a fungus disease that becomes established late in the season on the lower leaves of the parsnip plant. Fungus spores fall to the ground and to the top portion of the parsnip root, working downward. Once inside the parsnip, they cause the rusty spots which you see. Control: Spray or dust your plants with Bordeaux mixture using anywhere from 4 to 6 tablespoons to each gallon of water. Start in late summer and give at least 3 doses, continuing up to the time of harvest. Hilling up soil around parsnips as much as possible during the latter part of the growing season will help keep the disease out.

USES

Boil parsnips till tender. Or halve lengthwise and french fry in oil or fat.

PEA (*Pisum*)

Medieval Europeans relied on peas as a staple food to stave off famines and see them through wars. Until the 17th century, peas were used only in dried form. But once discovered, fresh peas became intensely fashionable among royal ladies of France. The ladies liked to partake of their green peas just before retiring, a practice which a contemporary writer considered not a fashion, but pure madness. At first it was customary to cook peas in their pods and lick them out at the table; in England, it later became the accepted rule to eat peas with a knife.

Sowing: Peas are a cool-season crop. In fact, light freezing in the spring will not harm the vines. It's best to sow early, medium, and late varieties all at the same time so as to have a succession. Or you can make a second sowing about 3 weeks after the first. Keep in mind that peas sown in summer rarely succeed on account of mildew and dry weather.

In the garden, peas are usually sown by hand. Make a trench 1 to 3 inches deep. If the ground is moist, as it usually is early in the spring, 1 to 1½ inches is deep enough; later, when the soil is dry, make deeper trenches and do not fill them quite up when covering the seed. Sow about 15 peas to the foot—about 1 pound to 100 feet of row. The dwarf varieties should be planted in rows 2½ to 3 feet apart and the tall varieties 3½ to 4 feet.

Tall varieties of peas are benefited by having some support for the vines. This may be supplied by placing brush or branches in rows. Some folks with limited space use chicken wire, but it might get hot and burn the tender tendrils (climbers) so use brush or string netting if you wish to stake up your vines. Many home gardeners prefer to grow the dwarf varieties, since no support is needed.

Inoculating Pea Seed: It might be a good idea to inoculate the pea seed with a bacterial preparation sold commercially. This preparation takes nitrogen from the air and converts it into plant food for peas and other members of the legume family. If you've had peas growing in the garden for the past several years, you probably won't get much response from extra inoculation, although it certainly won't hurt anything and it's mighty inexpensive and easy to do. You simply dust it on the seed and it's ready to go to work for you.

Heat-resistant Peas: Wando is a pea that laughs at hot weather. We have sown Wando as late as the first of July and still had good tender peas. One year we ate tender peas in September. Wando makes dwarf, sturdy vines and the dark-green pods are about 3 inches long, loaded with juicy, tender, sugar-sweet peas, ideal for eating raw, cooking, or freezing. A pound will sow about 100 feet of row and costs little enough to be a real bargain for folks who love to eat peas fresh from the garden, but cannot get their garden started early.

Edible-podded Peas: These peas can be cooked pod and all like green beans, or used in Chinese dishes. We like them raw. Pick pods when young, before peas are lumpy. Light-green pods are 2 to 3 inches long, flat, meaty, sweet, and tender when young. Purple blossoms. Wilt-resistant.

Southern Peas: Try the Purple Hull Crowder Pea, also called "knuckle hulls. Easy to gather pods as they tend to cluster and stay off the ground. About same culture as regular garden pea.

Harvesting: Peas stay at best quality for only a short time, so harvest them when in prime condition (before pods get too fat) and eat or preserve them as soon as possible after harvest. The higher the temperature, the more rapidly peas will pass the best edible state. If your vines are pulled, wet them down if you can't pull the pods off, and keep them in shade.

TROUBLES

Yellow Vines: Yellow, stunted plants, pods misshapen or curled.

Due to virus or mosaic. Aphids (plant lice) pick up virus from clover, alfalfa, vetch, etc., and carry the disease to young peas, causing the symptoms. Control: Next year, spray or dust with Malathion, right after the blossom period.

Wilt: Due to fusarium fungus, causes dwarfing, rotting and distortion of leaflets. No control. Use resistant varieties such as Freezonian or Early Perfection.

Root Rot Disease: Vines turn yellow or brown at the roots and die. Fungus lives in the soil for many years. Control is to plant peas in soil where this crop hasn't been grown for the past 4 or 5 years. This is difficult if you have only a small garden. We hope we can soon have a pea that's resistant to root rot, but until that time comes, planting in new soil is the only answer.

Pea Weevil: Adult beetle lays eggs on pods, larvae feed on pods. Overwinters in crop debris. Burn pea vines after harvest. This will do a lot to prevent the occurrence of the pea weevil the following year.

Bean Maggot: Sometimes troublesome, feeds on roots and young plants. Control: Dust seed and soil with Chlordane.

Pod Diseases: Downy mildew, scab (blotches on pod), worse in wet, damp weather. Don't pick while vines are wet. Dust with Captan.

Most troubles of peas (including seed rot and root rot) can be controlled by: (1) using treated seed, (2) rotating the area, (3) planting early, while soil and air are cool (4) feeding, and (5) keeping vines dusted with Sevin or Malathion to keep out aphids.

PEANUTS (*Arachis hypogaea*)

Although peanuts are a long-season crop, they can be successfully grown in central New York State. They like a fairly rich and sandy soil. An early fall frost will injure them so you should harvest the crop as soon as possible. In northern regions, try the Early Spanish, sowing first of June, if possible. They can be planted either in hulls or shelled. Shelled nuts can be placed 3 to 6 inches apart. If in the hulls, plant about 8 inches apart. Cover about 1½ inches deep and cultivate freely.

The pods or nuts are formed underground. After the flowers are fertilized, the short stalks which bear them become elongated and bend down and push the flower into the soil, where it develops into a peanut. Before frost in the fall dig or lift the entire vine and hang under an open shed to cure.

TROUBLES

None.

PEPPER (*Capsicum frutescens*)

The pepper is a vegetable which has mystified most gardeners. Sometimes they bear and sometimes they don't. Early blooming varieties are more likely to bear successfully.

Peppers need more heat than tomatoes, and a longer growing season. They are usually started indoors and transplanted outdoors when all danger of frost is past.

Varieties: There isn't any variety which can always be depended upon to bear heavily. Some are better than others. Pennwonder is a good variety and you can buy seeds or plants. This is a dark-green pepper, turning bright red when ripe and always sweet and mild. It's one of the best all 'round peppers we know of. It's a husky grower, bearing heavy crops of thick-meated blocky fruit right up until fall. Sometimes it misses and refuses to bear. Vinedale, All-America pepper which won the bronze medal for 1952, resembles the Pennwonder with its blunt ends and rather thick walls. Bears fruit upside down, early in the season and is good for areas where the growing season is a bit short. California Wonder, a good thick-walled pepper but refuses to bear in many areas—especially those in which the growing season is short. Not recommended for most northern areas.

As for hot peppers, all of them are prolific and equally pungent. Sometimes sweet peppers turn "hot." That's because the sweet ones grew in the vicinity of hot ones and the plants crossed, or pollinated with each other. The hot flavor is passed through the seed. Planting peppers close together is useless and does not insure fruit set. All hot peppers are edible, including the ornamental Christmas pepper, often used as a houseplant.

Both black and white pepper of commerce are made from the pepper fruit of a different species of plant. If the fruits are ground whole you get black pepper. If the pericarp (outer skin) is removed before grinding, you get white pepper.

Starting from Seed: Start your seed early indoors (February or March) in seed flats filled with loose soil (muck, vermiculite, sand and peat mixture, perlite, sphagnum are all good). Sow the seed lightly and cover with a fine sifting of peat, muck, or vermiculite. Place the flat in a shallow pan of water and allow water to come up from below. Put a pane of glass or plastic over the box until seed starts to sprout. Keep germinating temperature between 70° and 80° or seed will be slow to germinate or may rot. After seeds sprout remove glass and put the box or flat in a bright window.

Peppers are also sold already started in flats. Buy from a dependable grower. Transplant 1 foot apart in rows 2 feet apart, in loose, well-drained soil. Use paper collars to protect the young plants.

Why All Bush and No Peppers?: Gardeners are often disappointed to have their plants produce all bush and no fruits. The reason is this: loss of water from the tops, due to high temperature, low relative humidity, and hot, drying winds at blossom or bud time. These factors, or any factor which causes a shortage of water in the plant, will cause the buds and blooms to "absciss," or drop off. An abundance of water in the soil will not guard against bud shedding when water loss from the plant surface is rapid on a hot or windy day. In Arizona, 1 or 2 drying days in the middle of blooming often ruins the entire crop.

Does it pay to plant the plants close together for pollination? No. Cross-pollination is unimportant. In fact, tests show that most of the shedding takes place after pollination and even after fertilization of the ovary. Richness of the soil (too much nitrogen) has been blamed for all bush and no fruit, but this is seldom true.

It all boils down to the fact that peppers are sensitive to hot weather, low relative humidity, and drying winds. When the weather is favorable at blooming time, you get a good set of fruit. One reason why an early blooming pepper like Vinedale is more dependable in most areas than, say, the California Wonder is that being an early bloomer, it does so before hot, drying weather sets in and therefore shows less shedding of blossoms.

Pruning: Does it pay to prune a pepper plant? I doubt it. Pruning removes the leaves (food factories) and thus reduces the possible fruit load of the plant. Old-fashioned gardeners are inclined to prune, but modern gardeners are hesitant. You may get a stockier plant, but I'm afraid that pruning will delay bearing.

Harvesting: All red peppers are green before they are ripe and turn red or scarlet upon maturing. That red coloring is there all the while, masked by the green pigment. When gathering peppers, cut them off with a sharp knife, leaving a short piece of stem. This protects the plant and enables the peppers to last longer in storage.

TROUBLES

Phytophthora Blight, Anthracnose (see illustration), Cercospora Leaf Spot, Ripe Rot: Spray with zineb or Maneb, use treated seed. Do not plant peppers in garden location which had peppers the previous year.

Virus Diseases: Cause stunting, mottling, and curling of leaves. Do not use tobacco while handling pepper seedlings. Yolo Wonder is resistant to tobacco mosaic.

Bacterial spot on pepper. On the leaves the spots are brown and the larger spots have a light center and dark margins; the spots on the fruit are slightly raised and have a cracked, roughened surface. (USDA Photo)

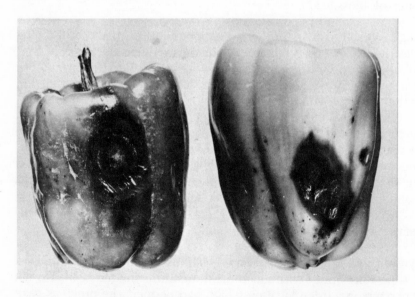

Anthracnose spotting of pepper. The centers of the spots show numerous dark specks, bodies that contain spores of the fungus. These spores are washed or spattered by rain to other fruits, thus in rainy seasons losses may be severe. (USDA Photo)

Mildew: Use zineb or Maneb.

Bacterial Leaf Spot: (see illustration) On the leaves the spots are brown, and the larger spots have a light center and dark margins. Control difficult. Try zineb.

Poppy Seed (*Papaver somniferum*)

Poppy seed is sold in grocery stores, and poppy plants are grown in many backyards for their spectacular flowers. Many ask me if the poppy seed we eat is from the same poppy from which opium is made.

Opium is obtained from the opium poppy (*Papaver somniferum*), a plant native to Asia Minor. Opium is commercially produced in Turkey, India, Iran, and Yugoslavia, and its cultivation is controlled by the United Nations. None of it is grown in this country. The alkaloid narcotic is obtained from sap scrapings of the green seed pods. The poppy plants grown for garden flowers (*P. orientale*) are a different species.

The poppy seeds used on buns, bread, and other baking items are the dried seeds of the opium poppy. But eat all you want, because the seed itself is harmless and contains no form of narcotic.

USES

Poppy Seed Dressing: ½ cup sugar, 1 level teaspoon each salt, dry mustard, celery seed, and poppy seed, 2 tablespoons grated onion, 1 cup cooking oil, 4 tablespoons vinegar or lemon juice.

Mix sugar, dry spices, and onion together. Then add the oil slowly, beating well (I use an electric beater). Add vinegar or lemon juice. A good dressing served with all fresh garden greens.

Potato (*Solanum tuberosum*)

Many home gardeners are yearning for a good eating potato, since many store potatoes lack quality. Considering the space that potato plants require, ordinarily we don't recommend growing potatoes in the small garden, or if you live in an area where you can buy good potatoes.

Soil: Potatoes like a well-drained soil, sandy loam, well supplied with humus. If you have a clay soil don't try to grow spuds. Potatoes do well when following alfalfa or clover crops. Rye, planted in August or September and plowed down the following spring when 6 to 12 inches tall, adds organic matter and reduces damage from scab disease. Potatoes should not be planted in old grass sods because they are often infested with grubs.

Seed Potatoes: BUY CERTIFIED SEED STOCK! This is your guarantee of quality, as it means the potatoes are grown just for seed use. U.S. No. 1 (seen on bags) is not a grade for seed potatoes, but for table potatoes.

Certified seed stock means that the seed tubers must be inspected at least twice while growing in fields, by an official state inspector, and again in the bin after they have been dug. Certified stock must be practically 100% pure in type and free from late blight, rot, blackleg, powdery scab, leaf roll, ring rot, and many other diseases. Don't be afraid to spend a little more money for certified seed.

You can also buy potato seed sets. Each set has a small amount of "meat" with the eye, or bud, to insure good germination, and has been treated, ready to plant. Potato seed sets are inexpensive.

You can also buy seed potatoes, these being small potatoes from 1¼ to 2 ounces in weight. They are planted whole. Larger potatoes may be cut into blocky pieces about 1½ ounces each. There should be 1 eye on each piece, and it is safer to have 2 or more eyes to the piece. If you're going to cut seed pieces, do so at least 1 day before planting. Soon after cutting, put the pieces into a container and keep it covered in a warm room for a day to assist healing.

It's a good idea to dust your seed with a good fungicide such as Semesan or Captan. Note: Those tiny tomato-like fruits you see on top of a mature potato plant are the potato seed. Do not plant seed from these. Some people call them "potato balls" or "potato apples," but they are nothing but seed pods of potatoes, not edible, and not the result of potato crossing with tomatoes.

Planting: Plant seed pieces 18 inches apart, 3 or 4 inches deep in furrows or in holes dug with a hoe. They'll come up quickest and make best growth if covered only about ½ inch deep. The rest of the hole may be filled in after plants are 3 or 4 inches high.

Varieties: Let's take the red-skinned ones first. Red Pontiac has shallow eyes, white flesh, does well on muck or upland soil, is medium-early. Bliss Triumph is round, extra-early, deep eyes, may be hard to peel. Red La Soda has white flesh, waxy red skin, high-yielding. Among white varieties, Irish Cobbler is a popular early white spud. Early Gem is scab-resistant. Rushmore is a new early long white. Kennebec, high-yielding, good flavor, resistant to late blight and mosaic. Chippewa, midseason white, best for northern climates. Cooks white. For late white varieties, try Russet Rural, Sebago, and Katahdin. Sebago is blight-resistant and scab-resistant. Russet Burbank (sold as the Idaho Baker) does not yield heavy, but is good for baking, oblong with a netted skin. For a yellow-fleshed potato, try Fingerlings, skin and flesh yellow. Boil with jackets on and cut up for salads. Blue potatoes: Blue

Victor, large, round, and blue-skinned, white flesh. Good keeper, high-yielding, and fine-tasting.

One reader and potato grower, Jack Tomion of Stanley, New York, wrote: "Last spring I planted 3 bushels of Blue Victor and 8 pounds of Blue Cristy potatoes. From the 3 bushels of Blue Victor I harvested 68 bushels and the potatoes were real nice. I now have 1 acre growing and expect 400 bushels to sell for seed. I'm also growing 5 new blue varieties from the State Agriculture College in Maine." Another blue potato is Cowhorns, tubers long like a finger (similar to Fingerlings). There's also a blue-fleshed potato that cooks blue. It tastes like a potato, but the flesh is the color of a red beet when raw, and when cooked it is "true blue." German Purple is a variety with purple skin, yellow flesh, round tubers. Boil with skins on. Nice for salads.

Culture: Keep soil cultivated well during first few weeks after planting so that all grass and weeds are destroyed. Cultivate shallow, and stop when plants begin to blossom and set tubers. Weeds appearing late in season should be cut off at the surface of ground with sharp hoe. Not necessary to hill up spuds unless soil is poorly drained or potatoes appear above ground. Delay harvesting until vines mature or until after they've been frost-killed. Well-matured potatoes are of better eating quality than immature stock, keep better in storage.

Digging and Storing: Potatoes may be dug whenever they reach edible size, or you can leave them until fall when the vines turn brown and have practically died. Dig crop on clear day when soil is not wet. Dig with a potato hook or fork and store in a cool place which will not freeze. Potatoes keep best at temperatures between 36° and 40°, an impossibility in our modern homes. Cover with bags or papers to keep out light. Light causes skins to turn green and ruins flavor.

How to Keep Stored Potatoes from Sprouting: Did you know that you can keep stored potatoes from sprouting by mixing apples with them? Tests at Ohio State University have found that apples form ethylene gas, which halts the sprouting. One apple per bag, if the bag is paper or paper-lined, is enough. You can use about 10 pounds of apples per bushel of potatoes if the spuds are stored loose. Potatoes and apples, incidentally, shorten the life of cut flowers, so don't keep posies in the vicinity if you want them to last.

You can also control sprouting in the cellar by spraying maleic hydrazide on the vines a week after the blossoms fall, or 4 to 6 weeks before the potatoes are ready to harvest. This will prevent stored potatoes from sprouting for 4 to 6 months longer than untreated potatoes, even at storage temperatures of 55° to 65°.

Maleic hydrazide is valuable for table potatoes which must be stored several months, and it has a distinct advantage for the potato-chip makers by allowing potatoes to be stored at relatively high temperatures which prevent accumulation of sugars in the tubers. Warning: Don't use maleic hydrazide on potatoes grown for seed because it will hold up their sprouting in the ground next spring.

Another material used to inhibit sprouting is a hormone, methyl ester of alpha napthaleneacetic acid. It's usually stocked in powder form by garden-supply houses under various trade names. Be sure to follow manufacturer's directions.

To be effective it must be used *before sprouting begins*. Most potato tubers have a 2- to 3-month dormancy after the vines have matured. After that they may begin to sprout.

The use of this hormone probably won't keep potatoes from sprouting all winter unless they are also kept at a storage temperature of less than 50°.

Potato Poisoning: During the spring, potatoes in storage have a tendency to send up sprouts, and when left in a well-lighted room they take on a greenish cast. Without being an alarmist, I'd like to point out that potato sprouts, potato tops, and greened portions of the tubers are poisonous to humans, since they contain an alkaloid known as solanine. To be on the safe side gouge out the eyes of all old potatoes before cooking, and remove greened portions.

TROUBLES

You can avoid a lot of troubles by using certified seed only. Pull up and burn volunteer potato plants in garden.

Seed Piece Rots: When potato seed pieces rot instead of sprouting, may be due to cold, wet soil.

Early Blight: Fungus causes black, target-shaped spots on lower leaves. Bad in wet seasons. DOES NOT AFFECT TUBERS. Weekly spraying with zineb, ziram, or Bordeaux mix controls disease.

Late Blight: Serious fungus disease which affects tubers and tops. Appears suddenly, like premature frost injury to plants. Blighted tubers have corky, brown, firm rot layered just under skin. Fungus is seed-borne, may overwinter in potato cull piles. Favored by cool temperatures. Control: Maneb, zineb, or Bordeaux mixture helps to control blight. If late blight has appeared, do not harvest tubers until 10 days after tops have dried. Dig on dry, sunny day.

Wilts: Potatoes get fusarium and other wilts. Leaves appear mottled, droop, tips turn yellow, plants die prematurely. Vines also wilt on hot days, and from insect trouble. Control: For disease wilts, plant certified seed, collect and burn old vines after harvest. Grow wilt-resistant types like Katahdin.

Virus Diseases: These include leaf roll, mosaic, yellow dwarf. Look for rolling of lower leaves, mottling, stunting of plant. Virus diseases are carried in infected seed by sucking insects. Do not save seed from your own plants. Use certified seed.

Bacterial Ring Rot: Plants wilt in day, recover at night. Causes rotted tubers. Look for yellow cheesy ring about ¼ inch below skin. Sprays ineffective. Use certified seed.

Black Rot: Roots with dark, round spots, which extend to tubers, giving them a bitter taste. Spreads in storage. Control: Treat seed with Captan.

Green-skinned Potatoes: Due to sunburn or too much light in storage or cellar. Cover roots in garden with more soil to exclude light. Store spuds in dark room. (See Potato Poisoning.)

Hollow Hearts: Due to fast growth, especially in wet seasons. No control. Space plants closer together next year.

Rhizoctonia: Look for hard, coal-black spots on tuber. Not much you can do once it sets in. Use certified seed.

Potato Scab: Scabs or pits on tubers. A bacterial disease, seed and soil borne. Scab is favored by alkaline (sweet) or neutral soils and is stopped in soils below pH 5.6 (acid). Soils having lots of chicken or barnyard manure produce scabby spuds. Too much lime will, too. Terraclor gives partial control when mixed into upper 6 inches of soil at rate of 1 pound per 100 square feet. Moist soils reduce scab, thus early irrigation is helpful.

While we have some resistant varieties, such as Cherokee and Ontario, available for the home gardener, usually varieties which are resistant to scab are unsatisfactory so far as eating quality is concerned. Your best bet is to treat the soil so that the pH reading is below 5.6 (see Liming and Soil Acidity). If your soil is sweet (alkaline), sulfur will lower the pH reading to the point where scab organism cannot live.

One gardener wrote: "We raise about 10 acres and use sulfur to keep them free of scab. After the seed potatoes are cut we put a good big handful of sulfur on per bushel, and shake thoroughly to make sure each seed piece is coated with sulfur. After we plant the potatoes we add some more sulfur, just to make sure each piece gets plenty of sulfur. Home gardeners can get dusting sulfur from seed stores or a drugstore, and if they've been having trouble getting clean, scab-free potatoes, I suggest they try using sulfur."

Storage Rots: Wet or dry rots in storage with sweet or foul odors. Control: Avoid bruising or skinning tubers. Cure potatoes 10 to 14 days at 80° to 85° to decrease losses in storage.

Dark Potatoes: What causes potatoes to have black spots and streaks after you cook them? This disorder is known as "after-cooking darkening." It's worse in some years than in others, and some varieties are more susceptible than others. The Katahdin, a common variety, is fairly susceptible, whereas Sebago is quite resistant. Of the varieties commonly grown, Russet Burbank is the most resistant to blackening.

Blackening is due to a combination of iron with certain phenolic compounds inside the spud. The coloring compound formed is sensitive to acidity changes, so housewives can reduce after-cooking darkening by adding some form of acid, such as vinegar or lemon juice, to the cooking water. However, addition of such acid usually has a somewhat undesirable effect on the appearance and texture of the potato.

A better corrective is the addition of sodium acid pyrophosphate, a leavening agent commonly used in certain types of food products. Adding ½ teaspoon of the chemical per quart of cooking water will reduce or eliminate after-cooking darkening. This chemical, available at your drugstore, is effective because it ties up the iron so it's not available for the color reaction.

By the way, after-cooking darkening in no way affects the nutritive value or flavor of potatoes, so if you can put up with the color, forget the treatments.

Research scientists have discovered why some potatoes used in making potato soup turn dark when coming in contact with milk. It appears that storage temperature is the most important factor in the development of undesirable color. Potatoes kept at 40° for 245 days had an acceptable color when processed. Those stored at 50° to 75° for varying periods of time up to 129 days showed a tendency to darken.

This is important, not only to processors, but to growers who store their potatoes before marketing them. Storing tubers at 40° appears to keep off-color potatoes to a minimum.

Potatoes grown in loam soils are whiter than potatoes grown in sandy soils.

Colorado Potato Beetle, Aphid, Flea Beetle: Colorado Potato beetle (see illustration p. 186) eats the foliage. Flea bettle (see illustration p. 185) makes small holes in the leaves. Aphids suck plant juices from undersides of leaves and clusters on flower stalks. Control: Methoxychlor or Malathion will check these pests. Apply to top and undersides of the leaves every 2 weeks.

Potato Leafhopper: A tiny, green, jumping, flying pest which often appears in dry spells. Causes leaves to turn brown, curl, and die. Control: Dust with Sevin or methoxychlor every 2 weeks.

Potato Stalk Borer: Slender, naked, 1-inch caterpillar attacks the stems. Control: Keep weeds down within 25 feet of planting.

Most garden stores have a potato dust which will control beetles, leafhoppers, thrips, and aphids. Sevin is a pesticide which works well on potato insects.

POTATO, SWEET (*Ipomoea batatas*)

The yam is a large starchy tuber, a native of Africa, grown in a wide variety of forms throughout tropical regions of the world. True yams are not considered edible by modern man unless he is faced with starvation. Those "yams" you see in stores are sweet potatoes. You can grow sweet potatoes anyplace where there is a frost-free period of 150 days or more.

You can grow beautiful crops of sweet potatoes in spite of the cold season using plastic mulch (see Mulches). This not only holds in the soil moisture and controls weeds, but raises the temperature of the soil. Soil temperature is very important in the production of sweet potatoes. (However, our neighbor raises sweet potatoes weighing up to 3 pounds each, without the use of plastic mulch.)

Planting: Your best bet is to start sweet potatoes from plants. Sweet potatoes have many eyes, as many as 50 to a medium-sized potato. If you should cut these up as you do white potatoes you would still have several eyes on each piece, all of which would grow if planted. The plants would be so crowded that no sizeable sweet potatoes would be produced.

To overcome this problem, sweet potatoes are "bedded," placed close together in a bed and covered with sand. The bed is kept moist, and when the plants are large enough the bed is opened and the plants carefully broken off from the potatoes and bunched for sale. About 100 plants will fill a 150-foot row.

Varieties: Orange Jersey, Orange Little-Stem, and Nemagold are common dry-fleshed types. New Centennial is a sweet, golden variety, with copper skin, orange flesh. Another good one is All-Gold Bunch Puerto Rico, ideal for backyard gardens. No vines to run all over the place. Goldrush and Puerto Rico are 2 moist types. Puerto Rico has orange skin, deep, rich, yellow flesh.

Soil and Planting: Sweet potatoes, being a root crop, like deep, sandy loam. Clay soils encourage formation of long stringy roots. Keeping this in mind, you should choose the lightest soil you have. After plowing and fitting, lay out the rows 4 feet apart and apply a good grade of commercial fertilizer where your row is to be, at the rate of 7 or 8 pounds per 100 feet of row. With a small plow, cultivator, or hoe throw a ridge of soil over the fertilizer, 8 inches high and a foot across at the base.

Cut a twig a foot long with a small ¼-inch crotch at 1 end. Take the potato plant in the left hand, place the crotch of the twig near the end of the root and shove the plant down into the center of the ridge until only 1 or 2 leaves are above ground. Set the plants 15 to 18 inches apart. After the plants start, more soil may be thrown up on each side of the ridge.

Harvesting: Dig a short time before frost, on bright, dry day when soil is dry. Let roots dry in sun 2 or 3 hours, then cure for storage.

Curing: Once you're fortunate enough to harvest a crop of sweet potatoes you can store them for the winter in baskets or hampers lined with paper so they'll be handled as little as possible. Place near a furnace for 10 to 20 days at a temperature of 80° to 90°. Then move them to a cooler part of the cellar or into a storage room, where they will keep best at 50° to 60°. Furnace room is a good place to store them.

One of my readers in Eden, New York, has a different method for growing sweet potatoes. He writes: "I've raised sweet potatoes for years and start my own plants. Usually, in January, I get 1 good-sized sweet potato and put it in water, allowing it to grow into a decorative vine. About June first I take each vine from the potato and plant it.

"I've had almost a bushel of sweet potatoes from the 1 vine. They're the easiest thing in the entire garden to raise, and so far no bug or insect has attacked them. I leave them growing just as late as possible in the fall, and I use no mulch. Just plant the vines and keep watered."

Incidentally, the sweet potato makes a good vine indoors. Place in jar of water and it'll sprout. Some may not sprout, if they have been treated with a hormone to prevent sprouting in storage.

TROUBLES

Yellow Dwarf Disease: A constant nuisance. Stunts size of plants and tubers, reduces yield. Control: Plant yellow-dwarf-free seed stock.

Failure to Mature: Due to cold seasons. Sweet potatoes, like peanuts, prefer a rather warm growing season. Use plastic mulch to hasten ripening.

Rot: Anytime your sweet potatoes are subject to temperatures below 50° for a period of more than 24 to 48 hours they become chilled and are more subject to decay.

PUMPKIN (*See Squash and Pumpkins*)

RADISH (*Raphanus saturis*)

Radishes are easy to grow and quick to mature. They grow best in cool weather, become "hot" in hot weather. Small round varieties mature more quickly than long ones. Good round types are Cherry Belle and Champion. Icicle is best long white type, grows 4 to 5 inches.

Planting: A single packet of radish seed will sow 25 to 30 feet. Sow seed in rows and cover ¼ inch. Thin plants to about ½ inch apart. Irrigate every day in hot weather. Make additional plantings every few weeks for a continuous supply, except during hot, dry weather, when they don't do well.

Winter radishes are sown in the summer, in rows 18 inches apart, and thinned to 6 inches. They can be stored in moist sand for winter use.

The best radishes are those raised in greenhouses or hotbeds, as they are not as sharp-tasting as those grown outside. Sow in rows 4 inches apart, thin plants to ½ inch apart, and water often.

A few radish seeds mixed in at planting time with such vegetables as carrots, parsley, and parsnips will mark the rows for the slower-growing crops, help break the surface crust for fine seed. Be sure to pull up radishes as soon as they are ready to eat, to keep them from competing with the main crop.

TROUBLES

No Bottoms: Due to too rich a soil, or failure to thin out plants.

Root Maggots: Mix a small amount of Sevin or Chlordane with soil before sowing seed, and dust a little along the rows just as plants come up. Fall crops of radish are much less apt to be injured by maggots but some protection will still be needed.

Flea Beetles: Dust tops with Sevin to check flea beetles.

Hot-tasting roots: KEEP RADISHES WELL WATERED IN SUMMER AND THEY WON'T BE HOT!

RHUBARB (*Rheum rhaponticum*)

A good patch of rhubarb or "pieplant" will last 25 years or more. Stalks are highly prized for sauce and pies. Spring is best time to plant rhubarb. McDonald and Valentine are good varieties to try.

Planting and Care: Starting from seed not reliable. Buy roots from a nursery, or wait till your neighbor divides his old plants. Plant 4 to 5 inches deep, with eyes up in well-drained soil. Rhubarb likes big doses of rotted manure or compost, 3 to 6 bushels per 100 square feet, and about 5 pounds 10–10–10 fertilizer plus 1 pound of nitrate of soda to

100 square feet. Remove seed stalks before they have a chance to develop, as they are a drain on the plant. Loosen up the soil around your rhubarb and give them a good feeding in spring, again in late summer. Give lots of water in spring.

Harvesting: Don't harvest any stalks till the third year, but after that a full crop may be harvested in 2 months each spring. Pull the stalks from the plant, don't cut. It's always a good idea to wash the stalks off before eating. Never eat the leaves of rhubarb as they contain a poison.

Propagation: Divide your plants by cutting the old crowns into pieces with strong buds ("eyes").

Early rhubarb can be had by covering a hill with glass sash or cold frame just before growth starts in spring. Rhubarb may be forced in a box of soil in cellar during winter, if roots are brought in after experiencing a hard freeze. Exclude light.

TROUBLES

Pink Stems Turn Green: Pink rhubarb should remain pink after transplanting. If the plants get full sun, they will develop the pink color. If grown in the shade, the pink goes out and the stems are green.

Spindly Stems: Usually a sign the plants need dividing. The best time to divide a rhubarb patch is in early spring.

If your stalks are spindly, or dwarfed, they may also need feeding. Use previously described food. Hot days and lack of moisture are causes of poor growth and seed stalk development. Cut seed pods off just as quickly as you see them popping out. Seed stalks weaken the plants.

Wilt: Rhubarb has a wilt disease. Drench the root with formaldehyde (may kill it, if too strong), 1 teaspoon to 2 quarts of water. Dust root with Fermate.

Borers: Will burrow in stem. Cut them out with knife.

Crown Rot ("Foot Rot"): Dig up diseased clumps and burn. Plant disease-free clumps in soil that has not grown rhubarb for 4 years.

Curculio: Stings stalks and leaves, making unsightly mess. Control: Dust with rotenone in May before the pest comes along.

USES

Rhubarb Conserve: Cook 2 quarts cubed rhubarb for 5 minutes. Add 2½ cups sugar, pulp and juice of 2 oranges, 1 pound seeded raisins, 2 cups chopped nutmeats. Boil till thick, stirring to keep from burning. *Rhubarb Marmalade*: 2 quarts cubed rhubarb, 1 to 2 cups sugar, depending upon desired richness, pulp and juice of 2 oranges, 1 cup blanched almonds, chopped fine. Boil all ingredients slowly to desired thickness, 2½ to 3 hours.

Rhubarb can be combined with other fruits, such as strawberries, gooseberries, pineapple, and so on.

RUTABAGA (*Brassica napobrassica*)

Rutabagas or "Swede turnips" aren't too popular with home gardeners, but if you're interested you can get a heavy crop by sowing the seed June 15 to July 1, in rows 2 feet apart. Rutabaga needs a heavy soil for best growth. Thin to 1 foot apart. Dust the plants with Sevin to repel flea beetles. Rutabagas are similar to turnips except they have smooth instead of hairy leaves. They also have a larger root and need a month longer to mature.

Rutabagas will stand considerable frost. After heavy frosts have come, lift them, top the plants, and store the roots in moist sand in a cool part of the cellar. Or wax for storage.

Waxing for Storage: The rutabaga is the only root crop I know of that is waxed to last longer in storage. Paraffin can be used, although commercial companies use a special vegetable wax which is not as conspicuous. For home use simply melt the paraffin, dip the rutabagas, and let them dry. Rutabagas retain their quality in storage better than turnips.

TROUBLES

Flea Beetles (see illustration p. 185): Dust or spray with Sevin or Malathion as soon as seedlings break through the ground.

Corky Growth: Too much nitrogen or hot weather causes corky growth and pithy plants.

Bitterness: Due to hot weather.

SALSIFY (*Tragapogon porrifolius*)

Salsify or "vegetable oyster" is one of the unsung vegetables. The long, fleshy roots have an oyster-like flavor, and are ideal for late fall, winter, and early spring use.

Salsify is easy to grow. Sow in May, preferably in light, rich soil, which produces the largest and best-shaped roots. Any good garden soil is satisfactory, however, if deeply worked. The roots may be used whenever large enough. For winter use, dig them in the fall, trimming the tops at least 1 inch above the root, and store in moist sand in the cellar. Digging should be delayed until the ground begins to freeze. Salsify may be left in the ground over winter if covered with straw.

USES

Boil roots till tender, serve with a cream sauce.

SPINACH (*Spinacia oleracea*)

Spinach is still a leading "greens," rich in iron, calcium, and vitamin A. Spinach is a quick-growing, hardy crop which thrives best in cool weather.

Soil and Planting: Any good fertile soil is satisfactory. Spinach should be planted just as early in the spring as possible in rows 14 to 18 inches apart, covering the seed about ½ inch. Thin the plants to 5 or 6 inches apart in the row. Successive plantings will give you a supply throughout the season, but after the middle of May, use only long-standing varieties since others do not do well in hot weather. For fall use, sow in August, and to winter over sow the seed about the first of September.

Spinach will respond well to nitrate of soda or high-nitrate fertilizer applied alongside the rows.

TROUBLES

Since spinach usually gets blight in the fall, a blight-resistant variety should be used for sowing after the middle of July.

Leaf Miner: Maggot eats between leaf tissues. Use Sevin.

Aphids: Dust with Malathion or nicotine sulfate. Tough to control.

Mildew: Control difficult. Practice 3-year rotation. Burn refuse as soon as crop is harvested.

SPINACH, NEW ZEALAND (*Tetragonia expansa*)

The low-spreading "summer spinach" or New Zealand spinach is quite different from other varieties as it is not a true spinach. It may be sown in the early spring or summer, and will grow during the hottest weather. The seed germinates slowly and it is a good plan to soak it for 24 hours before sowing. The rows should be 3 feet apart, as the plants spread out nearly 2 feet each side of the row. The tender new leaves at the tips of the branches may be picked off as wanted in summer and fall. This spinach is killed by hard frost.

TROUBLES

None.

Squash and Pumpkins (*Cucurbita*)

No vegetable exceeds the squash in variety of form and color. The hard-rinded winter squashes are considered true squashes; summer squashes, usually eaten immature, should correctly be called summer pumpkins. Don't worry too much about classification. Summer and winter squash and pumpkins have about the same culture as melons and cucumbers. If you don't have much space, grow the bush types.

Culture of Summer Squash and Pumpkins: Sow seed in hills (clusters) 3 or 4 feet apart. Plant 8 or 10 seeds in a hill and cover with about 1 inch of soil. Later, thin plants to 3 in a hill. Cultivation should be shallow to avoid injuring the roots. Use a plastic mulch around plants to keep weed growth down. Side-dress with sodium nitrate during the season. Modern summer squash hybrids take little space and produce abundantly.

Will pumpkins and squash cross or mix in the garden? All the varieties within a species will mix or cross. So all varieties of *Cucurbita pepo* (summer squashes and most pumpkins) will cross, but this is no problem to the average gardener unless he saves his own seed. Pumpkins and squashes cannot be crossed with cucumbers, muskmelons, or watermelons, so you can't blame poor taste on cross-pollination with these.

For best eating, pick summer squash fruits while still small, young, and tender. Keeping fruits picked will make the vines bear throughout the entire season. Pumpkins can attain tremendous sizes and weights; specimens over 100 pounds have been produced. Many gardeners grow pumpkins with their corn. It works fine as a space-saver.

See your catalog for pictures and descriptions of best varieties of pumpkins and summer squash.

Winter Squash: Needs more space to grow than summer squash. Plant in rows 7 to 8 feet apart for smaller types such as butternut, acorn, and buttercup, and in rows 9 feet apart for the larger types such as Hubbard. Plant in hills 4 feet apart in the rows with 8 to 10 seeds to the hill. Then thin to 3 plants per hill after plants are up. The most popular winter squash is the acorn or Table Queen.

Tricks With Squash and Pumpkins: Growing pumpkins with kids' names on the outside is a lot of fun, and quite simple. It's done by cutting the pumpkins with a knife when the vegetable is about ½ formed. The cut must be made deeply enough—about ¼ inch—so that the skin is adequately wounded. The scar tissue which forms over the cuts will produce raised letters, spelling out the name. Children are delighted to find their names inscribed on pumpkins.

Another trick is to grow giant-sized pumpkins. Secret is to remove all the blossoms or young fruit except 1 or 2. Let all the strength go into the 1 remaining pumpkin and you'll get a giant. Or you can put the tip end of a pumpkin runner into a solution of sugar and water. This helps grow giants that will amaze your next-door neighbor.

The question of feeding pumpkins or squash with milk to make them grow to giant size pops up every now and then, but I have never found an authority who believes that there is anything to it. The theory is that if you cut off the tip of a vine and keep it in a bowl of milk, the pumpkin or squash will suck up the milk and grow to blue-ribbon proportions. Most people who grow large fruit for shows, however, just give the plants extra-wide spacing, furnish plentiful fertilizer and water, and pick all but 1 or 2 fruit off the vines as soon as they appear.

Harvesting Squash and Pumpkins: Acorn squash is ready to harvest when the skin takes on a dark-green color, becomes hard, and develops an orange or yellow spot where it lies on the ground. Butternut squash will change from a creamy yellow color with faint green markings to a buff or tan color when fully matured. The skin will become hard. Buttercup squash will change to a dark-green color, with perhaps a few small yellow or orange striations in the "cap." The rind will become very hard.

The same applies to the larger varieties of squash—Hubbard, Delicious, banana, etc., and to pumpkins. The change in color intensity and hardness of the rind are the best indications of maturity.

Winter squash should ripen thoroughly in the field, until the shell is quite hard and resists the pressure of a thumbnail. But do not leave them exposed to frost as this injures their keeping quality. A good fungicide applied during the season to keep the vines healthy will help produce long-keeping squash.

The secret of picking summer squash is to pick them while they're young, nearly cylindrical, before the rind hardens. Skins should be dark, glossy green or yellow, according to the variety.

Storage of Pumpkins and Squash: Both pumpkins and squashes can be kept in the cellar for several months, if properly stored. You can leave them outside for a while in the fall, if protected from frost. A couple of handfuls of straw over them will work well to protect from light frost. Pile them outdoors and cover at night to harden them. Squash and pumpkins store best under warm and fairly dry conditions.

Winter squash such as the butternut, buttercup, and any of the Hubbard varieties may be stored in the basement if the temperature is around 55° or so. Store only fully mature squash, those that have developed their characteristic color and have a hard outer rind. Fruits that have been subjected to anything more than a very light frost will not keep well. Carefully handled and stored at about 55° in a fairly dry place, the squash should keep well until February.

Pumpkins won't keep as long in storage as some varieties of squash. Hubbard and Delicious squash are good keepers, but Table Queen and other acorn varieties do not keep as long. Some gardeners prefer to cure their squash by storing them for 2 or 3 weeks at a temperature of 70° to 80°, them moving to a dry room at about 50° to 60°.

Pumpkins and squash store best if part of the stem is left on. Nothing spoils faster than immature or unripe vegetables. Immature squash will break down within a month.

TROUBLES

Pumpkins and squash fall heir to practically the same diseases. Avoid working among plants when they are wet. Do not water overhead. Keep down weeds. Plow under, or better still, burn debris after harvest. Keep vines dusted or sprayed as soon as they start to run, using zineb, Maneb, or Captan with Sevin, Malathion, or methoxychlor added. This will prevent scab, pox, leaf spots and blights, and discourage insects.

Bacterial Wilt: Causes plants to wilt fast. Pull up and destroy affected vines.

Blossom Drop: Blossoms which dry up are no cause for alarm. Squash and pumpkins produce 5 to 10 male blossoms to 1 female, and only a small percent of the female blossoms naturally develop into normal fruits. The males and excess or unused female blossoms dry up and fall, their romance shattered forever. (See Squash or Pumpkin Blossom Fritters.)

Mosaic: Virus disease manifested by yellow-green and dark-green mottling or distortion of leaves. Leaves are wrinkled or stunted, vines dwarfed and bunchy, and fruits are mottled, stunted, warty (knobby), and have bitter taste. Control: Keep weeds pulled nearby. Pull up first infected plants after you apply Sevin or Malathion. Control aphids, leafhoppers, and cucumber beetles (with Malathion) as they spread the virus. Use resistant varieties.

Powdery Mildew and Downy Mildew: White furry growth on foliage, worse in moist areas. Apply Karathane 1 to 3 times, 10 days apart. Some varieties are mildew-resistant. (These will be mentioned in reliable seed catalogs.)

Squash Vine Borer: Causes wilting and death of vines. Small piles of a sawdust-like material ("frass") on ground indicate presence of borers. Control: Spray vines at base of runners during late June and early July (after the blossom shucks have fallen), using 2 tablespoons of 50% methoxychlor to 1 gallon of water, or Sevin or Malathion. Give 2 doses, 7 days apart. Borers already inside a stem may be stabbed with a penknife. The wounded stalk is then placed on the ground and covered with soil for root formation.

The mature stage of the borer maggot is a day-flying moth which looks like a wasp. The moth lays its eggs on the stem and the young borer penetrates the vines. Decay sets in and the vine wilts and dies, giving the impression it has been hit by a disease. Spraying or dusting prevents this.

Since the insect passes the winter in the ground, it isn't a good idea to grow squash or pumpkins in the same spot year after year. Deep plowing in the spring helps check the pest. Also, vines should be collected and destroyed as soon as harvest is over to prevent the later caterpillars from reaching maturity. It's interesting to note that the butternut squash is partially immune to the borer, due possibly to its woody stems. Table Queen and Blue Hubbard are highly susceptible to borer attack. But don't let this discourage you from raising these squash.

Squash Bug (see illustration p. 186): In some years squash, cucumbers, pumpkins, and gourds are bothered by the squash bug (sometimes called "stink bug"), a difficult pest to control during the growing season because it feeds by piercing the vines and the undersides of the leaves, sucking out the plant juices. It also deposits a poisonous substance while feeding, causing the leaves to show light-colored areas that turn brown and die.

Control: Try spraying entire vines with nicotine sulfate, 1 teaspoon to 1 quart of soapy water, once a week, or use Malathion. The simplest way to kill the bug is to clean out and burn all vines and leaves of pumpkins, squash, etc., which are bothered by squash bugs. This destroys both insects and their winter shelters. Some gardeners fight the squash bug by placing a shingle-like board at the base of each plant to trap the grown bugs at night where they can be found and killed in the early morning. Nicotine sulfate or Malathion is more effective but be sure to spray both top and bottom sides of leaves.

USES

Acorn Squash Seed: Cut squash, scoop out center, mash in strainer, removing strings and pulp. Place seeds on paper towel to dry. Then bake in flat pan or pie tin at 325° for 20 minutes, in 2 tablespoons of salad oil and salt to taste. Stir, bake till seeds are brownish and crisp. These are really great, better than pumpkin seeds. If you don't want to bake them, feed them to birds. Attract cardinals!

Canned Squash: Can your squash. Flavor is not too important in selection of canning varieties as it can be controlled by the canner. Spices, and other ingredients influence the original flavor. Winter squash can be used like pumpkin for a fine pie.

Cooked Pumpkin Seeds: Separate seeds from yellow fibers to which they cling, and DO NOT WASH. Spread in shallow baking pan, sprinkle with salt. Coat with melted butter or oil and brown lightly in a very slow oven (250°), 1 to 1½ hours.

Dried Pumpkin: Another gardener writes: "Years ago I used to help Mother dry lots of pumpkins for winter use. We took off the tops, cleaned the insides, then cut the pumpkins into rings about 1 inch thick. These rings were strung on heavy clothesline to dry. When good and dry, we broke the rings up into pieces and put them in flour sacks to be hung on walls in rooms where it was warm and dry. Always had nice dry pumpkins for winter use."

Edible Squash or Pumpkin Vine Feelers: You can eat squash or pumpkin vine feelers or "clingers." Just take the runners and a few leaves with clingers, and boil them for about ½ hour, then drain and put in a frying pan. Fry just a little, then add 2 or 3 scrambled eggs.

Squash or Pumpkin Blossom Fritters: First, pick the false blossoms (male ones, there are about 20 males to 1 female blossom on the vines). These false or male blooms can be distinguished from the female blooms, since the "she" blossoms have a small nub at the base, and male flowers don't. Pick plenty of male blooms because nature was generous and left plenty for pollination. Soak the blossoms in salt water to remove any insects, drain, and dip in batter made from 1 egg, 2 tablespoons flour, salt, pepper, and finely chopped parsley. Fry in deep fat until brown. Let drain on absorbent paper and serve with meat. Makes a fine breakfast dish served with butter and syrup.

If you'd like to make squash blossom soup, use a good beef stock, bring to boil and add the blossom petals whole or cut into pieces. Continue to boil for 20 or 30 minutes. Blossoms keep their nice light-yellow color, and you'll have a pretty as well as tasty dish of soup.

Squash or Pumpkin Blossom Salad: Cook a large basket of male blossoms not more than 5 minutes, then let drain. When cool, squeeze out water and chop. Then add salt, pepper, chopped onion, parsley, and chopped hard-boiled egg, serve with salad dressing or mayonnaise.

If you'd like squash blossoms in a hot dish, cook up a batch and keep in refrigerator. After frying pork chops, pour off most of the fat. Pile the chops to one side, and add some cooked squash or pumpkin blossoms to pan. Season and allow to simmer until warm, serve with pork chops.

Pumpkin blossoms also go well with cheese. First, brown up some butter, add a little chopped onion. Add some drained, cooked blossoms and fry for about 5 minutes. Serve with grated American or Italian cheese. Some folks add well-beaten eggs to this recipe with the cheese, for a good omelet or croquettes.

SUMMER SQUASH

Baked Tomato-Squash: 2 small summer squash, 3 tomatoes, sliced, 1 medium onion, sliced, 1 teaspoon salt, dash pepper, ¼ tablespoon butter, ⅓ cup grated cheese. Wash and cut squash into thin slices, arrange with tomatoes in alternate layers in greased casserole. Sprinkle with salt and pepper. Dot with butter and add grated cheese. Cover and bake in preheated 350° oven for 45 minutes. Remove cover last 10 minutes to brown the cheese.

Candied Summer Squash: Wash and chop yellow summer squash in skillet containing a small amount of butter or shortening. Chop small onion into squash, add salt, black pepper to taste. Add sugar (prefer brown sugar flavor) to taste and cook until brown and candy-like. Experiment with amounts of ingredients used.

Creamed Mashed Summer Squash: 3 medium-sized summer squash, 1 teaspoon salt, 1 teaspoon sugar, 2 tablespoons butter or margarine, ¼ teaspoon pepper, 1 tablespoon flour, ½ cup top milk or light cream. Select very tender squash so the rind and seeds do not have to be removed. Slice and barely cover with boiling water containing the salt and sugar. Boil until tender, about 30 minutes. Drain well and mash. Add the remaining ingredients in order given and heat to boiling point, stirring constantly.

Sautéed Summer Squash With Sour Cream: Peel 4 squash and cut in matchlike strips. Sprinkle with 2 teaspoons salt and let stand 1 hour. Drain well. Sauté 2 sliced onions in ¼ cup butter, simmer till nearly done, then add squash and cook till tender. Stir 2 tablespoons flour into a little sour cream, stir into squash mixture. Add more sour cream, using 2 cups in all. Simmer 5 minutes. 1 teaspoon paprika may be added. If squash is tender, use unpeeled.

Scalloped Yellow Squash: Take tender summer squash (I use my fingernail for test), wash and cut in pieces. Put a little water in a pan, add squash, and cover tightly. Watch carefully to prevent burning when partly cooked. Add butter, onion, seasoning. When cooked (slightly brown), mash and serve.

Southern Style Summer Squash: A reader wrote: "An old Southern lady kept a large black iron skillet on her stove all the time, carefully covered. This she never washed, but drained the grease and wiped the pan each time it was used. First she carefully laid 6 thick strips of bacon in the pan, browned it carefully, then removed the bacon and added a layer of thinly sliced onion. On top of this she placed about 1 quart of squash, diced in 1-inch cubes. This was cooked, covered, over low heat until the squash was tender. She served this with small parsley potatoes, sliced tomatoes, and 2 slices of the bacon. Seasoned with salt, black pepper to taste."

Stewed Summer Squash: 2 large summer squash, seeded and diced, 1 teaspoon sugar, 2 tablespoons butter, 6 tablespoons water, 2 thinly sliced onions, 2 teaspoons salt. Cook in tightly covered utensil until ingredients melt into perfection.

Summer Squash Special: 1 pound pork sausage, 1 clove garlic, crushed, 4 cups sliced summer squash, ½ cup dry bread crumbs, ½ cup grated Parmesan cheese, ½ cup milk, 1 tablespoon chopped parsley, ½ teaspoon oregano, crushed, ½ teaspoon salt, 2 beaten eggs. Cook sausage and garlic till meat is brown, drain off excess fat. Cook squash, covered, in small amount of water till tender. Drain, stir squash and next 6 ingredients into meat, fold in eggs, transfer to 10"x6"x1½" baking dish, bake at 325° for 25 to 30 minutes. Serves 4 to 6.

Tender Squash and Corn Stew: 2 tablespoons bacon fat, 1 pound (cups sliced) summer squash, 1 cup fresh corn cut from cob (about ears), 1½ cups diced fresh tomatoes, 1 tablespoon diced green pepper 1 tablespoon sugar, 2 tablespoons salt, ¼ teaspoon ground black pepper grated cheddar cheese. Use a 2-quart saucepan. Mix first 7 ingredient well, cover, and cook 12 minutes. Stir in pepper. Serve hot, covered with grated cheese. Serves 6.

WINTER SQUASH

Baked Squash: Boil winter squash (peeled and cut in small pieces) unt almost done in small amount of water. Put in greased casserole and add salt, pepper, butter, and American cheese, chopped or shredded and a small amount of milk. Bake for 30 minutes, or until cheese i brown.

Butternut or acorn squash can be baked in halves. Place in a dis with a little water in bottom after cutting in half and removing seeds Place sausage or bacon in center, bake at 375° for 1 hour or until ten der. Makes a tasty dish.

Cornmeal and Squash: Peel and slice squash ¼ to ⅜ inch thick. Bea an egg and add salt and pepper to taste, making it slightly salty. Dip slices of squash in the egg and then into a mixture of cornmeal an flour, about 2 tablespoons of cornmeal to 1 of flour. Then drop in inch of hot fat in skillet, and fry until nicely browned. Works with scalloped, butternut, and buttercup varieties, as well as zucchini Some like the scallop the best. You can prepare the winter crookneck squash the same way, except lay the slices on a greased cookie shee and bake until tender and brown.

ZUCCHINI

Baked Zucchini: Slice thin, dip in melted butter or margarine, sprea on large baking pan or rimmed cookie sheet. Sprinkle generously with grated Parmesan cheese and bake at 350° for 15 minutes, or unti tender.

Southern Style Zucchini: Northern recipes call for large squash, South ern ones use the squash when 3 to 5 inches long, even 5 inches being a little too large, for you don't want the seeds showing or skins tough Just cut off the ends of the squash and slice them up. For 2 servings cut up about 6 squash, put 1 tablespoon bacon grease or butter in fry pan, toss squash around, add 1 tablespoon water, cover, and lower heat Turn over once or twice, add pepper and salt, chop with spoon, serv when all "squashy." Another method is to cut up medium onion, sauté in fat until transparent, then add squash and continue as before. Do not let the squash cook till transparent, it is better crisp. If you don't want to watch the cooking, put them in a double boiler and cook. To make a casserole, cook as described, add coarsely crumbled crackers, milk, and an egg, if you like—bake, but always use the tiny squash. Some like them cut up raw in vegetable salads.

Stuffed Zucchini: 4 small, or 2 large zucchini (about 1 pound), 2 tablespoons butter or margarine, 2 tablespoons chopped onion, 2 tablespoons chopped anchovy fillets (optional), 2 cups soft bread cubes, ¼ cup grated Swiss cheese. Place squash in a pan, cover, and bring to a boil. Continue cooking 5 to 10 minutes or until barely tender. Scoop out the centers from squash and reserve for stuffing. Melt butter in a skillet, sauté onion and anchovies until tender. Combine bread cubes, centers from squash, and onion mixture, fill squash shells. Bake in a shallow pan at 350° for 25 minutes. Sprinkle with cheese. Serves 4.

Vegetable With Zucchini Casserole: Amounts depend on number in family. Zucchini, thinly sliced, potatoes, thinly sliced, onion, thinly sliced, green peppers, cut in pieces, fresh tomatoes, quartered or sliced, semi-hot green peppers (or a few drops hot pepper sauce). Butter a large casserole dish, put layers of vegetables in dish, in order given. Dot each layer with bits of butter and sprinkle with salt and pepper. Bake 1 hour 20 minutes in 375° oven, or until potatoes are done. Some may not care for the tang of hot pepper, but it truly does a lot for the casserole. With the addition of hot rolls or biscuits and a light dessert, this is a meal in itself.

Zucchini and Eggs: Put a little olive oil in skillet and heat. Wash zucchini and cut into small chunks. Add to olive oil, cover, and cook till tender, adding a little water if necessary. Beat about 6 eggs (amount depends on amount of squash used and number in family). Add eggs to squash and mix in. Season to taste. Good too, when onions are cooked in oil before adding squash. Pour off excess water before adding eggs.

Zucchini Cakes: 2 cups coarsely shredded, unpeeled zucchini, ¼ cup shredded onion, 1 egg, beaten, ⅔ cup pancake mix, ½ teaspoon salt, ⅛ teaspoon black pepper, ⅓ cup milk, vegetable oil. Mix all ingredients together and drop by tablespoon onto an oiled hot griddle. Cook over slow heat until brown on both sides. Serve at once. Serves 4.

Zucchini Sauté With Sweet Basil: 4 medium-sized zucchini, 1 tablespoon butter, 2 tablespoons olive oil, 1 clove garlic, minced, 1 small onion, minced, 1 bay leaf, 1 teaspoon sweet basil, minced, salt and pepper, ½ boullion cube dissolved in cup of water, 2 tablespoons tomato sauce or 1 peeled tomato, cut up. Wash squash and cut into thin rounds without peeling. Melt butter and mix with olive oil in frying pan. In this, cook garlic and onion for 10 minutes without browning. Add zucchini and herbs and seasoning, stir well, and add boullion. Cover and cook 10 minutes, then add tomato or sauce and finish cooking. When almost done add more salt if needed. A tablespoon of grated cheese stirred in at serving time adds a fillip.

Zucchini Stuffed and Fried: Excellent with rather simply seasoned meat. No matter how many you cook, they won't go begging. One 6-inch zucchini for each serving, 3 slices of bread, cooked in milk, 2 eggs, 1 clove of garlic, minced, ½ cup grated Romano cheese, ½ teaspoon thyme, salt, pepper, olive oil, and butter. Parboil zucchini, cool and split lengthwise. Remove pulp, chop finely, and add to it bread from which milk has been squeezed, eggs, garlic, cheese, thyme, salt, and pepper. Mix well and stuff zucchini, gauging amount by number of zucchini used. Brown completely and serve while hot.

Zucchini With Onion Rings: 4 zucchini, 6 to 8 inches long, 1 onion, sliced, 2 tablespoons water, salt, pepper, 1 tablespoon butter, grated Parmesan cheese. Slice zucchini into pan, add the onion, water, and salt to taste. Cover and cook over medium heat for 15 minutes. Drain, add butter and pepper to taste, and serve with cheese.

Zucchini With Rosemary Sauce: 4 medium zucchini, 1 sliced onion, 1 clove garlic, minced, ½ teaspoon minced rosemary, 2 tablespoons olive oil or butter, stale end of French bread loaf, salt and pepper, cup of broth or hot water, 1 tablespoon grated Romano cheese. Wash and slice zucchini without peeling. Fry onion, garlic, and rosemary slowly in oil for 10 minutes. From the stale French loaf shave enough thin shavings to make ½ cup. Add to oil mixture and fry slowly, until bread slivers are browned. Add zucchini slowly, and cook until zucchini are tender, stirring frequently. If necessary to keep from burning, add small amount of water. Just before serving, stir in cheese.

SUNFLOWER (*Helianthus anthus*)

Sunflowers are some flowers! You don't need a green thumb to grow them. While not a vegetable you'd be surprised to see how many gardeners raise this item for ornamental use and food, as well as for bird feed. A row of sunflowers makes a fine "living fence."

Sunflowers grow in any type of soil. Seed is sown outdoors in spring, and by late summer you're apt to have plants 15 feet tall. Sunflowers like the heat and plenty of moisture in summer. In hot weather the heads will droop, but upon watering, they'll freshen up again. You've probably heard the story about sunflowers following the sun each day. That is, in the morning the heads face the sun and follow it around until in the afternoon, they face west. Sometimes they do this, and sometimes they don't.

Harvesting: Sunflower heads should be cut as soon as the seeds start to take on a brownish tinge. If you wait too long to harvest, the birds will beat you to it. You can keep birds out by covering the heads with plastic bags (perforated). One problem is mildewing or rotting of seed in the head. Prevent this by picking the heads when seeds are fully ripe (just before they are shed) and hanging upside down in warm, dry place. Better still, dry the heads off quickly by placing them in front of an electric fan to drive off moisture.

TROUBLES

Sunflowers have few insects or diseases to bother them. Sometimes aphids (plant lice) are troublesome but these can be knocked out by spraying with Malathion or nicotine sulfate.

USES

Sunflower seeds are highly nutritious, contain phosphorus, calcium, iron, potassium, and some vitamins. Seed can be purchased ready to eat from various food centers, and you can also buy sunflower-seed meal to sprinkle on foods. Russia produces the most sunflower seed, Argentina second.

Roasted Sunflower Seeds: In October, soak sunflower seeds overnight in strong salt water. Drain off the water in morning and spread the seeds on cookie sheets. Roast in a 200° oven for 3 hours, or until crisp. They are easy to shell if roasted long enough. Pumpkin seeds can be treated same way.

Sunflower or Pumpkin Seed Snack: 1 pound sunflower or pumpkin seeds, 1 cup salt, 1½ pints water. Wash the seeds, let drain in a colander. Clean off membrane from seed. Add salt to water, stir until dissolved, then place salt water and seeds in an enamel pot. Let boil for 15 minutes, stirring occasionally. Drain seeds and spread in a flat pan. Whenever you use your oven for baking and have finished, put seeds in warm oven to dry. Turn the seeds over after they've been in oven for a while. Repeat process several times, until seeds are good and dry. Then put a cupful or more seeds into a frying pan on low heat, keep turning till you hear some of them popping. Then they are ready to eat.

Tomato (*Lycopersicon esculentum*)

Even the hard-pressed suburbanite, his time for outdoor activities ever chipped away, saves a place in his garden and schedule for the raising of tomatoes. Related to the pepper, eggplant, and potato, dear to American palates, this acid fruit is a heavy-yielding staple of the home garden.

What's the Best Tomato?: Home gardeners often ask which tomato is the best-tasting, heaviest yielding, least acid, least seedy, sweetest, meatiest, thinnest-skinned. The answer is that there is no single variety which meets all the demands of all home gardeners. Varieties are developed with particular properties in mind. It's impossible to rate a single variety in every category, and even a well-established variety will vary in its performance. A tomato which does well in your own garden might do differently in your neighbor's, 20 feet away, due to differences in soil, culture, etc. (does your neighbor spray, water, feed, fuss more than you do?).

My advice is to try 3 or 4 different kinds. There are early, midseason, and late varieties. Tomatoes have size and shape differences, too. Most folks like a medium-sized tomato which is fairly early and has an extended fruiting season. There are differences in color. Numerous variations are found, from bright scarlet red to a rich brick red. There are some who prefer the pink-type tomatoes (often called "blue" tomatoes). Then there are the yellow-orange and tangerine types. There is even a range of mildness: Some like an acid tomato, others like a flat, subacid type.

Remember that quite often the performance of a variety is directly dependent upon the kind of care given it. No variety will perform well on an underfertilized or overfertilized soil (see Feeding of Tomato Plants).

Hybrid Tomatoes: You don't need a big backyard to grow a big crop of tomatoes. One of my gardener-readers planted 6 hybrid tomato plants and picked 4½ bushels. Most of the fruits were "as large as grapefruits." When he dug up the ground, he put in sheep manure, nothing else. When the plants started to blossom he sprayed each blossom with a blossom-set hormone spray. Plants were staked to a 12-foot trellis, and after he got tired of tying them he just let the vines hang. Five of the plants were 14½ feet high.

Another told me he grew a different hybrid, using liquid plant food, and obtained 200 tomatoes from 2 hybrid plants, which grew to 7 feet. One gardener, who did not believe in hybrids, planted 2 hybrid plants and had vines 17 feet 2 inches tall. He used liquid manure, 1 bushel soaked in a 30-gallon barrel of water.

One of the greatest developments in the vegetable world is the hybrid tomato. Why hybrids? The vines are husky, flavor is high-quality, and the plants produce tremendous clusters of fruit all season. While hybrid seed and plants cost more, many believe the extra price is off-set by yield and quality. There are many good hybrids on the market, such as Harris' Moreton and Burpee Big Boy. While hybrid tomatoes are a great introduction, it does not mean that the open-pollinated or regular types are obsolete. There's still a place for these, and many of them are worthy of a spot in your garden. Try both types, compare their yields and flavor, and then you be the judge as to which does best for you and your pocketbook.

Novelties: If you're looking for novelties, try colorful tomatoes such as Snow White (white when ripe), Evergreen (green when fully ripe), and the blue tomato. For orange tomatoes, try either Jubilee on wilt-free soil or Sunray on wilt-infected soils. There are many other ornamental and novelty tomatoes, but my advice is to try only a few from seed. Do not plant a lot of them, because a little goes a long way.

You might like to try growing cherry tomatoes. Just 1 or 2 plants will bear profusely, and supply the average family with plenty of tiny, round, bright-red fruits for salads and appetizers.

Resistant Varieties: If your tomatoes wilt every year you should try to rotate (grow plants in a new spot), but if this is not possible, then be sure to grow disease-resistant varieties. MAKE SURE YOUR GREENHOUSE OPERATOR HAS NAMED VARIETIES. Some unscrupulous fruit stand operators may tell you they have such-and-such variety just for the sake of making a sale. If you're not sure, buy seed and start your own plants.

Galaxy is a new early disease-resistant type, ripening a few days later than Fireball, an extra-early tomato. Galaxy's fruit is larger than Fireball's and the vines are larger, but are not adapted to staking. For a full-season disease-resistant variety, try Heinz 1350 (also crack resistant) and Campbell 1327. Both are resistant to disease, and both ripen in about 75 days. Tomatoes are good-sized, well colored, and good yielding. Moreton Hybrid is resistant to verticillium wilt. If you've had trouble with plants wilting, poor quality (and yield) of mid- and late-season tomatoes, I suggest you grow Heinz 1350 or Campbell 1327.

There are other good resistant varieties listed in your seed catalog. There is no single variety free from all diseases. A variety that is resistant to a particular disease may have its share of certain other diseases.

Soil: Tomatoes grow in almost any type of soil, provided it's well drained. For midseason and late crops, heavier soils are good because they hold moisture better than do the lighter soils. Also, on heavy soils there is less likely to be blossom-end rot of the fruit, a trouble brought about by fluctuations in the supply of soil water.

Setting Plants: Don't set your plants out until danger of frost is over. There is nothing to be gained by setting out in a cold, wet soil, and while plant protectors are generally helpful in producing earlier fruit, in such soils little is gained by their use. In small plantings, baskets are good protectors on frost nights, but they must be removed in the morning, otherwise plants will suffer from lack of light. A sprinkling system or irrigation system may prevent plants from freezing simply by allowing water to fall on the plants during the period of frost—usually during a few hours in the early morning. Potted plants may be set out pot and all (in the case of peat pots), set a little deeper than the pot soil surface.

Although spacing of the plants will vary according to the system of growing used (staked plants are set closer), a good general practice would be to set plants 2 to 3 feet apart each way. An ideal tomato plant should be 6 to 9 inches high, with strong stems and a well-developed root system. Foliage should be a healthy green. Don't worry too much if the plant is rather tall because it can be set in deeper and still make good, husky growth. Roots will form all along the stem. Some gardeners like their plants 18 to 24 inches tall, so they can be set in holes made with a crowbar. Others prefer short plants. We've tested both and find that there is no difference in yield or maturity date. Just make sure the plants are free from disease. The virus causing mottled or mosaic disease is carried and spread on workers' hands. Loss from these forms of mosaic can be prevented if growers will wash their hands thoroughly in soapy water before handling tomatoes, peppers, and similar plants, especially after smoking.

Start Your Own: Tomato plants can be started from seed sown indoors about the first of April. Perlite, sterilized muck, vermiculite, or a mixture of sand and peat moss make a good starting medium. Sow seed in a small box or flat, cover lightly with ½ sand and peat, sifted, and cover with newspaper or plastic until seed starts to germinate. Water the flat from below, NOT FROM ABOVE, or you'll encourage damping off, the fungus disease of seedlings. Just as soon as seedlings appear, give lots of light and grow in a cool temperature, 60° to 70°. Without these conditions, your plants will be leggy or spindly. Thin to 2 inches apart each way. Transplant to individual peat pots or boxes.

Harden Your Plants: Don't let your tomato plants grow too fast or tall. This is avoided by withholding water, checking their growth so they become toughened and stunted. A certain amount of this "hardening-off" is necessary.

Greenhouse operators harden or toughen up their plants by placing them outside in a cold frame, without heat. There they are checked in growth by cooler temperatures and less watering.

Tomatoes in the Compost Pile: Some home gardeners who throw tomato vines on the compost pile in fall find that tomato plants grow voluntarily. Many tell us that the plants were hybrids and ask if the seedlings which sprout will also be hybrids. The answer is no. Actually, plants which came up from last year's hybrid's are known as F_2's— that is, they are the second generation of an F_1 hybrid.

One of the advantages of an F_1 hybrid is its extra vigor. An F_2 will generally produce more and better fruit than a regular non-hybrid variety but not as much as an F_1 hybrid.

When seed is saved from an F_2 to produce an F_3 just about all the advantage of hybridization is lost.

What all this boils down to is: You shouldn't save seed from a hybrid. But if you do, the F_2 generation will do a better-than-average job.

If you plant early and late-bearing tomatoes close to each other, don't worry about them cross-pollinating. The fruit you harvest won't be a bit different, even if the flowers have been cross-pollinated. You're interested in the fruit, not the seed.

Tomato plants have both male and female parts in the same flower. That's why even the city dwellers with only a foot of space can get fruit on a single plant.

Direct Seeding of Tomatoes: While the seeds of most tomato varieties must be started indoors, weeks ahead of frost-free date in the garden, there are new varieties which can be planted (seeded) right out in the garden, and still produce bountiful crops within your growing season. This is called direct seeding, and many commercial growers are doing this now. Time to plant is after May 10 in the north, after March 20 in the south, and after April 15 in the middle states.

The secret: Start only *early* varieties such as Fireball, New Yorker, and others in this class. You cannot direct-seed later varieties, since they take too long to mature. Fireball is an early self-pruning variety with good internal color. It sets fruit well at relatively low temperatures, is less subject to cracking and blossom-end rot than most varieties, and has acceptable fruit size when grown from young transplants. Disadvantages include sparse foliage cover, which means trouble from sunburning in warm seasons, a low yield, a tendency to develop severe blotchy ripening or graywall in cool periods or years, and only fair external fruit color. (To increase yield of Fireball when *not* growing by direct seeding, plant the plants closer, give them lots of nitrogen, water, and pest protection.)

After soil has been prepared by spading, preferably to a depth of 1 foot, clods broken up, and the area leveled and smoothed with a rake, seeds of these tomatoes may be planted.

Make furrows ⅛ inch deep, spaced at least 18 inches apart. Seeds of Fireball should be scattered about 1 inch apart in the row. Cover all seeds with ⅛ inch of soil.

When seedlings are 3 or 4 inches high, thin so they are spaced from 2 to 3 feet apart. If you have planted seeds of Fireball allow plants to remain 6 to 8 inches apart.

We tell gardeners who try direct seeding of tomatoes to try only a short row of 10 to 12 feet the first time, and to also plant their regular supply of tomato plants. This will give them a chance to compare the 2 systems, and will also give them their usual supply of tomatoes. Fruit from the transplanted plants, since they have a head start, will be ready for harvest sooner than garden-seeded tomatoes of the same variety.

Feeding Tomatoes: As the tomato sets fruit and begins to make size, the demand for nitrogen changes and changes fast. Plenty of nitrogen is needed at this time, so apply about ½ pound of ammonium nitrate per 50 feet of row when the first tomatoes on the plants attain the size of a golf ball.

Repeat this application 2 more times, at 3- to 4-week intervals. You will find that you get higher yields of larger fruit if you follow this side-dressing program, providing the other essential plant food elements are at their optimum levels.

If you're a gardener who likes to use liquid plant foods to boost growth along, use a commercial grade made specifically for liquid feeding (such as Ra-Pid-Gro), with a 23–19–17 formula. Apply it over the foliage, or at the base of the plant. Apply with a sprinkling can, sprayer, or hose feeder. Mix at rate of 1 level teaspoon to 1 quart of water, 4 level teaspoons to 1 gallon.

Gibberellic Acid: This is a growth-promoting stimulant which is still a laboratory tool and not recommended for the home gardener, unless he wants to experiment.

Insurance Plantings of Tomatoes: Some gardeners tell me that every year they set out 2 dozen extra tomato plants, "1 for starlings, 1 for cutworms, and a dozen for ourselves." You can eliminate damage from starlings and cutworms by placing tomato cans around each plant after setting them out. Coffee cans with plastic tops are even better. You cut the bottom out, set the can halfway into the soil around the young transplant, place the plastic lid over it and presto!—your plant is enclosed in a greenhouse which lets in light and keeps out cutworms and birds. The tin collar around the plants not only keeps the birds out, but is a barrier to cutworms and rabbits. Remove the lid on hot, dry days for ventilation. When plant grows tall, lid may be permanently removed.

Some gardeners fill the cans half-full of sand, and water the plants by filling the cans each time they are dry. Liquid plant food can be poured on top of the sand all during the growing season. Do not bother to remove the can. The plastic ½- or 1-gallon jugs which household bleach comes in are useful for getting an early start in setting out tomatoes. Indeed, these can be successfully used to protect against frost and cutworm activity. Trim top and bottom off with shears. On real hot days they should be ventilated a bit, as they may cook inside. They act as miniature greenhouses and are useful for getting plants off to a quicker start than if they were set outdoors without any protection.

One gardener tells us he uses No. 10 vegetable and fruit cans (such as those used by restaurants and school cafeterias) for covering tomato plants. He takes a hatchet and cuts a cross in the bottom, and turns the points up enough to give the plants more room and ventilation. These cans will cover a larger plant than the coffee cans mentioned earlier, and will protect transplants against freezes. The same cans can be kept from year to year. Bushel baskets or crates can also serve to keep out crows, starlings, and other robbers.

Cultivate Tomatoes Carefully: Probably more tomatoes do not produce the maximum yield because of improper cultivation than any other single factor. Cultivation is performed for 3 distinct reasons: to control weeds and grass, to introduce oxygen from the air into the soil, and to prevent erosion and leaching. This has to be accomplished without injury to the root system of the plants. Improper cultivation results in damage to the root system.

If you are a gardener who prefers to mulch tomatoes with straw, sawdust, hay, etc., they will not need cultivation the rest of the season. Mulching reduces fruit cracking and blossom-end rot, common troubles. (See section on Mulches.)

Pruning Tomatoes: There are several methods of pruning tomato plants. To avoid confusion only the single-stem system will be described here. In the single-stem system of pruning tomatoes, all the suckers or side-shoots are removed and the plant is trained to a single stem (see illustration).

You will note that as your plant grows there are shoots which appear in the axils of the leaves (where the leaf attaches to the stem). These shoots are called suckers and should be removed when 2 to 4 inches long. They can be pulled off easily by grasping the sucker with thumb and forefinger and pulling outward and downward.

It is not advisable to cut the suckers with a knife as you can transmit virus diseases from one plant to another in this way. Should the suckers get away from you and reach a length of a foot or more, you can still remove them without causing too much injury to the plant. It is best to remove them while they are small.

About the time you start picking your first tomatoes, it might be advisable to discontinue pruning or suckering the plants. Allow the late suckers to grow and provide shade for the 5 or 6 hands of tomatoes below.

Note: If pruning tomatoes sounds "Greek" to you, then forget the job! You can grow all the tomatoes you want without resorting to any pruning whatsoever.

How to sucker your tomato plants. (University of Missouri)

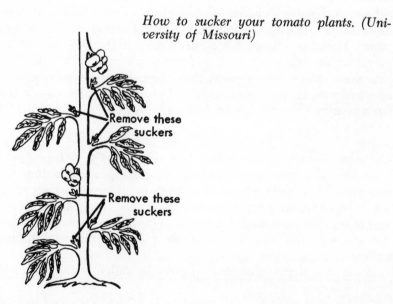

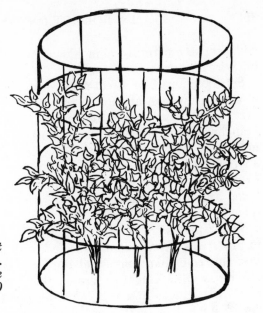

Another variation is to plant tomatoes inside a wire corset. A single plant inside a wire corset will give up to 60 pounds of fruit.

Tricks to Get Lots of Tomatoes from a Little Space

Some gardeners like to stake their tomatoes to save space over the mulching and sprawling method. The latest wrinkle among gardeners is the "Chinese Tomato Ring," known also as tomato trellising, growing tomatoes on a corset, and many other descriptions. Many commercial growers in southern areas find it advantageous to grow tomatoes on trellises, just as grapes are grown. This enables them to grow more plants in the available space, and the fruit is kept free from snails and other pests. Tomato plants grown on trellises will bear heavily until frost, and in tests, a single plant has produced as much as 62 pounds of tomatoes. According to the University of Maryland, 25 tomato plants produced over ¾ ton of fruit, with the corset or trellis method.

Steps in the Chinese Ring Method: After the soil is well worked with organic matter (peat, compost, leaf mold), you rake in 2 pounds of a complete plant food (such as 5–10–10, or similar analysis) per 100 square feet. Or you can wait and feed your plants liquid plant food (such as 23–19–17).

Basically, this method amounts to keeping each plant inside a wire cylinder, 1½ feet across and 5 feet tall. The result is a column of vine growth held in place and supported by a wire cylinder. Wire with a 6-inch mesh is best because it makes it easy to reach in and pick the tomatoes. Concrete reinforcing wire is ideal because it is rigid enough to be self-supporting. You can get this in lumberyards. Cylinders or other wire supports only half as tall may be used to give partial support to the plants. If the wire is weak, a few stakes around the cylinders

will keep them from being blown over. I like the concrete reinforcing wire because it is so sturdy.

Set the plants 3 or 4 feet apart, water them well, then apply a mulch
of straw, sawdust, aluminum foil, plastic, etc. Place the wire cylinder
over each plant soon after transplanting and keep all the tomato
branches inside the wire framework. The tomato plants will eventually grow over the top of the cylinders and down the outside making
a vine length of about 10 feet. DO NOT PRUNE OFF ANY OF THE BRANCHES.
From time to time you'll have to keep training the top as it climbs.
Some folks tie the shoots to the wire with soft cloth, others just weave
them in and out of the mesh.

Water plants frequently during early part of season but later only
in dry spells. Keep plants watered with liquid plant food from time
first cluster of blossoms is set until end of summer. Once a month or
oftener is O.K. Tomatoes grown this way are clean, bright-red, free
of growth cracks and rots, and the plant is capable of producing a
larger amount of food over a longer period than any other vegetable
in the home garden. If you don't want to grow the plants individually
in cylinders, you may vary the idea by using a large corset and growing several plants on it. Another trick is to keep adding a mulch of
leaves, sawdust, grass clippings, etc. around the cylinder and pour water as needed inside the cylinder. No weeds, no snails, nothing to trouble the fruit. Add a mulch of leaves, straw, sawdust, peat moss, hay, or

*Some gardeners train tomato vines on a wire fence. Plants are
set 2 feet apart and trained to 3 strands of wire. Snail injury is
avoided, picking is easier, fruit is cleaner.*

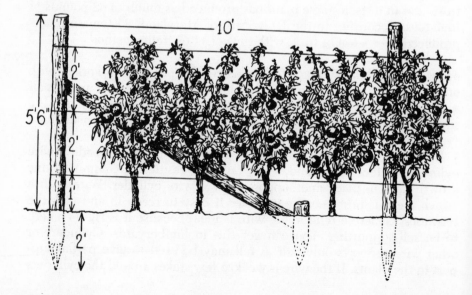

anything you can get, on outside to save moisture. Add water to inside of ring.

Keep plants covered with Maneb or zineb, 3 tablespoons to a gallon of water, when first fruits set. Use Malathion or Sevin, 2 tablespoons to a gallon of water, for insects.

Grow Tomatoes on a Straight Fence: Another trick is to grow your tomatoes on a straight wire fence. You can buy the fence from your farm-supply dealer. Mesh can be 4"x5" or something close to it. Train the vine up and through each mesh, then tie with soft cloth or wire twists.

Should You Stake Your Tomatoes?: Home gardeners are divided on whether to stake tomatoes or let them ramble over an area and keep them mulched with straw. One reason for staking tomatoes is psychological—it looks impressive to see the cluster of tomatoes hanging on the vine. Tomatoes lying on the ground are hidden. Some advantages of staking are:

1. Earlier fruiting and ripening.
2. Fruit will be clean and free of ground spots.
3. Fruits will average larger.
4. Ease of picking.
5. You can get higher production per unit of garden space, but it will take more plants to achieve this.

Some real disadvantages to staking are:

1. More work involved in pruning and tying.
2. Less fruit per plant.
3. More tendency for sunscalded fruits and cracking.
4. Greater likelihood of blossom-end rot in most seasons.
5. More plants required for the same total production compared to growing plants on the ground.

How to Stake Tomatoes: 1"x1" stakes, 5 or 6 feet long, are fine for stakes. Place them about 3 to 5 inches from the plant and drive them about 10 inches into the soil. It's best to place the stakes at the time of setting out the plants or within a week or 2 thereafter.

When the tomato plant reaches a height of 10 to 12 inches make your first tie to the stake. Tie the plant with strips of cloth, binder twine, or any soft cord, or you can use plastic-covered wire twists. Kite string is generally not strong enough and may cut into the stem. Tie the string or cloth securely to the stake. Take the free end and bring it around under a stem and tie securely to the stake again.

You will probably have to tie your tomatoes every 10 days or 2 weeks, depending upon the growth rate; 4 or 5 ties are usually all that are necessary. As you tie your plant to the stake, try to keep the flower

Vigorous, high-yielding varieties of tomatoes such as ForeMost E-21 (pictured) will bear from seed only 10 days to 2 weeks later than greenhouse-grown plants. When seedlings are 6 inches high, thin to 1 strong plant per hill. Transplant the thinned seedlings if you need more plants. Drive long stakes 2 feet deep, leaving 4 feet for tomatoes to climb on. (Ferry-Morse Seed Co.)

clusters away from the stake. This will prevent the tomatoes, as they enlarge, from being injured or misshapen by crowding between the stem and the stake.

WAYS TO GET EARLY TOMATOES

Defoliation to Hasten Ripening: Removing some of the foliage may hasten maturity by 3 or 4 days. Ripening and coloring of tomatoes depends upon fruit temperature, not light. Removing some of the foliage allows more direct sunshine to reach the fruit, raises the temperature, and thus hastens maturity. Once a tomato has reached the "mature green" stage (full development except for red color) the most desirable color develops at temperatures from 75° to 80°. Tomatoes do not color up well at temperatures below 65° or over 85°. Putting green tomatoes in a bright window does not hasten coloring, since light has little effect on ripening. Some late varieties are naturally slow to ripen and your best bet is to avoid the late ones.

Removing foliage to hasten ripening may offer some advantages as well as disadvantages.

Advantages:

1. Picking is easier and faster if some of the foliage is removed to expose the fruits, especially in fields with heavy vines.

2. The fruits and soil under the vines may dry off faster in mornings or after rains, thus reducing the development of rots and mold.

3. The amount of cracking may be reduced (although some maintain it has no effect).

Disadvantages:

1. Exposed fruits may sunburn if a hot spell follows treatment.

2. More fruits will be exposed to damage by early light frosts that normally would not harm fruits protected by leaves.

3. Defoliation might cause an increase of anthracnose (see Troubles) on the fruits.

4. Also, exposing the fruit may cause poor shoulder ripening of green-shouldered varieties.

Start With Early Varieties: There are early, midseason, and late tomatoes. If you live in a region where frosts come early in the fall, then select an early maturing variety. If you don't, you'll have green tomatoes at harvest time. You can use what are known as "potted" tomatoes. These are started early indoors and after the seedlings are up, they are transplanted to individual pots. These can be "plant bands" —made of veneer or paper. Or you can use fertile pots, made of peat and manure. These can be set in the garden without any check of growth, as plants need not be removed from the pot. Pots will decay and furnish plant food as they break down in the soil. Or you can use ordinary florist's clay pots, and these can be used year after year. Fireball, New Yorker, and Moreton Hybrid are good early varieties.

Potted tomatoes may grow tall and have blossoms at transplanting time. Open blossoms should be removed as they may check growth but unopened blooms may be left on. Don't worry about the length of the stem. You can set them into the ground deeply and they'll form roots all the way up the stem. When the plant "takes hold" you'll see it practically jump. Some folks like to use a booster solution or transplanting solution of a high-analysis water-soluble complete fertilizer at planting time. This helps give the plants a quick send-off. We use

23–19–17 at planting time and again after the plants have started to take hold. When you set out potted plants, it's a good idea to break the pot gently (without disturbing the roots), so that the roots can grow directly into the soil. We've found that if the pot goes dry, roots will sometimes actually curl up inside the pots, instead of growing out through the organic container.

Hormone Sprays: Another way to have earlier fruit is to use "blossom-set" hormone sprays. These will ripen tomatoes 1 to 3 weeks earlier. The spray comes in aerosol cans, or in liquid form, ready for dilution. You spray the flower clusters when they are open or partly open. We spray the flower clusters as soon as 2 or more blossoms are open, with repeated sprayings weekly to set flowers opening later. Unpollinated or incompletely pollinated tomato flowers often fail to set fruit and drop off the plants, especially in the early part of the season, due to cool nights (below 59°), or short, cloudy days and lack of sunlight—all conditions unfavorable for pollination. The blossom-set hormone sprays make the fruit set, hold it on the plants. The hormone chemical starts fruit development by chemical stimulation of the flowers. Many of the tomatoes will be seedless, because fruit is set by chemicals, not by pollen.

Hormones are perhaps most effective early in the spring when temperatures go below 60° as the first or second "hands" (flower clusters) are blooming. Their value in setting fruit is questionable in tempera-

A healthy potted plant ready to set in the garden. Potted plants bear earlier.

tures over 95° or when night temperatures continue at levels above 80° for several days. The hormones can be bought under several trade names and are generally inexpensive. Use them if you wish, but be sure to follow directions on the label. Don't expect them to substitute for good cultural care such as irrigation, fertilization, and insect and disease control.

Chilling the Seedlings: Another way to produce more early fruit on tomato vines is to chill the tomato seedlings. This is a new concept in planting. Studies show that flowering is stimulated in the tomato and other vegetable plants if the seedlings are exposed to cold. You get remarkable benefits by chilling the seedlings 2 or 3 weeks at 50° to 55° (night temperature). This is done after the seed leaves, or cotyledons (first leaves to appear) unfold—and first true leaves have begun to show—plants being about 1 to 1½ inches tall.

Chilling the young seedlings not only increases the flower numbers, but results in early yields. Chilled plants are blockier (stocky), have thicker stems, and their survival following transplanting is greatly favored. Also, flower numbers in the first and second clusters are more than doubled. Fruit clusters are larger and early yields may be greater. The idea behind chilling young tomato seedlings to stimulate flowering. The flower number and the position of the first cluster are determined 4 to 6 weeks before the first flowers open. Flower formation occurs during the 2- or 3-week interval immediately following the expansion of the seed leaves and chilling is effective during that time.

Pruning and Staking: The chief argument in favor of staking and pruning tomatoes is early maturity. There are some who do not go along with this theory. A garden full of staked plants often does not yield more than an equal area of plants not staked, but it normally produces a larger percentage of the fruit early in the season (see Should You Stake Your Tomatoes).

Tomatoes grown in a dry soil often will bear riper tomatoes than plants grown in a loose, wet soil. Irrigated tomatoes will usually bear a bit later than plants in a dry soil. Tomatoes growing in soils high in nitrogen (too much nitrates) will mature later. During dry periods, soaking the soil prevents checking the growth of plants, thus helps to eliminate blossom-end rot. Some believe soaking also encourages early maturity of fruit, although I do not go along with that thought. But remember that ample moisture at all times is necessary for a good crop.

Mulching: Placing a 4-inch layer of sawdust, grass clippings, straw, wood chips, leaves, plastic mulch, or anything you have available, around the base of the plant conserves moisture and may hasten ripening. Remember to add a handful of dry fertilizer or 1 quart of liquid plant food per bushel of undecomposed organic mulch. Be sure to use an early variety of tomato such as Fireball (60 to 65 days), Galaxy, or Moreton Hybrid. Mulched tomatoes have less blossom-end rot (brown spot on bottom). (See section on Mulches.)

Pull Roots: To get ripe tomatoes ahead of your neighbors, try this trick a gardener sent me. When the first or second fruit develops to a good size on the vines, reach down and grasp the main stem firmly at ground level. Pull upward until you hear and feel the roots snap. By disturbing the root system, the fruit nearest to maturity will ripen faster. The pulled plant will show wilting, but don't worry as it will re-root and go on producing the balance of its fruit with no ill effects. I wouldn't pull this trick on all your plants, but suggest you try it on 1 or 2 until you catch on.

Raising Tomatoes in the Window: Gardeners can raise cherry tomatoes indoors, but the plants may turn yellow, although the fruit itself is delicious. Yellowing of the plant can be due to dry soil, poor drainage, too much water, or high room temperature. These windowsill tomatoes will bear profusely, the fruit being the size of marbles or larger. Some will bloom when plants are 6 inches high. They need full sun, ample water, and feeding once or twice with liquid plant food. Failure to set fruit is due to lack of pollination. You have to help nature along and tickle each flower with a camel's-hair brush (or tip of your finger) and then transfer pollen from one bloom to the next. Outdoors, insects and the wind do this job. Tiny Tim is a good windowsill tomato to try.

Indoor Tree Tomato: The so-called "tree tomato" isn't really a tomato and it's not as great as its promoters claim it is. It's much cheaper to start them from seed. In late spring your plant should start to set blossoms (or fruits). This item grows about 12 feet high, with large elephant-ear-like leaves. During the winter it'll have to be cut back to get it into flowering shape.

Tricks for Storing Green Tomatoes: Many gardeners like to pull up their tomato vines before frost and hang them upside down in a garage, where the green tomatoes gradually turn red. A reader passes along a "better" idea. He writes: "For years I used to pull up our tomato vines and hang them in the garage. A better trick is to pick the green tomatoes and place them on a wire tray in a cool cellar. We place a piece of paper over the tray, then put the green fruit on the paper. Some of them last until Thanksgiving." DO NOT STORE TOMATOES IN A BRIGHT, SUNNY WINDOW.

If you pick green tomatoes, best temperature to store them is about

55°. At this temperature color development will take place slowly and fruit will keep longest. Keep ripe tomatoes in one container, fruit developing red color in another, and those that are green in a third container. Ripe tomatoes can be kept in a refrigerator at about 40° for 2 or 3 weeks. Store them 1 layer thick. Sort them out every 2 or 4 days, and discard bad ones. Handle them carefully, and they're better with stems off.

Another reader tells us he keeps green tomatoes a long time after frost by using a weak solution of household bleach (1 teaspoon bleach to 1 quart water) to disinfect the fruit. First wash the green fruit with the bleach solution, then dry with paper towels. The tomatoes are then packed in fresh newspapers, in bushel baskets, and stored in a cold part of the cellar.

Freezing Tomatoes: Some gardeners freeze tomatoes for use in flavoring soups, roasts, and stews. When you pick them in fall, wipe off each fruit, place in a freezer just as they are. When ready to use, take the tomatoes from the freezer, put under cold-water faucet, and the skins will come right off. You can also freeze tomatoes in plastic containers.

TROUBLES

Tomatoes—called "oranges of the garden" for their high vitamin C content—fall heir to countless troubles, but that's no reason why you should not grow them. The following list of the most common troubles will help you diagnose and avoid tomato troubles this year and next year.

Poor Fruit Set: Due to too low or too high temperatures. Night temperatures between 70° and 75° and day temperatures between 80° and 90° are ideal for fruit setting of tomatoes; such temperatures will also produce larger fruit. Night temperatures either below 60° or above 80° and day temperatures above 90° are unfavorable to fruit set.

Just what low night temperatures do isn't too clear, but they seem to reduce the fruit set of tomatoes by affecting pollen formation. If tomato plants are in the bud stage, a drop in night temperature might injure the plants' ability to form pollen and ovules.

Spraying with hormones will offset the effects of the cold night temperatures and increase fruit set. As the season advances and the weather gets warmer, later flowers aren't affected too adversely by low night temperatures and you should get enough tomatoes.

Many gardeners believe that poor fruit set can be attributed to too much nitrogen, vegetative growth, irrigation, or rain. It is doubtful that any of these factors is a direct cause, although under certain conditions excessive amounts of nitrogen may be a contributing factor.

Large vine growth is more often the result of poor fruit setting than the cause. Young tomato fruits have a high food requirement and drain off the food reserves that otherwise would go to producing new plant growth. After a period of fruit setting, vine growth is usually retarded or stopped.

Maintaining a good level of moisture in the soil is essential for obtaining good fruit set and high yields. A serious shortage of moisture will reduce fruit set. Many growers believe sprinkler irrigation harms fruit setting, perhaps because while irrigating they have seen the flowers fall off the plants.

Actually, the failure of a flower to set is determined 10 to 14 days prior to the time the flower actually falls off. Thus irrigation at the time of blossom drop has nothing to do with the fruit-set problem.

Poor light due to cloudy weather reduces photosynthesis, resulting in low food production. It is almost impossible to set tomatoes in greenhouses, for instance, during the cloudy, short days of late fall and early winter regardless of temperature. Do not grow tomatoes in the shade! When the conditions are borderline, especially the food re-

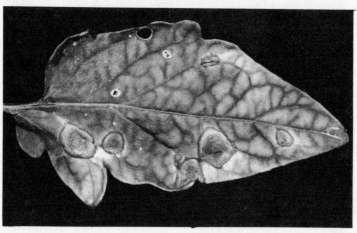

A

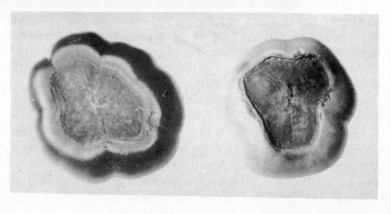

B

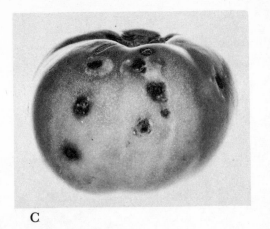

C

D

A. Early blight of tomato. B. Blossom-end rot of tomato. C. Bacterial spot of tomato. D. Septoria leaf spot of tomato. E. Anthracnose of tomato. (Dr. Arden Sherf, College of Agriculture, Cornell University)

E

serves, then nitrogen may become a factor in distributing the balance. Ordinarily, however, it is doubtful that nitrogen directly affects setting unless there is a deficiency or a serious excess of this nutrient.

Varieties vary in their ability to set fruit. Fireball and Pearson are 2 examples of varieties which set under somewhat adverse conditions.

It must be remembered that a tomato plant produces many flowers over a long period of time. It is not uncommon for a period of poor setting to follow a period of heavy setting. Usually, it is not possible or even desirable for a plant to set all of the flowers produced.

All Vines, No Fruit: Due to shade, poor pollination, rich soil. It is possible to get a variety such as Rutgers into an over-vegetative state much more easily than some of the earlier varieties. In general, if any nitrogen need be applied, it should definitely be withheld until after the main portion of the fruit on the plant is set. Earlier applications may result in all vines and no tomatoes.

*F. Tomato plant showing symptoms of fusarium wilt. Some shoots
are dead, but others show only drooping leaves. (USDA Photo)*

Anthracnose: Ripe rot, worse on plants in poorly drained and in-
fertile soils. You see it when fruit is ripe, first coming on as small,
round, sunken, water-soaked spots. Control: Pick ripe fruits at each
picking, for if left in field will rot and spread disease to remaining
fruit. Apply zineb or Maneb.

Blossom-end Rot: Physiological disease caused by moisture fluctuations. The blossom (bottom) end takes on a flaky, black, leathery look,
involving bottom half of the fruit, and secondary fungi will enter and
cause further rotting. Control: Keep plants watered and mulched with
straw or other suitable material. In dry weather, do NOT cultivate, and
avoid heavy doses of nitrogen. Staked tomatoes get it worse than
mulched ones, so be sure and mulch your staked vines to save moisture. Rutgers and Marglobe are resistant to blossom-end rot.

Botrytis Fruit Rot: Spotted fruit which eventually rots, worse in
damp, cloudy weather. Avoid syringing foliage. Bordeaux mixture
will check it.

Buckeye Rot: In wet weather you see a water-soaked spot near
blossom end of fruit where it touches soil. Stake plants to keep fruit
off the ground.

Catfacing: Fruit badly malformed and scarred at blossom end,
swollen protuberances, bands of scar tissue. May be due to extreme
heat and cold, drought, or pesticide injury.

Cracking of Tomatoes: There are 3 types of tomato cracking: radial, concentric, and "skin-cracking." Cracking occurs after heavy rains or heavy irrigation. Probably humidity has more to do with it than anything. When you have a rain with the humidity high for a few days, cracking is more likely to occur than if the humidity drops right after the rain and there are some clear, dry days following it. Glamor and Heinz 1350 are resistant to cracking.

Fruit Spots and Soft Rots: Often anthracnose (which see). Control: Remove rotted fruit and bury or burn. Keep fruit off soil by mulching or staking.

Graywall: Blotchy ripening with internal browning. Various causes but not fully understood. Use resistant varieties such as Manalucie or Manapal.

Hard Cores or Centers: Due to temperature fluctuations, especially low night temperatures. The core is hard and you have to peel away a lot of tomato to get enough to can. No control. Some varieties are more susceptible, although all will get it in low temperatures.

Hard White Tissue Inside: Known as blotchy ripening and from what we've been able to gather, this is tied up with a shortage of plant food (potassium) in the soil. Blotchy ripening has no effect on yield, but it does make a lot of fruit useless. Try feeding your tomatoes with a balanced plant food when the plants are about 1 foot high. An easy

G. Tomato showing advanced symptoms of gray mold, caused by fungus (Botrytis cinerea). (USDA Photo)

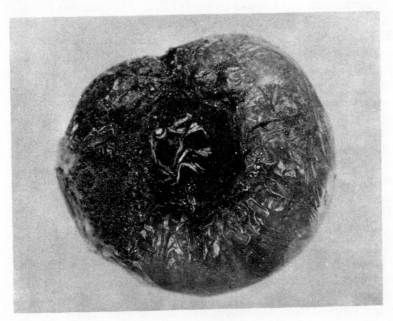

way to get potassium into the soil or plant is to apply a liquid plant food such as 23–19–17 directly on the foliage.

Sunscald: Worse in hot weather, light-gray scalded spots on fruits, often followed by attacks of fungi. Control: Do not prune plants heavily, avoid varieties with sparse foliage.

Scabby Fruits: Caused by bacterial spot, canker, speck, wildfire. Control: Use Bordeaux mixture, 1½ tablespoons to 1 gallon water, plus 1 tablespoon Maneb or zineb.

Bacterial Wilt: Infected plants wilt fast and die, without spotting or yellowing of leaves. If stem is cut lengthwise near ground level, a water-soaked or brownish discoloration of the central tissue (pith) can be seen. A slimy ooze appears from cut stem. This is one way to distinguish disease from fusarium and verticillium wilts. Cavities form in the pith in later stages of disease. Control: Do not grow tomatoes in same area for 4 or 5 years. Rotate soil with grains or corn to burn disease out. Never rotate with potatoes, peppers, or eggplants.

Chlorosis: Foliage turns yellow, especially between veins—may be due to excess lime, or lack of iron. Test the soil for acidity, add iron sulfate if soil is sweet (see Liming and Soil Acidity).

Collar Rot: Disease of seedlings and transplants at soil surface. Dip in Maneb solution before transplanting.

Curly Top: Twisting, upward curling, or cupping of new leaves. Flowers malformed. Caused by virus, usually spread by leafhoppers. Spray plants with Malathion. Avoid planting tomatoes near beets.

Damping-off: Young seedlings flop over in flats or boxes, the result of various fungi. Use Captan or zineb (1½ tablespoons per gallon water) or dust lightly (see Starting Seed Indoors).

Early Blight or Alternaria: Causes browning and dropping of lower foliage in late summer. This is a foliage blight, may also cause a fruit rot around stem end. Look for brown spots with concentric rings in a target pattern on lower leaves. Spots soon enlarge to ¼ to ½ inch in diameter, run together, cause the leaf to turn brown and usually to drop off. If your tomato leaves turn brown, dropping from the bottom of the plant in early fall or late summer, it is fungus known as alternaria or early blight. Control: Spray regularly with Maneb fungicide, 2 tablespoons per gallon of water, applied when first fruits have set and then every 7 to 10 days throughout entire season. This spray also handles anthracnose nicely.

Gray Spot: Small spots on leaves and stems, become shiny and glazed as they enlarge, caused by fungi. Control: zineb or Bordeaux mixture will check.

Hollow Stem: Noninfectious. Avoid by hardening seedlings before you transplant them. Do not transplant them into dry soil. Avoid overcrowding.

Late Blight: High humidity, cool nights, warm days bring on late blight. In few days time kills vines and rots all green and ripe fruit. Look for irregularly shaped, dark-brown, water-soaked areas on stems and leaves. Fruit rots at or near the stem end and soon spreads over entire fruit. Rotted areas are green-black with firm but wrinkled surface. Control: Bordeaux, zineb will do fine job, applied before the disease comes.

Leaf Mold: Yellowish or green spots on leaves, followed by gray-purple mold growth. Worse in damp, rainy season. Control: Keep plants covered with Bordeaux mixture, zineb, or Maneb. Avoid watering leaves, especially at night.

Leaf Roll and Curl: Curling or rolling of leaves is a common problem. This is a physiological disease, follows extended periods of wet weather and most likely to occur on plants in poorly drained soils. It has also been seen after close cultivation and extremely close pruning. Leaf curl and roll may also be caused by prolonged dry weather. Some early varieties have genetic leaf curl. Aster yellows disease also causes curl.

Rolling starts on lower leaves, proceeds upward and almost all the leaves are affected. In severe cases rolled leaves are thick and tend to rattle when plant is shaken. Plants bear a near-normal crop, but may lose ⅛ to ½ of their leaves, with loss in fruit quality. Worse on staked tomatoes. Heavy rains and winds which whip and riddle older rolled leaves may be responsible for plants losing leaves. Control: Plant on well-drained soil, don't cultivate deeply, and stop staking tomatoes. Use a mulch of straw, sawdust, etc. (see section on Mulches).

Leaf Wilting: Most common cause of wilt is fusarium, a fungus that lives in soil for many years. It enters root system and plugs up plants' pipes. First, there's a slight wilting of tips during hot afternoons, followed by yellowing and dying of lower leaves. A sure method of diagnosis is to cut into a branch. If inside is brownish-black, you have fusarium wilt. Control: None, once it has set in. You can avoid fusarium by planting wilt-resistant types. Most garden soil harbors the fungus of the fusarium wilt disease. This lives for many years in the soil, so rotation is of little value. Grow resistant varieties such as Manalucie, Homstead, Heinz 1350, Campbell 1327, or New Yorker.

Walnut wilt, which is confused with fusarium or verticillium wilt, might be the trouble, if a walnut tree is close. The other possible cause of wilted leaves is verticillium wilt, a disease that affects many types of plants, characterized by a brown spotting of leaves. Verticillium is internal, hence no spraying is effective. Most home gardens are so small it's not practical to rotate crops, thus the disease builds up in the soil. Control: Plant disease-resistant types such as Heinz 1350, Galaxy, Campbell 1327.

Mosaics (Streaks, Yellows): Leaves mottled, sometimes curled, crinkled, puckered, deformed, shaped like fern leaf or shoestring. Plants may be stunted and have a yellowish cast. Control: Pull up and destroy affected plants. Remove and burn all crop debris. Keep down all weeds (ground cherry, plantain, horsenettle, milkweed, burdock, wild cucumber, bittersweet). NEVER HANDLE TOBACCO WHILE WORKING WITH TOMATOES, POTATOES, PETUNIAS, AND OTHER PLANTS IN SAME FAMILY. Viruses such as mosaic can be lessened by spraying tomato and pepper plants with milk several hours before transplanting. Use 1 gallon of whole or skim milk or 1 pound of dried skim milk mixed with 1 gallon of water. Apply to 20 square yards of garden or plant bed. When handling tomato plants dip hands in whole or skim milk, or 4 ounces of dried skim milk per quart of water, every few minutes. Milk deactivates the virus.

Purple or Bluish Leaves: Purple or bluish tints in tomato foliage on dwarfed or spindly plants could indicate deficiency of phosphorous, although not always. Cold weather may give same discoloration, or extremely dry soils, or anything which stunts growth. Hot sun with high temperatures may yellow fruit on the exposed side. A marked shortage of potash may cause dark-green, stunted plant and uneven fruit ripening.

Shoestring Disease: When leaves get stringy and narrow, it's a virus or mosaic (which see). Pull up and burn the plants. Also pull nearby weeds, as these are reservoirs for infection. Spraying does not help, although it will control insects which spread virus.

Short Vines, Poor Growth: Could be due to lack or excess of plant food, cold temperature, hot winds, drought, mechanical injury, insects, soil-borne diseases, leaky gas main, robber tree roots, too much shade (especially in the morning), or poor drainage.

Walnut Poisoning: Tomatoes, potatoes, corn, eggplants, and other vegetables growing in the close vicinity of walnut tree will show wilting or dwarfed effect due to walnut poisoning. Roots of walnut secrete a toxic material, juglone, out as far as the tree's edge. Control: Don't plant near walnut. Not all plants are affected. Wood chips, sawdust, and bark from walnut trees are not toxic and may be used in compost or mulch. Dead walnut trees do not produce juglone.

2,4-D or 2,4-5-T Weed Killer Injury: Tomatoes very sensitive to all weed killers. Tiny amounts in spray drift may cause injury: leaves twisted or frilled, fruit cone-shaped, cracked, or catfaced. Control: Try to nurse plants along with water, then feed. Never use pesticide sprayer for weed killers. Always have a separate sprayer for weed killers and be careful of drifting spray.

Aphids (Plant Lice): Spray with Malathion.

Colorado Potato Beetle: Oval, hard-shelled insect ⅜ inch long, feeds on foliage. Dust with Sevin.

Cutworms: Smooth gray or greenish caterpillars that curl up when disturbed, cut off young plants at ground level. Control: place paper

collar around each transplant, or dust soil with Chlordane after planting. If stem is cut off at slant, this is rabbit injury. Scatter mothballs or
blood meal around base of plants. (See section on Animal Control.)

Eelworms or Nematodes: Cause lumpy knobs on roots. Pull out
plants and burn. Sterilize soil using methyl bromide or chloropicrin,
following directions. Use Nemagon.

Flea Beetles: Cause holes in leaves. Spray with Sevin or Malathion.

Hornworm: This is a large, fat, ugly, cigar-shaped worm, ravenous
eater. Handpicking is best control, or dust with Sevin. A tiny wasp
parasite feeds within body of hornworm and kills the worm. You
can tell a parasitized hornworm by white cocoons on back. Do not
disturb the parasites as they will emerge from cocoons and attack other
hornworms.

Slugs: Worse in wet weather and on mulched tomatoes. Stake tomatoes to keep them off ground. Use metaldehyde baits at base of
plants. Hydrated lime, stoker ashes, wood ashes at base of plants will
discourage slugs.

Symphylid: Tiny white worm in soil, shortens plants, causes them to
turn yellow. Dust soil with Sevin or Chlordane.

Tomato Fruit Worm: Same as corn earworm, feeds mainly on tomato
fruit, moves from one to another, damaging crop. Control: Dust with
Sevin or handpick and destroy.

White Flies: Tiny white insects that swarm off plants when touched.
Spray with Malathion to check.

Flea beetles, tomato fruit worms, cutworms, and aphids are worst
insect pests of tomatoes. Methoxychlor or Sevin applied on both tops
and bottoms of leaves will check them. Also, Malathion, or general-
purpose garden sprays or dusts.

General Trouble Control Measures: Buy tomato plants from a good
grower, one who practices plant sanitation. Do not plant any which are
spotted or hardened, sickly or yellow. If you use southern-grown
plants, loosen the bundles so air can get to them, dip roots in water,
but leave stems and foliage dry.

If you save your own tomato seed (don't save hybrid seed), be sure
to treat seed with hot water (122° F.) for 25 minutes, or you can use
improved Ceresan dust or Captan.

Plant seed or plants on clean soil, and rotate your crops. Once every 3
years is enough to plant tomatoes on same land. Do not rotate with potatoes, eggplants, okra, or peppers. Do not place diseased tomato plants
on compost pile. Destroy all weeds near tomato plantings.

Stay out of tomato patch when leaves are wet. Do not irrigate tomato plants from above, as this spreads disease, especially at night.

Apply fungicides and insecticides BEFORE pests appear.

Maneb (80%) is a good fungicide. Apply at rate of 1 tablespoon to 1 gallon of water, starting 4 weeks after setting out in garden. Repeat at 7- to 10-day intervals. Prevents most foliage diseases. Zineb, sold under various trade names, also good. Spray every 7 to 10 days. Bordeaux is still a good spray, but "old-fashioned," may burn plants; cover both top and bottom of leaves. Spray young seedlings with Captan to prevent damping-off. Give them fresh air and do not crowd them in seed flat or cold frame.

For a dust, use zineb (5 to 8%) every 5 days, covering both top and bottom of foliage. Sevin or Malathion will check most insects.

Many old-time gardeners still like to use copper sprays for tomato diseases. Use as dust or mix with water to spray. Use fixed copper at the rate of 3 tablespoons per gallon of water.

Planting disease-resistant varieties is the most effective way to control some diseases of tomatoes. For control of fusarium wilt, try Campbell 1327, Homestead, Kokomo, Manalucie, Manapal, Floradel, Roma. Also Sunray, a yellow tomato. For verticillium wilt control, try VR-9 and Red Top (pear-shaped), Heinz 1350 and 1439, Galaxy, Moreton Hybrid, and Campbell 1327. For early blight try Manalucie, New Hampshire Surecrop. Rutgers and Pritchard are somewhat resistant to disease, but Manalucie, Manapal, Manalee, and others are more resistant to fusarium. For late blight try New Yorker.

There is no such thing as a totally disease-resistant variety of tomato.

USES:

Tricks for Using Green Tomatoes: Some gardeners live in areas where tomatoes do not ripen. Weather, growing conditions, varieties, all have an effect on ripening. If you happen to get a lot of green tomatoes each season, don't despair, because they do make fine food. Here are some recipes sent to me by gardeners who use green tomatoes. Try them!

Canned Sliced Green Tomatoes: Wash and slice green tomatoes. Boil in solution of ½ vinegar and ½ water. Add pinch salt. Boil till tender but not mushy. Drain in colander. Measure drained liquid to gauge amount of sweet pickle syrup to make. Syrup: Add 1 pound brown sugar to 1 pint liquid (vinegar diluted with water according to taste), bring to boil. Pack hot drained tomato slices in hot jars with stick cinnamon (broken) and cloves. Fill with hot pickle syrup and seal.

Dilly Green Tomatoes: Select firm green tomatoes, leave stems on. Pack 1 stalk celery and 1 hot green pepper in sterilized quart jars. Combine 2 quarts water, 1 quart white vinegar, 1 cup salt, cook 5 minutes. Fill jars to within ½-inch of top, add 1 head dill to each jar, seal.

Easy Green Tomato Pickle: Slice green tomatoes and allow to stand in weak salt brine overnight. Next morning rinse and pack directly into fruit jars. Place the jars uncovered in the steamer and steam for 2 hours. Have ready at the end of the time a sweet-spiced vinegar made exactly as you do for pickling peaches (see following). After draining all the juice that cooked from the sliced tomatoes, fill cans brimful with vinegar-syrup and seal. Syrup: 1 pound brown sugar, 1 stick cinnamon, 1 pint vinegar diluted with water according to taste.

Fried Green Tomatoes: Slice firm green tomatoes, dip in flour, salt, and pepper to taste. Fry until tender, turning to brown both sides. Bacon or ham grease may be used for a good flavor.

Frozen Sliced Tomatoes: Slice green tomatoes ¼ inch thick. Dip in batter and stack in cartons. Or you can stack them plain.

Green Canned Tomatoes for Winter Frying: Slice green tomatoes, pack into quart jar, put in 1 teaspoon salt, fill with cold water, seal, and boil for 3 minutes in canner (time from when water bath begins to boil).

Green Tomato and Apple Chow Chow: 6 large green tomatoes, chopped, 4 cups chopped celery, 4 cups chopped carrots, 2 chopped green peppers, 4 chopped red peppers, 4 tart apples, chopped, 3 cups granulated sugar, 3 cups vinegar, 1 teaspoon mustard seed, 1 teaspoon cinnamon, 1 teaspoon salt. Add a little water to finely chopped tomatoes, celery, and carrots, cook until almost tender, then add finely chopped peppers and chopped apples. Now combine sugar, vinegar, and spices, bring to boil. Add the hot vegetable mixture and bring to a boil again. Pack in hot jars and seal.

Green Tomato Catsup: 1 peck of green tomatoes, 2 large onions, sliced. Place tomatoes and onions in layers, sprinkle salt between, let stand 24 hours, then drain off. Add ¼ pound of mustard seed, 1 ounce allspice, 1 ounce cloves, 1 ounce ground mustard, 1 ounce ground ginger, 2 tablespoons black pepper, 2 teaspoons celery seed, ¼ pound brown sugar. Put all ingredients in a preserving pan, cover with vinegar, and boil 2 hours. Strain through a sieve and bottle for use.

Green Tomatoes for Pies and Cookies: 1 peck green tomatoes, 4 cups brown sugar (4 pounds), 2 cups sweet cider (or water and vinegar), 1½ pounds seedless raisins, 1 tablespoon allspice, 1 tablespoon each cinnamon, ground cloves, salt. Chop the tomatoes in food chopper and drain off green water. Boil 15 minutes, then add sugar, spices, and salt, boil 2 hours. Pack in jars while hot and use as needed.

Green Tomato Mincemeat: 1 peck green tomatoes, chopped fine and drained, 3 lemons, chopped rind and all, 1 pound raisins and 1 pound currants, chopped, 5 pounds sugar, 1 teaspoon nutmeg, 2 teaspoons each cinnamon, cloves, and allspice, 6 tart apples, chopped, 1 cup butter, 2 tablespoons salt. Boil all ingredients together over medium heat, stirring almost constantly to keep from sticking. Boil until tender, dark, and thick. Can in clean sterile jars. Makes a delicious mincemeat pie. Sometimes called mock mincemeat.

Green Tomato Mincemeat #2: 3 pounds green tomatoes, 3 pounds apples, 2 pounds raisins, 1 cup suet, 1 cup vinegar, 4 pounds brown sugar, 2 pounds salt, 2 tablespoons cinnamon, 2 teaspoons cloves, 1 teaspoon nutmeg. Put tomatoes and apples through food chopper, mix with balance of ingredients. Boil until the syrup is thick. Can, makes 10 pints, will keep indefinitely.

Mincemeat Drop Cookies: ¾ cup shortening, 1½ cups sugar, 3 well-beaten eggs, 3 cups flour, ¾ teaspoon salt, 1 teaspoon baking soda, 1½ cups canned green tomato mincemeat, 3 tablespoons water, 1 cup broken nutmeats. Don't add any more flour than called for in recipe. Bake 10 minutes at 400° or till brown.

Green Tomato Pie: Take medium-sized green tomatoes, pare and cut out stems; have your pie tin lined with pastry or biscuit dough. Slice tomatoes very thin, filling pan somewhat heaping. Then grate over it a nutmeg (or sprinkle ground nutmeg), put in ½ cup butter and 1 cup sugar. Pour in ½ cup vinegar before adding top crust. Bake ½ hour in a moderate oven (350°), serve hot.

Green Tomato Relish #1: About 8 quarts tomatoes, proportionately twice as many green as ripe ones (and several half-ripe), 1 dozen green peppers, 1 dozen red peppers, a chili pepper or 2, 9 stalks of celery, all washed, trimmed, and chopped fine. Place chopped vegetables in a large enamel pot or basin, cover with a thin layer of granulated sugar, pour over a modest quantity of white vinegar. Brought to simmer and cooked gently 5 minutes, the relish is ready to serve and can. Men eat this with a tablespoon at beef dinners.

Green Tomato Relish #2: 2 quarts chopped green tomato, 2 medium onions, chopped, ½ cup salt, 2 quarts cold water. Combine ingredients, let soak 3 hours, drain and rinse well with cold water. Then use: 1½ cups vinegar, ½ cup boiling water, 1½ cups sugar, 1½ teaspoons celery seed, 1 tablespoon mustard seed, ½ teaspoon tumeric, ¼ teaspoon mustard. Boil 3 minutes and add the tomato-onion mixture. Simmer 10 minutes uncovered. Pack in sterilized jars. A little red pepper can be added for color.

Green Tomato Relish #3: 1 gallon green tomatoes, 6 onions, 6 red sweet peppers, 6 green peppers. Grind all together. Add 1 cup salt, let stand overnight, drain. Add ½ gallon vinegar, 3 cups sugar, 1 cup flour, 1 pint prepared mustard, cook ½ hour or till clear, and seal in jars. Ideal for sandwiches, hamburgers, hot dogs.

Green Tomato Sandwich Spread: 2 quarts ground green tomatoes, 9 red or green peppers, 1 pint ground onions, ½ cup salt. Let all ingredients stand 2 hours, squeeze out as much juice as possible (which you throw away). Add 1 pint sugar and 1 pint vinegar. Cook ½ hour with cover off. A pint of celery can be added but cook ingredients longer. When cold, add 1 pint mayonnaise dressing, and small jar of mustard, stir well and can. If too juicy after adding mayonnaise, drain.

Preserved Green Tomatoes: Take 1 peck green tomatoes, slice 6 fresh lemons without removing the skins, but take out the seeds. Add 6 pounds granulated sugar, and boil until tomatoes are transparent and syrup is thick. Ginger root may also be added.

Sliced Green Tomato Pickles: Slice green tomatoes ¼ inch thick. For 7 pounds tomatoes make a syrup of 1 pint vinegar, 3 pounds (6 cups) sugar, 1 teaspoon cinnamon, 1 teaspoon cloves, and 2 tablespoons salt. Pour over tomatoes and boil softly until tomatoes are tender and juice thickens slightly. Can in sterile jars.

TOMATO, HUSK (*Physalis pruinosa*)

The husk-tomato is a low, bushy plant that bears a papery husk-like structure enclosing a yellow or greenish 2-celled berry. Another name for the husk-tomato is strawberry tomato, dwarf Cape gooseberry, or ground cherry.

Husk tomatoes and cherry tomatoes are 2 different species. The small cherry tomatoes grow the size of a quarter and are a real tomato, whereas the husk-tomato is not. (It belongs to genus *Physalis*.)

Start seeds of the husk-tomato indoors. Set plants outdoors in well-drained soil in full sun when girl-watching weather comes.

USES

Ground Cherry Preserve: 2 pounds ground cherries (about 8 cups husked), 4 cups sugar, 1 cup water, grated rind and juice of 2 lemons. Husk and wash ground cherries carefully. Measure sugar and water into large kettle. Bring to full rolling boil, and boil for 2 minutes. Add cherries, lemon rinds and juice. Bring to full rolling boil. Reduce heat and simmer for 5 minutes. Remove from heat, cover with clean towel, and let stand overnight. Next day, return to heat and again bring to boil. Reduce heat and cook gently until transparent, about 15 minutes. Immediately pour into hot, sterilized glasses, seal at once. Yields 5 to 6 cups.

TURNIP (*Brassica rapa*)

Turnips have the same cultural requirements as rutabagas. Turnip roots have lighter flesh than rutabagas. You can plant seed in late July for a fall crop. They do best on rather light soil of high fertility. Check your seed catalog for varieties.

Turnips sown in July or August will be of much better quality than those sown earlier. Turnips are usually planted on land from which an early crop such as peas or spinach has been harvested earlier in the season. The soil should be worked up fine and smooth. Sow in rows 12 to 15 inches apart, cover lightly, and thin to stand 3 or 4 inches in the row. Or you can just broadcast the seed, sowing thinly.

Harvest in late summer, when roots are about 3 inches in diameter. Plants are hardy and may be left in ground until severe freezing weather comes in fall.

TROUBLES

Flea Beetle: Tiny black beetle (see illustration p. 185) that eats holes in the small new leaves. Apply rotenone or Sevin to control.

WATERMELON (*Citrullus vulgaris*)

You don't have to live in the South to grow good watermelons. In general, watermelon culture is similar to muskmelon culture, but except for the midget types, watermelons should have more space: 8 feet between rows and 2- to 3-feet spacing in the row are recommended. Some gardeners prefer to plant them in hills 6 feet apart, preferably in a loose soil. In cool-season areas, they do best on light sandy soils with a southern slope. Watermelons are more tolerant of acid soils than muskmelons. Fertilize well and irrigate if needed.

For a yellow-flesh variety you might try Golden Honey, or you can try the New Hampshire Midget, a tiny "icebox" melon. Another early, small, and productive watermelon is Takii Gem (pronounced Tocky).

Most of the small icebox melons have thin rinds and must be harvested promptly.

Giant Watermelons: Tremendously big specimens of watermelons can be had if you're willing to fuss with them. A friend of ours in the West, credited with raising the largest watermelons in the world (nearly 200 pounds each), tells us that persistent thinning of young fruit is the keynote to success. Never cut off any vines!

After several small melons have started to develop on lateral vines, he pinches them all off except the most perfect ones. Any formed subsequently are pinched off at 3- or 4-day intervals, eventually permitting only 1 properly shaped fruit to grow to maturity. In this way, only about 50 watermelons are grown on 1 acre, 1 to each vine. He also feeds heavy applications of manure and fertilizers since watermelons are gross feeders.

Quite a few gardeners tell us they coax their melons along (also pumpkins) with the bottle method, which consists of feeding a sugar

Watermelon vine grown on black plastic. (Monsanto Plastic Products Division)

solution through a cotton wick taped to a hole anywhere on the stem. I doubt if such a method could produce bigger fruit than you get through the thinning process previously mentioned.

Bush Watermelons: Home gardeners who like to raise their own watermelons will be interested to know that new varieties of the bush-type melons are available. Where a normal vine melon takes several feet to run, the bush type can now be grown in ¼ of the space.

Seedless Watermelons: A few years ago seedless watermelons came on the American scene and we were one of the first to grow them. This novelty has been tried by many gardeners. Some have been disappointed to find that when the melon is cut open there are whitish translucent seeds in the seedless melon. In eating the fruit you'd never notice them, and they aren't worth worrying about. Sometimes the seeds are absorbed in the flesh to a degree where they are scarcely visible. Sometimes a normal-sized black seed will develop in the seedless melon, but usually it's hollow. In spite of these, it's still fun to grow the sterile hybrid seedless watermelons. Such seed is harder to germinate and needs extra heat for best results.

How to Tell a Ripe Watermelon: It's a little tougher to determine when watermelons are ripe or mature when grown in the average home garden. Rich soils found in most gardens will delay maturity of watermelons. Cool, wet conditions will also delay ripeness. Watermelons in heavy soils lack flavor.

Here are some indicators of ripeness: Brown tendrils on the stem near the fruit. A yellowish color where the melon touches the ground. A rough and slightly ridged feel as you rub your hand over the melon. You can see the ridges if you look closely. The thump? I wouldn't rely on it! It can really fool you!

Usually, most varieties give a metallic ringing sound when they are green, and a muffled or dead sound as they become mature. Experience is your best bet. Watermelons should be cut, not pulled from the vine.

TROUBLES

Same troubles as muskmelons (which see), scab, pox, anthracnose, leaf spots, blights, angular leaf spot. Dust plants with Captan, Karathane (for mildew), or zineb. Malathion checks most insect pests.

Anthracnose: Worst disease of watermelons, round, grayish-brown, sunken spots on fruit. Do not work in patch when vines are wet. Cover foliage with Captan or zineb.

Wilt: Due to fusarium fungus. Causes vines to wilt and turn brown. Control: Try to plant watermelons in different spot every 3 years. May not help as the disease will live in soil for at least 16 years. Use resistant strains.

Stem-end Rot: Handle watermelons with care.

Blossom-end Rot: Due to moisture, high temperatures. Apply mulch of straw.

Downy Mildew: Causes powdery foliage. Dust with Karathane.

Important control measures for watermelon diseases are:

1. Rotation with other than vine crops.

2. Destruction of mosaic-carrying weed hosts, such as wild cucumber, catnip, motherwort, pokeberry, ground cherry, plantain, flowering spurge, and white cockle.

3. Keeping plantings away from such flowers as petunia, gladiolus, phlox, hollyhock, and from such crops as tobacco, soybean, and old alfalfa fields.

4. Treatment of the seed with corrosive sublimate, and then just before planting, dusting with an appropriate chemical dust.

5. Spraying or dusting both in the seedbed and in the field.

6. Planting fusarium-resistant varieties (listed in your seed catalog).

USES

Don't believe the story that the white flesh of watermelon rind is poisonous. Many use the rind to make preserves and for sweet pickles.

In southern Russia a beer is made from watermelon juice. The juice can also be boiled down to a heavy syrup like molasses. In many parts of Asia, the seeds are roasted, with or without salting, and eaten from hand.

CHAPTER IX

GREENHOUSE GARDENING FOR VEGETABLE GROWERS

THE HOME GREENHOUSE

Time was when a small greenhouse in the backyard was for the rich only, but today a small greenhouse is within the reach of nearly all gardeners. You can not only use it for starting your own vegetable plants, but also for raising annuals and perennials, starting evergreens and flowering shrubs. There are greenhouses you can put up by yourself right in your own backyard. The cost will fit the pocketbook and be an excellent investment for health, fun, and profit. And by raising your own vegetable and flower plants, and a few extra to sell to the neighbors, you can easily get your money back on your investment.

Many greenhouse construction companies have hobby-type greenhouses that are relatively inexpensive. They can be purchased in kit form to construct yourself, or can be erected by the company. Before building or buying it is best to contact a greenhouse construction company. They can furnish plans and materials for the most satisfactory structure, and can outline the best arrangement of benches and walks.

Gardeners who are handy with a hammer and saw can build themselves a small lean-to greenhouse attached to their home. This makes a true winter garden and you can step from a warm house into a warm greenhouse, without sloshing through snow or mud. Besides this, electricity, water, and drains are usually handy for connecting to the greenhouse. If you heat with hot water, the house heating plant can be extended for heating the greenhouse. The best location of the

338

greenhouse is on the south or east side of your home so the plants will receive as much sun as possible. It should be located away from trees and buildings so that light from the south, west, and east is not blocked off. It is recommended to buy or build the largest greenhouse you can afford because you'll find your family of growing plants will increase rapidly.

Plastic Greenhouses: When greenhouse construction is considered, the use of plastic as a substitute for glass should be investigated. By and large, many of the commercial growers who have them find the plastic houses quite satisfactory and practical. Many home gardeners are completely satisfied with plastic houses. Plastic is not as durable as glass, but a plastic house can be built for ⅓ the cost of a glass house.

The details of framing need not be elaborate for a plastic house, but the frame should be strong and adequate. Simple designs using 2x4's and 2x2's can be erected without highly skilled labor.

Flexible sheet plastics are used for covering the frame. The cheapest plastic on the market is polyethylene. The estimated life of polyethylene is 3 months during the summer and 9 months during the winter. The breakdown of polyethylene and many other plastics is caused by the ultraviolet rays of the sun. Sheet plastics may be obtained in any thickness and width. The thickness normally used for covering greenhouses varies from 2 mils (.002 inches) to 15 mils (.015 inches). The thicker the plastic, the more expensive per square foot. The width of a plastic sheet varies from 2 feet to 40 feet.

Plastics may also be obtained in comparatively thick (1/16 to 1/8 inch), rigid panels. The cost per square foot of this material is greater than for flexible sheet plastic, but the rigid panels last much longer. Rigid plastic panels are not as transparent as sheet plastic. This would not be a problem in the summer, but when the light intensity is naturally low in the winter months only those plants that require low light intensity, such as African violets, orchids, and some foliage plants, can be grown successfully. Because promising new plastics are coming on the market every day, it is best to check with your county agricultural agent about the type best suited for your needs.

A large number of plastic houses have been designed. Three major types are conventional, sash, and quonset.

The conventional plastic greenhouse is built with the same general design as the familiar rectangular, peaked-roof glass greenhouse. Sheet plastic is rolled on and stapled to the roof and sash bars. When the plastic has been applied, wood lath is tacked over the bars. If the plastic house is to be used during the winter months and a snow load is expected, roof bars should be no farther than 20 inches apart.

Ventilation of the conventional plastic house is similar to a glass house except the vent mechanism is simpler. Exhaust fans can be substituted for ventilators, but they must be large enough to remove all the air in the house once each minute in summer, and once every 10 minutes during the winter.

The sash greenhouse resembles the conventional type except for the roof, which is made up of panels or sashes. The panels may range in size up to 4'x15' and are constructed to slide in channels on the roof. The panels are covered with sheet plastics and thus easy to handle. Ventilation is achieved by sliding the panels up and down. The important and outstanding advantages of this house are that the panels can be removed and stored in a dark room when the greenhouse is not in use. This greatly increases the life of the plastic.

Quonset greenhouses are patterned after the quonset huts of World War II and were designed for plastics. The half-circle frames are made of either wood or metal (aluminum). They are covered with a single piece of plastic. This type of house is constructed up to 20 feet wide. The greatest advantage is the ease of erection and covering with plastic. Ventilation is only by exhaust fans at the ends of the house.

In all types of plastic greenhouse, 2 layers of plastic are better than 1, since the dead air spaces between the layers have insulation value which cuts down on heat loss. This also reduces condensation of moisture on the inside of the plastic.

Soils and Soil Treatment for the Home Greenhouse: A soil mixture for the small greenhouse may consist of 1 part garden soil, 1 part peat moss, and 1 part sand or perlite. Perlite holds large quantities of air and moisture, and is usually better adapted to heavy soils than sands. Superphosphate (20%) should be added to the soil mixture at the rate of 4 ounces to the bushel. This soil mixture is also recommended for starting seeds.

In a small greenhouse, since disease organisms tend to build up, the soil should be changed every 2 years unless there is equipment to steam-sterilize. While commercial growers steam-treat their soils, this is hardly practical for the small greenhouse operator. A recommended treatment is the use of formaldehyde to control soil fungi. The disadvantages are that the soil cannot be planted for 10 to 14 days after treatment, and the soil must be diluted with large volumes of water. Formaldehyde does not control nematodes or insects.

The treatment is as follows:

1. In the bench or the ground of hotbed work up the soil thoroughly to a depth of 6 inches.

2. Make a solution of 1 part commercial formalin to 50 parts of water.

3. Apply the solution with a watering can at the rate of 2 quarts to 1 square foot of bed.

4. Cover the bed with moist sacks, canvas, or several layers of newspaper. Keep moist for 2 to 3 days.

5. Uncover the soil at the end of 3 days and air for 10 to 14 days or until no odor exists.

Seed flats or pots of soil are treated in the same manner. Treating the soil and flat together prevents contamination from putting sterilized soil in dirty, fungus-infected flats or pots.

Heat sterilization of soil mixtures is very satisfactory and easily accomplished when only small quantities are needed. The soil must be heated to 180° F. for 30 minutes.

A good soil drench can be made by mixing 2 ounces each of Captan Terraclor, and ferbam in 12 gallons of water. Pour this on bare bench soil or hotbed soil, to help eliminate fungi prior to planting.

Watering: When watering your greenhouse plants, use a sprinkler attached to the hose, or a sprinkling can, and water quite thoroughly. If plants are allowed to go dry, they'll be checked in growth and become stunted. Plants in small pots dry out faster than those in larger pots, so they may need watering a second time during the day. Don't let your peat pots dry out.

Feeding: Every 3 weeks apply a water-soluble plant food to potted and benched crops at the rate of 1 teaspoon to 2 quarts of water, after the crop has started. Liquid feeding is easy because the food is applied with a hose attachment as the plants are watered.

Ventilation and Temperature: Good ventilation is important in a greenhouse. Leave the ventilator open a crack at night to provide air drainage. During hot summer days, ventilate well and apply a shading compound to your glass roof to keep the sun out. Most garden-supply houses handle shading compounds. A low night temperature (45° to 50°) is ideal for most plants. During the day, a temperature range of 65° to 80° is suitable.

Insect and Disease Control: Most greenhouse pests can be licked using smoke generator bombs, effective against spider mites, aphids, and white flies. Malathion sprays will banish scale and mealybugs. Sanitation is the best way to keep diseases from flaring up among your vegetable plants.

The most discouraging part of growing plants in the small greenhouse is getting seeds to germinate and grow. When seedlings die after germination before they are transplanted, the cause is damping-off disease. There are several methods to avoid damping-off and these include soil sterilization, starting seeds in sterile media such as perlite, vermiculite, or a sand-peat mixture, and using liquid soil drenches (see Starting Seeds under "Plant Propagation").

Gardeners interested in greenhouse gardening should subscribe to *Under Glass* magazine, published bimonthly by the Lord and Burnham Company, Irvington, New York, or *Grower Talks*, by George J. Ball Company, West Chicago, Illinois. These firms will tell you the best ways to keep insects and diseases at a minimum in your little greenhouse.

Don't hesitate to study literature offered by commercial suppliers of greenhouses, seeds, and related products. There's a wealth of information available free for the asking.

Pay a visit to a successful commercial greenhouse operator and learn tricks from him. He's in a business to make money, and his experience can help you get more mileage from your greenhouse efforts.

A Poor Man's Greenhouse

Every homeowner has an ambition to own a small indoor greenhouse. You don't need a lot of glass to grow and experiment with vegetable and flower plants. An empty corner in the basement, a few dollars worth of wood, a couple of used fluorescent fixtures and you can build an indoor greenhouse.

Here are the details:

Bench Construction: A 30-inch high bench can be erected with 1″ by 6″ boards forming the sides for the table top or bed. Redwood lumber or pine treated with cuprinol will be adequate. The frame should be made of 2x4 lumber for stability. The table bottom of the bench can be made from ¼-inch tempered Masonite, or better still "Transite," an asbestos-and-cement board commonly used for greenhouse benches. The soil tray should be 4 inches deep. The bottom should be cross-braced every 16 inches with 2x4 lumber. For pot culture a 3- to 4-inch layer of sand is placed on the bottom of the bench for drainage. Stop in at your local greenhouse and study the construction of the benches for helpful ideas for constructing your own.

Lighting: It would be advisable to start growing plants by use of a 4-foot, 2- or 3-tube, 40-watt industrial fixture with a reflector. For convenience and efficiency a poultry-type clock switch should be placed in the circuit. If the temperature is abnormally low, i.e., lower than 50° at times, provision should also be made for a heating cable to provide bottom heat. Probably a separate circuit will have to be provided for the heating cable. Follow the instructions given for installation of heating cable under Hotbeds Construction.

Daylight or cool white fluorescent tubes are preferred for plant growth. Intensity is another factor to be considered, because each type

Homemade cold frame with roll-down plastic top. (USDA Photo)

of plant has its own requirements. To provide maximum flexibility, the fixture should be hung on pulley arrangements. Raising the fixtures lowers the light intensity at plant level, while lowering the fixtures increases the intensity. For starting seeds of vegetable and flower plants, it's advisable to lower the fixture to within 6 inches of the seedling plants. The light should be gradually raised as the plants grow to keep it at about the same distance above the tops of the plants. Spring bulbs are forced at low intensities, perhaps calling for a smaller fixture. Since the light requirements of plants are based on the duration of that light, it may be necessary to give a longer light period to compensate for too low an intensity. Twenty-four-hour lighting of plants is not harmful except where the length of "day" would affect the flowering of "short-day" plants, such as garden mums, which start to form buds in fall when days get shorter.

Watering: Plants will require more watering if there is low humidity in the basement. A 4-inch layer of sand kept moist will help raise the humidity. If high humidity happens to be a problem, an electric fan located nearby will keep the air in motion and help prevent disease.

Soil: The same type of soils and mixtures as suggested under The Home Greenhouse can be used for the poor man's greenhouse. Sterilization of the soil is important and can be accomplished by the heat method or by use of formaldehyde. However, perlite, perlite-and-peat-moss mixture, sphagnum moss, or vermiculite can be used without sterilization.

Disease and insects should be no problem provided good sanitation and culture are practiced. If trouble occurs, however, treat as described in Insect and Disease Control in the Home Greenhouse.

Cold frames and hotbeds are similar in construction, with the principal difference being in heating and insulation.

COLD FRAMES AND HOTBEDS

Cold Frames:A cold frame utilizes the sun's heat, with no artificial heat supplied. The soil is heated during the day and gives off the heat at night to keep the plants warm. The frame may be banked with insulating material like straw, sawdust, or leaves to insulate it from the cold outside air. Mats of straw, paper, or cloth may be placed over the sash at night to conserve the heat.

Cold frames are used to harden plants which have been started in the greenhouse or hotbed before transplanting to the garden. The process of hardening matures succulent tissues. This reduces injury from sudden temperature drop and from conditions which favor rapid drying after transplanting.

Early lettuce and radishes as well as bulbs and perennials are forced in a cold frame a few weeks before normal season. Cold frames are also used to give a head start to tomatoes, corn, peppers, melons, and other tender vegetable and flower plants. The plants may be set directly in the soil of the cold frame or in pots or flats. Cuttings of red raspberries, blueberries, grapes, gooseberries, etc., may be rooted in a cold frame. Chrysanthemum stock plants and biennials are placed in a cold frame for winter protection. Cyclamen, azaleas, and some houseplants may be grown in a cold frame during the summer. Partial shade should be given to these plants in the summer by using lath sash or roll of snow fence in place of the glass sash.

Since cold frames are movable, they can be erected or set over beds of rhubarb, pansies, violets, primroses, etc., in very early spring to bring these plants into bloom ahead of normal season. Just set the frame over the plants which are to be forced and bank the outside with leaves or straw to keep out the cold. Dandelion greens can be forced a couple of weeks earlier in the same manner.

Construction of Hotbeds: Hotbeds or heated frames are similar in construction to cold frames except for the addition of an 8-inch board below ground. The walls are sometimes insulated and are usually higher than those of cold frames to permit tall-growing plants to be placed in them.

Artificial heat is supplied by electricity (light bulbs or electric cable), steam, or hot water.

Heated frames or hotbeds are used for all vegetable plants, bulbs, azaleas, hydrangeas, and chrysanthemums. They are ideal for starting vegetable and annual flowering plants from seed. Summer propagation of cuttings from woody plants and ground cover like pachysandra is also accomplished in a hotbed.

A lead-covered electric cable is the most frequently used method

A small, electrically heated hotbed may be made from scrap material about your home. You can buy a heating cable from any greenhouse specialty company. Left illustration shows hotbed heated by cable. On the right, light bulbs are used to generate heat. Manure may also be used as a source of heat.

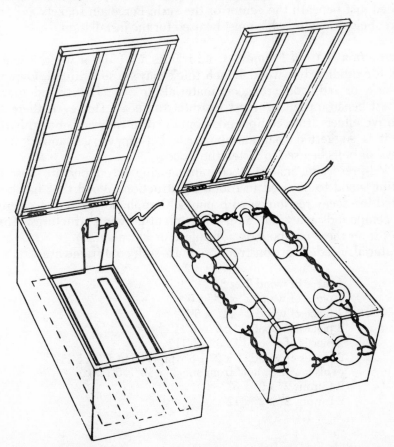

of heating hotbeds. The lead covering is necessary to resist soil corrosion. This heating cable is operated by a thermostat which controls the hotbed automatically, saves electricity, and assures constant temperature.

Heating cable is purchased in lengths of 60 to 120 feet, with 60-foot length being used on a 110-volt power supply and 120 feet of cable on a 220-volt power supply. Each 60-foot length of cable will heat 36 square feet of frame space. Both heating cable and thermostats can be purchased from garden-supply houses.

To install the cable in a frame put a 12-inch layer of fine gravel or cinders below the hotbed to provide both insulation and drainage. Next, add a 1-inch layer of sand or soil, which acts as a bed for laying out the electric cable. Loop the cable back and forth across the bed, 3 inches from the sides and with the lines 6 inches apart. On top of the cable place hardware cloth (¼-inch mesh) to act as a heat conductor and for keeping uniform temperatures. Soil or coarse sand is then placed on the hardware cloth to a depth of 4 to 6 inches.

For less expensive heating use electric light bulbs. Use 8 25-watt bulbs for heating a 3'x6' frame, mounted on a strip of wood spanning the bed just beneath the center of the sash. Porcelain sockets and waterproof electric wire cable must be used for the installation.

Construction of Cold Frames: Cold frames are built of wood 2 inches thick for rigidity, but wood 1 inch thick may be substituted. Cypress, hemlock, or redwood are good materials to use. Heartwood grades are best because they are most resistant to decay. However, there are corrosive effects from compounds contained in redwood. For this reason, it is suggested that aluminum or hot-dipped galvanized nails, screws, or bolts be used to fasten the wood.

Wood-preserving materials containing zinc or copper are best for treating wood to be used in frame construction. Wood that has been treated for decay resistance with pentachlorophenol, mercury, or creosote compounds must not be used in plant-growing structures. Toxic fumes from these compounds will injure or kill plants.

Materials needed for construction of a 2-sash cold frame are:

1 piece of wood 2" x 8" x 6'
1 piece of wood 2" x 14" x 6'
1 piece of wood 2" x 2" x 6'
2 pieces of wood 2" x 6" x 5'11"
2 pieces of wood 1" x 3" x 5'11"
2 pieces of wood 2" x 2" x 8" (tapered to 2") x 5'11"
(This may be made from one 2" x 10" x 5'11")
2 L-irons 2" x 2" x 6"
2 L-irons 2" x 2" x 12"

24 round-headed bolts 3/8″ x 3″, with washers
30 #8 nails

The standard sash for covering cold frames and hotbeds is 3 feet wide by 6 feet long with 3 rows of glass panels lapped to allow rainwater to run lengthwise. Construction can be made simpler by using plastics. The various materials available for glazing of sash are discussed under Plastic Greenhouses.

Care of Hotbeds and Cold Frames: Seeds started in a cold frame or hotbed are sown directly in the earth of the frame or in flats or pots. If the seed is sown directly, the soil is prepared by spading and raking to provide a finely pulverized bed. A 4-inch layer of fine peat moss added before spading is beneficial.

For sowing in pots or flats, 3 to 4 inches of the soil is removed and replaced with cinders. This provides drainage for the bed and prevents earthworms from entering the pots or flats.

Cuttings may be started in the frames during the summer months by using sand, sand and peat, or perlite instead of soil.

Ventilation of cold frames and hotbeds during the spring months and on hot, bright days, is important. The temperature inside the frames should not rise above 70° during periods of sunshine. Wooden blocks are used to raise or lower the sash on the side opposite the direction of the wind. The sashes are closed before sundown to conserve heat. If the night temperature is expected to fall below 40°, insulating mats are used to cover the sash.

Watering must be done in the morning so that the plants will dry off before the frame is closed for the night. Care must be taken to avoid getting the soil too wet during periods of low temperature and cloudy days. Such conditions favor damping-off fungus, which quickly kills young seedlings.

Index

349